GOVERNING
THE AMERICAS

GOVERNING THE AMERICAS

Assessing Multilateral Institutions

EDITED BY
Gordon Mace
Jean-Philippe Thérien
Paul Haslam

LYNNE
RIENNER
PUBLISHERS

BOULDER
LONDON

Published in the United States of America in 2007 by
Lynne Rienner Publishers, Inc.
1800 30th Street, Boulder, Colorado 80301
www.rienner.com

and in the United Kingdom by
Lynne Rienner Publishers, Inc.
3 Henrietta Street, Covent Garden, London WC2E 8LU

Library of Congress Cataloging-in-Publication Data
Governing the Americas : assessing multilateral institutions / editors,
    Gordon Mace, Jean-Philippe Thérien, and Paul Haslam.
    p. cm.
    Includes bibliographical references and index.
    ISBN 978-1-58826-533-3 (hardcover : alk. paper)
    1. International agencies—America. 2. Pan-Americanism.
3. Inter-American conferences. I. Mace, Gordon. II. Thérien, Jean-Philippe.
III. Haslam, Paul.
JZ5331.G68 2007
341.24'5—dc22   2006102807

British Cataloguing in Publication Data
A Cataloguing in Publication record for this book
is available from the British Library.

Printed and bound in the United States of America

∞   The paper used in this publication meets the requirements
     of the American National Standard for Permanence of
     Paper for Printed Library Materials Z39.48-1992.

5 4 3 2 1

Contents

Part 3 Democratic Governance

Part 4 Trade and Economic Development

Part 5 Conclusion

Acknowledgments

This book would not have been possible without the collaboration of a great number of people. First, we would like to thank all the contributors for their professionalism and willingness to follow our suggestions in the writing and revising of their chapters. As editors, one of our main preoccupations was to give a unified focus to this collection. It is due largely to the individual authors if that goal has been reached.

We also gratefully acknowledge the help of our research assistants Valérie Bouchard, Ariane Chenard, Isabelle Jetté, Raphaëlle Lapierre, Chantal Lacasse, Danny Lepage, Marjolaine Pigeon, and Gary Winston, who were involved at various stages in the evolution of the manuscript. Their meticulous work and dedication made our job much easier. We want to thank particularly Chantal and Danny for their precious contribution in the last phase of the project.

Financial assistance was generously provided by the Fonds québécois de recherche sur la société et la culture and by the Social Sciences and Humanities Research Council of Canada. We are grateful to both institutions for their support to our research team over the years.

Finally, we want to express our gratitude to Lynne Rienner for her encouragement. Thank you also to Shena Redmond at Lynne Rienner Publishers for her work as project editor, Beth Partin for her meticulous copyediting, and Sally Glover and Karen Schneider at Lynne Rienner, all of whom contributed to making this book possible. We are of course responsible for any remaining errors.

—*Gordon Mace,*
Jean-Philippe Thérien,
and Paul Haslam

1

Introduction

Gordon Mace, Paul Haslam, and
Jean-Philippe Thérien

Why are the Americas in general and the inter-American system in particular so fascinating for those interested in the study of international institutions? One reason has to do with the complexity of a regime that strives to achieve a common destiny for so many different societies living in so many different environments. Another may be linked to the "historic mission" that the Charter of the Organization of American States (OAS) entrusted to the countries of the New World. A third may have to do with the resilience of a system whose member countries have weathered recurrent periods of crises and conflicts among themselves. Finally, this fascination may result from the discrepancy between the initial expectations of what the system could achieve and the difficulty of finding the right mix of instruments to fulfill these expectations.

According to Arthur Whitaker, the Western Hemisphere Idea incorporated the notion of a special relationship between the peoples of the United States and Latin America, constructed on the basis of shared ideals developed in the common fight for independence against European powers (Whitaker 1954: 1). As pointed out by historian Gordon Connell-Smith (1974: 27), the concept of a Western Hemisphere united by common values was an illusion in much the same way as was the myth of Latin American unity pursued by Simón Bolívar and his followers. Nevertheless, the twin concepts of the Western Hemisphere and pan-Americanism reflected expectations about the development of a regional system of the Americas through which the peoples of the region would prosper in a peaceful environment (Bernstein 1961). This vision of the future was deemed possible despite a unique context of asymmetry absent in the other regions of the world.

From Pan-Americanism to the Inter-American System

Since 1889, when the US government convened the First International Conference of American States, the architects of hemispheric regionalism have devoted considerable time and resources to building a panoply of institutions that are almost as diverse as those of the European Union. Far from being instantaneous, this construction has resulted from a long evolution of successive waves of institution building.

The agenda of the first pan-American conference, as was the case with most of the subsequent conferences until World War II, dealt exclusively with commercial matters and peaceful settlement of disputes. In institutional terms, the Washington conference created the International Union of American Republics with a Commercial Bureau acting as a kind of secretariat. In 1910, the Commercial Bureau became the Pan-American Union (Carnegie Endowment for International Peace 1931; Inman 1965). Consequently, the beginnings of hemispheric regionalism were relatively modest, in terms of both institutional capacity and scope of agenda setting, since little progress was made on the themes discussed at the various conferences.

It was only after World War II, following the reorganization of the international system, that pan-Americanism experienced a substantial facelift. The new inter-American system established at Bogotá in 1948 was much more ambitious than what had existed previously. The Bogotá Conference adopted major documents, among them the Charter of the OAS, which became the constituent document of the inter-American system, the American Declaration of Rights and Duties of Man, and the American Treaty on Pacific Settlement (Pact of Bogotá), although the latter included numerous reservations and ultimately applied only to those states that had ratified it. The Rio Treaty, which came into effect in 1948, added a previously nonexistent security dimension to the inter-American system (Fenwick 1963; Inter-American Institute of International Legal Studies 1966; Stoetzer 1993).

The charter described the main organs of the OAS, some of which were profoundly modified by the Protocol of Buenos Aires in 1967 and the Protocol of Cartagena de Indias in 1985. The Inter-American Conference became the General Assembly, subsequently acting as the supreme organ of the OAS. The Meeting of Consultation of Ministers of Foreign Affairs remained the same over the years but was given more visibility by Resolution 1080, which was adopted in 1991. The resolution made it mandatory for the foreign ministers to hold an extraordinary session in the event of "any sudden or irregular interruption of the democratic institutional process" (Bloomfield 1994: 16). The Council of the OAS became the Permanent Council and the General Secretariat became an ever more central component of the OAS (Atkins 1989: 207–213; Connell-Smith 1966).

These major organs were supported by a complex network of commissions, councils, and specialized conferences supervised by the OAS or working closely with the organization. In addition to the initial apparatus, the institutional capacity of the inter-American system was substantially increased in the 1950s and 1960s. Institutions were established, such as the Inter-American Development Bank (Dell 1972) and the Inter-American Commission on Human Rights, both created in 1959, and the Inter-American Court of Human Rights, established in 1969 by the American Convention on Human Rights (Pact of San José), which came into force in 1978 (Buergenthal, Norris and Shelton 1983; Cerna 1987; Cerna 1992). The Pan-American Health Organization succeeded the Pan-American Sanitary Bureau in 1958 (Howard-Jones 1981).

Consequently, the second wave of hemispheric institution building resulted in a much more robust institutional structure and a more sophisticated system for collective action. After 1948, the inter-American system had the instruments to intervene, should the members have wished to do so, not only on issues of health and security but also in relation to democracy and human rights, development and education, business relations, agriculture, and so on.

Although the overall robustness of hemispheric regionalism had increased considerably from one period to the other, the performance of the system was far from optimal. Arguments were put forward to support the thesis that the OAS was still an appropriate political forum for the hemisphere (Vaky 1981) and that it had been relatively successful at peacefully settling disputes (Ball 1969). Yet a majority of analysts were much more critical of the performance of the OAS and of the overall achievements of the inter-American system between the mid-1950s and the 1980s than they were later. Criticisms took many forms, ranging from a direct attack on the OAS as being essentially an instrument of US foreign policy (Aguilar 1965) to a more balanced analysis of the inefficiencies of an institution that had lost its purpose (Slater 1969; Scheman 1988; Dreier 1968). Whatever the angle of analysis, the global appreciation was negative.

The underperformance of a regional system well endowed with instruments for action can be explained in a number of ways. Some have to do with the behavior of the member governments, but others are associated with the functioning of the institutions themselves. In the case of the inter-American system, the overthrow of the Arbenz government in Guatemala in 1954 (Gleijeses 1991; Immerman 1982) and the US intervention in the Dominican Republic in 1965 (Connell-Smith 1968; Lowenthal 1972; Slater 1970) stand out as particularly significant episodes. In each case, manipulation by the US government and the inefficiency of the OAS combined to destroy the legitimacy of the main political forum of the inter-American system and, more broadly, hemispheric regionalism itself.

For the twenty years following the Dominican crisis, hemispheric regionalism became largely irrelevant as a political space for managing regional affairs in the Americas. Inter-American relations were so stagnant that Latin American and Caribbean governments started to create their own regional institutions. In addition to the subregional economic integration arrangements, such as the Andean Group, the Central American Common Market, and the Caribbean Community, regionwide entities were established. The Special Commission for Latin American Coordination (CECLA), the Latin American Economic System (SELA), and the Rio Group, among others, were created to facilitate the discussion of regional affairs among Latin American governments and to support negotiations in international forums such as the United Nations Conference on Trade and Development (UNCTAD).

In the early 1980s, the inter-American system stood on the brink of collapse. The institutions created in the 1940s and the 1950s had proven incapable of resolving the main problems and crises of the hemisphere that had occurred since the establishment of the OAS in 1948. The social and economic conditions in many parts of the region were dire, and the return to democracy in a limited number of countries had little to do with OAS intervention. Not surprisingly, calls were made for a renewal of the inter-American system and of its flagship organization (Muñoz 1993; Molineu 1994; Ezeta 1992; Scheman 1994).

A New Institutional Design

The first Summit of the Americas, held in Miami in December 1994, signaled the start of another wave of institution building for the inter-American system. In a fashion similar to what had happened in 1948, the new push toward institutionalization responded to changes in the regional and international environments and to the need for more efficient instruments to deal with a novel situation.

First of all, as in the 1940s, the structure of the international system was considerably altered. The bipolar system of the Cold War dissolved, which had a tremendous effect on the foreign policy calculus of the governments of the Americas. Second, the structure of the regional system was also modified by the arrival of Canada and the Caribbean states as new members of the OAS. And finally, the hemispheric problems of the 1990s were very different from those of previous decades. The issues of security, democracy, the economy, and the environment were now much more complex, and the existing institutional structures were judged inadequate to deal effectively with this new agenda of inter-American relations.

In 1994, therefore, a new institutional design was introduced that considerably changed the structure of hemispheric regionalism. A "nesting" operation (Aggarwal 1998) was undertaken to create a dual structure to govern inter-American relations. Since this restructuring, the Summits of the Americas process (SOA) has been composed of three principal entities:

the summits of heads of state, the ministerial conferences, and the Summit Implementation Review Group (SIRG). In this new executive structure of the inter-American system, the summits periodically (approximately every four years) define the upcoming agenda for hemispheric regionalism, the ministerials adapt and build the agenda for each sector, and the SIRG supervises the execution and reporting to the ministers of foreign affairs.

Alongside the decisionmaking structure is an administrative one composed of the existing regional institutions, among them the OAS, the Inter-American Development Bank (IDB), and the Pan-American Health Organization (PAHO). A Secretariat, housed within the OAS, is charged with keeping track of the implementation of summit mandates and liaising with the SIRG to ensure a smooth flow of information between the two structures.

In terms of the scope of the agenda covered, it would appear on the surface that the issue areas addressed in the framework of hemispheric institutions have changed very little since the 1980s. The themes discussed still relate to democracy and political affairs, institutions, trade and labor, security, and education and culture. The environment has become a major issue area, but what has really changed is the variety of themes being dealt with in each sector. In the case of security, for example, discussion is no longer limited to insurgency and external threat but also includes corruption, drugs, crime, terrorism, and civil-military relations.

So the third wave of hemispheric institution building has once again expanded the capacity of the inter-American system as well as the scope of its agenda. Hemispheric regionalism has now become a highly institutionalized system of governance. But for what purpose? How has this new institutional design performed? What has it achieved in relation to initial expectations, and what significant contributions has it made to solving the collective action problems that the old design failed to address?

The literature on inter-American relations in the era of summitry has increased over the years, but it is very uneven both in terms of the issues covered and its analytical content.[1] There are a few general studies on the subject. Some address only the era's initial years (Atkins 1999; Mace and Bélanger 1999), whereas others adopt a foreign policy perspective (Tulchin and Espach 2001; Roett and Paz 2003). In addition to the documents available from the Summits of the Americas Information Network website, research has been conducted on the new institutional design of hemispheric regionalism (Rosenberg 2001; Mace and Loiseau 2005), on partial assessments of summitry itself (Feinberg 1997; Leadership Council for Inter-American Summitry 2001; Lagos and Rudy 2002), and on the role of the OAS and multilateralism (Pellicer 1998; Thomas and Magloire 2000).

There is also a real discrepancy in the analytical treatment of the topics addressed in the study of hemispheric regionalism. Free trade (Salazar-Xirinachs and Robert 2001; Schott 2001; Weintraub, Rugman, and Boyd

2004) and democracy and human rights (Cooper and Legler 2006; Harris and Livingstone 1998; Tickner 2000) have been examined quite extensively. But other themes, such as the security dimension (Franko 2000), have received far less attention.

Consequently, knowledge of the functioning of inter-American institutions in the era of summitry is still quite limited. The main contribution of this book, therefore, is to provide the first systematic assessment of the institutional setting of hemispheric regionalism since the introduction of the summit process. In order to do this, the book is organized around a few key questions: What is the role of the new institutions, and how are they linked with the ones that predate summitry? What are the problems that the new institutional design was supposed to solve more efficiently, and did it manage to do so? In purely institutional terms, did the "nesting" succeed, and if not, why? On the basis of the existing record, how effective has hemispheric regionalism been as an instrument for collective action, and what does that entail for the future of the inter-American system?

These questions shape our examination of contemporary hemispheric regionalism, which focuses on four main dimensions: general institutional setting, security, democracy and human rights, and trade and growth. In providing answers to these questions, we seek to offer a contextualization of inter-American institutions that will contribute not only to a better understanding of governance in the Americas but also to the larger theoretical study of international institutions.

Summary of Chapters

This collection is organized around a problem: understanding the governance of the inter-American system and how it has been transformed by the latest cycle of institution building in the summit era. It takes a broad approach to governance and institutions. Governance, as understood by James Rosenau, implies that control or steering may, but does not necessarily, occur through mechanisms that involve governments. It may occur through government regulation, international organizations, nongovernmental patterns of behavior, and the diffusion of ideas (Rosenau 1995). The Americas, enchanted by pan-Americanism and the Western Hemisphere Idea but under the influence of the world's hegemon, present just such a tapestry of governance and institutionality.

In this respect, the use of governance and institutions in this book is explicitly inclusive of the wide range of approaches apparent in the literature on the inter-American system. Chapters echo the major approaches to governance and institutions, including the transaction-cost analysis of neoliberal institutionalism, the power-based approach of the neorealists, the ideational and normative concerns of constructivism, the historical perspective of economic neo-institutionalism, and the deductive thinking of rational design and legalization. The authors in this collection address the asymmetry of power, the disconnect between principals and agents, informal links between bureaucracies, the role of subnational and civil-society actors, and the impact of ideas. The governance and new institutionality of the inter-American system are examined through four issue areas: the overall governance of the inter-American system; the security institutions of the Americas; democracy, human rights, and civil society; and trade and economic development.

L. Ronald Scheman's overview of the inter-American system brings the insight of a longtime practitioner to the challenge of improving cooperation and institutional design. Scheman's description of the organizational structure of the OAS underlines several problems that hamper its efficiency, particularly the asymmetry of US and Latin American objectives and structural power, the politicization of the OAS, and the failure to allocate budgets commensurate with its vast mandates. Gordon Mace and Jean-Philippe Thérien further investigate the issue of divergent objectives in their comparison of the summit period with two earlier moments of institutional renewal, 1889–1910 and 1947–1954. They ask why institution building in the inter-American system rises and declines in what appears to be a cyclical movement. Mace and Thérien draw particular attention to the problem of the ambiguous consensus and incompatible expectations that eventually weaken the political will to further inter-American cooperation. Richard Feinberg and Paul Haslam address the coordination problems between the new institutionality of the summits and the two principal institutions of the inter-American system, the OAS and the Inter-American Development Bank (IDB). Feinberg and Haslam ask why the OAS and IDB have responded differently to mandates emanating from the summits process.

The problematic interaction between new and older institutions is also evident in security. Margaret Daly Hayes examines the renewal of the hemispheric security architecture in the summit era, the interaction of new and older institutions, and the obstacles to deepening security cooperation. She underlines the extensive dialogue on reform, which was buttressed by the SOA process and energized the expanded security agenda. However, she underscores that fundamental questions about how to reform the relationship between the OAS and the traditional security institutions, particularly the Rio Treaty and the Inter-American Defense Board, proved difficult to resolve. David Mares examines one element of the new security agenda in detail: confidence- and security-building measures (CSBMs). He asks if CSBMs are efficient and relevant institutions in the unique security environment of the inter-American system, where a superpower that interprets conflicts in terms of its global interests coexists with small and medium powers that view conflict locally. For Mares, CSBMs are the key element contributing to the institutionalization of security cooperation and moving the Americas away from conflict-prone balance-of-power politics. This portrait of hemispheric security institutions reveals a complex system of overlapping institutions embodying divergent normative values based on both collective and cooperative security designs and diverse national interests.

The institutional consolidation of the inter-American regime for protection of democracy and human rights has been one of the fundamental achievements of the summit era. Nonetheless, the uneven application of the Inter-American Democratic Charter, since its adoption in 2001, leads Tom Legler to ask if it is a "living document" or an "empty piece of paper." On the one hand, this new instrument filled many of the holes in the hitherto existing defense of democracy regime. On the other, its implementation has revealed a number of shortcomings—particularly in terms of preventing authoritarian backsliding. Legler asks if the fundamental problems with the charter are geopolitical and normative rather than legal and procedural. In a similar manner, the human rights regime has also evidenced considerable development and institutional consolidation during the summit era. Bernard Duhaime assesses the performance of the Inter-American Commission on Human Rights and the Inter-American Court of Human Rights up to 1994 and the impact of summitry afterward. Duhaime underlines, however, that the impact of summitry on this process has been marginal and that human rights has developed as an autonomous regime within the inter-American system. William C. Smith and Roberto Patricio Korzeniewicz examine the increased engagement between civil society organizations and inter-American institutions in the summit era. They observe insider and outsider strategies deployed, respectively, by civil society organizations targeting the summit and Free Trade Area of the Americas (FTAA) negotiations. The increased participation of civil society organizations in the third cycle of inter-American institution building remains a dramatic and encouraging departure from past practice. Nonetheless, it is still unclear to what extent civil society organizations have played a role in democratizing and legitimizing inter-American institutions.

The FTAA was the cornerstone of the Summits of the Americas process. Maryse Robert presents an overview of the evolution of regional integration and the free trade idea in the Americas. In particular, she asks whether the profusion and institutional overlap of bilateral and subregional agreements furthers or hampers the move toward an FTAA. She reveals a dynamic and complicated process at the subregional level, where policy coordination and harmonization drive integration and institutional innovation forward despite stalemate at the regionwide negotiations since the Miami ministerial of 2003. But the issue of the consistency and compatibility of this institutionalization remains salient. In his chapter, Louis Bélanger analyses the institutional design of the North American Free Trade Agreement (NAFTA) and its inability to adapt to changing circumstances through the problem of institutional "delegation." NAFTA was deliberately designed without the independent decisionmaking power that permits adaptation. The result has been institutional dysfunction leading to the inefficiency and erosion of NAFTA benefits, as this 1994 agreement is surpassed by latest-generation agreements that offer better market access or improved dispute settlement. In contrast to the chapters by Robert and Bélanger, Al Berry underlines the extent to which existing trade and development institutions are inadequate to the task of alleviating poverty and inequality in the hemisphere. In this respect, he explicitly asks the question, What are institutions for? By his criteria, inter-American institutions charged with alleviating poverty and inequality cannot be judged favorably. Despite improved education and social security nets in some countries, the period since the mid-1980s in Latin America has been characterized by low rates of economic growth, income and job instability, and an overall increase in regional inequality.

Kenneth W. Abbott draws the analyses of the other contributors together in his chapter on the theoretical implications of international relations theory for the study of the inter-American system. He asserts that power asymmetry is the defining feature of the inter-American system, generating both US efforts to use the OAS to further its own interests and Latin American reluctance to attribute significant independence or efficiency to inter-American institutions. Thus, Latin America finds itself caught between committing to the OAS as a way of constraining or engaging the regional hegemon and fearing the hegemon's ability to manipulate the organization. As Abbott puts it, this complex system results in "Goldilocks" institutions, neither too strong nor too weak.

Despite the immense heterogeneity of the hemisphere and diverse and unstable national interests, periodic domestic convergence has permitted shaky institutional advances in democracy, human rights, and security. Shared ideas and norms create opportunities for compromise and institution building. The phantoms of pan-Americanism and the Western Hemisphere Idea float over the inter-American system, not strong enough to challenge national identities and interests but repeatedly drawing the hemispheric nations back to the imagined space of the Americas. This collective work on the third wave of institution building in the inter-American system examines in detail a complex regional system that has received relatively little attention from scholars of international relations and institutions. As discussed by the editors in the final chapter, the inter-American system did achieve some success over the years but significant obstacles still remain. We hope that this book provides not only a thorough assessment of contemporary hemispheric institutions but also useful insights for the study of international institutions in general.

Note

1. It is not possible in the space provided to make a complete review of all the material that has been produced on post-1994 inter-American institutions. The literature is both diverse and uneven. References included here should only be considered as illustrations.

PART 1

The Inter-American System

2

The Inter-American System: An Overview

L. Ronald Scheman

International cooperation has been called a political decision in search of a framework. It is no more effective than the underlying political relations among the participating nations. The relationship, however, is reciprocal. The institutional framework that the nations establish to implement their cooperation deeply influences the nature and efficacy of that cooperation. Since the 1970s, the nations of the Americas have had a difficult time defining the purpose of the institutions they have designed to promote inter-American cooperation. Do they really seek more intensive regional cooperation, or are the regional institutions merely adjunct to a growing commitment to global engagement? Do they seek to advance regional development cooperation to improve the quality of life for all the Americas, or are their underlying motivations more political, to foster a continuing dialogue to air national differences and contain intervention?

The forefathers of inter-American cooperation at the beginning of the twentieth century sought both political and development goals. They were filled with the zeal and idealism of the historical significance of the Western Hemisphere in world history. The dramatic changes of globalization and the reach of technology, finance, and power in the twentieth century, however, have been a major challenge for the Americas, sharply contrasting with their relative isolation in earlier decades.

In this chapter, I examine the framework of inter-American institutional cooperation, looking first at the historical roots and then examining the current institutional structure with particular emphasis on the Organization of American States (OAS) and the new architecture of inter-American cooperation emanating from the high-level Summits of the Americas. I then review the issues and trends currently of concern to the nations of the hemisphere and the roadblocks to greater institutional cooperation and conclude with some conjecture on how to overcome these roadblocks in order to address the challenges of the future.

The Backdrop

Since the beginning of the twentieth century, the nations of the hemisphere have worked to shape a credible network of inter-American institutions to achieve a more integrated hemisphere that would reinforce democracy and sustainable development on a continuing basis. When the pioneers of inter-American cooperation conceived of an international system binding all the nations of the hemisphere, from the first conference summoned by Simón Bolívar in Panama in 1826 to the First International Conference of American States in Washington in 1889, they were responding to the political realities of their day. At the same time, they were setting the base for modern international organization. The agenda of that first inter-American conclave in 1889, seeking to spur international commerce in the Americas, was an innovative undertaking emphasizing commerce, free trade, and, in the political sphere, the goal of arbitration of international controversies among the American states.

Subsequent institution building among the American nations built on those foundations in two waves. The first took place at the turn of the twentieth century. The International Union of the American Republics, soon to be rechristened the Pan-American Union, was the product of a small elite from Latin America who sought practical machinery to engage the United States to balance the overwhelming European influence in the hemisphere. At the time of the Washington conference in 1889, Latin America's trade with Europe was four times that of trade with the United States. The implications of the resurgent imperialism of European powers, such as France, England, and Germany, actively expanding their colonial empires were not lost on the still unstable American republics. The successes of the early years of inter-American cooperation in articulating a framework for relations with the United States and adopting the principles of nonintervention and the juridical equality of states were major achievements in their time.

As frequently happened in the ensuing century, idealism for cooperation was repeatedly tempered by practical geopolitical issues, followed by periods of retrenchment and isolationism. Latin ardors for association with the United States in the early twentieth century were rudely shattered by the Roosevelt Corollary to the Monroe Doctrine in 1904, which asserted the unilateral US right to "exercise an international police power" if necessary to preserve order in the hemisphere. President Teddy Roosevelt's intervention in Panama, followed in the next decade by several unilateral interventions in Caribbean countries, set the tone for the new realities. With the attention of the United States diverted by World War I and the rejection of the League of Nations, the initial flush of cooperation ended, and the political goals of the Latin American countries turned from cooperation to a struggle to constrain their rambunctious northern neighbor.

Faced with the new realities, the nations of Latin America embraced initiatives for advancing nonintervention, self-determination and the sovereignty of states, and the peaceful resolution of disputes. A spate of inter-American treaties was signed, following the 1929 Washington Conference on Conciliation and Arbitration. The efforts rapidly faded as the Great Depression of the 1930s overwhelmed the economies of Latin America. Spurred by the growing attraction of national socialist ideologies and fascist ambitions in Europe, the United States again began to look more carefully at its weaker neighbors in the Americas. Franklin Delano Roosevelt's (FDR's) Good Neighbor Policy and acceptance of nonintervention and self-determination were important in restoring good relations. The era of good feeling caused the Latin American bloc, led by Alberto Lleras Camargo of Colombia, to insist on including provisions for regional organizations in the drafting of the UN Charter, over the resistance of the United States.

The second great wave of institution building in the Americas occurred after World War II, when the Cold War prompted the United States to forge a network of alliances to compensate for the weakness of the United Nations. The postwar period, from 1948 to 1960, found nations busy cooperating to apply the newly invigorated inter-American machinery to the widespread instability in the Caribbean region and beginning to focus on the long-term goals of economic growth. In this period, which was the apogee of inter-American cooperation, South America and the United States began to pursue similar interests in reducing tensions in the region. It was the period of the Marshall Plan, the Bretton Woods agreements, the North Atlantic Treaty Organization (NATO), and the General Agreement on Tariffs and Trade (GATT). The United States addressed what it perceived as its exposed southern flank with a new political structure to bring the nations of the Americas under the US umbrella. The old Pan-American Union morphed into the Organization of American States, and its charter was signed in Bogotá in April 1948. New agreements for security and peaceful resolution of disputes were implemented with the Inter-American Treaty of Reciprocal Assistance (Rio Treaty), signed in September 1947, and the American Treaty on Pacific Settlement (Pact of Bogotá), signed in April 1948. A formidable infrastructure was created to attend to political affairs, highlighting covenants for nonintervention and respect for self-determination, a long-sought goal of the Latin American members. The Inter-American Defense Board and the specialized organizations were merged into the OAS to structure a more comprehensive and coherent framework for cooperation.

The ensuing period was one of the most intense and successful in the history of inter-American cooperation. In the 1950s occurred the peaceful resolution of over forty disputes, mostly in the Caribbean and Central America, by the Inter-American Peace Commission, operating out of the OAS's Washington headquarters. The successes generated a sense of optimism that helped to motivate President John F. Kennedy (JFK) to propose the Alliance for Progress, which built on an earlier proposal for stronger inter-American cooperation by Brazilian president Juscelino Kubischek in 1958, which he called "Operation Pan-America."

The newly formed Alliance for Progress focused heavily on building institutions to address the onerous social problems plaguing Latin America. The Inter-American Development Bank and the Inter-American Commission on Human Rights were established, and the nations embraced a new Inter-American Committee for the Alliance for Progress (CIAP) under the OAS to assist each nation of the Americas in its economic planning. CIAP was a major innovation and incursion on the powerful shibboleths of national sovereignty. It held annual economic reviews patterned after the institutions of the Marshall Plan, in which all aid agencies, global, regional and bilateral, conducted weeklong reviews of the status and condition of every nation's domestic economy, made specific policy recommendations, and set the agenda for international economic assistance.[1]

By the early 1960s, however, with Fidel Castro's adventurism and the Cold War poised to expand to the Americas, sharp divisions had reappeared in the political and economic thinking of Latin America. The United States again awoke to its security interests and embarked on an effort to reinforce its alliances in the hemisphere, but the pressures of global realpolitik intervened with the Vietnam War. Henry Kissinger's Cold War assessment of Latin America's strategic importance as "a giant dagger pointed at the heart of Antarctica" left the region to fester under the protectorate of cooperative military dictatorships. A more significant event, however, the US intervention in the Dominican Republic in 1965, severely undermined the rhetoric of inter-American cooperation. The United States was clearly not to be "contained" when it considered its national interests at stake, especially in the Caribbean.

The changes in Latin America's attitudes toward the OAS occasioned by the events of that era were vividly reflected in the policies of Mexico and Brazil. In the 1940s and 1950s, when the OAS began to prosper, Mexico was one of the strongest advocates of inter-American cooperation and perceived it as the main line of defense against the United States. The Mexican foreign minister, Ezequiel Padilla, proposed a hemispheric economic union, and the Mexican ambassador to the OAS, Luis Quintanilla, took the lead in making the Inter-American Peace Committee an active force for peaceful resolution of disputes, avoiding unilateral intervention. As the United States began to turn to the OAS forum for Cold War purposes, beginning in 1954 with the Guatemalan revolution and more markedly in the Dominican intervention in 1965, Mexico balked and cast strong dissenting votes. The efforts to isolate and eventually expel Cuba from the system found Mexico a lonely dissenting voice. Immediately following the Dominican intervention in 1965, Mexico's policy perceptibly changed. From that time until the major change in direction with the approval of the North American Free Trade Agreement (NAFTA), Mexico became intransigent regarding the use of the OAS as a channel for dealing with Latin American issues. Instead of seeing the inter-American machinery as a defense, Mexico saw its vulnerability to US pressure. That was one of the major reasons for the use of other ad hoc conclaves outside of the OAS, such as Contadora, to address Central American civil strife in the 1980s.

Today, the mantle of resistance has been assumed by Brazil. In this context one of the most decisive events of recent times was the US attempt to interfere with the Brazilian plans for nuclear energy in 1977. The US unilateral action caused Brazil to sever its military treaties with the United States and accelerate the development of its own national armaments industry. The aftershocks, still reverberating, have influenced Brazilian perceptions far deeper than diplomacy could ever address.

The civil wars in Central America and the debt crisis in the 1980s reminded the United States once again of the dangers that poverty-plagued neighbors posed to political stability in the Americas. President George H. W. Bush launched an innovative Enterprise for the Americas Initiative and took steps to reduce the overwhelming debt of the region, conditioned on instituting economic and trade reforms. He and President Bill Clinton embraced access to US markets as a way to propel economic development in the region. A new wave of prospective institution building centered on trade was to ensue with the signing of NAFTA and an agreement to begin negotiations for the Free Trade Area of the Americas (FTAA), an ambitious goal for which the political will is still to be proven.

The Evolving Framework of Inter-American Institutions

The current institutional structure among the nations of the Americas is comprehensive, covering political, financial, and development issues. It involves a plethora of agencies, specialized organizations, and commissions that have evolved over decades rather than a coherent political framework for cooperation.

Periodic presidential summits provide the overarching forum for political and development direction at the highest level. Among the agencies, OAS covers the political sphere, including human rights, drugs, and terrorism. The Inter-American Development Bank (IDB) addresses financial needs, assisted by a cluster of subregional development banks, such as the Andean Development Corporation, the Caribbean Development Bank (CDB), and the Central American Bank for Economic Integration (CABEI). Technical assistance and training are addressed by both the OAS and IDB. A cluster of specialized organizations attend to specific sectoral development issues, including health, women's rights, and agriculture. The mandates of the combined entities cover the entire gamut of cross-border issues that concern nations, except for trade, which is currently on the agenda with the negotiations over the FTAA. On the subregional level, trade is addressed by a cluster of agencies and financial institutions dedicated to economic integration but having only limited membership. Military/security issues were meant to be addressed by the Inter-American Defense Board, but that fell into disuse after the US intervention in the Dominican Republic in 1965 and the newly admitted Caribbean nations and Canada declined to join the board. A more complete listing of the principal agencies and commissions can be found in Appendix 2.1.

Supplementing the above, innumerable subcommissions and independent entities group clusters of nations or specialists in various sectors.[2] In the private sector, hemispheric organizations are prevalent in the banking community, with the well-organized Latin American Federation of Banks (FELABAN) and ad hoc entities such as the Latin American Business Council (CEAL), the Inter-American Council for Commerce and Production (CICYP), and the hemispheric gatherings of the various chambers of commerce. Civil society has innumerable multinational arrangements and ad hoc hemispheric meetings in various social and economic sectors, such as environment, human rights, indigenous issues, and microenterprise, all of which have been greatly enhanced by the Internet and modern communications.

The OAS

The structure of the OAS is a fine theoretical model of all that inter-American cooperation might desire. It covers the three critical areas: politics, development, and regulation. The political arena is under the aegis of a Permanent Council whose country representatives are stationed in Washington with ambassadorial rank. It addresses issues relating to the strength of democracy, peacekeeping, human rights, juridical issues, and drugs and terrorism. These matters do not require large budgets. The promotion of development is governed by the second OAS council, the Inter-American Council for Integral Development (CIDI).

The OAS structure in the political field also encompasses a cluster of independent commissions with their own governing bodies that establish policies in their respective fields. The major peacekeeping machinery is set forth in considerable detail in the Charter of the OAS, placing responsibilities in the hands of the Permanent Council and meetings of consultation of the ministers of foreign affairs that are summoned by the council on an ad hoc basis. The Inter-American Commission on Human Rights is composed of experts in the field elected by the governments in their individual capacity. An independent Inter-American Court of Human Rights resulted from a pioneering effort to codify basic human rights in the Inter-American Convention on Human Rights in 1978. The Inter-American Juridical Committee, created in 1942, is charged with formulating recommendations relative to international organization. At the meeting creating the committee, Mexico's foreign minister, Ezequiel Padilla, pronounced that an attack on the United States would be considered an attack on all countries of the Americas, a declaration that set the basis for the subsequent Inter-American Treaty of Reciprocal Assistance (Rio Treaty) in 1947.

Although democracy is enshrined in the OAS Charter as one of the basic principals of inter-American solidarity, efforts to create a framework for collective action to support and reinforce democracy have been tempered by the pervasive concerns about placing too much authority in a body that was malleable to US influence. A series of actions that began with Resolution 1031 of the OAS General Assembly in 1991 and culminated in the Inter-American Democratic Charter, ratified on September 11, 2001, set the basis for specific collective action in the event of the interruption of democratic continuity in any American state. The interpretation and implementation of the Democratic Charter is relegated to the Permanent Council. To meet cross-border threats from narcotics traffic and terrorism, the Permanent Council established special commissions, the Inter-American Drug Abuse Control Commission (CICAD) and the Inter-American Committee Against Terrorism (CICTE), with delegates appointed by the nations specifically for those purposes.

The body that governs development efforts, the Inter-American Council for Integral Development (CIDI), theoretically an independent council that reports directly to the General Assembly, is peopled not by development specialists but by the same ambassadors that cover the Permanent Council. It has two charges, making policy recommendations in the economic and social fields and managing direct technical assistance. Under its wing is one of the largest foreign fellowship programs in the hemisphere, on which smaller nations rely heavily. The council has so many different token programs huddled under its wing, however, that none of them has any meaningful capability to accomplish anything. The CIDI stands as an ungainly model of a multifunctional organization with huge mandates and no money. International institutions may achieve considerable results in single-function entities with small budgets or may manage multiple functions with a large budget. It is not possible, however, to manage multiple functions with a miniscule budget. Consequently, the CIDI is essentially dysfunctional. It is largely inward-looking, incessantly entangled in internal discussions to apportion miniscule amounts in a scenario reminiscent of the proverbial bald men fighting over a comb. It is not treated seriously by the very ambassadors charged with its oversight, who delegate responsibility to junior diplomats who have little experience in overseeing development programs. In contrast to Canada, which selects its representative from the Canadian International Development Agency (CIDA), the United States is represented by State Department officials, instead of the development professionals from the US Agency for International Development (USAID).

The policy-oriented focus of CIDI relates to its responsibility as secretariat for periodic hemispheric ministerial meetings in the areas of education, labor, social development, environment (sustainable development), and science and technology. The Pan-American Health Organization (PAHO) and the Inter-American Institute for Cooperation on Agriculture (IICA) unite the health and agriculture ministers in annual or biannual meetings. Treasury ministers convene annually at the IDB meeting. Several other ministerial summits lie outside the orbit of the OAS or any other inter-American secretariat, including energy, transportation, commerce, and justice ministers. There is no rationale as to why some are serviced by the OAS and others are not.

With regard to direct technical assistance, the OAS experimented with a new initiative when it created the Inter-American Agency for Cooperation and Development (IACD) in 1999. The agency was an attempt to breathe new life into stagnating development programs of the OAS by attracting outside resources to amplify hemispheric technical assistance. The agency's mandate was limited from the beginning, however, when the OAS Permanent Council declined to put the substantive development programs of the secretariat under the IACD aegis. Without authority to direct even the internal resources of the OAS General Secretariat, it had no credibility with the country development authorities or any of its partner inter-American institutions. Given the sharp budgetary constraints, the experiment failed to motivate the countries to submit the quality projects required to attract new resources to the OAS.

The OAS role in cross-border regulatory collaboration relates primarily to the Inter-American Telecommunications Commission (CITEL), which serves as the regional voice for the International Telecommunications Union (ITU), and the Inter-American Ports Commission (CIP), which convenes regular meetings of port managers. These bodies focus entirely on policy issues. They convene the experts in their respective fields for exchanges of information and ad hoc cooperation without secretariat intervention. The absence of technical assistance functions enables them to play an influential convocational role in spite of minimal budgets. In other subjects, however, the creative impulses of inter-American cooperation have spawned institutions outside the traditional structure. In two areas, taxation and auditing, other inter-American commissions have been formed entirely outside the OAS. These are the Inter-American Center for Tax Administration (CIAT), with the

US Internal Revenue Service playing a key role, and the Council of Securities Regulators of the Americas, which was initiated under the aegis of the US Securities and Exchange Commission (SEC).

The role of the OAS in development is controversial and increasingly under fire. It is seen as a marginal player because of the overwhelming resources of the international financial institutions (IFIs). The OAS's principal problem in development policy, however, is not the need for more money. It is governance and staffing. Its role of convoking and providing secretariat functions for the preparation and follow-up of the mini-summits of ministers in the area of social development gives the OAS a unique potential in the policy arena. However, the foreign ministries dominate the organization's decisionmaking, whereas responsibility for the substantive issues falls to other ministries. Generally, these technical ministries do not want the foreign ministries meddling in their affairs. This causes them to keep the OAS secretariat at a distance. This can be clearly discerned in the United States, where departments such as education, health and human services, and commerce totally reject the intermediation of the Department of State in their substantive issues. The most conspicuous example is the Department of the Treasury, which sets its policies for Latin America totally independent of and frequently without regard to the concerns of the Department of State.

Structural issues in international governance have become increasingly acute due to unlimited modern communications. Technical experts talk regularly to their counterparts in other nations without intermediation. Not only are they far more effective in direct communication, but they resist any effort by outside institutions that do not have technical credentials to impose unnecessary procedures. The world of modern communications has accelerated the trend to decentralized cooperation. Only a few decades ago, one could hardly get a president or minister on the phone, much less travel to see him without considerable protocol. Today direct communications are routine. Technical meetings to share information and discuss cross-border issues take place on a regular basis, many of them emanating from technical meetings of multinational corporations or sponsored by the private sector. The Internet empowers experts to share each other's databases. Many of them meet so frequently they even know each other's families. This evolution has been one of the strongest elements to which traditional institutions such as the OAS have to adapt.

The New Architecture: Presidential Summit Meetings

Meetings at the highest political level of the American states began with the presidential summit convoked by President Clinton in 1994. With it came a new dynamic in inter-American cooperation. As a conclave of the highest authorities of the Americas, the summit meetings instantly generated new excitement about regional cooperation. Their deliberate creation outside of the OAS orbit was intended to give it broader reach to engage multiple entities, including mandating periodic mini-summit meetings of ministers from different sectors to encourage senior officials and technical experts to interact among themselves.

The presidential summit machinery, however, had a serious contradiction. It was centralized at the highest level but relied on decentralized machinery to implement its mandates. No systematic linkage, however, bridged the two. The ministerial meetings theoretically address the issues raised in the summit, but they are neither responsible to nor report to the summit. A similar problem exists with the implementation agencies, the regional and subregional financial institutions, and the inter-American specialized organizations. No directives are issued to the technical ministries to guide their proposed programs, and no feedback mechanism allows them to offer their advice or technical expertise to the presidents. The summit stands in splendid isolation, and its agendas are solely in the hands of foreign ministries, whose knowledge of the technical issues is only theoretical and who prefer to address the issues with rhetoric rather than defer to the responsible parties with experience.

To foster meaningful and systematic regional cooperation from these high-level conclaves, some institutional mechanism will be required to ensure that summit development mandates are funneled into the ministerial agendas in a structured, coherent manner. Credible machinery that engages the other development agencies and development banks, both regional and subregional, in the summit process is also essential. Only if the IFIs are given a systematic role in the process will their staffs engage seriously in financing programs to fulfill the mandates. This means establishing well-structured preparatory committees for the ministerial meetings and inviting the IDB and the subregional development banks as full members, not as observers. A Summit Implementation Review Group (SIRG) was wisely created as a preparatory committee for the summit. However, no similar preparatory mechanism exists for the ministerial meetings.

The OAS has the capability to do this for the ministerial meetings under its aegis, but its reach is too limited to provide a meaningful solution. To exercise this function successfully, the other inter-American agencies must be convinced that participation in the preparatory committees is part of an officially sanctioned two-way street—mandates traveling down from the summit to the ministerials and recommendations rising from the ministerials to the summits. This has never been achieved, and it is a remote possibility so long as foreign ministries dominate the OAS machinery.

The Future of Inter-American Cooperation

Overcoming the Roadblocks

Institution building and reform involve patient analysis to define real needs and consensus on practical ways to meet them. In times of transition in the international arena, as occurred after World War II, a natural momentum builds for change. In more tranquil periods of history, conflicting issues and interests overwhelm the agenda.

The realities of official inter-American cooperation today belie its uninhibited agenda. There are several reasons for the weaknesses: divergent interests, unrelated development institutions, inarticulate development priorities, and lack of funding. First and most complex are the divergent political purposes distinguishing South America from Central America and the Caribbean. Central America and the Caribbean are composed of small vulnerable economies that are highly dependent on trade and tourism from the United States. South America's economies are more diverse, with global trade patterns that extend equally to the United States, Europe, and Asia. The economic and political realities of the two regions also vary dramatically. The fourteen English-speaking Caribbean nations have relatively stable democratic institutions. Their weakness is economic vulnerability. A small tax base and recurrent natural disasters make them highly dependent on external cooperation. The South American nations have stronger, more self-reliant economies. Their major issues relate to unstable political structures. Thus the needs and aspirations of the representatives from the two areas for the inter-American community are entirely different. The goals of Central America and the Caribbean are to engage and co-opt the United States for economic assistance. The political orientation of South America is to contain the United States.

The US agenda stands in sharp contrast to both of them. The overarching thrust of US policies in the hemisphere has been dominated by security concerns. That holds true for US-sponsored initiatives to improve inter-American relations as well as interventionist incidents. For example, FDR began to pay attention to Latin America with his Good Neighbor Policy to counter the growing strength of fascism in the 1930s, and JFK's concerns about the growing following of Fidel Castro in the early 1960s spawned the Alliance for Progress. President Ronald Reagan reacted to the perceived inroads of Fidel Castro in the Caribbean with a military intervention in Grenada and the Caribbean Basin Initiative. And, as we noted, the interventions in the Dominican Republic in 1965, in Nicaragua in the 1980s to support the contras, and more recently in Haiti have deeply influenced the attitude of most of the nations of the Americas as to how much political or policing authority they are willing to cede to inter-American institutions. Indeed, many Latin Americans sense deeply that the only foreign intervention they need fear is from the United States.

The interests of the United States, however, play the most decisive role in the capacity of the system not only because the United States finances the system but because Latin American and Caribbean members shape their policies to the institutions largely by their reaction to or fear of US motivations. When such divergent motivations meet in one multifunctional organization such as the OAS, the political considerations inevitably divert attention from developmental and humanitarian goals.

Second, the structure is burdened with a plethora of unrelated development institutions, many of which have outlived their historical usefulness and have spawned an atmosphere of frustration that impedes new initiatives. The OAS has six specialized organizations and a range of special committees that have little relationship to each other in their structure, budgeting, or governance. The specialized organizations are intergovernmental organizations with their own charters ratified by the governments. Only two, PAHO and IICA, have budgets reasonably commensurate with their mandates. The others have independent governing bodies but negligible budgets. OAS members have yet to devise, much less apply, any criteria for sunset provisions. However, new cross-border issues emanating from summit mandates, such as cooperation with regard to energy, the environment, or education, go unattended.

The third gap is the inability of the nations to establish priorities among their development goals. Agendas are overcrowded with trivia. Every possible issue is addressed, no priorities are set, no directives compel the independent governing boards of the multiple institutions, and no plan of action sets guidelines or goals for the succeeding time frame. In Europe, mandates from the highest political level of the European Union are directed to specific bodies and firmly followed up. In the Americas, the OAS has no such authority. The redundancy of summit declarations, which set no priorities or indicate how they are to be followed up or financed, has generated an environment of cynicism. Moreover, there is little that is new in successive summit pronouncements. Paragraphs are reshuffled but generally contain little more than what was said in the lofty declarations of the Alliance for Progress or even the Economic Agreement of Bogotá, signed at the time of the adoption of the OAS Charter in 1948. No one is listening any longer—not even the staff of the institutions, and certainly not national political leaders.

The fourth and perhaps greatest failure of inter-American cooperation is that the nations fail to appropriate adequate budgets to accomplish the high-sounding goals. An observation in the 2005 UN Human Development Report sounds a note that strongly applies to inter-American institutions. It observed that "the currency of pledges from the international community is by now so severely debased by non-delivery that it is widely perceived as worthless" (p. 40). Except for the regional and subregional banks, which are self-financing, the OAS, its commissions, and specialized organizations have virtually no resources. That has paralyzed the entities' ability to act, not only in the development field but in the political arena. For example, when the OAS played a major role in the El Salvador–Honduras border dispute in 1969 and again in 1976, it did so because the United States unilaterally put up the funds to finance peacekeeping forces. When similar peacekeepers were needed in Haiti and Nicaragua in the 1980s, the United States sought to diffuse its financial burden in the midst of the huge budgetary deficits of the Reagan years and turned to the UN. The action was a major setback to the prestige and potential of the OAS in inter-American peacekeeping.

The funding issue has much broader implications for inter-American cooperation. Latin American nations have neither the will nor the resources to sustain international cooperative efforts, especially given the priority of democratic governments to respond first to the pressing social demands of domestic constituencies. The disconnect between resources and rhetoric became most evident in the efforts of the Latin American nations to form their own institutions for development cooperation without the United States. The most famous of these examples were the Latin American Economic System (SELA), set up in the 1970s as a policy agency to counterbalance perceived US domination of OAS economic policy pronouncements, and the Latin American Organization for Energy Development (OLADE). In contrast, the subregional agencies dedicated to forging policies for integration, such as Mercado Común del Sur (Mercosur), Andean Group, and the Caribbean Community (CARICOM), have had more impact where their activities relate to influencing policy among a more coherent grouping of nations than undertaking specific activities that require major funding.

Setting the Patterns for the Future

If American nations are to garner the political will to strengthen their institutional infrastructure, several issues must be addressed. They include defining the objectives of the nations for inter-American cooperation, finding practical ways to engage the technical experts and real actors in the countries, providing adequate funding, and linking American organizations more closely to the global institutions of the UN. Let me address each of these briefly.

- *Mission.* In spite of an OAS Charter that articulates coherent goals, many inter-American institutions have historically outdated missions or only token programs. These remnants of the past crowd out resources for current priorities. Their token programs subvert public confidence in the nations' ability to address more urgent issues. For example, the summit repeatedly enunciates priority issues of energy, environment, and education, yet no special resources are allocated and no specialized organizations exist to address these objectives.

- *Engaging the real actors.* The foreign ministries in many Latin American countries are often divorced from and unfamiliar with the forces shaping the vital economic and social interests of their countries. Principal among them are the major economic and social actors, the private sector and civil society. Machinery to engage these sectors in forging policies to address the issues would inject new energy into the process. Similarly, it would be useful to consider means to engage legislators who have to adopt legislation that gives substance to inter-American cooperation.

- *Funding.* Unlike the UN, which has many donor nations, the Americas have only two, the United States and Canada. Fifty-nine percent of the OAS budget comes from the United States, and 84 percent comes from five nations: the United States, Canada, Mexico, Brazil, and Argentina. There is little economic capacity in the Americas to support inter-American programs unless the United States agrees. However, the larger Latin American nations, Brazil and Mexico, have also played a major role in restraining OAS capacity for reasons that relate mainly to their perception of the role of the United States in the hemispheric forum. During the 1970s, Mexico weighed in heavily on refusing to allow increases in the OAS budget, and since the turn of the twenty-first century, Brazil has vetoed any increases. These limitations, played out over larger political issues as noted above, have crippled the OAS role in peacekeeping and severely handicapped the ability of the secretariat to implement regional programs to benefit the smaller of its member nations.

- *Limited interface with the UN and global institutions.* Communications, not to speak of coordination, between UN agencies and the regional entities are virtually nil. Models of how regional organizations can complement and enhance global efforts, however, do exist. PAHO entered into an agreement with the World Health Organization (WHO) shortly after the formation of the UN, by which PAHO became the regional executing agency of WHO in the Americas. Today all programs approved by the WHO for the Americas are turned over to PAHO for execution, greatly enhancing the authority and engagement of the hemispheric ministers of health, who comprise the board of PAHO. Similarly, CITEL has carved out a role for itself as the regional policy forum feeding into the ITU. Both are important examples that deserve further study of how global and regional organization can work together, allowing the global agency to set policies and delegating implementation to the regional entity that is closer to the scene (UNITAR 1984: 1–5). No other inter-American agency, either in the political field (human rights, women's issues, narcotic traffic) or the development field (agriculture, education, and environment), has replicated such cooperation.[3] Overlapping and even competitive programs thrive in this environment, diluting the meager resources available to both the OAS and the United Nations Development Programme (UNDP) and impeding more meaningful programs to address overwhelming social and economic development issues.

- *Unresolved staffing issues.* Cross-border programs in international cooperation are huge and complex. They require technical experts experienced in management. Training and dedication to mission are a sine qua non for effective managerial response. In comparison with private sector corporations in which training is always the highest priority, meager international organization budgets leave virtually no money available for training. The OAS has a more serious problem, in that it has not come to grips with the tension between the need for experienced career staff and the desire for more energetic and innovative younger people from a rotating staff. The issue of training and motivating an innovative international civil service is the Achilles' heel of meaningful international institution building.

What Works

A diagnosis of the success and shortcomings of inter-American institutions must begin with a pragmatic analysis of what has worked among institutions that have merited the support of the governments in the Americas and beyond. It is useful to review these issues as they apply to the current state of institutional engagement in the Americas.

- *A clear consensus among the participating nations.* As I stated at the beginning of this chapter, international cooperation is a political decision. It must have strong backing from the highest technical levels of government. Such a consensus occurred most dramatically with the Inter-American Commission on Human Rights but faltered with the more ambitious Inter-American Court of Human Rights. The commissions to address narcotics and terrorism derived from a consensus on need, but the specific actions to be undertaken were limited because of the divergent interests of the governments. In the current inter-American environment, any serious institutional reform must emanate from the summit.

- *Strong secretariat or governmental leadership.* The Inter-American Human Rights Commission serves as an extraordinary example of the success that can be had when a consensus exists and the governments agree to delegate the responsibilities to recognized experts to exercise their judgment in their individual capacity, not as representatives of their government. Leadership by one or more governments that have a special interest in an issue also serves as a viable catalyst, as took place with the Inter-American Peace Commission in the 1950s. This works particularly well when one of the major contributing governments assumes leadership.

- *Technical issues addressed by technical agencies.* We have noted that international collaboration works best when nations allow the experts directly involved in substance to represent their governments. In the inter-American environment, CITEL, the regional entity coordinating policy for the ITU, and PAHO in health, both attended by experts in their fields, have made extraordinary technical contributions. In contrast, the Special Committee on Trade Consultation and Negotiation (CECON), which was mandated to manage trade discussions in the 1970s, is an important example of the causes of failure. Its location under the OAS in Washington left representation to foreign ministry officials, who made it more of a rhetorical and contentious forum than a constructive one. The Office of the US Trade Representative, whose mandate was separate from that of the US State Department, considered the entity unconstructive and paid it little attention. It met irregularly until the FTAA established a new process directly under the trade ministries.

- *Practical applications.* CIAT, COSRA, and CITEL are important models of entities focused on practical issues that require cross-border collaboration. Military and police collaboration in Interpol is another example, but the levels of their collaboration are hidden from public view and in many countries from the foreign ministries.

Issues for the Future

In my view, three issues will greatly affect the evolution of Inter-American cooperation in the coming decades: (1) the potential of the FTAA, (2) the latent need to embrace more practical cooperation in areas that are of direct concern to the American nations, and (3) the role of the various actors and interests influencing inter-American issues.

Trade

The most important new development on the horizon relating to the continuing evolution of inter-American cooperation is trade. The prospect of a Free Trade Agreement of the Americas, if such an agreement is adopted, will give rise to an entirely different set of issues among the nations than those presently addressed by the OAS or IDB. An FTAA secretariat will overshadow and in some areas conflict with the OAS on issues of trade and economic development because it will have tangible substantive issues to address. This will enable it to attract higher-level and more engaged representation from its member states. In time it could well replace the OAS in its development role as these issues atrophy under the limited OAS budget. If, however, agreement on a hemispheric FTAA fails, leaving a series of bilateral or subregional agreements among the nations, the OAS will remain as the principal inter-American forum, and its limitations will be more evident in a new context.

Cross-Border Cooperation

The second issue is inter-American machinery that places practical cross-border issues under the aegis of those components of national governments that bear direct responsibility for them. Two areas that stand out are energy and transportation. In the field of energy, the complementary needs of the energy-rich and energy-poor countries of the Americas are not being addressed. Mexico and Venezuela have agreed to supply oil at reduced prices to the nations of Central America and the Caribbean under the Acuerdo de San José, but their initiative addresses only part of the needs. Something like an American Energy Community, patterned after the European Coal and Steel Community (ECSC), would provide a pragmatic mechanism for American nations to spark the development of the hemisphere, to finance energy development, as well as to facilitate capital investment and greater inter-American cooperation (Scheman 2003: 209–213).

A long-term plan for the Americas to achieve energy security means adopting policies to harmonize legislation and taxation of different types of energy sources and developing the economic and financial infrastructure to provide generating and transmission networks. Such an entity could provide funds to develop each nation's most economic sources of supply, help finance rural electrification or energy conservation measures, and become self-financing by securitizing its investments without calling on governmental guarantees.

Transportation infrastructure is another area in which cooperation results in more coherent investment, reduces costs, and enables the countries to be more competitive in global markets. With advances in electronic technology, improvements in the quality of education, especially in the sciences, can be achieved by hemispheric distance-learning courses for teachers. Practical issues such as these are more likely to galvanize greater cooperation and thus build confidence among the general public, analogous to what the ECSC did for Europe in the 1950s.

Real Interests and Diverse Actors

The third issue that demands attention is engaging the actors whose attitudes, outreach, and decisionmaking responsibilities have a direct impact on the success of inter-American cooperation: civil society, the private sector, and, in representative democracies, legislators. Any meaningful measure of inter-American cooperation, especially in trade, must sooner or later receive their approval. Their ignorance of the issues being discussed in inter-American forums and lack of involvement in the debates are often major hurdles to meaningful fulfillment of an inter-American agenda.

Reference to the need for public-private sector partnerships is standard rhetoric at every summit and Permanent Council meeting. Both the OAS and the IDB have made impressive strides in engaging civil society in dialogue and in program formulation in the early stages. Similar progress has not been made with the private sector, which remains relatively aloof from the process. However, in the political context of the summit meetings, the participation of civil society and the private sector is limited to short, highly structured meetings, frequently held after decisions have already been made.

Finding more meaningful ways for them to participate at the various levels of inter-American discussion and decisionmaking could enhance the effectiveness of and support for inter-American cooperation and could mobilize their considerable energies into real, constructive proposals. Their imagination and experience add depth to the official committees that presently receive input principally from the narrow perspective of the foreign ministries.

Conclusion

Numerous conflicting currents presently flow through the inter-American system. In the political arena, the agreement of the American nations on the Inter-American Democratic Charter in 2001 opened a new chapter of potential collaboration in favor of democracy, even though populist leaders who weaken democracy through disregard of its underlying institutions continue to hamper genuine cooperation.

In the economic field, the clash of the United States and Brazil over agricultural subsidies has, at the time of this writing, stymied the efforts toward an FTAA. However, the magnet of US market remains. Tension among the nations of the Americas analogous to those we are addressing today were prevalent when FDR's Good Neighbor Policy and, three decades later, JFK's Alliance for Progress successfully reversed attitudes. The attraction of the markets cannot be underestimated in evaluating long-term political trends.

Given concerns about the flow of drugs and illegal immigrants in relation to the overriding issue of terrorists taking advantage of the weaknesses those activities represent, it is timely for the nations of the Americas to consider more pragmatic, sustainable policies for inter-American cooperation. This might require a disaggregation of hemispheric arrangements, separating the relationship between the United States and the Caribbean, through which most of these threats flow, from that between the United States and South America. It could mean the adoption of a new subregional arrangement between the United States and the Caribbean Basin nations to supplement or supersede the Rio Treaty, which has been virtually moribund since the Falkland/Malvinas war in 1982 (Scheman 1987). It could also enable the United States to focus more realistically on the needs of the smaller nations of the Caribbean, of which many of the English-speaking nations were not admitted to the IDB (although they all were admitted as full members of the World Bank). Such a policy would conform more effectively to the diverse interests of the nations of the hemisphere. Since such an arrangement would not include South America, the diverse interests of those nations that have stymied the OAS action in these fields could be addressed more coherently.

In sum, it is time for a new look at the fundamental interests of the nations of the hemisphere. If the more developed nations of the hemisphere abdicate this responsibility, they will leave wide latitude to populist leaders. The ensuing chapters in this book will analyze these issues in greater depth. They come at a very propitious time. The year 2005 marked a milestone in the leadership of the principal inter-American institutions. José Miguel Insulza, elected secretary general of the Organization of American States, and Luis Alberto Moreno, as president of the Inter-American Development Bank, represent a generational change. They bring a new perspective to inter-American institutions in an environment in which democracy and free market economics in the hemisphere continue to face fresh but familiar challenges. It is important to appraise carefully how their initiatives have met the issues that this book seeks to address.

Appendix 2.1 The Component Institutions of Inter-American Cooperation

- **Overarching Inter-American Cooperation:**
  The Presidential Summits of the Americas
  - o Ad Hoc Mini-Summit Meetings of Ministers with Sectoral Responsibilities
- **Political**
  - o Organization of American States
    - ■ Democracy and Juridical Issues
      - ❑ OAS Permanent Council[a]
      - ❑ Inter-American Juridical Committee (IAJC)
      - ❑ Inter-American Commission on Human Rights (IACHR)
    - ■ Military
      - ❑ Inter-American Defense Board (IADB, the Board)
      - ❑ Inter-American Defense College
    - ■ Narcotic Control
      - ❑ Inter-American Drug Abuse Control Commission (CICAD)
    - ■ Combating Terrorism
      - ❑ Inter-American Committee Against Terrorism (CICTE)
  - o Rio Group
- **Development**
  - o Inter-American Council for Integral Development (CIDI)
  - o Specialized Organizations
    - ■ Pan-American Health Organization (PAHO)
    - ■ Inter-American Institute for Cooperation on Agriculture (IICA)
    - ■ Inter-American Commission of Women (CIM)
    - ■ Inter-American Children's Institute (IIN)
    - ■ Inter-American Indian Institute (III)
    - ■ Pan-American Institute of Geography and History (PAIGH)
  - o Latin American Economic System (SELA)
  - o Latin American Organization for Energy Development (OLADE)
- **Finance**
  - o Inter-American Development Bank (IDB)
  - o Andean Development Corporation (CAF)
  - o Central American Bank for Economic Integration (CABEI)
  - o Caribbean Development Bank (CDB)
  - o Latin American Export Bank (BLADEX)
- **Regulatory and Advisory**
  - o Inter-American Telecommunications Commission (CITEL)
  - o Inter-American Ports Commission (CIP)

- **Trade and Economic Integration**
  - ○ Subregional
    - ■ Mercosur
    - ■ Andean Community of Nations
    - ■ Central American Integration System (SICA)
    - ■ Caribbean Community (CARICOM)
    - ■ Latin American Integration Association (ALADI)
  - ○ NAFTA
  - ○ Central American–Dominican Republic Free Trade Agreement (CAFTA-DR)

Notes: This list does not include the United Nations inter-American agencies, such as the Economic Commission for Latin America and the Caribbean (ECLAC).

a. The OAS Charter, which established the modern framework of the OAS in 1948, provided only for the Permanent Council. Charter amendments adopted in Buenos Aires in 1967 provided for three governing councils, the Inter-American Economic and Social Council and the Inter-American Science, Education, and Cultural Council, with the objective of dealing more coherently with the issues addressed by the Alliance for Progress. The two development councils were merged into one Inter-American Council for Integral Development in the charter amendments adopted in Nicaragua in 1998.

Notes

1. For a complete discussion of the institutional arrangements fostered by the alliance, see L. Ronald Scheman, *The Alliance for Progress: A Retrospective* (New York: Praeger, 1988), and the bibliography therein.

2. For a more comprehensive listing as of 1988, see L. Ronald Scheman, *The Inter-American Dilemma* (Praeger, 1988), 28–29.

3. When the issue was broached that the newly formed Inter-American Agency for Cooperation and Development (IACD) enter into a formal agreement with the United Nations Development Programme, it was quickly discouraged by political elements in both entities. Even more significant, the staffs of the OAS and IDB, who work within a few city blocks of each other, have consistently been unable to cooperate on projects addressing similar issues.

3

Inter-American Governance: A Sisyphean Endeavor?

Gordon Mace and Jean-Philippe Thérien

In the early 1980s the inter-American system went through a period of such turbulence that some observers believed its main institutional base—the Organization of American States (OAS)—was on its last legs (Bloomfield and Lowenthal 1990: 869; Gannon 1984; Vaky 1993: 11). The Falklands crisis, the unending civil wars in Central America, the perpetuation of authoritarian regimes in a number of countries, and the disinterest of political elites appeared at the time to be insurmountable obstacles to the development of dynamic hemispheric cooperation.

Due largely to the end of the Cold War, this climate of pessimism shifted in a surprisingly short space of time. Held in Miami in December 1994, the first Summit of the Americas ushered in a new era in inter-American relations amid feelings of shared values, new and renewed friendships, and revitalized hope in the future of regional cooperation.[1] A high point of that new era came in September 2001 with the adoption of the Inter-American Democratic Charter on the very day the United States was hit by extreme terrorist attacks. Yet, within a year after the agreement on the Inter-American Democratic Charter was reached, the general impression was that the inter-American system had reentered a period of relative paralysis, which the Fourth Summit of the Americas, held in Mar del Plata, Argentina, in November 2005, did little to attenuate.

Broadly speaking, in this chapter we seek to better elucidate why hemispheric relations constantly oscillate between periods of innovative institution building and periods of near-stagnation. Within this general context, our more specific objective will be to provide an analysis of the current state of inter-American governance and explain why the new institutional design introduced in 1994 did not achieve the success that had been anticipated.

Our study is grounded on three key ideas that can be summarized as follows. First, it is important to acknowledge that since the first pan-American

conference of 1889–1890, the history of the Americas has been characterized by the slow construction of a hemisphere-wide system of governance.
Granted, this construction has always been ridden with conflict, strewn
with stumbling blocks. Evidently, the inter-American regime of governance
is not as strong as that associated with European integration. In comparison
with the European experience, dominated by the European Union, the inter-
American system is limited by allowing the coexistence of several levels of
interstate governance in the region: a hemispheric structure under the aegis
of the OAS and its related agencies and a variety of subregional structures
such as the North American Free Trade Agreement (NAFTA), the Caribbean Community (CARICOM), and the incipient South American Community of Nations. Yet inter-American governance involves a complex set of
institutions, norms, and rules that cover almost every aspect of international
relations. That is why the Americas provide a potentially fertile source of
instruction for anyone interested in the development of "sub-global international societies" (Buzan 2004: 18).

Second, our analysis is based on the observation that the inter-American system of governance has evolved in a cyclical rather than a linear
fashion. The notion of "cycles" was notably used by historian Arthur Schlesinger (1986), who suggested that the foreign policy of the United States
underwent profound changes roughly every thirty years. More closely
related to the theme of this chapter, the concept of "cycles" was recently
taken up by Javier Corrales and Richard Feinberg, who described hemispheric cooperation in terms of its "many-steps-forward-some-steps-back-
ward trajectory" (1999: 9). Opinions naturally vary concerning the peri-
odization of this trajectory, but there is a fairly widespread agreement on
three moments of significant consolidation of hemispheric governance—
1889, 1948, and 1994—which represent turning points on the road to an
institutional and normative renewal of the inter-American system. Although
the regression of the recent years was certainly not unavoidable, it is consistent with a logic of déjà vu that has continued to render the advances of
regional cooperation in the Americas highly tenuous.

Third, our analysis stresses the idea that inter-American governance is
to a large extent shaped by the social and political environment. Of course,
institutional variables also exercise a decisive influence on hemispheric
politics. In this regard, it is clear that the introduction of summitry in 1994
generated a strong impulse for the renewal of the governance of inter-
American relations by creating a new institutional design (Aggarwal 1998).
In addition, the notion of "nesting" proposed by Vinod Aggarwal provides
a stimulating insight for an account of some recent difficulties of inter-
American governance. Nevertheless, as we shall see, the divergence of values and the absence of political will no doubt do more than any institutional
variables to explain, ultimately, the hindrances blocking the development of
inter-American cooperation.

The rest of the chapter is divided into two parts. The first looks at the 1889–1994 period and examines how inter-American governance underwent two distinct cycles of expansion and decline. The second part of the chapter focuses on the latest cycle of hemispheric cooperation, which began in 1994. Following an analysis of the new institutional design that was established at that time, the section examines four variables to account for the current paralysis of inter-American cooperation: the inefficiency of the institutional design, the confusion in priorities, the lack of resources, and the absence of democratic legitimacy.

Inter-American Governance Until 1994

A Cyclical Evolution

For the past 100 years or so, inter-American relations have evolved in cycles. Each cycle was composed of a short period of institution building, followed by a longer period of paralysis. In each case, institution building was made possible by a combination of several factors, in which three elements seem to have been particularly decisive: a favorable international context, US leadership, and the capacity to reach a "historic compromise" in US–Latin American relations. Stagnation, however, arose from a blend of misperceptions and divergent expectations regarding what inter-American cooperation implied in terms of rights and responsibilities.

The first cycle started with the First International Conference of American States, which took place in Washington from October 1889 to April 1890, and lasted until the end of the 1930s. Although limited, institution building lasted twenty years. It ended with the fourth pan-American conference of 1910, which transformed the Commercial Bureau of the American Republics into the Pan-American Union. The emergence of an inter-American system of governance resulted essentially from the ascendancy of the United States on the international scene as of the end of the nineteenth century. Propelled by the determination of Secretary of State James Blaine, the US government played an instrumental role in the organization of the first pan-American conference. Most importantly, Washington proved able to convince Latin American countries that they could enhance their status in world politics by joining in a regional system of the Americas.

Despite its promising beginnings, hemispheric cooperation subsequently went through a long period of stagnation in which, to quote the respected historian Gordon Connell-Smith, "Pan-Americanism had not achieved a great deal" (1974: 127). The perception of shared interests that may have existed on the eve of the 1889 conference had all but disappeared in the 1930s, after years of US unilateralism and military interventions in the region. US behavior served only to illustrate the ambiguities of the 1889 compromise: Washington had hoped for the establishment of a regional customs union, whereas Latin American leaders were mostly interested in an agreement that would have made the right of conquest illegal (Moreno Pino 1977: 75–76; Corrales and Feinberg 1999: 5–7). The ensuing events left both parties with the confirmation that their feelings of disappointment had been justified.

Post-1948 Institution Building

The second cycle of inter-American cooperation lasted over forty-five years, starting in 1947–1948. The period of institution building, however, lasted only seven years, ending more or less with the US-supported coup in Guatemala in 1954. The transformation of pan-Americanism in the 1940s was again engineered by the United States. In fact, the restructuring of hemispheric cooperation was part and parcel of the new world order established after World War II under US leadership. The new order was, of course, largely shaped by the East-West divide, but it also very quickly came to be distinguished by the burgeoning of international institutions. Beginning with the establishment of the UN system, this phenomenon soon spread to the regional level. It is against this background that the OAS was founded in 1948, becoming the world's first regional organization. The "historic compromise" on which the OAS was based took the form this time of an agreement by the Latin American governments to take part in a regional security regime in return for the US support in favor of the principle of nonintervention.

From 1945 to 1948, five conferences enabled the governments of the region to create a complex set of institutions that would govern inter-American relations (Atkins 1989: 207–236). With its council, its meeting of consultation of foreign ministers, and its specialized conferences, the OAS emerged as the main political component of this new system. The OAS nurtured extremely high expectations: its charter, adopted in 1948, declared that America's "historic mission" was to "offer to man a land of liberty and a favorable environment for the development of his personality and the realization of his just aspirations" (OAS 1989).

It also became possible in the 1940s to consolidate the inter-American architecture through the addition of regional norms in the areas of security and human rights. With respect to security, the 1947 Inter-American Treaty of Reciprocal Assistance (Rio Treaty) instituted a system of regional collective security, and the 1948 American Treaty on Pacific Settlement (Pact of Bogotá) committed the parties "to settle all disputes without resort to force" (Ball 1969: 426). Concerning human rights, the American Declaration of the Rights and Duties of Man, adopted in 1948, earned the distinction of being the first legal instrument designed to set up an international regime in this sphere of activity (Stoetzer 1993: 245).

Overall, quite a lot was done between 1945 and the end of the 1950s to restructure inter-American governance around a dense network of institutions and norms. But institutions do not automatically equate with cooperative behavior. Many analysts have argued that inter-American governance, and particularly the OAS, entered a state of crisis starting in the 1950s (Stoetzer 1993: 295). Again, the "historic compromise" behind hemispheric cooperation appeared to be fraught with ambiguity. From the Latin American viewpoint, the OAS was supposed to be a shield against US hegemony, whereas for the United States the organization was perceived as a vehicle for its foreign policy interests (Thérien, Fortmann, and Gosselin 1996: 232). Because of these differing outlooks, hemispheric governance was stymied for three decades.

Toward the Paralysis of the Inter-American System

The period from the mid-1950s through 1985 was a difficult one for the inter-American system. Regime building did occur in some areas, as witnessed by the creation of the Inter-American Development Bank (IDB, 1959), the Inter-American Commission on Human Rights (1959), and the Inter-American Court of Human Rights (1978). Treaties were signed and conferences were held. In particular, the 1967 Meeting of American Heads of State in Punta del Este, Uruguay, attracted the attention of the diplomatic community and the media. But this gathering, which was supposed to relaunch hemispheric cooperation and help Latin American economic integration (Connell-Smith 1974: 248–249), simply confirmed that the OAS and the inter-American system had little relevance for regional politics.

A number of reasons explain this long period of decline in hemispheric governance. A major factor had to do with the US interventions in Guatemala in 1954 and in the Dominican Republic in 1965. They reminded Latin Americans that US unilateral behavior was still a dominant form of Washington's foreign policy in the region. Each time the United States considered its national interests to be at stake, the logic of power prevailed over the principles of international law. Some observers have summed up this situation by stating that the OAS was governed by the principle of "la mayoría de uno" (Ezeta 1992: 25).

Other factors linked to the international context were also at work. One of them was the Cuban Revolution of 1958, which introduced a Cold War dynamic in the Americas, thereby creating a difficult environment for regional cooperation to develop. From then on, the Cold War poisoned inter-American relations for a whole generation. Blinded by its East-West reading of the civil wars that ravaged El Salvador and Nicaragua during the 1980s, American diplomacy sought for a long time to resolve these conflicts through military rather than political means. As this strategy had practically no support elsewhere in the hemisphere, it greatly contributed to undermining any form of inter-American dialogue.

Another international factor was the nascent North-South confrontation over a new international economic order. In the various forums where economic issues were heatedly discussed, the Unites States was on one side of the fence, and Latin American governments were on the other. The North-South cleavage, along with the mood of economic nationalism spreading in many subregions of the Americas, had a structuring effect on diplomatic relations across the hemisphere. Regional integration schemes were flourishing while Latin American governments created subregional institutions, such as the Special Commission for Latin American Coordination (CECLA), the Latin American Economic System (SELA), and the Rio Group, to better defend their own specific interests. For Latin American governments, these organizations rapidly came to be seen as more appropriate instruments of representation and expression than hemispheric institutions, whose legitimacy was significantly reduced.

The external environment thus goes a long way toward explaining the paralysis of inter-American governance that started in the second half of the 1950s. International rigidities might have been reduced if initial expectations had been fulfilled, but that was never the case. Washington used hemispheric institutions as a way to legitimize its own unilateral behavior in pursuit of its interests, while equitable economic partnership never succeeded. The "historic compromise" had failed again, and the hopes that had emerged in the 1940s for a new era for inter-American cooperation were shattered.

Understanding the Present Cycle of Inter-American Governance

A New Institutional Design

A new cycle of inter-American cooperation was made possible by a series of events that occurred in the 1980s, both at the international and at the regional level. The end of the Cold War and the implosion of the Soviet Union had a significant impact on inter-American dynamics. These events considerably strengthened the hegemonic position of the United States in world affairs and limited the options for anti-US policies in Latin America. The perception of emerging trade blocs, particularly in Europe, also played a catalytic role in the renaissance of hemispheric cooperation. But the external debt crisis of the early 1980s was probably the main engine for change because of the tremendous effect it had on economic policies in all of Latin America and the Caribbean (ECLAC 1992, 1994).

The debt crisis not only had severe economic consequences for the populations involved, but also caused a psychological shock. Under strong pressure from international financial institutions such as the International Monetary Fund (IMF) and the World Bank, decisionmakers in most countries of the region had to rethink the old ways of doing things and to adopt new patterns of behavior. All over the hemisphere, neoliberal policies replaced economic protectionism, and representative democracy became the political model to follow.

The victory of "market democracy" was warmly received by the US administrations of the first part of the 1990s. The US discourse on inter-American politics was studded with references to "shared values" and a "convergence of interests," and unrealistic expectations emerged. From Washington's point of view, policymakers all over the Americas now had to "seize the moment" and use the "window of opportunity" so that the new regional consensus could become instrumental in remodeling hemispheric relations (Aronson 1996: 184; Bush 1989: 505; Gore 1994; Christopher 1993: 625; Watson 1995; see also Leiken 1994 and Shaw 2004: 1–5). More than anything else, it is this apparent consensus that explains the upsurge of hemispheric regionalism during the 1990s and the introduction of a new institutional design for inter-American governance. This design created two parallel structures: a political, decisionmaking structure centered on the Summits of the Americas (SOA), and a technical, administrative structure centered on the OAS and other bodies involved in regional affairs (Mace and Loiseau 2005: 124–129).

Given the dismal record of the OAS up to the 1980s, US policymakers—who were the prime movers of summitry—did not feel that the OAS had the organizational capacity to support and sustain by itself the renewal of inter-American regionalism (Feinberg 1997: 101). Consequently, they convinced their counterparts in the hemisphere to create a twin structure where the general orientations of inter-American governance would be adopted during summits of heads of state. Closely integrated with the leaders' summits, sectoral ministerials in the fields of defense, justice, and labor, for instance, would act as a kind of follow-through mechanism and take care of decisionmaking in specific areas.

Alongside this decisionmaking structure would be another one of a more administrative nature. Composed of the OAS, its specialized agencies, and other regional organizations such as the IDB and the Pan-American Health Organization (PAHO), this technical structure would be charged with implementing the decisions made during summits and ministerials, as stipulated in the plans of action adopted by the heads of state at each summit. Though the new institutional design might regrettably weaken the OAS as the only permanent diplomatic forum of the region, many gains were expected from the new organizational architecture of hemispheric regionalism.

Indeed, the introduction of summitry in hemispheric affairs in 1994 had four very positive effects. The first was the personal involvement of the heads of state. From 1948 through 1994, with few exceptions, the OAS had dramatically failed in its role as the driving political force behind inter-American governance. Robin L. Rosenberg (2001: 83) has noted that the organization was perceived by many as "a 'talk shop' for unqualified diplomats sent to pasture in a place where nothing meaningful could or would be done." Summitry had the potential to change that perception dramatically by having the presidents and prime ministers define the course of hemispheric regionalism and, in so doing, provide greater authority and legitimacy to inter-American cooperation.

A second effect of summitry was to give unprecedented visibility to the inter-American system. Up to 1994, public interest concerning OAS affairs was essentially limited to the small policy community around the organization. What summitry did was to put regional affairs on television and in front-page news, thereby placing hemispheric issues before the public of the Americas as never before. A third, related effect was to foster civil society involvement in inter-American governance. Before the Miami meeting, interest groups and nongovernmental organizations were largely ignored by governments and regional bodies in the conduct of hemispheric politics. By institutionalizing mechanisms for civil society participation, the summit process sent a message that civil society should be considered as a legitimate partner in the management of inter-American affairs.

Finally, summitry breathed new life into the whole of inter-American cooperation. Not only did it generate discussions on the machinery of inter-American governance, but it also developed an agenda for various dimensions of hemispheric regionalism in relation to the economy, the environment, security, health, education, and so on. Although hemispheric relations had begun to warm up as of the late 1980s, it was the summit process that justified the references to a "new cycle" in inter-American cooperation.

The introduction of hemispheric summitry in 1994 had all the potential to create a "nested substantive linkage," as defined by Aggarwal (1998: 20–1). It could have allowed the reconciliation of a new institution (summitry) with an older one (the OAS and related agencies), thereby modifying inter-American governance so as to give a new impetus to cooperation in the Americas.[2] As we shall see in the next section, however, the promise was not fulfilled.

Roadblocks to Hemispheric Cooperation

After more than ten years of coexistence between the SOA and the OAS, the efficient merging of these two structures remains problematic. In fact, the new institutional design of inter-American governance is affected by at least four significant problems.

Inefficiency of the institutional design. When one examines the organizational charts of inter-American governance, there is some logic to the institutional design that has been adopted. In principle, coordination between the SOA and the OAS structures is carried out in the following way. The agenda of hemispheric regionalism is determined primarily by the summits. With its declaration and its plan of action, each summit sets the course of action for the period leading up to the next summit. In ten to twelve policy areas, ministerial meetings are held periodically in order to set a more specific agenda.[3] Regional organizations and national governments are then responsible for the concrete implementation of summit mandates. Implementation is monitored by the Summit Implementation Review Group (SIRG), which reports annually to foreign ministers. Finally, the Summits of the Americas Secretariat, hosted by the OAS, acts as an information clearinghouse by collecting, archiving, and disseminating information related to implementation. On paper, then, the "nesting" operation alluded to above makes sense, and the new institutional architecture seemed promising at first. The results, however, have been mixed at best.

On the plus side, it is true that under the stewardship of Secretary-General César Gaviria, the OAS made substantial efforts to adapt itself to the new division of labor among regional institutions. By becoming the main administrative arm of inter-American governance, the OAS turned into a much more results-oriented organization (Rosenberg 2001). Among the important changes initiated by Gaviria were the creation of thematic "units" directly accountable to the OAS secretary-general and the establishment of the Office of Summit Follow-Up, which changed its name to Secretariat for the Summit Process in 2002 (and later was transformed into the Summits of the Americas Secretariat) (OAS 2002a: 2). In 2001, the OAS was also instrumental in establishing a Joint Summit Working Group comprising the OAS, IDB, PAHO, UN Economic Commission for Latin America and the Caribbean (ECLAC), and the World Bank. Finally, the Summits of the Americas Secretariat was afforded a special link to the Office of the Secretary-General in 2005 after a reform that had somewhat downgraded the secretariat as a subunit of the new Department for Democratic and Political Affairs.

On the minus side, however, the new institutional design is weakened by two significant problems. The first, arising largely from lack of resources, is the difficulty of coordinating the behavior of the main actors of inter-American governance. Connection either between the summits and the ministerials or between the ministerials themselves is not always self-evident. The link between the summits and subregional groupings such as CARICOM or Mercosur (Mercado Común del Sur) also appears to be non-existent, while the relationships among the summits, national governments, and the OAS remain dramatically weak.

The other problem lies in the major discrepancy between the coordination role given to the Summits of the Americas Secretariat and the resources provided by member states. With a staff of fewer than ten officers and an annual budget of $700,000, the secretariat has to accomplish several key functions, which include providing technical and administrative support to the SIRG, managing the Summits of the Americas Information Network, coordinating with other OAS organs on the execution of summits mandates, acting as secretariat of the Joint Working Group, and coordinating civil society participation in the summits process. Clearly, there is a major gap between the funds available and the tasks to be fulfilled by the Summits of the Americas Secretariat.

The new institutional design of hemispheric regionalism has not been able to deliver on its initial promises. The impact of this situation appears all the more serious when it is examined within the context of the implementation of summit decisions and the overall funding of inter-American governance.

Confusion of agenda setting and lack of implementation. Confusion of agenda means that goals are often undefined and that the mandates given by the summits and the ministerials to regional institutions and national agencies lack clearly identified priorities. A good illustration of this problem is provided by Gordon Mace and Hugo Loiseau (2005: 115–121) in relation to the three plans of action issued by the Miami, Santiago (1998), and Quebec City (2001) summits. With these three documents, the heads of state gave mandates concerning more than 550 action items covering more than forty policy areas ranging from transparency and good governance to corporate social responsibility and management of disasters. In all three documents—and the same can be said for the plan of action that came out of the 2005 Mar del Plata summit—one finds something for everyone but no pinpointing of the priorities during the period leading up to the next summit (Fourth Summit of the Americas 2005).

Furthermore, what became apparent during the drafting of the declaration and of the plan of action of the Mar del Plata summit was the widening divergence between the priorities of the United States on the one hand and those of Latin America and the Caribbean on the other. Washington wanted to put the accent on economic growth, democratic governance, private enterprise, and the fight against corruption, whereas Latin American and Caribbean governments insisted on employment, reduction of inequalities, the role of the state, and the responsibility of industrialized countries to adopt concrete measures, such as the elimination of agricultural subsidies, as a contribution to Third World development (US Department of State 2005; SIRG 2004). Given such a polarized environment, it is hardly surprising that the Mar del Plata summit was described as "the least successful" of the four summits held since 1994 (Graham 2005a: 14).

A related issue is the lack of implementation of decisions. This situation has already drawn some attention (Leadership Council 2001) but needs to be restated, if only briefly. The problem is that about one-half of the summits' mandates are given to regional bodies, whereas the other half must be acted upon by national governments. In the first case, it was only in June 2001 that regional institutions started to coordinate their actions through the establishment of the Joint Working Group. Results so far have been limited, as shown by Richard Feinberg and Paul Haslam in Chapter 4 herein, because the resources needed to implement the mandates can come only from the IDB, an institution whose agenda is set independently from that of the summits. In any case, the performance of the Joint Working Group is hard to assess because of the lack of guidelines to monitor the implementation of the mandates.[4]

In the second case, tracing the implementation of summit mandates at the domestic level is well-nigh impossible. Even though summitry recognizes the "primary role of governments" in the implementation of the plans of action, in 2003 only half the countries had submitted a national report on summit implementation to the SIRG (Summits of the Americas Secretariat 2003b: 137). In addition, when national reports on implementation have been submitted, the link between national actions and summits mandates has been left largely unexplained (see, for example, Summits of the Americas Secretariat 2003c). Such a lack of information clearly suggests that some member states do not take their participation in the process of summitry very seriously.

Lack of resources. Funding has been a problem throughout the history of the OAS (Ball 1969: 465; Scheman 1988: 40–41; Vaky 1993: 39–40; Feinberg 2004: 26). In one way the OAS is not very different from other international bodies where burden-sharing among member states is always the result of delicate arbitration. Yet the OAS remains in a class of its own due to the particular weight of the United States within the institution. One can understand, for instance, how a crisis arose in the 1980s following Washington's unilateral decision to reduce its portion of the OAS budget. In the space of a few years, the US share of total assessments dropped from 66 percent to 59.5 percent (Vaky 1993: 39). With the introduction of summitry and the new role given to the OAS in that context, the financial problems of inter-American cooperation have only grown worse.

From 1996 to 2006, the annual regular budget of the OAS was frozen at $76 million. To put the OAS budget in perspective, it is useful to recall that in the last few years US bilateral assistance to Colombia alone amounted to more than $700 million annually (US Conference of Catholic Bishops 2006). It should furthermore be stressed that the bulk of the organization's budget is earmarked for staff salaries and pension plans (OAS 2004b). As a consequence, several inter-American programs can survive thanks only to special contributions (Graham 2005b). In a surprising show of candor, acting OAS secretary-general Luigi Einaudi put the organization's financial situation in 2005 in these stark terms: "everybody knows that the Organization is largely bankrupt" (Einaudi 2005: 3). A year after this urgent appeal, the member states agreed to increase the OAS's budget to $81.5 million in 2007 (OAS 2006b: 1). Though most welcome, the OAS budget increase will obviously not suffice to meet all the funding requirements of inter-American cooperation. Under the present circumstances, the IDB is the only regional institution to have at its disposal the resources necessary to make a difference. For the moment, however, the IDB's involvement in the mandates defined by the summits remains timid.

In sum, the institutional design put in place in 1994 in order to renew hemispheric regionalism runs the risk of becoming completely irrelevant because of a serious lack of resources. What Viron Vaky wrote in the pre-summit era remains valid today: if regional governance is not supported financially, "it cannot be effective" (Vaky 1993: 40). In other words, if inter-American governance is to have any impact in the future, governments will need to provide hemispheric organizations with a capable bureaucracy and adequate funding.

Democratic deficit. Be it on the national, global, or regional level, governance needs legitimacy in order to be socially relevant. Compared with the pre-1994 period, important steps have been taken in hemispheric governance to achieve such legitimacy. Several recent initiatives thus encourage the participation of civil society in OAS and summit-related activities. These initiatives include the adoption of the Guidelines for Participation by Civil Society Organizations in OAS Activities (1999); the establishment of the Committee for Civil Society Participation (1999), which was transformed into the Committee on Summits Management and Civil Society Participation (2002); the adoption of the Strategies for Increasing and Strengthening Participation by Civil Society Organizations in OAS Activities (2003); and the creation of the Inter-American Civil Society Partnership Initiative (2004) (OAS 2004e).

These measures expressed the will of the OAS and its member states to open up the process of regional governance to nongovernmental actors. And indeed, they succeeded in generating some innovative inputs from civil society actors during summits, OAS General Assemblies, and other hemispheric meetings. But as William C. Smith and Roberto Patricio Korzeniewicz argue in Chapter 9, the net effect of OAS initiatives on democratization and access to decisionmaking still remains extremely limited, in terms of both participation and influence.

Regarding participation, only 165 civil society organizations (CSOs) were registered at the OAS by 2006. Not only is this number very low in comparison with the number of CSOs throughout the Americas, but their attendance at specific events has also been small, as reported by the Summits of the Americas Secretariat (Cole 2003: 17). Furthermore, these organizations are not representative from a geographical point of view, and many among them lack the information and resources needed to be really effective.

With respect to influence, several observers share Grugel's position that CSOs can have no more than a minor influence on regional decisionmaking processes (Grugel 2004: 2). It seems that many government officials attribute no great value to CSO participation in summits or OAS-related events. In this connection, in 2005 the International Coalition of Human Rights Organizations of the Americas circulated a document among all the CSOs registered in the OAS, protesting the indifference displayed by government representatives toward the process of consultation with civil society. As of 2007, the openness of inter-American governance regarding civil society often appears to be more an exercise in public relations than a genuine effort at democratization.

CSOs are not always authentic democratic representatives of the societies they come from, and some of them promote narrowly defined interests. But in the absence of parliamentary representation, civil society participation, however imperfect, is the only mechanism currently available for societal intervention in inter-American governance. One of the obvious challenges facing hemispheric regionalism is thus to carve out more adequate channels for the expression of public concerns. Otherwise, regional governance will remain weakened by a democratic deficit that will undermine the legitimacy of the whole enterprise.

Conclusion

Three years into his term as secretary-general of the OAS (1994–2004), César Gaviria was extremely optimistic about the future of hemispheric regionalism:

> The good news is that fresh evidence is being produced every day, and in places like the OAS, that each government in the Hemisphere is engaged in actively seeking solutions to the issues that either (1) affect the health of their country directly or (2) help to improve the environment in which the Hemisphere is already beginning to build its place in the twenty-first century. (Gaviria 1997: 10)

At the end of his mandate, however, Gaviria's judgment was far more sober concerning the possibility of deepening hemispheric governance. Criticizing the deficiencies in regional cooperation, the secretary-general stated, "We cannot say that we have a system that operates with solidarity"

(Gaviria 2004: 361). But even more fundamentally, César Gaviria went so far as to query the true objectives of the inter-American project: "Perhaps the final question we have to ask ourselves is: Do we really want to unite our peoples in a common destiny?" (Gaviria 2004: 362).

More than ten years after the first summit of the Americas, hemispheric relations are once again confronted with a grim prospect. In a curious repetition of history, a third phase of institution building has again been followed by a period of stagnation, and, according to a longtime observer, the decline is unlikely to end anytime soon (Hakim 2006: 41). It is thus unavoidable to ask why inter-American governance is so difficult to construct.

Analysts have identified many factors explaining the slow progress of hemispheric cooperation. The political, social, and economic heterogeneity of the region itself and of its subregions is often mentioned (Banega, Hettne, and Söderbaum 2001: 247). Some experts have also pointed to the cultural divide between North America and the rest of the region (Harrison 1997) and to the persistence of "contrarian ideas" against hemispherism (Corrales and Feinberg 1999).

Looking at the recent evolution of inter-American relations, a factor that needs to be emphasized is Washington's gradual loss of interest in the region since September 11, 2001 (Hakim 2006: 39). It has been fueled in part by the Bush administration's perception of a lack of support from many Latin American governments for US foreign policy and especially the intervention in Iraq. On the other side of the equation, there is a sense of estrangement, of being left out, on the part of Latin American governments who believe that their views—on the economy, immigration, drugs, or aid—are given short shrift by Washington. Ultimately, however, as John Graham has pointed out (2005b: 4), the fundamental problem of inter-American cooperation, now as in the past, has to do with the lack of political will of governments. This in turn is a direct result of the ambiguities of the consensus that is supposed to underpin inter-American cooperation.

This ambiguous consensus can be explained by two patterns of behavior, one associated with the United States and the other with Latin American governments. In the first case, what readily comes to mind is the US policymakers' misreading of beliefs and attitudes in Latin American countries. Periodically, but most particularly during phases of inter-American institution building, decisionmakers in Washington have believed that a "convergence of values" had appeared. In these periods of rapprochement, it is falsely assumed that Latin American and Caribbean governments have come to accept the US vision of the problems of the hemisphere and the solutions that are needed. Such misperceptions naturally create expectations that cannot be met, leading the US government, again, to lose faith in hemispheric regionalism.

The other pattern of behavior involves what Peter Hakim (2006: 53) fittingly calls the "fundamental ambivalence" of Latin American and Caribbean governments toward US policies in the region. Most governments south of the Rio Grande are attracted by the US market and the potential benefits that could result from closer economic ties with the United States. That attraction prompts gestures of compromise, suggesting that things have changed fundamentally in US–Latin American relationships. But when the hope of commercial and diplomatic gains fades, attitudes of compromise are replaced by benign opposition or, as can be seen in Hugo Chavez's Venezuela, by more confrontational gestures. Latin America's ambivalence toward US policies then leads to noncommitment to hemispheric governance.

The paternalistic self-assurance of the United States and the absence of commitment among Latin American countries go a long way toward accounting for the current period of stagnation in inter-American cooperation. The way out of this situation is far from self-evident. For hemispheric regionalism to regain legitimacy among the governments and the publics of the Americas, stopgap measures to fix the institutional workings of inter-American governance will certainly not suffice. Sooner or later, two fundamental issues will have to be addressed.

The first of these issues has to do with regional inequality. No other region in the world features such a high level of economic disparities as the Americas. The experiences of small countries such as Luxemburg and Denmark within the European Union have demonstrated that regional cooperation can adapt to a considerable asymmetry in structural power. It remains to be seen whether regional governance can be extended in an environment where the economic asymmetry is as pronounced as that which exists between the United States and Haiti or Bolivia. It is difficult to imagine that a "true community of nations" could emerge in the Americas until the unequal distribution of wealth is dealt with more seriously. Of course, the redistribution of wealth will for a long time continue to be above all a national and not a hemispheric responsibility. That being so, it is hard to see how American states could share their values if they can't share their wealth. Thus, the needs targeted by US president John F. Kennedy's Alliance for Progress or, more recently, by Venezuelan president Hugo Chávez's Social Fund are far from having disappeared.

The other unavoidable issue concerns democracy. The promotion of democracy has been a centerpiece of hemispheric regionalism and of US policy in the region since the early 1990s. But the United States—along with a few other countries like Canada and Chile—can hardly push for democracy at the national level and not support it at the regional level. Granted, efforts have been made in the framework of the new institutional design of inter-American governance to respond to this challenge. The results, however, are still a long way from being satisfactory. If the social groups and the citizens of the Americas cannot find a proper channel to support the initiatives they like or oppose those they dislike, then regionalism will severely lack the legitimacy it needs to develop and flourish. So long as inter-American governance fails to become a more transparent, more inclusive process, its future will no doubt remain very bleak indeed.

Notes

1. Canada and the English-speaking Caribbean states had been active partici- pants in hemispheric affairs since the start of the 1990s.
2. The situation of the IDB is quite different, as shown in Chapter 4.
3. Many are held every two years.
4. For an illustration, see Summits of the Americas Secretariat, 2003a.

4

Problems of Coordination: The OAS and the IDB

Richard E. Feinberg with Paul Haslam

The two main institutional pillars at the heart of the "system" of inter-American relations are the Organization of American States (OAS) and the Inter-American Development Bank (IDB). With nearly 100 years of history between them (not including the OAS's predecessor organization, the Pan-American Union), both are firmly established entities with highly articulated institutional norms and detailed bureaucratic routines. Moreover, prior to the Summits of the Americas process, the division of labor between the OAS and IDB was clear and noncontroversial: the OAS had jurisdiction over security, diplomacy, and politics, and the IDB had responsibility for advancing economic development. The "system" was orderly and understood, lines of authority were clearly drawn, and parallel jurisdictions were well demarcated.

In late 1993 US president Bill Clinton invited the other thirty-three democratically elected heads of state and government of the Western Hemisphere to attend a Summit of the Americas with a broad, multipurpose agenda covering political, economic, and social issues (Feinberg 1997). The 1994 Miami summit was the beginning of an ongoing, increasingly institutionalized series of such high-level meetings connected by a web of follow-up activities. The Miami summit was the first such gathering of national leaders since 1967, the first since the collapse of the Soviet Union and the end of the Cold War. Neither the OAS nor the IDB played major roles in the preparation of the December 1994 summit (although the heads of both organizations were consulted during the preparatory meetings and addressed the gathering in Miami). Nevertheless, the assembled hemispheric leaders signed a Declaration of Principles and a Plan of Action replete with twenty-three separate initiatives detailed in some 164 action items—that stepped all over the jurisdictions of the OAS and IDB.

However, the summit leaders did not establish a new bureaucracy to implement their Plan of Action. Rather, they chose to rely heavily on existing institutions. In a detailed appendix, the Plan of Action explicitly assigned many of its mandates to the OAS and IDB for implementation. This raised the question of how the preexisting institutions would be reconciled or reformed to adapt to the new institutionality of summitry. Nor did the summit leaders place price tags on their ambitions, or promise to authorize significant new monies to fund their many mandates. Subsequent summits persisted in this process of unfunded mandates. Other than occasional and very modest special contributions, the OAS and IDB were left largely to address summit mandates within their existing budgetary resources.

The leaders that signed the Miami Plan of Action are the supreme political authorities in their governments and are the direct superiors of the ministers of foreign affairs and finance that, in turn, govern the OAS and IDB. At first blush, therefore, the lines of authority would appear evident: the governing organs of the two central regional institutions would follow the orders of their leaders and take up the responsibility of turning the energies and resources of the OAS and IDB into instruments of summit compliance. The actual story, however, is much more complex. In fact, there has been considerable slippage in the effective transmission of commands from leaders assembled at summits to the OAS and the IDB. Initially, many political appointees and staff in both regional institutions perceived the summit process as a threat to their institutional autonomy and resisted encroachment.

With the passage of time, the summit process became more consolidated and institutionalized. Summits were held periodically (in Santiago, Chile, in 1998; Quebec City, Canada, in 2001; Monterrey, Mexico, in January 2004; and Mar del Plata, Argentina, in 2005). As it became apparent that summits were a permanent institution, the OAS and IDB became more responsive to summit mandates. Institutional responsiveness, however, has been unequal. To an impressive degree, the OAS has embraced the summit process and mandates and has significantly revamped its mission and agenda to conform to summit plans of action. In contrast, the IDB has been much more hesitant to adjust. In the construct of Vinod Aggarwal, the OAS has become "nested" under the hierarchy of summitry, whereas the IDB has eschewed subordination in favor of a "parallel" relationship pursuing largely convergent activities (Aggarwal 1998). However, for both regional institutions, there remains a wide gap between the pledges and directives emanating from the summits and what the two regional institutions have been—and could be—accomplishing.

In this chapter we explore the reasons behind this slippage between the principals (the leaders) and the agents (the two regional institutions). Although understanding the creation of international institutions has long been central to the study of world politics, relatively little attention has been paid to the impact of new institutions on older ones (Aggarwal 1998: ix). Why and how have the regional bodies shirked many of the commands of their erstwhile superiors, even after their directors agreed, in their summit remarks, to the informal contracts that are the summit plans of action? In what circumstances have the preexisting regional agencies chosen to follow leaders' mandates? What are some of the key explanatory variables behind this behavior?

An Uneven Institutional Response

Institutionalized summitry is the highest form of multilateralism. It assembles the highest authorities of states to engage in collective action. Summitry among the industrialized nations was the subject of an early study by Robert Putnam and Nicholas Bayne (Putnam and Bayne 1984). *Hanging Together: The Seven-Power Summits* drew attention to the annual summits of the leaders of the seven major industrial nations that had begun in 1975. Western Hemisphere summitry has exhibited some of the problems that Putnam and Bayne identified and that are also common to ministerial multilateralism (Feinberg 2000; Simmons and de Jonge Oudraat 2001, especially chaps. 17–18). There is the tendency to make decisions by consensus, which drives language toward a least-common-denominator acceptability and gives small minorities veto power, making innovation and boldness more difficult—and frustrating the more powerful members. Logrolling among member states quickly adds up to long laundry lists of initiatives: the Miami summit logged 164 action items, Santiago 141, and Quebec 245 (Mace and Loiseau 2002). Mar del Plata followed with a reduced but nonetheless additional list of seventy.

Most importantly, regional summitry often lacks its own instruments to implement its decisions. For example, in Asia-Pacific Economic Cooperation (APEC), the Association of Southeast Asian Nations (ASEAN), and summitry in the Americas, there are no strong bureaucracies that have been created specifically to carry out the leaders' mandates. In addition, there is often a wide gap between the scope of approved initiatives and the allocation of funds for their realization. Unfunded mandates are common attributes of regional summitry where leaders are pressed by a wide array of pressure groups into making ambitious promises and where implementation instruments are underdeveloped, compounding problems of noncompliance (Simmons and de Jonge Oudraat 2001: 690).

In the Western Hemisphere, leaders have sought to overcome this absence of bureaucratic and financial underpinning by turning to preexisting regional institutions and assigning them responsibilities for following through on summit decisions. Yet neither the governments of the Western Hemisphere nor scholars have focused sufficient attention on the implications of this new source of authority for the already existing inter-American system.

The existing evidence on the implementation of summit plans of action by the IDB and OAS suggests that both institutions have taken actions that respond directly to some of the most important summit mandates. Certainly, the summits have given a boost to efforts to open select OAS and IDB activities to representatives of civil society organizations (Payne 2003). Importantly, together with the UN Economic Commission for Latin America and the Caribbean (ECLAC), the summits reinvigorated the Tripartite Committee, which has coordinated their respective trade units to advance hemispheric integration through research, publications, training, and backstopping the Free Trade Area of the Americas (FTAA) negotiations process (IDB 2002d; IDB 2005a).

However, the IDB and OAS have also shirked many summit mandates. Jeffrey Puryear has documented the failure—particularly of the IDB—to fulfill the education mandates that were a centerpiece at the 1998 Santiago summit (Puryear and Alvarez 2000). Studies commissioned by the Leadership Council for Inter-American Summitry have documented shortfalls in implementation of other important summit mandates, including counternarcotics and sustainable development (Leadership Council 1999, 2001; see also Mace and Loiseau 2002). A Canadian Foundation for the Americas (FOCAL) study of judicial reform found "uneven" progress (FOCAL 2002: 24). The OAS itself prepared an extensive internal "Implementation and Monitoring Chart" (2002c) that lists the initiatives of the 2001 Quebec summit, together with the institution or country assigned "lead responsibility." In many cases where the IDB or OAS shouldered such responsibilities, the "actions taken" were either minor (e.g., attendance at a meeting, preparation of a report, approval of small isolated loans) in comparison with the ambitiousness of the mandate, or the action boxes were empty altogether. Furthermore, where action was taken, it is sometimes difficult to attribute causality to summits per se.

Realistically, summits have a number of functions other than implementation of their plans of action. Summits underscore shared values, add legitimacy to certain ideas, help to fortify personal relations among leaders and their senior staffs, and may reduce tensions among states. But over time, if summit pledges of action remain unfulfilled, the whole summit process will increasingly be perceived as "only empty rhetoric," and the other functions of summits will also suffer. The entire edifice of summitry requires at least some degree of transformation of words into deeds.

To better understand the uneven implementation record of the OAS and IDB and to compare and contrast their respective behavior, this chapter examines the "black box" of institutional response to summit mandates. As a result of studying the bureaucratic process through interviews with the institutions' political authorities, senior management, and executive directors, the analysis privileges six explanatory variables for the differential response of the two institutions: ministerial authorities, competing mandates, institutional missions, internal structures, membership, and leadership.[1]

- *Ministerial authorities:* the source of political authority for the institution in question, particularly the consequences of linkage to different ministries in member countries;
- *Competing mandates:* the extent to which summit mandates are integrated or not with existing institutional mandates and alternative sources of authority;
- *Institutional missions:* the health of the existing institutional mission and the financing that supports it;
- *Internal structures:* bureaucratic and organizational rigidities that affect the institution's ability to adapt to new demands, and the impact of summits on units working on issues directly related to plans of action goals;
- *Membership:* the influence of extra-hemispheric voting members on institutional response to summit mandates; and
- *Leadership:* the role of leadership style on institutional response, particularly the personalities of former IDB president Enrique Iglesias (1988–2005) and OAS secretary-general César Gaviria Trujillo (1994–2004).

The research revealed a disjuncture in the response of the two institutions toward new summit mandates: the OAS acknowledged that the organization's activities were the direct result of summit mandates, whereas the IDB demonstrated more reticence in accepting summit authority. OAS officials interviewed for this study demonstrated awareness of the details of summit plans of action and allocated their own time and energies toward advancing specific summit initiatives. It was believed that senior management, in particular Secretary-General César Gaviria, recognized the summit plans of action as "authoritative mandates" that should guide the institution's work. Nonetheless, the day-to-day concerns of the Permanent Council with routine internal matters and the crisis of the moment (often Haiti) impeded the translation of these mandates into reforming important aspects of OAS behavior. Furthermore, the real decline in the OAS budget limited the organization's ability to reallocate resources in response to summit mandates.

In contrast, interviews with IDB officials revealed a very different story. Knowledge of summit mandates and commitments was lower, as was the allocation of time and resources on specific summit initiatives. Nor were these mandates viewed as "authoritative" for the hemisphere's finance ministers, although senior management recognized IDB president Enrique

Iglesias's personal engagement with the summit process. It was generally agreed that the IDB Board of Executive Directors had paid scant attention to summit plans of action and that the IDB had seldom reallocated resources to respond to summit mandates. In two published reports, for example, the IDB catalogues long lists of its projects that "coincide with" and "contribute to" summit goals without being specifically derived from that source (IDB 2001b and 2002c).

The Inter-American Development Bank

Ministerial Authorities and Competing Mandates

The IDB Board of Governors—the organization's supreme authority—is composed primarily of ministers of finance, though some countries are represented by ministers of economy or economic development. Ministers of finance have, for the most part, not attended the summits, and many finance ministries have not been very involved either in the diplomatic negotiations of the plans of action or even within their own governments' interagency summit preparatory committees. Ministers of finance may have been elbowed out by other parties or may have purposefully kept a distance from the summit process, precisely in order not to feel obligated by summit mandates. Finance ministries tended to see the summit process as being directed by the offices of the leaders or by ministries of foreign affairs. These agencies are, to varying degrees, bureaucratic rivals of finance ministries and may also be pursuing different agendas, interests, and even worldviews.

Within finance ministries and within the IDB, attitudes toward presidencies and foreign ministries are not always flattering, as they are often perceived as being "political" and not fully understanding the hard realities of the global economy. The summit process is frequently dismissed as "por la galleria"—for popular consumption. So it is not surprising that ministries of finance seek to keep their distance from diplomatic processes perceived as serving the interests of other agencies whose motives and capacities are questionable. Symptomatic of this disinterest in, or even hostility toward, summitry inside ministries of finance, one executive director remarked, "Many Latin American governments don't transmit to their Executive Directors the message that summits are important. After Quebec, my government conveyed nothing to me, and the same would be true for other borrowing-country governments." Other executive directors confirmed such an absence of instructions from their ministries.

There is another (but not inconsistent) explanation for why finance ministries and the IDB itself—its executive directors, managers, and staff—might not be fully responsive to summit mandates. The bank recognizes three sources of authority—none of which are summits:

1) the Agreement Establishing the Inter-American Development Bank (the Charter), which establishes the broad enduring purposes of the institution; 2) periodic replenishment agreements negotiated by the shareholders of the institution, which set priorities and targets for Bank action over a multi-year period; and 3) regular decisionmaking by the Board of Executive Directors on policy issues. (IDB 1999a: 3)

IDB officials repeatedly referred to these three sources of authority, in contrast to summits, which were described only as "guides" or "references to be taken into account." As one executive director affirmed, "Summits have no legal standing for the IDB. Mandates and issues become authoritative for the Bank only when they are incorporated into the Bank's official documents. If a summit Plan of Action includes something that is outside of the context of the Bank's activities, it would not be an authoritative mandate."

IDB documents make it very clear that summit mandates are not IDB mandates, by omission: summits are very rarely mentioned in IDB documents, whether public or internal, printed or electronic. In the IDB's two published reports on the agenda of the IDB and the Summits of the Americas, everything in the reports—from the titles to the graphics to the carefully crafted language—appears constructed to suggest that the Bank's ongoing activities "coincide with" summit mandates, but in the first instance derive from the mandates of the bank's own institutional mandates, as dictated by its Charter, Board of Governors, and most recent 1994 Capital Replenishment (IDB 2001a: 184; 2001b; 2002c). An IDB interviewee confirmed that there was a "purposeful de-linking" of key bank documents from summit mandates.

Why might the IDB prefer the three accepted sources of authority—its original charter, periodic replenishments that are accompanied by planning commitments and approved by legislatures, and the Board of Executive Directors? One explanation is bureaucratic: finance ministries and their executive directors are in charge of negotiating the replenishments, and it is hardly surprising that executive directors favor their own interest in their capacity as directors. In addition, senior managers are well positioned to have considerable influence over board activity. Summitry is a much more distant and less easily influenced phenomenon. In addition, the two sources of accepted authority outside the board—the charter and the replenishments—are at most very loosely binding. Current bank activity has diverged greatly from the language of the 1959 Charter, apparently without consequence, and the replenishment planning documents are so general and broad as to encompass almost any activity that the bank board and management preferred to pursue and so package. Thus, by paying homage to the charter and the periodic replenishments, the executive directors and management maintain a wide freedom of action for themselves. To accept summit mandates as binding would restrict that sphere of freedom.

Institutional Missions and Internal Structures

By coincidence, the first Summit of the Americas occurred just months after the IDB had successfully negotiated its eighth replenishment, which raised its capital base from $60 to $100 billion, guaranteeing it sufficient funds to increase its annual lending level to some $8.5 billion and to sustain activity at that comfortable level far into the future. The replenishment gave the bank a series of missions, including poverty alleviation, modernization of physical infrastructure, regional integration, environmental protection, and strengthening of the private sector. With this reaffirmation of political support, a big capital injection, and a negotiated mission statement, the IDB felt no need for additional political backing or further mission requirements.

At the same time, it was not surprising that the Miami summit texts mirrored many of the themes of the IDB's eighth replenishment, since both documents were elaborated by the same governments (if not necessarily the same agencies or officials) at the same moment in history. This convergence of themes made it easy for the IDB to embrace, at least at the rhetorical level, those summit themes that coincided with its own agenda. Further, select offices within the IDB did welcome the Miami summit Plan of Action because it helped to legitimize or give greater focus to their missions. The fledgling office in charge of democracy promotion—Modernization of the State (MOS)—was fortified by the summit. Governability was not within the traditional IDB mandates or agenda, such that summits have served the MOS office as a useful reference without having to amend the IDB Charter. Also within the IDB, the office dealing with regional integration and trade policy saw its salience sharply upgraded and its agenda reoriented as a result of the Miami agreement to pursue an FTAA.

If most of the IDB preferred to keep summit mandates at arm's length out of deference to other sources of authority, these officials had another reason to downplay summit mandates: the structure of the bank's internal decisionmaking procedures made it very difficult to implement *any* set of finely targeted programs across the breadth of the bank's clientele. The eighth replenishment mission statements set broad guidelines for the bank's main business—loans, grants, and technical assistance—but the preferences of the borrowing-country governments were at least as weighty a determinant. A 1999 internal bank document found that the focus of country programming has been on loan approval and that the proclaimed developmental policies and priorities were merely "ex-post rationalization of the project pipeline" (IDB 1999b: 37). As a result, the bank was not structured to run the sort of cross-country campaign that would be required to implement such summit targets as universal education through sixth grade by 2010 and a secondary school enrollment rate of at least 75 percent.

Another constraint on the bank's capacity to follow summit mandates is bureaucratic rigidities. As the 1999 Institutional Strategy noted, "Despite being a borrowers' Bank, the interplay of institutional checks and balances has built a stable bureaucracy with strong rules and procedures," and this consensual governance structure produces a "balanced approach across multiple sectors" (IDB 1999a: 6–7). Within the IDB, some refer less kindly to a "silo-ing" of activities by sector and geographic subregions, impeding coherent bankwide programming as well as any major reallocation of resources.

In sum, the very mixed record of the IDB in summit implementation is deeply rooted in the bank's internal structure and standard operating procedures. The power of the borrowing countries makes it difficult for the bank to drive specific development goals across the region. The bank's bureaucracy itself is internally fractured, in ways that, to at least some degree, reflect and reinforce borrowing-country power and impede effective programming. The bank does not generally pursue campaigns or quantitative outcomes. In any case, the Board of Executive Directors has purposefully chosen not to establish strong mechanisms to pursue or monitor the implementation of summit mandates, nor does it perform that task itself.

Membership and Leadership

The IDB's membership of forty-six nations includes "nonregional" nations in Europe and Japan. Might the nonregionals—who do not sign the summit texts—be major roadblocks to IDB follow-up of summit mandates? Formally, the IDB is governed by a system of weighted voting power that reserves only 16 percent for the nonregionals. The Latin American and Caribbean nations are guaranteed a slight majority—fortifying the image of a borrowers' bank—while the United States has 30 percent and Canada 4 percent (IDB 2001a: 19). In general, the nonregionals' influence, although difficult to measure, is not considered very great except where they have set up special trust funds with their own monies.

At the same time, the bank's Board of Executive Directors has tended to seek a broad consensus, and former president Iglesias was particularly known for his search for unanimity. Iglesias hesitated to bring a matter before the board if a consensus was absent, enlarging the power of minority voices and those who would exercise a veto. Although not necessarily an overriding problem, the presence of nonregional nations within the IDB—nations not included in Western Hemisphere summitry—is a matter that has been overlooked by summiteers.

In explaining IDB responsiveness to summits, the leadership style of Enrique Iglesias has likely been important. Having served as secretary-general of the ECLAC, as foreign minister of his native Uruguay, and as IDB president, Iglesias was the de facto dean of inter-American relations, quite possibly the most respected and beloved figure in hemispheric intergovernmental affairs. Iglesias's personal enthusiasm for summits has been frequently noted, particularly at board meetings immediately following summits. Iglesias attended each of the summits and on each occasion delivered speeches affirming that summit themes mirror those of the IDB and pledging that the IDB would help to carry out important summit initiatives. At the same time, Iglesias's consensual approach to politics may have meant that he did not have the inclination to overcome the various roadblocks, whether political or bureaucratic, to a more thorough IDB implementation of summit plans of action. As a successful accommodator, Iglesias may have preferred the degrees of freedom that obtain from denying summit mandates full authority, bestowing on him wider room for maneuver as he conciliated the diverse interests that bore on the bank. In the principal-agent framework, such ambiguous multiple-agency arrangements, where bureaucratic agents can play off one authority against another, tend to strengthen the agenda-setting autonomy of the bureaucracy (Moe 1984: 768–769).

The Organization of American States

Ministerial Authorities and Competing Mandates

OAS ambassadors believe that their ministers of foreign affairs consider the summit plans of action to be authoritative mandates that should guide the work of the OAS. The process of negotiating the plans of action is led by foreign ministries in most countries, giving them the buy-in that comes from participation and influence. Foreign ministers accompany their leaders to the summits. And foreign ministries take the lead in the follow-up processes of summitry. An internal 2001 OAS report noted this overlap of institutional authority: "The present agenda of the OAS is derived from the Summits of the Americas process, and the ministers of foreign relations are responsible for both the OAS agenda and the Summit process" (OAS 2001c: 26).

Foreign ministers comprise the OAS's supreme governing body, the General Assembly. In a series of formal resolutions passed at its annual meetings, the General Assembly has directed the OAS to consider summit mandates as binding on the OAS. Shortly after the Miami summit, the General Assembly (OAS Resolution AG/RES. 1349) set up a Special Committee on Inter-American Summits Management of the Permanent Council "to ensure follow-up of the activities assigned to the Organization by the Summit of the Americas" (OAS, *Annual Report 1995–1996:* 7, 11). Weakened over recent decades by the rise of specialized issues in international affairs where authority and expertise lie in other government agencies, foreign ministries welcomed this coordinating role.

Despite the powerful incentives for foreign ministries to link the OAS to summitry, there is evident slippage in the transmission of instructions or perceptions from ministers to ambassadors to senior management. It is also acknowledged that there are differential commitments to summitry among the various governments. One senior manager went so far as to suggest that some of the larger countries "could care less," whereas some other countries, notably Canada and Chile, that had hosted summits were very committed. More generally, the three major powers in the hemisphere, namely the United States, Brazil, and Mexico, have a very mixed record with regard to multilateralism in inter-American relations, and arguably that attitude translates, or is perceived to translate, into an ambivalent relationship with the OAS and summitry.

Traditionally, the OAS was governed by its originating document, the Charter of the OAS, signed in Bogotá in 1948, as amended on numerous occasions, and by its political organs—the annual ministerial-level General Assembly and the ambassadorial-level Permanent Council. Shortly after the April 1998 Second Summit of the Americas in Santiago, Chile, the General Assembly of that year resolved to fully incorporate the mandates of the Santiago Plan of Action into the organization's agenda. In his preface to that year's annual report, then secretary-general Gaviria remarked with some pride and satisfaction, "For the OAS, the [Santiago] Summit was a milestone, as the Santiago Plan of Action adopted by the heads of state and of government entrusted the Organization with no fewer than 31 mandates. This was almost three times the number entrusted to the OAS at the Miami Summit. . . . as a result, the OAS agenda today is cohesively linked to the one mapped out by the heads of state and government" (OAS, *Annual Report 1998–1999:* x). In marked contrast to the IDB, whose official documents (both internal and public) and website rarely mention summits, OAS documents are replete with positive references to summit mandates.

In the early years of summitry, there were some in the OAS who did question the authority of summit mandates. But this skepticism faded as ministers through the General Assembly made clear that they considered the summit plans of action to be binding on the OAS, as they instructed the OAS to implement summit mandates, and as they pressed the OAS to restructure itself to fulfill these instructions from the leaders. In 2002, during the General Assembly in Barbados, the foreign ministers momentarily constituted themselves as the Summit Implementation Review Group (SIRG), normally a working-level committee, to indicate that the foreign ministers themselves were serious about summit implementation and that, in their minds, the summit process and the OAS were increasingly joined. The foreign ministers reaffirmed this practice at the 2005 General Assembly in Fort

Lauderdale, Florida. With these senior-level signals, OAS ambassadors and staff also came to grasp that the summits were beneficial to the authority of the OAS.

Institutional Missions and Internal Structures

The OAS had been in decline since the fading of the Alliance for Progress and the attenuation of the Cold War. The old security agenda seemed largely irrelevant, and the United States considered the institution ineffectual and blocked by distrustful Latin American and Caribbean members, who in turn feared that the United States would abuse its power to bend the OAS to its will. As a clear sign of their discontent and disinterest, OAS member states had been slicing its budget and personnel. Thus, summitry came along at a fortuitous time for the OAS: an organization in search of a new agenda was met by a new process in need of implementing instruments (Rosenberg 2000).

The OAS annual reports provide solid evidence that the institution's agenda has been reinvigorated and molded by summitry. In a summary of his first five-year term, Gaviria wrote of "solid gains on the Hemispheric agenda," "an agenda configured on the basis of resolutions adopted by the political organs of the Organization and mandates approved at the 1994 and 1998 Summits of the Heads of State and Government" (OAS, *Annual Report 1999–2000:* xi). Interviewees offered testimonials to summitry: "Without Summits, the OAS would be virtually obsolete and limited to formalisms, the Summits give the OAS all of its new life and energy"; and "No doubt, the OAS has been revitalized by Summits—the Summits are the OAS." OAS senior management were extremely knowledgeable of summit plans of action and were convinced that summitry had enhanced the OAS's agenda and influence on matters that were central to inter-American relations, including the Unit for the Promotion of Democracy, the Trade Unit, the Inter-American Drug Abuse Control Commission (CICAD), the Inter-American Telecommunications Commission (CITEL), the Unit for Social Development and Education, the Inter-American Agency for Cooperation and Development (IACD), and the special committee responsible for drafting the Inter-American Democratic Charter, among others.

Gaviria modified the OAS's internal structure to strengthen units assigned important summit mandates. The Unit for the Promotion of Democracy was expanded to nineteen staff members. CICAD was given the responsibility for the Multilateral Evaluation Mechanism mandated by the Santiago summit. The Trade Unit was created in 1995 and by 2000 had twelve staff members (OAS, *Annual Report 1999–2000:* 246, table 16).

Since Miami, the OAS has gradually but continually been creating mechanisms dedicated to the oversight of summit implementation. Shortly after

Miami, the Permanent Council established the Management Committee on Inter-American Summits (later renamed the OAS Special Committee on Inter-American Summits Management). The OAS offered to host and, increasingly, to staff SIRG, an intergovernmental roundtable convened quarterly with the purpose of monitoring summit follow-up and preparing future summit agendas. Initially governments sent foreign ministry officials and sectoral experts from capitals to attend SIRG meetings, but over time many governments delegated representation to OAS ambassadors. Following the second summit in Santiago, Gaviria created the Office of Summit Follow-up (OSFU) to galvanize support within the OAS for the summit process and to coordinate the activities and follow-up on the mandates assigned in the Plan of Action of Santiago. This new office soon took on the technical secretariat functions of the SIRG (OAS, *Annual Reports,* various, reports of the Office of Summit Follow-up). However, the OSFU has been understaffed and underfunded, limiting its ability to effectively evaluate summit implementation, despite having its status upgraded in 2002 to "Executive Secretariat for the Summit Process" and its budget increased from $455,000 in 2002 to $748,000 in 2003.

In 2005 the OAS underwent a major administrative reorganization. The Office of Summit Follow-up was renamed the Summits of the Americas Secretariat and reports directly to the new secretary-general, José Miguel Insulza. The key summit implementation units were maintained, although some "units" became "offices," and a new level of senior management was added to rationalize decisionmaking by reducing the number of units reporting directly to the secretary-general. Several of the new department heads have been deeply involved in summitry, and Insulza played an important role as a senior host government official in the 1998 Santiago summit. It seems unlikely that the reorganization will reduce the OAS commitment to summitry.

However, the OAS budget has been frozen in nominal terms for some years and hence has been declining in real terms. The OAS's central budget for 2002, $76 million, fell well short of the $100.4 million level required just to have maintained the purchasing power in the 1995 budget when summitry began (OAS 2001c: 11). Gaviria complained, "Today it is extremely difficult to ensure the sustainability of the Organization's financial structure, and to reconcile the growing number of mandates and tasks with the current financial limitations" (OAS, *Annual Report 1999–2000:* xv). A very high proportion of the existing budget is consumed by tenured personnel and existing programs. OAS management has sought to direct the remaining discretionary funds toward summit mandates, but such funds are very limited. In 2001 Gaviria ordered his chief of staff to meet with every unit to review the budgetary implications of the mandates assigned to the OAS by the summit process, as a signal of the importance he attached to summit follow-up (OAS 2001c: appendix J), an exercise that underscored the misfit between mandates and resources.

Membership and Leadership

With thirty-four active members, the OAS membership is the same as summitry. Cuba remains a charter member of the OAS, even if its participation has been suspended since Fidel Castro rose to power, and it has been excluded from summitry for not meeting the "democratically elected" criteria established by President Clinton in his invitations to the first Miami summit. The OAS has granted permanent observer status to over forty-four states, including Japan and European states, but they have no voting power. So the OAS does not face the problem that the IDB has with voting members that do not participate in Western Hemisphere summitry.

The commitment of former secretary-general Gaviria to summit implementation and to binding the OAS to summitry has been pivotal. Before Gaviria took the helm, during the preparation for the 1994 Miami summit and in its early aftermath, some at the OAS not only questioned the authority of summits but saw summitry as a threat to the primacy of the OAS as the hemisphere's leading political institution. However, Gaviria grasped that far from being a threat, summitry was the means to rejuvenate the OAS, to enhance its authority, to remodel its mission, and to widen its agenda. He worked to seize that opportunity and used summitry to drive a process of permanent modernization and reform of the institution.

Whereas summitry began at a time when the IDB had a strong sense of mission and a capital base heading toward $100 billion, Gaviria inherited an OAS adrift and starved for resources. Gaviria therefore had good reason to reach out to summitry for a new agenda and, possibly, additional funding. History and personality may also have played roles in explaining Gaviria's embrace of summitry. As a former head of state, Gaviria may have identified more personally with the summit process and declarations signed by presidents. Gaviria's leadership style was more imperious, and he was less inclined to expend his time in building wide consensus. The former Colombian head of state was prepared to confront bureaucratic obstacles and bear political costs in order to reshape the organization under his aegis. To be sure, as compared with Iglesias, he had an important advantage: whereas Iglesias had to contend with ministers of finance often hostile to summitry, Gaviria's governing board consisted of "sympathetic" ministers of foreign affairs.

Comparing the Institutional Responses

The attitudes and responses of the two regional institutions to the imposition of summitry in inter-American relations, as suggested by the interviews and examination of institutional documentation, differ sharply. This differential response can be explained with reference to the six variables examined above: ministerial authorities, competing mandates, institutional missions, internal structures, membership, and leadership. Governed by the same foreign ministers responsible for organizing summits, the OAS is more prone to consider summit mandates to be authoritative, whereas the IDB, governed by ministers of finance who are inveterately suspicious of foreign ministries, is more likely to question the authoritativeness of summit mandates crafted by ministries that are, in more than one respect, foreign.

As the summit process got under way in 1994, the IDB was fully loaded with challenging mandates freshly approved by its governing board and member states, but the OAS was in search of new purposes that, it soon came to recognize, were being served up in abundance by summitry. The IDB was satisfied with its institutional missions as prescribed by its charter, replenishments, and governing authorities, and did not welcome additional constraints on its freedom of action. The OAS also had a charter and governing authorities, but rather than being showered with new resources via replenishment, governments were cutting its budget, rendering it more receptive to new missions that might enhance its prestige and, eventually, attract new resources. Furthermore, OAS membership is virtually identical to summit participation, whereas the IDB has to contend with nonregional voting members excluded from summits who are less ready to accept its instructions. Finally, leadership has played a role, as the secretary-general of the OAS energetically used summitry to empower and refashion his institution, while the president of the IDB accommodated the pressures devolving from the other causal variables. Not surprisingly, the OAS has moved much more expeditiously than the IDB to establish internal mechanisms to promote implementation of summit mandates, even as bureaucratic rigidities, budgetary limitations, and member interests have constrained adaptation in both regional institutions.

Assigning relative weights to these six variables in our two case studies is a hazardous exercise. But the importance of ministerial authority and robustness of institutional mission (and its corollary, budgetary health) stand out: governed by foreign ministries deeply involved in summits and desperately in need of new missions and financial resources, the OAS had good reasons to look favorably on summits, whereas the IDB, governed by rival finance ministries and already stuffed with mandates and replenished with resources, had good reasons to remain aloof. Competing mandates and internal structures might carry intermediate weight: they can be obstacles to adaptation but can be overcome in time with sufficient political will. When membership between institutions is identical, as it is between summits and the OAS, nesting is easier than when the overlap is imperfect, as it is with the IDB, even if deft diplomacy might well be able to ameliorate tensions. Although the decisive leadership of OAS secretary-general César Gaviria made a difference at the outset, it is possible that over time the other compelling factors would eventually have yielded a similar outcome.

Conclusions and Policy Proposals

Summitry is the newcomer to the emerging inter-American system and has not easily integrated with the other two preeminent hemispheric institutions, the Inter-American Development Bank and the Organization of American States—a fact that is expressed in the uneven adoption and implementation of summit mandates. If summits are to command the heights of the inter-American system and to better manage the principal-agent problem inherent in sending directives to separate institutions, some of summitry's major flaws need correcting (Leadership Council 2001).

The literature on principal-agent relationships suggests that summits need to improve the quality of information flow in both directions, pay more attention to monitoring and feedback mechanisms, and get the incentives right. Specifically, governments need to design negotiating modalities that contain the logrolling so common to multilateralism and produce a leaner list of priority mandates that command more legitimacy and authority at the regional institutions to which they are assigned. A more realistic, refined list of mandates would help to overcome the principal-agent shirking problem by making agent performance easier to monitor. Better monitoring and evaluation would help to add the element of accountability that has been lacking. Accountability—getting agencies to serve agreed-upon goals—would be further enhanced if summit mandates posited measurable indicators of outputs and outcomes (Wilson 2000: 154–175, 315; Moe 1984: 756; Pratt and Zeckhauser 1985: 5). With these improvements in communications, the summitry process, governments, and nongovernmental organizations would be better able to evaluate compliance by the regional institutions.

In 2000 the United Nations Millennium Summit Declaration generated the Millennium Development Goals (MDGs)—a broad global consensus around a set of clear, measurable, and time-bound development goals. Many goals, targets, and indicators repeat mandates contained in the plans of action signed by leaders at the Summits of the Americas. The IDB and ECLAC participate in the MDG monitoring exercise (IDB 2005b). The MDGs, suitably adapted to hemispheric realities, would provide inter-American summits with strong, clear consensual goals, ready-made quantitative indicators, resources, and evaluation mechanisms to alleviate poverty in the Western Hemisphere (Academic Roundtable 2005). Notably, at the most recent summit, in Mar del Plata, Argentina, the Declaration (items 7 and 72) includes references to meeting MDG targets on poverty reduction (Summits of the Americas 2005b). In this respect, there is some cause for optimism that the MDGs are gradually emerging as a quantifiable baseline integrated with summit-driven and other development programs in the Americas.

To nest the IDB more comfortably within summitry, its governing authorities—the ministries of finance—as well as its Board of Executive Directors and senior management, need to be engaged in the various stages of summitry, including the preparation of summit mandates. Just as the OAS General Assembly (the ministers of foreign affairs) and its Permanent Council signal to the OAS staff that summit mandates are authoritative, so should the IDB Board of Governors (the finance ministers) and its Board of Executive Directors formally endorse those summit mandates assigned to it, as a clear signal to senior staff of their authoritativeness for bank strategies and, ultimately, country programs.

The OAS has embraced summitry, but its ability to perform effective agency is constrained by its debilitating lack of resources (Graham 2005b). The OAS could engage in a reform-for-resources bargain, trading internal administrative reform as a condition for a bigger budget. The OAS needs to be much more aggressive in raising funds from a variety of sources, including member states, but also through partnerships with the private sector and nongovernmental organizations. In return for these resources, the OAS could cut overhead and revamp the Permanent Council to make it a more efficient governing body more responsive to the external environment. Furthermore, the OAS's existing summit follow-up mechanisms need to be expanded and funded more fully if they are to effectively monitor and evaluate the implementation of summit mandates. Although concrete action is yet to materialize, the Mar del Plata summit Plan of Action demonstrated that the leaders are cognizant of this problem: they agreed to "ensure that the OAS and other hemispheric organizations have the financial and institutional capacity to implement Summits commitment" (Summits of the Americas 2005a, item 70).

A more effectively integrated inter-American system requires deeper cooperation between the OAS and IDB. Officials at both institutions who are responsible for overlapping issues could form interagency working committees to exchange information and on occasion engage in joint projects. A good precedent for such interinstitutional cooperation is the Tripartite Committee (IDB, OAS, and ECLAC), which works to advance hemispheric trade integration. In June 2001, the OAS, IDB, ECLAC, and PAHO created a Joint Summit Working Group (JSWG) to better coordinate summitry activities among themselves. By 2005 the OAS-chaired JSWG had expanded to twelve institutional members and was meeting about every two months, mainly to exchange information on specialized summit-related meetings (OAS 2005d). The Mar del Plata Declaration instructed the JSWG "to continue, through their respective activities and programs, to support the follow-up and implementation of the Declarations and Plans of Action of the Summits of the Americas . . . as well as to assist in the preparations for future Summits" (Summits of the Americas 2005b, item 75). This joint coordinating and implementing responsibility, if taken seriously, marks a prodigious step forward.

Many of these proposed reforms face bureaucratic obstacles at the existing regional institutions, encumbered with their own interests and rigidities, but in the end the member states have the authority to further refashion the inter-American system. Only history will reveal whether the constituent states decide that it is in their respective national interests to fashion a more coherent, orderly, and effective inter-American system worthy of the name.

Notes

In preparing this chapter, Richard E. Feinberg benefited from informal conversations and from interviews with many former and current officials in the US government, Latin American governments, and especially in the OAS and IDB, who will remain anonymous. Their willingness to share their experience and insights was as gracious as it was essential for this research. For their valuable comments on earlier drafts, the author wishes to thank Vinod Aggarwal, Stephan Haggard, and Robin Rosenberg, as well as officials at the OAS and IDB. Kat Choi, Martha Garcia, and Leigha Cornett were very able research assistants. Donald Mackay's interest in the topic was a great stimulus, and the Canadian Foundation for the Americas (FOCAL) generously provided grant support for an earlier version of this study, *Unfunded Mandates in the Western Hemisphere* (2004). Important comments were also received at the colloquium "What Institutions for the Americas?" Université Laval, Quebec City, March 11–13, 2005.

1. Feinberg interviewed nine of the thirty-four ambassadors in the OAS and nine of fourteen executive directors in the IDB, with careful attention paid to geographic representativeness. In addition, eight IDB senior managers and five OAS senior managers were interviewed for a total of thirty-one respondents.

PART 2
Security Arrangements

5

Building Consensus on Security: Toward a New Framework

Margaret Daly Hayes

In Mexico City in October 2003, Latin American and Caribbean leaders declared a new concept of hemisphere security that is "multi-dimensional in scope, includes traditional and new threats, concerns, and other challenges to the security of the states of the hemisphere, incorporates the priorities of each state, contributes to the consolidation of peace, integral development, and social justice, and is based on democratic values, respect for and promotion and defense of human rights, solidarity, cooperation, and respect for national sovereignty" (OAS 2003a). A year later, at the Special Summit of the Americas in Monterrey, Mexico, they reiterated that "the basis and purpose of security is the protection of human beings" (OAS 2004a).

The consensus declared in Mexico was the result of long discussions among presidents and ministers of foreign affairs, defense, and other portfolios over the preceding decade, as well as debates going as far back as the nineteenth century.[1] The issues of security concern that are reflected in the declaration form four clusters, as seen in Figure 5.1.[2] They range from traditional threats from other states, insurgencies, and weapons of mass destruction to concerns about natural disasters and environmental accidents involving hazardous materials. The full range of transnational criminal activities, from drug trafficking to money laundering, arms trafficking, and terrorism, is front and center on the security agenda. In addition, the Declaration on Security in the Americas recognizes that profound political and economic structural disequilibria and inequities contribute to insecurity and instability in the region. Throughout the discussions, it has been clear that not all these "insecurities"—indeed, not even most of them—require a military response. Nevertheless, the set of issues on which consensus has been most difficult to find has been the disposition of the military components of the inter-American system, that is, the modernization of the hemispheric defense institutions created in the 1940s and of the relationships that accompany them.

Figure 5.1 Insecurities in the Americas

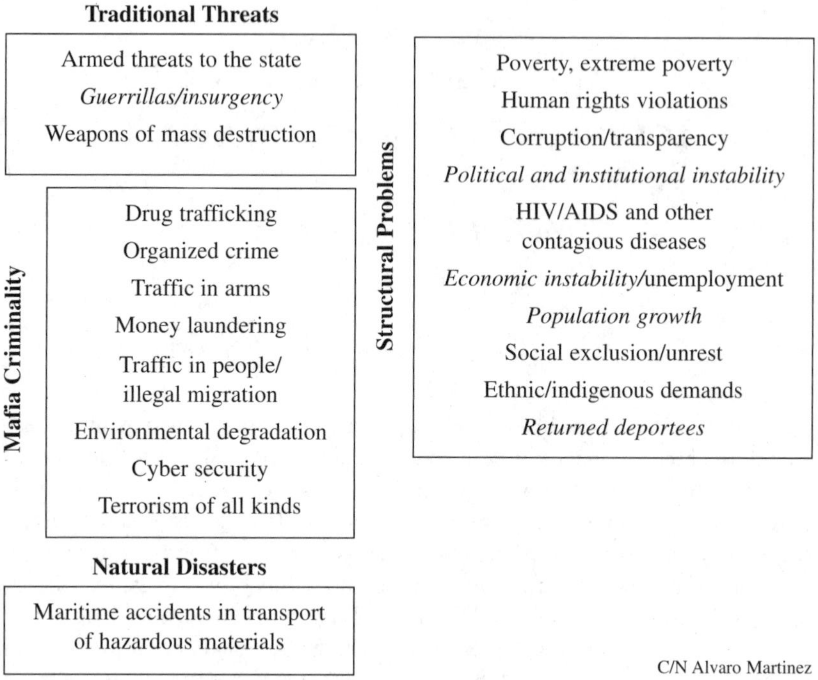

Traditional Threats

Armed threats to the state

Guerrillas/insurgency

Weapons of mass destruction

Mafia Criminality

Drug trafficking

Organized crime

Traffic in arms

Money laundering

Traffic in people/
illegal migration

Environmental degradation

Cyber security

Terrorism of all kinds

Structural Problems

Poverty, extreme poverty

Human rights violations

Corruption/transparency

Political and institutional instability

HIV/AIDS and other
contagious diseases

Economic instability/unemployment

Population growth

Social exclusion/unrest

Ethnic/indigenous demands

Returned deportees

Natural Disasters

Maritime accidents in transport
of hazardous materials

C/N Alvaro Martinez

The hemispheric security agenda is a still tentative framework agreed upon at the international level and implemented largely through institutions of the Organization of American States (OAS). That there is agreement is no mean feat, but there is still much to do. The renewal of the architecture of the inter-American system has evolved slowly and deliberately over fifteen years and has not yet reached conclusion. OAS members have identified common themes and created a preliminary institutional framework to coordinate the various components of the new security agenda. The challenge ahead is the effective execution of the high-minded and visionary goals expressed in the international agreements and treaties.

The new security agenda evolved in several different but mutually supportive tracks. At the hemispheric level there have been three: the OAS itself and its Committee on Hemispheric Security (CHS), the Summits of the Americas, and the meetings of defense ministers of the Americas. Parallel discussions have taken place in regions—Mercosur (Mercado Común del Sur), the Andean countries, Central America, and the Caribbean—and these talks have contributed importantly to the final agenda. Each of these tracks has added to the list of security issues of concern to the region, and each has reflected disagreements on the basic definitions of security, the scope of the security sector and its governance, historical civil-military tensions and bureaucratic rivalries, lack of agreement on how to use the extant inter-American institutions, and questions about the relative role and weight of the United States in a new security architecture.

In this chapter I review the security architecture reform that began in 1991 and explore the biases of this old debate. The chapter focuses mainly on hemisphere-wide institutions, but that choice should not be understood to diminish the importance of complementary actions at the subregional and national levels. In closing, I examine outstanding issues and address some possible next steps to strengthen the system.

Renewal of the Inter-American System

Agreement on the list of "traditional and new threats, concerns and challenges" evolved over a decade of discussion that began at the 1991 meeting of the OAS to consider the region's commitment to democracy and the renewal of the inter-American system. By the 1980s leaders in the Americas recognized that the inter-American system required profound revision and reform (see Vaky 1983; Farer 1988; Scheman 1988; Vaky and Muñoz 1993). By 1990, the Cold War having ended, circumstances seemed opportune. For the first time in decades, democratically elected governments ruled in every country in the hemisphere except Cuba. Chileans had voted in 1989 to end the exceptional government of Augusto Pinochet, and Patricio Aylwin's democratically elected government took office in 1990, marking the end of two decades of military governments in Latin America. In Central America, the Esquipulas Peace process led to the signing of the 1990 Oslo Accord, ending combat in Guatemala. A similar accord was in sight in El Salvador (it was signed in 1992). Violeta Chamorro was elected president of Nicaragua in 1990, ending the contentious Sandinista presence in the isthmus and making possible the consolidated Central American peace envisaged in Esquipulas.

Canada became a permanent member of the OAS in 1990 as well, bringing additional weight and a softer North American voice to deliberations, as well as experience in coalition peace operations. Canada was an important proponent of the human security focus being developed in Canadian and other foreign policy circles and at the United Nations (Lopez 2001; United Nations 1994a).

The fall of the Berlin Wall (1989) and the collapse of the Soviet Union (1991) were expected to generate a peace dividend that would permit nations to divert resources from defense to development. Latin American countries had already begun this process with a sharp downsizing of armed forces and their budgets, as democratic governments sought to assert control over their defense establishments. A cooperative security emphasis on confidence-building measures mirrored that of the Organization for Security and Cooperation in Europe's (OSCE) activities in Eastern Europe (see Carter et al. 1992; Nolan 1993; Zartman and Kremeniuk 1995).

This convergence of global trends and hemispheric events presented an opportunity to reexamine the purpose and nature of the inter-American system and to commit these institutions to new goals. The raison d'être of the extant inter-American security framework established during World War II, collective defense against external aggression by nation-states, had disappeared, as had the threat of international communism. The Inter-American Treaty of Reciprocal Assistance (Rio Treaty), generally perceived by Latin Americans to have been vitiated when the US supported Great Britain in the Falklands/Malvinas crisis of 1982, was ripe for either discard or dramatic revisions. The Inter-American Defense Board (IADB, but more often referred to as the "Board"), part of the system but not part of the OAS, required similar renewal. The region's policy focus in the 1980s had been on the resolution of the debt crisis and the return to democratic government. With a new decade beginning, the focus was on economic development, long a consistent theme in Latin American visions of the inter-American system, and the consolidation of democratic governments. Defense spending, which had risen dramatically in the 1970s and 1980s under military governments in some countries and as a consequence of the Central American conflicts in others, needed to be rationalized.

Track One: The Organization of American States and Committee on Hemispheric Security

The first step toward renewal and recommitment was taken with the announcement of the 1991 Santiago Commitment to Democracy and Renewal of the Inter-American System (OAS 1991b). The foreign ministers' declaration focused priority attention on promoting democracy, human rights, and economic development, as well as trade liberalization and measures against drug trafficking. In the preambles of the Commitment, delegates recalled that cooperation for peace and security was essential to democracy. In the declaration itself they committed to cooperate in the "adoption and execution of appropriate measures to begin to prevent and combat the illicit use and production of narcotic drugs and psychotropic substances and traffic therein, chemical precursors and money laundering, and related trafficking in clandestine arms, ammunitions and explosives," and, finally,

> a decision to initiate a process of consultation on hemispheric security in light of the new conditions in the region and the world, for an updated and

comprehensive perspective of security and disarmament, including the subject of all forms of proliferation of weapons and instruments of mass destruction, so that the largest possible volume of resources may be devoted to the economic and social development of the member states. (OAS 1991b: 3)

Thus, although the delegates' principal focus was on traditional themes of economic development and the new issues of expanding and deepening democracy, security issues lay close to the surface—with the emphasis on disarmament and reducing the "defense burden" on the one hand, and on the consequences of drug trafficking and related criminal activities on the other. These discussions would evolve to cover additional themes over the next decade.

New beginnings. The new look at the hemispheric security architecture began with vigor. The Santiago General Assembly entrusted the Permanent Council to create a working group to "examine the background, initiatives, experiences and instruments produced with the framework of the inter-American system" "for the purpose of making the pertinent revisions and adjustments" (OAS 1991c). The group would report to the next General Assembly.

The selection of chair for the working group, Argentine ambassador Hernan Patiño Mayer, was felicitous. In the 1980s Argentina had engaged in an important evaluation and recalibration of its own civil-military relations (see Huser 2002; Martinez 2002), in which individuals like Patiño Mayer had played an important part. Under the Menem administration, the Argentine military had become an important instrument of Argentina's and Foreign Minister Guido DiTella's foreign policy of reinsertion into the democratic world.

The Patiño Mayer working group's report to the 1992 General Assembly in Nassau was well received, and the ministers agreed to continue studying the security subject. Instructions in their resolution reiterated the focus on themes of disarmament, reporting of military expenditures and acquisitions, and restraint in arms transfers, among other issues. The concerns of small island states—disaster relief, arms smuggling, drug trafficking, and other transnational criminal activities—were included at the request of the Caribbean states (OAS 1992a). They agreed to a second, more ambitious statement, titled *On Cooperation for Security and Development in the Hemisphere—Regional Contributions to Global Security,* that addressed development questions as well as transparency in arms control and arms acquisitions. They also asked for recommendations defining the "legal-institutional relationship" between the OAS and the Inter-American Defense Board. A Special Committee on Hemispheric Security was created to pursue these concerns, and Patiño Mayer was elected chair.[3]

By May, Patiño Mayer had prepared a discussion paper (Patiño Mayer 1993) focusing on a "new concept" of cooperative security in the hemisphere that would replace the collective security concept inherited from World War II and the struggle against communism. He argued that the region must (1) reexamine its definitions of security and defense, (2) refocus the military dimension of hemisphere security, (3) build a positive civil-military relationship based on the premise of civilian leadership of the military, and (4) work for incorporation of the Inter-American Defense Board as an advisory entity of the Organization of American States. The first two themes fell clearly under the rubric of confidence-building measures on which all could generally agree. The second two issues would prove more difficult. The General Assembly, meeting in Managua, renewed the mandate of the Special Committee and instructed it to give special attention to OAS-UN cooperation in regional security (anticipating close cooperation in the Central American peace process), disarmament, transparency in acquisitions, confidence- and security-building measures, and military technical exchange, as well as civil-military relations. It agreed to continue to study the IADB-OAS relationship but stipulated that all political organs of the OAS could call on the IADB for "technical-military advisory services and consultancy."[4]

To further its work, the Special Committee organized a meeting of experts on confidence- and security-building measures (CSBMs) in Buenos Aires in March 1994 and a larger, regional conference on the same subject in Santiago in 1995. It commissioned the Inter-American Defense Board to prepare an inventory of confidence-building measures being practiced in the hemisphere.

The 1995 Declaration of Santiago on Confidence- and Security-Building Measures (OAS 1995) adopted a list of goals strongly influenced by the confidence-building measures of the ongoing Central American peace process in Esquipulas (as well as the board's inventory) (Herdocia Sacasa 2004; Villalta Vizcara 2002). The focus was on disarmament issues and on engagement among civilian and military forces, including the following:

- advance notice of military exercises as well as invitations to observers, visitors, and students;
- participation in the United Nations Register of Conventional Arms and Standardized International Reporting of Military Expenditures;
- exchange of information concerning defense policies and doctrines;
- limitation and control of conventional weapons;
- increasing security of transport by land, sea, and air;
- cooperation in natural disaster prevention and response;
- communications with civilian or military authorities of neighboring countries regarding border situations;
- seminars, courses, and studies on mutual confidence- and security-building measures;

- a high-level meeting on the special security concerns of small island states; and
- education for peace programs.

Despite his efforts, Patiño Mayer was not able to schedule the special conference on security explicitly called for in the 1991 Santiago Commitment. In 1996 he returned to Argentina, and leadership of the Committee on Hemispheric Security passed to others.

Expansion of the security agenda, 1996–1999. Under a succession of chairs from Brazil, Mexico, Antigua and Barbuda, and Chile, the committee continued to add new commitments to the security agenda. The 1998 San Salvador Meeting on Confidence- and Security-Building Measures anticipated extending discussions on security issues to parliamentarians and developing courses on CSBMs, disarmament, and other issues for a variety of academic venues that would include participation by "government, civilian and military officials and by civil society." Chile's success in developing a civil-military dialogue on defense policy through its white paper process was highlighted. Transparency in defense spending was promoted, and the special concerns of small island states were specifically addressed. Special attention was given to small arms trafficking in the region, and the Committee on Hemispheric Security was urged to "strengthen dialogue to manage questions related to conventional weapons" (OAS 1998).

Members committed to the removal of antipersonnel land mines from Central America (by 2000) and from the Peru-Ecuador border and promoted the Convention on the Prohibition of the Use, Stockpiling, Production, and Transfer of Anti-Personnel Land Mines and on Their Destruction (Ottawa Convention) and the Convention Against the Development, Production, and Stockpiling of Chemical and Biological or Toxic Weapons. The Inter-American Convention Against the Illicit Manufacturing of and Trafficking in Firearms, Ammunition, Explosives, and Other Related Materials (CIFTA) was signed in 1997 and ratified by most countries by the end of the decade. The committee established a working group on transparency in conventional weapons acquisition, and the Inter-American Convention on Transparency in Conventional Weapons Acquisitions was approved by the OAS General Assembly in June 1999 and entered into force in 2002 (Gaviria 2004).

In April 1999, the Committee on Hemispheric Security began discussions to redefine the concept of security and security threats in the hemisphere and of the role of the Inter-American Defense Board. As a result of the committee's presentation, the 1999 Guatemala General Assembly agreed to begin a review of the Rio Treaty and the Inter-American Defense Board. In addition, reacting to the tremendous collaboration of civilian and military organizations in response to the fall 1998 hurricanes, Mitch in Central America and George in the Caribbean, and to the Colombian earthquake in January 1999, the General Assembly expanded the range of cooperative issues on the security agenda to include cooperation in response to natural disasters and in humanitarian search-and-rescue operations. An Inter-American Committee on Disaster Reduction (IACNDR) was created. These issues would continue under discussion into the future.

Renewed energy on security, 1999–2003. The 1998 Santiago Summit and the 1999 Guatemala General Assembly each made a special point of calling on the OAS to convene the special conference on security, as called for in 1991. To ensure responsiveness to the summit mandates, the OAS secretariat appointed a coordinator for hemispheric security affairs to provide and coordinate technical support to the Committee on Hemispheric Security (which had no staff), to maintain and disseminate documents, and to advise the secretary-general on support for the committee.[5]

Following a series of conferences and workshops on hemispheric security, the committee developed a questionnaire to put to member states. The secretary-general's special advisor for hemispheric security took responsibility for formulating the questions and compiling the responses. Discussion of the questionnaire occupied the committee from 1999 to 2002, when the compendium of replies from member states was finally presented to the committee.[6]

In 2002 at Bridgetown, Barbados, the Caribbean states again introduced their concept of a multidimensional approach to security. This time they were persuasive.[7] The General Assembly declared that "the security of the Hemisphere encompasses political, economic, social, health and environmental factors" and that "Member States should seek to enhance and, where necessary, develop appropriate and relevant mechanisms to deepen co-operation and co-ordination in order to address in a more focused manner the new multidimensional threats, concerns and other challenges to hemispheric security" (OAS 2002d: 2).

At long last, the special conference was held in Mexico City in October 2003. In general, delegates were very pleased with the results. Nevertheless, the rapporteur's (minister of foreign affairs of Guatemala) final remarks leave clear that much remained to be done.[8] In particular, he noted, "Latin American democracies are vulnerable, flawed by a security problem. In my view it is a problem that needs to be addressed urgently, with actions undertaken in a spirit of solidarity that entail regional cooperation." He also noted that "we need to harp on the need for citizen and civil society participation. In terms of the institutional architecture for hemispheric security, one task remaining is to clarify the links between the OAS, the IADB and TIAR [the Rio Treaty]."[9]

Committee chairman and Mexican ambassador Miguel Ruiz-Cabañas described the enormous integrating task that had confronted the committee and its thirty-four members.

> From the very early stages in the negotiation process, it was clear that we all have different perspectives and different priorities when addressing the issue of security for our people, for our countries, and for our region. Some countries would put emphasis on traditional military threats to security, while others would focus more on natural disasters, extreme poverty or epidemic diseases. Thus our primary challenge consisted in identifying principles, shared values and common approaches to hemispheric security, that would serve as a basis for our understanding on the issue, in order to outline a road map for security in the Americas that could be flexible enough to respond to the security requirements of all member states.

He noted also that "in the preparatory process for the Conference we touched on the issue of the Inter-American Treaty of Reciprocal Assistance" and agreed to continue to study the issue, recognizing that "some security mechanisms that were useful in the past, do not necessarily reflect the security requirement we have today and must be updated according to our new conception of security" (Ruiz-Cabañas 2003).

The contentious issues. Three sets of interrelated issues have accompanied the discussion of the multidimensional security agenda: the role of the Inter-American Defense Board, the Inter-American Treaty of Reciprocal Assistance or Rio Treaty, and the role of the United States in the inter-American system.

Disposition of the Inter-American Defense Board has been a contentious issue since its founding. The idea of collective security was incorporated into the inter-American system in 1938 and further refined during World War II. The Board was created by the foreign ministers at their third wartime meeting of consultation in 1942 in the aftermath of the Japanese attack on Pearl Harbor. Set up as a planning body, it was charged with studying problems of hemispheric defense and recommending solutions (see Atkins 1999: 230). The Board was not mentioned in the 1948 OAS Charter, but along with a handful of other institutions, remained part of the overall inter-American system, operating with relative autonomy as a separate organization of the region's militaries, distinct and apart from the civilian OAS. This relationship is heir to and fraught with all the historical tensions of Cold War political divisions and civil-military relations in the region. Viron P. Vaky and Heraldo Muñoz (1993) reflect the diplomats' perceptions that the military "have tended to see the Board as their organization, independent of the 'political' organs of the OAS," and, at least in the past, preferred that relationship. In the worst case, some have seen the Board as a kind of golden exile for officers whose presence is undesired at home. Addressing these complaints, some countries have begun to send their OAS ambassadors to meetings, implicitly arguing for a civilian-military integration of the Board and potentially of the staff. In addition, the Board has opened its principal activity, the Inter-American Defense College, to greater civilian participation and has adjusted the curriculum to deal explicitly with disaster response, peace operations, and other contemporary issues. At the same time, the college's budget has been reduced sharply (the United States covers about 70 percent of the budget), and it has not been able to undertake a number of steps critical to enhancing its curriculum and acquiring a professional staff to meet the challenges of the multidimensional security agenda.

The United States presided over the Board from its inception, and as a consequence, some chose to view it as a "tool" of US policy, or at least not independent of US will. At the same time, in spite of its Washington location, the Board has limited standing as a focus of Pentagon defense policy initiatives.[10] With many of its assignments for demining and confidence-building inventories completed, the Board meetings lost their raison d'être. In the changed security climate of a region seeking to deepen democracy, in which countries have declared peaceful relations with their neighbors and see no global enemy, the Board's purpose was no longer clear.

The question of the legal disposition of the Inter-American Defense Board languished in the Committee on Hemispheric Security's agenda from the very beginning. Although the committee was able to absorb responsibilities for issues like disaster response, demining, terrorism, arms control, and other issues, it was simply not able to arrive at a consensus on the incorporation of the IADB as an advisory body of the OAS. Ernesto Lopez (2001) cites a Venezuelan diplomat, who said that "between 1991 and 1994 the deliberations of the working group and later of the Special Committee centered on the definition of the link between the OAS and the Inter-American Defense Board. Positions (never explicit) ranged between the extremes of converting the Board into an Inter-American Joint Staff in charge of the military of the region to the opposite extreme of simply eliminating it." Other commentators note the particular intransigence of individual countries—Brazil and Mexico are most often mentioned—as unwilling either to address the incorporation of the Board into the larger organization or to make any change in the status quo. More recently, this intransigence spread to most of the South American countries. Solutions presented to the Committee on Hemispheric Security all focused on adoption of a resolution that would make the Board either a "specialized organization" or an "entity" of the OAS. Finally, in March 2006, under the persistent leadership of Chilean ambassador Esteban Tomic, the committee presented its recommendations and revised Board Charter to the General Assembly. A resolution to incorporate the Board into the OAS as an "entity" with technical autonomy was adopted on March 16 in a special session called for that purpose (OAS 2006a). A rotating presidency was established, and in July 2006 a Brazilian general assumed leadership. The deed was done. The Board became part of the OAS, but its relationship to the Committee on Hemispheric Security and its tasking continued to remain unclear.

The Inter-American Treaty of Reciprocal Assistance (Rio Treaty), signed in Rio de Janeiro in 1947, is another cornerstone of the inter-American system. The treaty was the product of a series of meetings in the hemisphere in which the United States gradually set aside its traditional claim under the Monroe Doctrine to intervene unilaterally in Latin American countries for the purposes of restoring order.[11] Beginning in 1936, the US government proposed to abandon intervention if the Latin American states would accept collective responsibility for maintaining peace. The Latin American states issued a declaration to this effect at Havana in 1940 at the outset of World War II and formalized it by treaty in 1947. The Rio Treaty was concluded "in order to assure peace, through adequate means, to provide for effective reciprocal assistance to meet armed attacks against any American state, and in order to deal with threats of aggression against any of them." From its inception, the issues of collective security, peaceful resolution of disputes, and nonintervention in the internal affairs of states, as well as whose definition of threats of aggression should prevail, were in tension (see Fenwick 1962).

Either the Rio Treaty or the peace and collective security provisions of the OAS Charter (Chapters V and VI) were invoked on twenty-two occasions between 1948 and 1990 (Morales 2004). A majority of the invocations of the peace and security provisions involved disputes between Latin American countries. On several occasions the United States invoked the treaty to justify unilateral actions already under way, such as the interventions in Guatemala in 1954 and in the Dominican Republic in 1965. But the United States ignored the treaty when it supported Great Britain against Argentina in the Falkland/Malvinas crisis in 1982,[12] and on other occasions when it took unilateral actions in the area—Grenada in 1983, Panama in 1989, and in the 1980s Central American conflicts.[13] In lieu of the Rio Treaty framework, the Vatican provided mediation in the 1985 resolution of Argentine-Chilean claims in the Beagle Channel, and the Latin American guarantors of the 1942 Rio Protocol on the Peru-Ecuador border provided good offices (with US logistical support) in the resolution of the Peru-Ecuador border dispute that broke out in 1995.

Mexican president Vicente Fox called the 1947 treaty "obsolete and useless" in a speech to the OAS on September 7, 2001. Nevertheless, the treaty was invoked, at Brazil's initiative, in the aftermath of the September 11 bombings of the World Trade Center and Pentagon but was not mentioned in the November declaration on security in the hemisphere. On September 6,

2002, Mexico formally withdrew from the treaty. The treaty remains an "irritant" to some, as much in lore as in fact. The consensus may be to leave it "on the shelf," where it might be invoked when needed,[14] while crafting other instruments that address pressing present-day issues.[15]

There is no question that the US presence in the institutions of the inter-American system and as an actor in the hemisphere has an important impact on the discussion of the hemisphere security framework. The overwhelming military power of the United States, and its demonstrated willingness to use it at will within the region, makes any discussion of "collective" security seem pointless to some regional leaders.[16] The relegation of most military diplomatic relations to a unified commander based in Miami rather than in Washington, along with weak leadership on regional issues in the Office of the Secretary of Defense, is perceived as a lack of serious concern and respect for the region. The US Southern Command's reference to the region as its "Area of Responsibility (AOR)," which in US military jargon simply refers to its geographic region of focus, grates on Latin American and Caribbean ears, which hear these words as implying an infringement on their sovereignty. Regional diplomats and officers also lament the US Defense Department's "tin ear" and lack of knowledge of the region when promoting US interests while not taking into account regional interests or listening to regional opinions (see Diamint 2004; Chillier and Freeman 2005). US efforts to persuade countries of the region to sign Article 98 agreements regarding the International Criminal Court are acknowledged by many to have been ham-handed and resulted in many countries being cut off from US assistance and training. In 2006 hearings before Congress, the Pentagon and Department of State backed legislation that would permit waivers of sanctions mandated by the 2002 American Servicemen's Protection Act (ASPA).[17] Finally, the sheer volume of resources—aircraft, personnel, exercise and training money, and security assistance funds—gives the US military a highly visible and, for some countries, overwhelming presence in the region. Military resources far outweigh the resources of civilian agencies in Latin America and the Caribbean, and military diplomacy occurs alongside and often more visibly than civilian agency diplomacy. The result is an imbalance in the US presence—the iron fist of US power, rather than the soft glove of US diplomacy—in a region that is struggling to build civilian democratic government and to demonstrate civilian leadership in matters of defense and security. As one defense minister, trying to improve the professionalism of his ministry staff, observed, "there is always plenty of money for military training and education. There is hardly any money for civilian education." A Central American diplomat familiar with efforts to strengthen Central American security cooperation observed that US Southern Command's well-funded bilateral military-to-military programs made it difficult to advance poorly funded regional civilian security collaboration initiatives. Regional security cooperation, a US State Department responsibility under the Foreign Assistance Act of 1961, tends to take the face of military cooperation, as the military is the executive agent administering the funds.[18] Enormous obstacles, including both inertia and lack of political will, impede efforts to link military activities more closely with counterpart civilian political activities. Failure to do so results in sharply reduced civilian political-institutional capability to participate in or carry forward projects initiated by the military. At issue is the profile of shared, responsible civilian-military partnership throughout the hemisphere.

Track Two: The Summits of the Americas Actions on Security

The Summits of the Americas meetings have been the principal catalysts of discussions of hemispheric security. It is entirely possible that without a summit mandate, the OAS might never have succeeded in convening the Special Conference on Hemispheric Security called for at Santiago in 1991. The summit process was undertaken to give presidential and head-of-government impetus to OAS and other regional organizations' efforts to make progress across the broad range of issues of concern. From the US perspective, free trade was the most important agenda item. Latin American and Caribbean states and civil society observers added additional themes (see Hayes 1996; Feinberg 1997; Rosenberg 2001), and summit commitments have grown with each meeting.[19]

The Miami summit planners consciously excluded the security issue from their agenda, thinking that it would be too divisive.[20] Nevertheless, the summit action plan addressed the defense/security issue briefly, stating, "Our aim is to strengthen the mutual confidence that contributes to the economic and social integration of our peoples." The plan also called on governments to "support actions to encourage a regional dialogue to promote the strengthening of mutual confidence, preparing the way for a regional conference on confidence-building measures in 1995, which Chile has offered to host" (Summits of the Americas 1994).

Other broad security issues dealt with in Miami included drug trafficking and related crimes, eliminating the threat of national and international terrorism (terrorism was on the hemispheric agenda well before September 2001), and the creation of an emergency response corps of "White Helmets," an Argentine proposal. The military/defense issues were clearly intended to continue under discussion in the OAS Committee on Hemispheric Security, but the other security issues were initiated in other OAS or regional venues and gravitated to the Committee on Hemispheric Security and other agencies within the OAS. Argentina hosted a meeting on cooperation to prevent terrorism in August 1995 as a prelude to an OAS Specialized Conference on

Terrorism held in Lima in 1996.[21] The Declaration of Lima and its plan of action urged cooperation between and among states on issues of exchange of information, border security, transportation and travel documents, and other steps to eliminate terrorism. The declaration clearly extended security concerns to other government agencies and opened the door for security cooperation across the range of government portfolios.

The drug issue fell to the purview of the Inter-American Drug Abuse Control Commission (CICAD), which also was charged with strengthening efforts to control traffic in firearms and to consider a convention on money laundering (spearheaded by Central Banks). CIFTA was signed in November 1997.

The 1998 Santiago Summit of the Americas continued to press forward the broad set of security issues. A second Inter-American Conference on Terrorism was held in November 1998 in Mar del Plata, Argentina, with ministers of interior in attendance. The ministers adopted the Commitment of Mar del Plata (OAS 1998a), condemning terrorist acts as serious threats to the stability of elected governments. They also recommended creation of an Inter-American Committee Against Terrorism (CICTE), which would coordinate cooperation among states.[22] One of the committee's first tasks was to create a database of information on individuals, groups, organizations, and movements connected with terrorism. At the first CICTE meeting, OAS secretary-general Gaviria argued that countries must improve the capabilities and effectiveness of police, judiciaries, and investigative organizations as well as speed the exchange of information between government organizations and between governments. The United States noted the need to enhance border and airport security.

The Santiago summit also charged the OAS Committee on Hemispheric Security to

- follow up on topics related to confidence and security building,
- analyze the concept of international security in the hemisphere,
- examine ways of strengthening the institutions of the inter-American system that deal with hemispheric security,
- hold a special regional conference on security at the beginning of the next decade, and
- convene a follow-on regional conference on CSBMs.

The third summit, convened in Quebec City, Canada, in April 2001 continued to expand the range of issues of concern to the leaders. One of the new subject areas concerned justice, the rule of law, and the security of the individual; under this cluster were aligned goals to enhance coordination and collaboration among ministers of justice, combat drug trafficking, and implement a hemispheric antidrug strategy, as well as issues related to transnational organized crime, trafficking in persons and in firearms, and efforts to combat violence (gangs). Even though the fourth summit at Mar del Plata, Argentina, in November 2005 was plagued with controversy over trade issues, its declaration reiterated the growing list of multidimensional security issues that limit growth, equity, and job creation in the hemisphere.

Track Three: Defense Ministerials of the Americas (DMA)

The defense ministerial process was set in motion by former US secretary of defense William J. Perry, who chafed at the notion that defense and security issues had not been dealt with in full at the Miami summit and who recognized that defense ministers had not met as a group since an ill-fated meeting at Punta del Este, Uruguay, in 1961. Given the auspicious signs of democracy and the potential peace dividend, but also the surprising and shocking outbreak of armed conflict between Peru and Ecuador in January 1995, just after the hemispheric summit, Perry was committed to advance dialogue among his defense counterparts. The ministers and generals met for three days but did not agree on a declaration. Secretary Perry filled the gap with his own summary of the spirit of the meeting, which he termed the six "Williamsburg Principles" (Perry 1995):

- Uphold the promise of Santiago that the preservation of democracy is the basis for ensuring mutual security;
- Acknowledge that military and security forces play a critical role in supporting and defending the legitimate interests of sovereign democratic states;
- Affirm the commitments made in Miami and Managua that armed forces should be subordinate to democratic authority, act within the bounds of national constitutions, and respect human rights;[23]
- Increase transparency in defense matters through exchanges of information, reporting on defense expenditures, and greater civilian-military dialogue;
- Set a goal of the resolution of disputes by negotiated settlement and confidence-building measures, in a time frame consistent with hemispheric economic integration, recognizing that economic security profoundly affects defense security and vice versa; and
- Promote defense cooperation in United Nations–sanctioned peacekeeping operations and in a supportive role in the fight against narco-terrorism.

Participants could not decide how to follow up this initiative. Collaboration among military institutions was still a sensitive issue, and many countries did not have civilian-led defense ministries.[24] Most had found it a useful exchange, however, and Argentina's minister of defense, Jorge Dominguez, invited the ministers to meet again in Bariloche in 1996.

The Bariloche meeting advanced the debate on security and on relations with the armed forces considerably. Delegations divided into three groups to discuss the new dimensions of international security: the "end of the Cold War" theme (Group One), new roles for the armed forces (Group Two), and the institutional framework of defense in the region (Group Three).

The conclusions were not bold, but they were focused. Group One argued that regional stability was an important foundation for the advancement of democracy and that the armed forces' principal role lies in the defense of territory and sovereignty, with all roles being determined according to the legal and constitutional framework of each country. With the passing of old threats (the Cold War), it was agreed that new threats do challenge the region, including growing unemployment and the marginalization of large sectors of populations, drug trafficking, terrorism, organized crime, and human rights violations of various forms. It was recognized that these *new threats are not necessarily to be addressed from a military perspective* (my emphasis).

The delegations recognized that regional integration could be desirable but should not be understood to alter the existence or roles of national armed forces. Cooperation between and among armed forces (for example, in exchanges, exercises, peacekeeping operations), on defense issues, or in response to disasters was desirable. But military cooperation, whether bilateral or multilateral, "should not lead to the militarization of or handling of those threats that should be dealt with through other means" (DMA 1996). Unlike others, the ministers would always be clear on the limits to their portfolios.

Discussing new roles for the armed forces, Group Two reviewed the importance of and the positive experiences to be had participating in United Nations peace operations and the roles of the armed forces in environmental security (anticipating a US-sponsored conference on the subject scheduled for the coming year). Group Two recognized that although most countries held national exercises on disaster response, few participated in multilateral disaster preparation exchanges. The group discussed the need to pay greater attention to demining, especially in Central America; the roles of the armed forces in twenty-first-century defense; the different perceptions of risks, threats, and opportunities extant in the hemisphere; and science and technology exchanges.

Finally, Group Three focused on the questions of confidence building and transparency, as outlined at the Santiago CSBM conference the previous year. The group underscored the roles that defense and foreign ministries together play in the implementation of confidence and security measures. They echoed the Committee on Hemispheric Security's agenda of information exchanges:

professional and educational exchanges, combined military exercises, bilateral and multilateral meetings of civilian and military officers responsible for defense issues, and commitment to transparency by participation in the United Nations Register of Conventional Arms and the International Standardized Report on Military Expenditures. The group encouraged the development of defense white papers[25] that would make defense policies transparent and, finally, agreed on the desirability of developing "professional civilians proficient in defense issues."[26]

The third DMA took place in 1998 in Cartagena, Colombia, following the Second Summit of the Americas, which had urged countries to speed up efforts to meet on hemispheric security issues. It also operated in the shadow of the recently signed Peru-Ecuador peace accord and the Colombian government's own peace initiative with the Revolutionary Armed Forces of Colombia (FARC). Confidence-building measures, transparency, new threats, and the roles of the armed forces were again debated. Little new ground was covered. The white paper process was mentioned only briefly, even though Chile had just finished its white paper in August 1997 and Argentina had begun a similar deliberative process of its own.

Brazil hosted the fourth DMA in Manaus in 2000. The delegations again reviewed questions of confidence building, regional cooperation, the nature of the threats to security in the hemisphere, and the role of the armed forces in democracy. The Manaus declaration was more detailed than Cartagena's, making explicit reference to the continuing need for civilian education, participation in the UN Register of Conventional Arms, and the publication of defense white papers. Again, the declarations were hortatory, and no mechanisms were discussed to ensure follow-up.

When Chile hosted the fifth DMA in 2002, it sought to extend the scope of DMA-sponsored activities and to document the considerable progress achieved in defense and security cooperation in other venues.[27] The delegations recognized the need to modernize the "network of new and old security institutions and regimes, both collective and cooperative, and hemispheric, regional sub-regional and bilateral in scope" (DMA 2002).

Chile made a special presentation of the benefits of its exercise with Argentina to establish a "Common Standardized Methodology for the Measurement of Defense Expenditures" (ECLAC 2001),[28] and urged other countries in the region to follow a similar route.[29] The ministers also noted the Special Conference on Security to be held in Mexico in 2003 in accordance with the mandates of the second and third summits.

The sixth DMA was held in Quito, Ecuador, in November 2004 in the heady aftermath of the Special Conference in Mexico and its declaration of multidimensional security. Delegates made a concerted effort to underscore the multidimensional themes and renew previous commitments without entering into new substance. The three themes—"A New Architecture for

Hemispheric Security," "Mutual Confidence and Security," and "Defense, Development, and Society"—continued to provide the organizing principles behind the meeting, but increasingly, countries were becoming impatient with the absence of concrete progress across the range of subject areas.

From the beginning a number of observers have been included at the meetings.[30] Gradually, this number has expanded, and at Quito, it included representatives of civil society. Although the president of the Inter-American Defense Board is present at the defense ministerials, the meetings have never specifically dealt with the questions surrounding the Board, relying rather on euphemisms such as "institutions of hemispheric security" to refer to the ongoing mandate to address the issues.

Next Steps: Obstacles to and Options for Moving Forward

The hemispheric security agenda has expanded dramatically since 1991. Starting from discord and with a focus almost entirely on disarmament, demilitarization, and avoidance of state-on-state conflict, the security agenda now encompasses a full range of traditional and new threats, concerns, and other security considerations. It has taken a clear turn in the direction of democratic and human security, as reflected in the multidimensional concept first introduced by the Caribbean countries in 1992 and in El Salvador in 1998 and adopted at Bridgetown in 2002, as well as in the democratic security concepts announced in the 1994 Managua Declaration and in the Central American peace process. The new security agenda is consistent with the human security focus promoted by the United Nations since 1994. It is reflected in Colombia's Democratic Security Policy of 2003, which emphasizes citizen security (Colombia 2003). It is a security agenda for a twenty-first-century system of democracies focused on improving the security and well-being of their citizens, not just the well-being of the state.

The security agenda has been energized by a summit process that has given individual countries and the OAS "top cover"—presidential and head-of-government imprimatur—to move forward on difficult and contentious programs. Security is no longer only the subject matter of defense ministries, but the responsibility of a number of ministries and agencies. Defense ministerials have echoed the mandates of the summits and the OAS and have encouraged greater cooperation among ministries and armed forces, though many of these cooperative activities take place below the radar of international scrutiny.

The execution of this security agenda is diffuse. Different elements of the agenda have been assigned to a variety of OAS organizations that are responsible for coordinating; promoting information sharing; developing model regulations; and conducting conferences, seminars, and meetings of ministers of different portfolios on many of the broad security themes. Many initiatives are hampered by lack of funding and lack of people to effectively carry out programs at the subregional, national, and local levels, and there are few mechanisms to account for progress, communicate lessons learned, or identify weaknesses in one or another organization's capacity to execute. Many of the positive accomplishments are lost among the often negative headlines that capture the daily press.

Obstacles Deconstructed

The multidimensional security framework is complex. Coordinating efforts and achieving concrete results will never be easy. However, there are at least four underlying obstacles to moving forward with a comprehensive security agenda. The first is a continued failure, despite the 2003 multidimensional security declaration, to reach real closure on the expanded security definition. This contributes to the continuing debate over the "securitization" (read "militarization") of the agenda that focuses more attention on possible military roles than on the roles and capabilities of the many other key elements of the security sector. Second, continued tensions in civil-military relations and a pervasive failure to "turn the page" on the history of past military governments also impede dialogue. Third, there is a failure of imagination in defining purpose, roles, and missions for the defense sector, represented in part by the Board, within the OAS, but also at the national level around the region. Finally, greater political will is needed to move beyond debate on definitions and to focus on integrating the various elements, organizations, and actors with responsibilities in the multidimensional approach to security in the hemisphere.

What is security? Historically, Latin American countries have pursued a broad definition of security in their international relations. In their lexicon, security has always entailed economic development, political stability, and nonintervention in the affairs of neighbors, among other things. In contrast, the United States has focused on security as primarily a defense against external rivals, ideologies, and other challenges to US interests. These two different emphases have troubled hemispheric security relations since the beginning of the pan-American vision (Atkins 1999). The tensions between the IADB and the OAS also reflect the wartime origins of the former and its evolution during the Cold War, in contrast with the OAS's purpose of peaceful coexistence and the global world vision of the United States that contrasts with the more regional emphasis of most OAS members and of the OAS itself (Tomic 2006). These different understandings of security need to be reconciled.

All states and all peoples seek security for their economic, political, social, and military affairs. Security—protecting society from violence and foreign invasion—is the first obligation of the sovereign (or state), as Adam Smith argued more than 200 years ago.[31] Security is also a "state of mind."[32] The 1994 *Human Development Report* noted, "Most people instinctively understand what security means. It means safety from the constant threats of hunger, disease, crime and repression. It also means protection from sudden and hurtful disruptions in the pattern of our daily lives—whether in our homes, in our jobs, in our communities or in our environment" (United Nations 1994a). Economic development and globalization, with its potential for economic disruption, transnational crime, corruption, unemployment, and pandemic disease, all present challenges to the well-being of citizens in the Americas. They are security challenges in the contemporary understanding of individual, public, and state security.

While the multidimensional security framework is quite clear in stating that most of the identified insecurities do not require military response, it is not always clear which other organizations are responsible. In the absence of clear designations, critics have tended to raise the alarm about the "securitization," or militarization, of the agenda (Chillier and Freeman 2005; Diamint 2004). Chilean ambassador Tomic acknowledged the negative resonance of the word "security" in the region. "In the south . . . the word 'security' associated with the armed forces, awakens sinister echoes of a not distant past when [the military] used their intelligence and resources to combat an 'internal enemy' who spoke their same language, was born in the same country, perhaps prayed to the same God, but which had incurred the unpardonable crime of not having the same political ideas" (Tomic 2006). This historical caution notwithstanding, most of today's security threats have been identified by political leaders—presidents, prime ministers, and foreign ministers—as well as by citizens, and, quite explicitly, not by the military. Political leaders must begin to move the security debate beyond semantics to a discussion of the concrete actions needed to ensure results in the multiple different dimensions of security that they have defined.

The continuing civilian-military gap. Related to the definition of security and confounding the effort to bring consensus are the continuing civil-military gap and ongoing tensions in civilian-military relations in the hemisphere. No country is exempt from stress and rivalry between established hierarchical institutions. Edwin Dorn (2000) and Peter D. Feaver (2003) underscored the "gap" in political attitudes that supposedly exists between political elites and the military officer corps in the United States. Nevertheless, in a number of Latin American countries, the ghosts of the past have not yet been put to rest, despite considerable progress and general acceptance on the part of the military of subordination to civilian leadership. This persistent distrust translates into a reluctance to open channels for collaboration, to call on the military for assistance, and to recognize the useful contributions that the armed forces can make to specific situations. More specifically, it has translated into an unwillingness to bring the discussion of the role of defense and the military within the hemispheric system to closure.[33]

The expanded agenda and the role of the military and the Inter-American Defense Board. As the security agenda has expanded, civilian institutions have been given responsibility for most, if not all, of the new issues. The OAS coordinates these in part through CICAD, CICTE, CIFTA, its new Multidimensional Security Department, and other agencies. Some of these agencies work well, others less well. Inadequate resources, both financial and personnel, are ongoing challenges that limit their effectiveness. The Ministries of Interior, Justice, Finance, and Trade and the national and local police, to name only a few of the agencies involved, all play their appropriate roles in promoting security, and most meet regularly under different OAS committee or subregional auspices.

Defense ministries and the armed forces need to be folded into the overall multidimensional security architecture. At the hemispheric level, the IADB has a minimal role in most of the multidimensional security issues, though, to its credit, it has frequently delegated personnel to OAS civilian agencies to work on their issues, thereby addressing one of the agencies' major budget-induced constraints. Under the new statute, the Board may be called upon for advice. This is where new ground will be plowed: What advice will be sought? How will it be used? While subregional organizations like the Central American Conference of Armies (CFAC) send observers to Board functions, it has not taken, or been given, any mandate to encourage or facilitate collaboration on security issues at the subregional level. This is where many national leaders would like to focus in the near future.

Renewal and reorganization: Toward more agile security organizations. The hemispheric system now has a comprehensive security agenda. Still missing are a clear, integrated, and workable architecture of relationships and the political will to advance the security agenda. It is no longer sufficient to debate; the subject matter calls for action and results. With the important first step of folding the Board into the OAS, both organizations should begin to consider how best to restructure and refocus their activities to achieve results in appropriate subject areas. Instead of its current hemisphere-wide focus, the Board might organize to emphasize issues of importance to different subregions of the hemisphere, each of which has its unique specific interests as well as shared common interests. The Southern Cone countries, the Central American countries, and the Caribbean states already have regional cooperative structures that are beginning to address subregional issues, such as coordination of efforts against drug trafficking, control of illegal air traffic, and responding to disasters and preparing for peacekeeping operations. More robust coordination should be encouraged, facilitated, and financed. The Central American Integration System (SICA), a product of the Central American peace accords, explicitly seeks to coordinate the efforts of foreign, interior, and defense ministries. This kind of integration of effort is highly desirable in a number of security areas, particularly those involving transnational criminal activities. More opportunity for interagency coordination at the grass roots would strengthen local governance and deliver results more readily to the citizens of the region. Thematic emphases would likely vary from region to region and might include further disaster preparation and training, disaster medical response, assistance to CIFTA in identifying and controlling weapons, coordination and information sharing on illegal air and maritime movement, interregional education, gaming and simulation, and peacekeeping and humanitarian responses. All these activities have important civilian-police-military elements of collaboration. For example, the military would support other agencies, providing command-and-control facilities, communications, mobility, and surge response capability when needed.

Where the Board should not assume exclusive responsibility is in the organizing and staffing of the defense ministerial process. The institutionalization of civilian ministries of defense is still incipient, and it is not advisable that the military become the exclusive secretariat of the civilian ministers' processes. This is especially the case for a body that resides far away from the individual host defense ministries. The defense minister's civilian staff, with appropriate support from the military services as required and sought, should staff the Defense Ministerial of the Americas. To assist the host ministries, the Committee on Hemispheric Security might assume the role of DMA secretariat, tasking the Board for assistance.

To further civil-military and defense–foreign affairs coordination, individual countries might find it useful to assign a military officer to work on issues of the Committee on Hemispheric Security in the office of its OAS diplomatic mission. This liaison officer would provide advice and communicate with the Ministry of Defense and military services on relevant issues.[34] The liaison role would contribute to strengthening civil-military cooperation and confidence building at the national, subregional, and regional levels. By assigning more junior personnel to the liaison functions, countries would begin to build the long-term foundations for trusting civil-military relations.[35]

The defense ministerial process itself also needs more substantive focus and follow-up for it to continue to be a relevant component of hemisphere defense cooperation. DMA commitments advance slowly, in part because defense ministers change frequently, but also because there is no agreement to follow up on commitments made at the biannual ministerials.[36]

The ministers need to focus on themes that are within their realm of authority, rather than simply endorsing the broad multidimensional agenda. As the agenda expands, the ability to show results diminishes. In 1995, at Williamsburg, participants recognized that defense budgets would not likely increase in the foreseeable future. Argentina and Chile have touted the utility of their exercise of standardization of budget presentations as a confidence-building mechanism. Ministers know that the budget is their most important policy instrument. They might benefit immensely from a closer look at different countries' experiences in managing their budget process.[37] Countries of the region also have committed themselves to timely reporting of arms acquisitions to regional and UN arms registers, but there is little demonstrable progress.

Epilogue

The hemisphere's new security agenda is an important regional accomplishment, the first attempt to address the variety of security concerns of countries of the whole region. It is a first attempt to incorporate human security concepts into regional security policy while not discarding traditional security concerns. It opens a new chapter for regional cooperation, but it will require strong, committed leadership to create an effective hemispheric institutional structure capable of transferring creative energy from the international arena to the subregions and from nations and subregions to the regionwide forum. Leaders in this new architecture will need to focus on real security issues, rather than arcane debates over definitions, who is in charge, or whose agenda will take priority. Security priorities will vary from region to region. No single ranking of issues is likely. That should not be an obstacle to moving forward on different issues and agendas in different regions. Each will contribute to greater hemispheric security. The long debate on hemispheric security has resulted in an agenda, but the mechanisms for executing that agenda are still being worked out. The institutions of the inter-American system reconciled differences in security concerns largely by adding to the long list. The security framework is the product of the Committee on Hemispheric Security and other OAS agencies, prompted by the summit process. The Committee on Hemispheric Security does not have the resources to lead the agenda much further, and large elements of the agenda do not fall under its purview. Coordination and motivation of multiple OAS agencies and of the multiple actors at the subregional and national levels remain a daunting challenge for the hemisphere.

Whatever the security framework, countries of the region will have to confront the question of their own civil-military relations, for the success of any effort to further integrate all capabilities of the state (police, military, judiciary, etc.) in response to security threats, challenges, or concerns requires an a priori resolution of the fear, ignorance, and antipathy that have persisted between different participants, especially, but not only, between foreign and defense ministries. Decisionmakers must recognize that the multidimensional security agenda requires an approach that brings all players to the table in a collaborative mode, as well as committed leadership from the heads of government. It is time to end the debate and begin implementing activities that will lead to a more secure hemisphere.

Notes

I am very grateful to the many persons who assisted me in understanding the evolution of the new security framework. It was agreed that their observations would be "not for attribution."

1. This chapter deals with the evolution of the security architecture of the hemisphere since 1991. For an excellent review of the development of the inter-American system from its beginnings, see Atkins (1999).

2. Figure 5.1 is based on the research conducted by Captain Alvaro Martinez, Argentine Navy, while he was fellow in residence at the Center for Hemispheric Defense Studies, 2002–2003. Issues identified in the figure are based on the speeches and presentations to the OAS, the defense ministerials, summits, and other forums by presidents, ministers of foreign affairs, ministers of defense, and other national representatives.

3. Hernan Patiño Mayer served as chair of the Committee on Hemispheric Security from 1991 to 1996, that is, through the period of the working group and special committee. He is the only chair to have served longer than one year.

4. See the discussion of the Nassau and Managua General Assemblies in Vaky and Muñoz 1993: 21–22.

5. This would be Jorge Mario Eastman, a confidant of Secretary-General César Gaviria, and later vice minister of defense of Colombia (September 2004 to July 2006).

6. See Committee on Hemispheric Security website, Concepts of Security in the Hemisphere, Questionnaires and Responses, for details. http://www.oas.org/csh.

7. See Hurst (2003) for a discussion of the Caribbean Community's effort (led by Hurst) to influence the security agenda so that the concerns of small island states would be taken into account.

8. See the Committee on Hemispheric Security, Special Conference, Reports of Rapporteurs, for the text. http://www.oas.org/csh.

9. In fact, the Rio Treaty is not formally related to the OAS or to the IADB.

10. This is in part because the US unified command system allocates responsibility for policy execution to US Southern Command, based in Miami.

11. These meetings took place over the first half of the twentieth century, beginning in 1902. See Atkins (1999).

12. It should be noted that the treaty is nonbinding with respect to the use of force.

13. Central American peace was implemented in a combined OAS–United Nations effort.

14. This position was expressed to me by Brazilian ambassador Rubens Barbosa in the aftermath of September 11.

15. The Rio Treaty in fact permits countries of the hemisphere to respond collectively to "any fact or situation that endangers the security of the Americas" (see Morales 2004).

16. See Hayes (1983) for a discussion of reasons why "collective security" has not survived as a viable hemispheric security concept.

17. In 2006 General Bantz J. Craddock, commander of the Southern Command, and other elements of the Bush administration, including the secretary of state, began to speak out about the negative consequences of the ASPA. Strong appeals could not budge the White House to action. See *New York Times,* July 23, 2006, p. 23, "US Cuts in Africa Aid Hurt War on Terror and Increase China's Influence, Officials Say."

18. Ironically, many of the funds administered by the US military are State Department funds in law.

19. The OAS and Inter-American Development Bank, later joined by the United Nations Economic Commission for Latin America and the Caribbean (ECLAC), were charged with supporting the fulfillment of summit goals.

20. Latin Americans did not want it on the agenda. See Hayes 1996.

21. Argentina had suffered the terrorist bombing of the Argentinian-Israelite Mutual Association (AMIA) in July 1994. See http://www2.jus.gov.ar/Amia/.

22. The committee was constituted at the twenty-ninth meeting of the General Assembly in Guatemala in 1999.

23. Reference is to the Managua Declaration on Democracy and Development (United Nations 1994b).

24. Brazil, for example, did not have a single organization representing its armed forces at the ministerial level, but rather its joint staff organization, and all three services each held a cabinet (ministerial) position.

25. In 1995 Chile had just begun working on its White Paper, the Libro de la Defensa Nacional, which would prove to be an important exercise in reconciling civil-military relations in that country and would serve as a model for subsequent white paper exercises in the region. Argentina would follow suit.

26. This discussion was raised in part by the United States, which came to the meeting with an initiative on an "Inter-American Center for Defense Studies." Although it was initially intended to be a regionally supported program for civilian defense education, concerns about its financing, its support around the region, and its relationship with the Inter-American Defense College led the United States to move forward with the creation of the Center for Hemispheric Defense Studies at the National Defense University in Washington.

27. Chile has arguably the strongest defense ministry in the region, and then defense minister Michelle Bachelet (elected president in 2006) went out of her way to demonstrate the degree of cooperation between her ministry and Chile's armed forces, as well as to permit the Chilean armed forces to show off their skill and history. This was the first time the armed forces of the host country played a visible role in the set of events surrounding the ministers' meeting.

28. Chile and Argentina undertook the bilateral initiative to conduct a comparison of the two countries' defense expenditures as a confidence-building measure. Both countries, including both defense ministries and foreign ministries, were exceptionally pleased with the results of the exercise.

29. To date, Peru is the only country to have followed suit. Peru and Chile held the second meeting of their Permanent Committee for Consultation and Political Coordination, which is considering the ECLAC methodology, in July 2005.

30. This writer participated as observer in three DMAs while serving as the director of the Center for Hemispheric Defense Studies.

31. In *The Wealth of Nations,* Book V, Smith writes, "The first obligation of the Sovereign, which is that of protecting society from violence and from the invasion of other independent societies . . ."

32. This is an argument I have made in Hayes 1983 and 1986.

33. This is not a purely Latin American issue. Rivalries between the State Department and Defense Department are long-standing in the United States, too, and similarly preclude collaboration and coordination.

34. He or she could report to the military chain of command through his or her service attaché.

35. The example of exchange of liaisons might be copied in foreign ministries and defense ministries in the region. Chile has very successfully placed Foreign Service officers in its defense ministry and military officers in its foreign ministry to facilitate liaison between the two arms of national foreign policy.

36. The United States has been as guilty of failure to follow up as any.

37. A more open treatment of budgets would permit interested countries to share information on difficult problems, such as funding the maintenance of legacy systems, achieving economies of scale in routine acquisitions, and reforming military pensions—the latter an area in which there is much to be gained from sharing successful practices and lessons learned. There also are important opportunities to be exploited in cooperative programs for equipment procurement, repairs, and modernization within the region, particularly as applies to legacy systems.

6

Confidence- and Security-Building Measures: Relevance and Efficiency

David R. Mares

Western Hemisphere states and their organizations at the regional, sub-regional, and bilateral levels create and use confidence- and security-building measures (CSBMs) to move the region from a "negative" to a "positive" peace (Kacowicz 1998). Cooperative peace and security doesn't mean that interstate disputes disappear; rather, it means that such disagreements are actively managed through friendly diplomacy or ignored until they can be handled amicably. Mitigating the rivalry embodied in disputes through confidence and security building facilitates the mutual adjustment of policy positions that is necessary for cooperation to ensue.

CSBMs are institutions, in the sense that institutions are rules that guide behavior (North 1990). Interstate disputes in the Western Hemisphere (see Table 6.1), and the domestic instabilities confronting many countries in the region, stimulate efforts to increase confidence and build security. We should ask the same questions about these CSBMs as we do about the other institutions examined in this book: Are they efficient and relevant in the security environment facing the region today?

I begin this chapter with a discussion of the design of security institutions and then clarify structural and conjunctural factors influencing the development of CSBMs in the Americas and the criteria for evaluating their relevance and efficiency. An empirical analysis of hemispheric CSBMs' performances at the bilateral, subregional, and regional levels follows. The conclusion highlights key factors explaining the successes and limitations of CSBMs in the Western Hemisphere.

Designing Security Institutions

Past choices and events influence institutional design (Wendt 2001). Western Hemisphere institutional design borrowed heavily from the mythologized

Table 6.1 Traditional-Type Interstate Disputes in the Contemporary Western Hemisphere

Countries	Issue
Active Disputes	
Guatemala-Belize	Border demarcation
Honduras–El Salvador–Nicaragua	Maritime demarcation in Gulf of Fonseca; depletion of fisheries
Honduras-Nicaragua	Maritime demarcation in Atlantic; migration
Nicaragua-Colombia	Territorial dispute over San Andres and Providencia Islands
Colombia-Venezuela	34 points on border in dispute; migration; guerrillas; contraband, including drugs
Venezuela–Trinidad and Tobago	Maritime boundaries; natural resources
Haiti–Dominican Republic	Migration; border demarcation
Bolivia-Chile	Territorial dispute: outlet to the Pacific
Latent Disputes	
Venezuela-Guyana	Territorial: Venezuela claims 40 percent of Guyana
Guyana-Suriname	Territorial: Guyana claims almost half of Suriname
Antarctica (12 countries)	Treaty puts national claims on hold
Argentina–Great Britain	Malvinas/Falklands, Georgias, and Sandwich Sur
United States–Cuba	US naval base in Guantánamo

Source: Mares 2001b.

European experience with CSBMs (Desjardins 1996) and was influenced by structural and conjunctural factors peculiar to the Western Hemisphere (Cheyre Espinosa 2000).

The inter-American system has a unique structural feature: one great power coexists with multiple medium and small powers, many of whom have unstable governments. Disparities in national power and governmental abilities within this system create tremendous coordination and efficiency challenges for any security institutions (US Department of Defense 2005).

A great power's interests span the globe; it interprets each local or regional situation within that context. Consequently, commitments at the regional level will often take a backseat to responsibilities at the global level. Small powers, in contrast, don't have to relate the local context to their wider international commitments and challenges. This difference often produces distinct interpretations of events and their implications (e.g., nationalism and communism during the Cold War).

Unstable governments are challenging partners because they have little control over their polities. An unstable government's commitment may be problematic because its domestic situation is beyond its control: rebel groups, criminal organizations, and demagogic politicians may use the government's failures at home to question the existing international order, thereby producing a security issue for the great power who has created that international order.

Small powers can fear abandonment or domination by more powerful states. Unstable states that want the support of great powers desire institutions to strengthen security linkages between small and great powers. But stable small powers and governments that are advocating domestic reforms that frighten the great power fear increased opportunities for great power domination. Instead, these small powers seek to decouple great and small power security (Ikenberry 2001: 51ff). As members of the Regional Security System (Antigua and Barbuda, Dominica, Grenada, St. Kitts and Nevis, St. Lucia, and St. Vincent and the Grenadines) noted in replying to an OAS questionnaire:

> The increasing reliance upon a single power to provide military and developmental leadership, within the Western Hemisphere, poses one of the fundamental political hurdles which weak states face. The asymmetrical power relations in the Western Hemisphere, magnified by the presence of small island-states within the OAS, require a reliance upon international law that may not be a shared value among all members. Essentially, the Organization of American States is a tool that can be relied upon to manage disagreement and conflict among states, but at the pleasure of the lone superpower within it whenever that power is sufficiently magnanimous. (Committee on Hemispheric Security 2002b: 31)

Great powers want institutions to be binding on others but prefer not to be bound themselves. Consistently violating the institutional rules would, however, convince weaker states that there was no benefit to membership and they would not bind themselves through the institution. To facilitate this balancing act between commitment and independence, the scope of a security institution may be designed to allow great flexibility over where issues are negotiated (Koremenos, Lipson, and Snidal 2001: 770–771). The powerful state might pressure a weak state to eschew the institution and address an issue bilaterally. For example, the United States believes the drug trade threatens hemispheric security but prefers bilateral deals with key countries (Bolivia, Peru, Colombia, and Mexico). Each of these countries believes that it has specific assets that empower it in a bilateral negotiation but would diminish in a multilateral forum.[1] Whether this flexibility strengthens or weakens a security institution depends upon whether that institution would be abandoned by states seeking this flexibility. For example, a UN with Security Council vetoes is better than no UN at all.

Security institutions revolve around sovereignty and defense rights. Sovereignty rights stem from the nature of the international system of sovereign states, whereas defense rights are specified by international law (e.g., the rules of war) and by states' domestic institutional arrangements. The fundamental questions about security institutions revolve around their *relevance to* and their *efficiency in* producing the outcome for which they were either originally designed or used in a specific case (Lachowski 2004: 89).

Relevance results from their influence on the coordination of the important security interactions that fall within the security institution's purview. CSBMs, by eliminating misperceptions about aggression, providing credible assurances about defensive intentions, and decreasing military options, are expected to minimize interstate conflict and defuse it without violence when it does occur.

The efficiency challenge arises because CSBMs might contribute importantly to the desired outcome, but the costs of creating and maintaining those CSBMs could be more expensive than if security were defended by some different means (e.g., military alliances and unilateral defense policies). Alternatively, the outcomes might not have been achieved, or only minimally so, while the costs paid were high (Borner, Bodmer, and Kobler 2004). Paradoxically, CSBMs could be efficient and yet irrelevant if states paid low costs and used the CSBMs simply for rhetorical or domestic purposes.

Transaction costs of international institutions arise from negotiating and concluding institutional arrangements, monitoring the behavior regulated by the institutions, and enforcing the agreements. The administrative costs of negotiating CSBMs are not negligible since OAS, foreign and defense ministries, and perhaps other bureaucratic/diplomatic infrastructure are devoted to them, but costs are impossible to even estimate with currently available information.

Negotiating about self-defense rights means impinging upon sovereignty since the institutions limit how a state is legitimately able to defend itself. How much of a cost diminished sovereignty turns out to be depends on the relevant security environment and the specific terms of the security agreement.

CSBMs must be based on variables that are observable to the relevant parties and measurable in order to avoid disagreements over whether the terms of the CSBM are being met. If the variable is defined too narrowly, variations in behavior quickly produce breaches of contract. If a variable is defined too broadly, its relevance is at risk because the conditions for initiating action are never met. To build confidence in the security arena, one would expect institutions to define key terms fairly narrowly.

A treaty with strict implementation provides information about the preferences of states that do and do not ratify the treaty (Kydd 2001). However, an extremely costly treaty will have few signatories, diminishing its ability to provide information about state preferences. One of Latin America's earliest CSBMs, the American Treaty on Pacific Settlement, or Pact of Bogotá (1948), required signatories to follow certain procedures in a conflict. Only fourteen of the thirty-four active members of the OAS are signatories, and some did so with reservations that call into question its relevance (Committee on Hemispheric Security 2002b: 50).

Penalties for breach of contract vary. For Latin American countries, behavior that escapes the bounds of inter-American institutions generates more US interference. The United States pays some costs for institutional irrelevance or weakness as well. When the United States intervenes in the domestic and foreign affairs of its neighbors, they become suspicious of US motives and commitments. Consequently, they may try to balance with Europe or Asia or pull back from security institutions, weakening them further.

The Move Toward Confidence Building in the Americas

Latin America's security context has been competitive; deterrence and militarized bargaining have predominated (Kacowicz 1998; Mares 2001a). Efforts to resolve the Central American civil wars and bring the military under civilian control in the 1980s brought a new appreciation for confidence- and security-building measures throughout the hemisphere. Owing to the influence of the Rio Group (Rojas Aravena 1994) and supported by the United States, the OAS in 1991 declared democracy the sine qua non for interstate confidence to develop within the region.

Inter-American CSBMs confront challenges in defining the "security" toward which they are building. It is difficult to know how to build confidence on security matters when definitions of security and what constitutes a threat are ambiguous, if not outright contradictory. After a decade of discussion about the post–Cold War security environment and a year after the terrorist attacks of September 11, 2001, an OAS survey reveals the wide disparity in the region in the area of security.

Brazil distinguishes between "defense issues" (which involve the armed forces) and "security issues" (which incorporate many government agencies) (Pecly Moreira 2002). The United States includes drug trafficking and organized crime, but not the environment, development, or public health (Noriega 2003). Chile includes under "new threats to security" the transportation of hazardous substances (Committee on Hemispheric Security 2002b: 25), whereas the Regional Security System identifies "the transshipment of nuclear waste through the Caribbean Sea" as an "intention, implied or express, to severely damage or destroy" and, consequently, a threat to hemispheric security (Committee on Hemispheric Security 2002b: 30).

The OAS "solved" this definitional issue with the Declaration on Security in the Americas in October 2003 (OAS 2003a). The document reforms security institutions to address the post–Cold War and post-9/11 security environment. Multidimensional in character, the Western Hemisphere's security concept facilitates the development of a flexible security architecture. The OAS now has a Department of Multidimensional Security, whose purview includes terrorism, arms trafficking, explosives, demining, transportation ports, and illicit drug control. Subregional groupings are free to utilize any of the dimensions enumerated in the declaration, which should facilitate cooperation at the subregional level.

Critics argue that the multidimensional security concept represents the least common denominator. The declaration also "securitizes" a variety of important problems, to the detriment of effective solutions (militaries can do little to help solve many of them) and the undermining of citizen security, civilian control of the military, and, ultimately, democracy. The declaration is also criticized for accepting the precedence of state sovereignty with regard to prioritizing security threats and selecting which means can be used to address those threats (Chillier and Freeman 2005).

CSBMs in the Americas function across the levels of interstate relationships: unilateral, bilateral, subregional, regional, and global. Most CSBM efforts fall between the unilateral and global; a few examples at the ends of the continuum are worth noting. Unilateral measures, by the very nature of the security arena, are rare. Chile's publication of a defense white paper detailing its presumptions about the security environment the country faces, and its defense structure, goals, and policies, provides confidence-building information to neighbors in a transparent fashion and serves as an example to the rest of Latin America. The subsequent call by the OAS and the summit process for the development of defense white papers illustrates the utility of the Chilean unilateral act (nine states have published white papers of varying quality and utility). Participation by Latin American countries in UN peacekeeping efforts and the decision to become a party to the Convention on the Prohibition of the Use, Stockpiling, Production, and Transfer of Anti-Personnel Mines and on Their Destruction (Ottawa Convention) represent global CSBMs with spillover effects and reinforce CSBMs at the regional level. As the chairperson of the fifth defense ministerial (Santiago 2003) put it: "the region has gradually advanced toward a complex security system made up of a network of new and old security institutions and regimes, both collective and cooperative, of hemispheric, regional, subregional and bilateral scope, which have in practice made up a new flexible security architecture" (Bachelet Jeria 2003: 4).

Bilateral CSBMs

Bilateral efforts at confidence and security building proliferated in the 1980s in the aftermath of the Falklands/Malvinas war; the Central American civil wars; and the war scares in 1978 among Argentina, Chile, Peru, and Bolivia. After its defeat in the Falklands/Malvinas war, Argentina was involved with its traditional rivals Brazil and Chile in the most far-reaching bilateral measures ever with its neighbors. These initiatives covered nuclear policy, border delimitation, and military movements. Chile, in turn, embarked on CSBMs with its traditional rivals, Peru and Bolivia, but the territorial dispute with the latter has limited the relationship (Escudé and Fontana 1998; Varas, Schear, and Owens 1995).

Although more activity is occurring with CSBMs at the subregional and regional levels today than ever before, the daily activity of confidence and security building continues to be at the bilateral level. But in the absence of a methodology to distinguish between mere contact and the actual building of confidence, it is difficult to evaluate the impact of activities such as a military ski championship between Chile and Argentina, Peruvian efforts to spur tourism by military personnel with its neighbors, or Brazilian military students taking courses in Mexico. Even the countries that are ostensibly building confidence with each other do not agree on what measures build confidence. Hence Colombia listed five CSBMs of a military nature with Ecuador in 1995, whereas the latter reported nine such measures between them; Peru did not list Argentina as a country with whom it was engaged in such measures, but the latter listed Peru eleven times in its inventory (Inter-American Defense Board 1995). OAS efforts to provide guidelines are virtually useless: their experts came up with five single-spaced pages listing measures that could be considered CSBMs (Committee on Hemispheric Security 2003). The efficiency of this level of detail (in terms of the manpower used to track and report it) undoubtedly exceeds its benefits since the lower level of reporting by other countries is deemed to have met the requirements.

Subregional CSBMs

A consensus exists in the Western Hemisphere that many security issues or threat characteristics are peculiar to only parts of the region, that priorities may differ across the hemisphere, and that neighboring states may find it easier to cooperate on particular security issues than would states at opposite ends of the hemisphere. Consequently, the hemisphere has had a veritable explosion of subregional CSBMs. Among the most important are Mercosur's (Mercado Común del Sur's) democracy requirement for membership and the Framework Treaty on Democratic Security in Central America. The latter has explicit sections detailing conflict prevention and early warning measures that will create or strengthen existing Central American conflict resolution mechanisms. The treaty's CSBM provisions, however, were found wanting in 1998–1999, when the OAS had to mediate a conflict between Nicaragua and Costa Rica (Rojas Aravena 2001: 137–141).

The small eastern Caribbean island-states grouped in the Regional Security System have been particularly successful in getting regional attention.

Two high-level meetings on the special security concerns of small island-states have been held under the auspices of the OAS.

Not everyone has been happy with the proliferation of subregional groupings and CSBMs specific to them. Panama noted the potential problem for "adequate, effective coordination" of not clearly spelling out the relationship between subregional and regional instruments: Are they duplicating efforts? Do they have overlapping functions? Are they relatively autonomous? (Committee on Hemispheric Security 2002b: 75). What has remained unspoken is perhaps the most pressing question: Can CSBMs at the subregional level actually be destabilizing for other subregions or the region as a whole?

Regional CSBMs

By 1991, the OAS had picked up on the bilateral and subregional CSBM experiences of the 1980s in Latin America and the European experiences in the Helsinki Process. At the twenty-first regular session of the OAS that year, the General Assembly adopted a far-reaching document on security, the Santiago Commitment to Democracy and the Renewal of the Inter-American System (OAS 1991b). With this declaration, the member states took the step of using democratic standing as an indicator of whether a state could be a credible partner in the search for security and articulated a desire to renovate the OAS, including getting it involved in CSBMs.

The first Summit of the Americas (Miami, 1994) "endorsed CSBMs as a means of sustaining democracy and economic development in the region" (Bloomfield and Lincoln 2003). Two regional CSBM conferences were held, in Santiago, Chile, in November 1995 and in San Salvador, El Salvador, in February 1998. The second Summit of the Americas (Santiago, 1998) "mandated" the implementation of the results of the Santiago and San Salvador meetings. The presidents highlighted the need for increased transparency in defense policy and once again advocated the peaceful resolution of conflict (Summits of the Americas Information Network n.d.). The latter was particularly timely in view of the 1995 war between Ecuador and Peru and the peace negotiations that dragged on until the end of 1998. The presidents also instructed the OAS Committee on Hemispheric Security to begin considering an agenda for a special conference on security. The third Summit of the Americas (Quebec City, 2001) set the special conference on security for 2004.

The defense ministerials of the summit process are considered valuable confidence- and security-building venues because security issues are discussed and policy recommendations promoting cooperation are offered. They have played an active role in promoting CSBMs. But the defense ministerials are running into the same question confronting other CSBM efforts at the subregional level: What should be their relationship to the regional organization? Some states see the OAS as the implementer of summit agendas, but others believe that the defense ministerials themselves are redundant and want a hierarchical relationship in which they fall under OAS jurisdiction (Committee on Hemispheric Security 2002b: 68–73).

Examining Some Evidence on CSBM Relevance and Efficiency

Arms Treaties

Three main regional CSBM arms treaties have been adopted since 1991. Cooperation on conventional weapons acquisitions and illicit production and sales of weapons and ammunition has been less than universal, with some major players, including the United States, absent. The antipersonnel mine prohibitions have produced near-universal cooperation among the relevant parties, although the final elimination of such mines will still take a few more years (2011 is the target date).

The Inter-American Convention on Transparency in Conventional Weapons Acquisitions was developed in 1999 and entered into force in 2002. The treaty has twenty signatories, but only ten have ratified it (Argentina, Canada, Guatemala, Ecuador, El Salvador, Nicaragua, Paraguay, Peru, Uruguay, and Venezuela); the United States has not. The Committee on Hemispheric Security has called for a meeting in 2009 to review implementation of the convention and to promote membership (Committee on Hemispheric Security 2005).

Thirty-three of the thirty-four active members of the OAS (except Cuba) have signed the Inter-American Convention Against the Illicit Manufacturing of and Trafficking in Firearms, Ammunition, Explosives, and Other Related Materials. Only twenty-six governments have ratified the convention; among the seven that have not are the United States and Canada.

The conventional weapons and illicit arms trafficking CSBMs may play an important role in the coming years as Latin American militaries modernize equipment and training (Bruno 2005). The efficiency and relevance of these measures are currently being tested in Venezuela's modernization efforts. Hugo Chávez's government is purchasing 100,000 Kalashnikov rifles and forty helicopters from Russia and is seeking Brazilian attack airplanes and Spanish naval corvettes. The United States and Colombia are worried about Chávez's goals in modernizing the Venezuelan armed forces, as well as the possibility that the older rifles might be smuggled to guerrillas in Colombia (Economist 2005).

Under the Convention on the Prohibition of the Use, Stockpiling, Production, and Transfer of Anti-Personnel Mines and on Their Destruction, the Latin American countries with antipersonnel mines have all eliminated their stocks and begun efforts to demine areas (Nicaragua, Honduras, Ecuador, Peru, and Chile). The OAS provides financial support for demining, and the United States and other countries have contributed material aid, which is often preferred by recipients. Nicaragua, Ecuador, and Chile have cooperated with each other in building their antimining capabilities (Landmine Monitor 2004). The OAS also passed a resolution affirming the Western Hemisphere as an antipersonnel landmine–free zone in 2001 (OAS 2001a). The United States, however, is not a signatory to either the global or regional landmine conventions. The conventions do not address the issue of antitank mines (Landmine Monitor 2003).

Peaceful Resolution of Conflict Mechanisms

Peaceful resolution of conflict is promoted both generally through diplomatic initiatives and specifically through the Fund for Peace of the OAS. The Honduras-Nicaragua and Belize-Guatemala conflicts are the main targets of the Peace Fund now that the El Salvador–Honduras conflict has been successfully resolved. The purpose of the fund is to "assist with defraying the inherent costs of proceedings previously agreed to by the parties concerned." Argentina and Brazil provided experts to help implement the Civil Verification Mission in Honduras and Nicaragua. The fund has such great potential that financial support for it has come from observer countries (Denmark, Spain, the United Kingdom, Israel, and Italy) as well as from member states (OAS n.d.).

Eight boundary settlements have occurred so far during the era of CSBM attention at the regional level (post-1991) (Mares 2001b). It's difficult to assess the impact of current CSBMs on these settlements. Scores of disputes have been settled in the past through both arbitration and negotiations (Gros Espiell 1986). Perhaps these latest disputes were the "most difficult" to solve and required CSBMs. My own publications on the Ecuador-Peru and Argentina-Chile rivalries illustrate the tremendous obstacles to resolution that had kept the disputes alive and militarized. I've demonstrated that Ecuador's willingness to settle required a process of militarized bargaining and that they used CSBMs to lull Peru into vulnerable military and diplomatic positions (Mares 1996–1997).

The final settlement between Argentina and Chile in 1999 was the culmination of a bilateral process of confidence and security building that began much earlier. Shortly after the 1984 peace agreement that settled the Beagle Channel dispute, which had taken the countries to the verge of war, the navies and air forces of the two countries engaged in meetings and joint rescue operations. Democratization contributed to better relations, as did Argentina's decimation of its military establishment. In 1990 the two countries signed an agreement pledging cooperation in the pacific use of nuclear power and entered into a tripartite security pact with Brazil. The following year the three countries signed the Mendoza Compromise, prohibiting the development, production, storage, or transfer of chemical or biological arms. The Argentine and Chilean defense ministers established annual meetings for the joint chiefs to discuss coordination and cooperation on defense matters (Varas, Schear, and Owens 1995; Caro 1992).

Unfortunately, the CSBM process did not reduce militarized interstate disputes (MIDs) throughout the region up to 2000 (more recent data have not been compiled). In the decade of the 1990s, the years with the fewest MIDs were the years before the summitry era (Mares 2001b).

Terrorism

The OAS convened an Inter-American Specialized Conference on Terrorism in Lima in 1996. It appeared that the topic of terrorism was unlikely to be a contentious one for the hemisphere. The meeting adopted the Declaration of Lima to Prevent, Combat, and Eliminate Terrorism. In 1998 the OAS established the very active Inter-American Committee Against Terrorism (CICTE).

The committee confronts a fundamental problem in the wake of the post-9/11 US determination to fight a unilateral war on terrorism. States disagree on how hemispheric institutions should facilitate the pursuit of terrorists. Mexico, Brazil, and Argentina want Inter-American Commission on Human Rights guidelines, but the United States opposes letting the human rights community have such a major role (Bachelet 2005). The Inter-American Convention Against Terrorism was signed by thirty-three of thirty-four members of the OAS on June 3, 2002, but only twelve have since ratified the treaty; the United States has not (Department of Legal Affairs and Services n.d.). At the sixth defense ministerial in 2004, the United States attempted to broaden the definition of security threats to include terrorism and drug trafficking but was voted down. US and Central American efforts to give the Inter-American Defense Board priority over assertions of national sovereignty on security issues were also defeated, as was its proposal that countries should collaborate on compiling lists of terrorist organizations to facilitate the arrest of suspected members (Osava 2005). There is a degree of skepticism in Latin America vis-à-vis US reports and Central American fears that Al-Qaida is recruiting among local gangs, the *maras* (United Press International 2004; Blume 2004).

Conclusion

Regional CSBMs have been developed around three arms control agreements and a process to promote transparency in defense policy. The demining agreements represent the high points, as all the major mine-using countries in Latin America have begun the demining process. Yet a number of states, including the United States, have not yet ratified these agreements, thereby undermining their potential contribution to building confidence and security in the region. A number of interstate disputes have been settled, though that is not unique to the summitry era; a number of important disputes remain quite active, their periodic militarization remains a reality, and, at least until 2000, the frequency of occurrence of militarized interstate disputes had not diminished relative to previous years. Terrorism remains the area that is most problematic for inter-American security cooperation. The subregions where the most confidence has been developed are the Southern Cone and Central America.

Evaluation of the impact of CSBMs in the Western Hemisphere at this time, despite a fifteen- to twenty-year history of activity, has to be incomplete and ambiguous. The number of CSBMs created is not a particularly useful metric. The Americas are flush with these instruments, but it is not clear that they are being used in a number of circumstances that require confidence and security building (e.g., the United States refuses to be swayed by the legitimate elections that brought Evo Morales to the presidency in Bolivia). While bilateral, subregional, and regional CSBMs have helped resolve a few interstate conflicts (e.g., Argentina-Chile, Argentina-Brazil and El Salvador–Honduras), they continue to fail in Haiti and have done nothing to end the Bolivian stand-off with Chile over the outlet to the sea issue. And, as Canada noted in commenting on regional CSBMs promoted by the OAS, there has been a "lack of action . . . on the most serious conflict under way in the hemisphere, that in Colombia" (Committee on Hemispheric Security 2002b: 34).

These limitations to CSBMs in the Western Hemisphere negatively affect their evaluation on both relevance and efficiency criteria. CSBMs become irrelevant either when states can violate the agreements at low cost or when the criteria for establishing violations are ambiguous. The power disparity in the region continues to allow the United States to avoid being bound by CSBMs. The continued emphasis on sovereignty constrains the possibility of defining key terms in line with what is necessary for *confidence* and *security* to be constructed in certain important arenas. Without defining those terms and evaluating the degree to which states are meeting their obligations under the well-defined CSBMs, these security institutions can evolve into irrelevance.

Notes

I thank Gordon Mace for helpful comments.

    1. Mexico has a 2,000-mile-long border with the United States through which much illegal migration passes; Bolivia is the poorest country in South America; Peru was for a time the largest producer of coca and was fighting a communist insurgency; and Colombia is home to the groups that the US government believes control the production and initial trafficking of cocaine and heroin.

PART 3

Democratic Governance

7

The Inter-American Democratic Charter: Rhetoric or Reality?

Thomas Legler

On September 11, 2001, the thirty-four member states of the Organization of American States (OAS) made history by signing the Inter-American Democratic Charter. Less than two decades before, at the height of the Cold War, the human rights and democracy record of the countries of the Americas seemingly mattered less to inter-American diplomacy than their commitment to the struggle against communism. The charter enshrined the right of the peoples of the Americas to democracy and the obligation of their governments to defend it. It provided the diplomatic tools necessary to defend and promote democracy wherever it might come under threat, whether from would-be coup conspirators or incumbent elected leaders who reneged on their democratic obligations.[1]

In a keynote speech to the OAS in January 2005, Jimmy Carter challenged "all governments of the hemisphere to make the Democratic Charter more than empty pieces of paper, to make it a living document" (Carter 2005). After the initial challenge of creating the Inter-American Democratic Challenge in 2001, the member states of the OAS and civil society in the Americas face the problem of putting its noble principles into practice. Although the charter's provisions address many of the shortcomings identified in the OAS's emerging collective-defense-of-democracy regime during the 1990s, the document has been used only peripherally at best in OAS efforts to defend democracy in Bolivia, Ecuador, Haiti, Nicaragua, and Venezuela during this millennium. It would seem that after the initial enthusiasm that led to the creation of the Inter-American Democratic Charter, OAS member states find themselves at an impasse in terms of applying it.

What explains this impasse? On the surface it would appear that the answer has to do with design flaws in the Democratic Charter itself, the confusing situation on the ground in many countries in political crisis, or the shifting regional democracy problematic. Nonetheless, if hemispheric leaders are basically unwilling to invoke the Democratic Charter, textual modifications will not in the end enhance its implementation. In this chapter, I argue that a combination of the clash of democratic, multilateral, and sovereignty norms and geopolitical tensions between the United States and Latin American and Caribbean member states have contributed to the charter's less than spectacular debut. These constraints have underpinned a weak OAS mired in financial difficulties and suffering from a lack of sustained leadership and initiative on the democracy front.

This chapter is divided into four parts. The first section explores the origins of the Democratic Charter. The second part examines how it has been employed since its adoption in 2001. Third, the chapter considers various possible explanations for the impasse over the charter. In section four, I present my interpretation of the charter's difficulties: the twin problems of norm tension and the geopolitical strains of contemporary US–Latin American relations.

The Democratic Charter: A Noble Document

Entering the new millennium, OAS member states faced a number of challenges in strengthening the fledgling collective-defense-of-democracy regime, despite the important and historic advances that had already been made.[2] On the one hand, significant progress was made in elaborating the new regime. Beginning with the *Protocol of Cartagena de Indias* in 1985 (OAS 1986), the OAS Charter was amended to elevate the promotion and consolidation of representative democracy as a principle of the organization. In 1991, Resolution 1080 gave the OAS for the first time an automatic, rapid-response mechanism against coups d'état in the region (OAS 1991a). Accordingly, in the event of a coup, member state foreign ministers henceforth would automatically convene a special General Assembly within ten days of the occurrence and undertake all measures deemed appropriate to counter it. The resolution was invoked on four occasions, in response to political crises in Haiti (1991), Peru (1992), Guatemala (1993), and Paraguay (1996). In 1992, the Protocol of Washington amended the charter to give the OAS the authority to suspend a member state whose government had been overthrown by force (OAS 1992a).

OAS elections monitoring advanced the practice of external validation of member state electoral processes. Since 1990, the Department for the Promotion of Democracy (formerly the Unit for the Promotion of Democracy) has observed more than 100 elections in half the OAS's member states. These missions have the potential to deliver an external seal of approval or even disapproval, as evidenced by the OAS's criticism of the Peruvian second-round elections and Haiti's legislative elections, both held in May 2000.[3]

By the turn of the century, however, OAS efforts to defend democracy had achieved only mixed success. In 1989, OAS inertia prompted the United States to invade Panama unilaterally. OAS efforts failed to resolve the crisis in Haiti that was triggered in 1991 by the ouster of democratically elected president Jean-Bertrand Aristide in a coup led by General Raoul Cédras. The OAS imposed economic sanctions that were not enforced effectively and only punished the innocent. As in the case of Panama, OAS members could not agree on the use of force to restore Aristide; that job fell to a US-led peacekeeping force authorized by the United Nations Security Council in 1994.

In Peru and Haiti, the threat of coups was replaced by a new one: authoritarian regression or "backsliding" by incumbent democratically elected presidents. In Peru, OAS pressure in 1992 failed to compel President Alberto Fujimori to restore the status quo prior to his self-coup. Instead, Fujimori succeeded in rewriting the Peruvian Constitution to strengthen his own presidential power. Over the course of the next eight years, Fujimori systematically undermined representative democracy in Peru while maintaining electoral trappings. In Haiti, electoral fraud during legislative elections in 2000 seriously damaged the democratic credentials of President René Préval and his successor, Jean-Bertrand Aristide. In both these cases, the OAS could do little to stop the erosion of democracy by democratically elected authorities.

Resolution 1080 had been designed to counter coups d'état, not authoritarian backsliding. Moreover, member states could not agree on a single definition of representative democracy. Mexico, for example, was instinctively suspicious of the imposition of such a definition, not only because of some of the questionable democratic credentials of the ruling Party of the Institutional Revolution (PRI) that had governed Mexico since 1929, but also because the United States had periodically intervened in the past in its and other member states' internal affairs under the pretext of championing democracy. Without a consensus on what representative democracy meant, it was truly difficult to gauge at what point an incumbent, elected state leader could be considered to erode democracy. The criterion of free, fair, and transparent elections remained one of the few areas where a consensus existed on a benchmark for representative democracy; what happened in between elections continued to be the domain of sovereign, democratically elected leaders.

In the case of Peru, Resolution 1753 provided an ad hoc response by the OAS to the ultimate transgression by Fujimori, his attempt to rig the second-round presidential election in May 2000, in which he ran on constitutionally dubious grounds for a third term. After the Fujimori government finally departed in the wake of the "Vladivideo" scandal during the fall of 2000, the interim Peruvian government of President Valentín Paniagua and the Peruvian democratic resistance to Fujimori were determined that the OAS would have the means necessary to prevent and/or respond to the rise of future "democratic dictators" like Fujimori.[4] The Inter-American Democratic Charter was born out of their determination. The former opponents of Fujimori, now in positions of power under first Paniagua's and then Alejandro Toledo's government, crafted the initial draft of the Democratic Charter.

The original idea for a democratic charter was officially presented at the Summit of the Americas at Quebec City in April 2001. It was cosponsored by Peru, the United States, Canada, Costa Rica, and Argentina but was quickly embraced by almost all member states except for Venezuela. The Chávez government criticized the vision of representative democracy contained within the charter as insufficiently participatory but ultimately conceded to its creation. From an original grounding in the Democracy Clause of the Declaration of Quebec City (2001), the Democratic Charter underwent numerous drafts stemming from an elaborate process of negotiations among member states in consultation with civil society groups across the hemisphere. After early setbacks at the annual OAS General Assembly in San José in 2001, the Inter-American Democratic Charter was officially adopted on September 11, 2001, in a special General Assembly suitably held in Lima, Peru. On the same fateful day, of course, terrorists launched their attack on the twin towers of the World Trade Center. Under pressure to return rapidly to the United States, Secretary of State Colin Powell was able to secure rapid closure of debate and agreement on the charter, in what seemed at the time like a propitious show of hemispheric solidarity and consensus.[5]

On paper (see Table 7.1), the Inter-American Democratic Charter (OAS 2001b) filled many of the holes in the existing collective-defense-of-democracy regime. Article 1 formally established democracy as a human right that member states had an obligation to promote and defend. By framing democracy as a human right, the charter also potentially linked countries' obligation to defend democracy to an existing body of international human rights law and treaties.[6] Articles 3 and 4 for the first time ever established the equivalent of a detailed definition of or set of criteria for representative democracy. It finally became much clearer what exactly member states and the Unit for the Promotion of Democracy (now the Department for the Promotion of Democracy) were defending and promoting.

For the first time in the inter-American system, Articles 17 and 18 contained provisions for *preventing* political problems from escalating into full-blown crises. As a "self-help" provision, Article 17 could be invoked by governments under threat to seek outside assistance in defending their constitutional orders. Article 18 served as a "community watch" measure, whereby other member states or the OAS secretary-general could call for a collective assessment of the situation in a country under threat, with the prior consent of the host government.

Table 7.1 Inter-American Democratic Charter

Diplomatic Tools and Capabilities	Article
"Right to democracy" and action imperative for governments to promote and defend it	1
Definitional criteria for representative democracy	3–4
Linkage between representative democracy and human rights	7–10
Linkage between representative democracy and combating poverty	11–16
Crisis prevention (self-help and community watch)	17–18
Democratic membership criterion in OAS	19
Differentiation between coups and authoritarian backsliding	19
Authoritarian backsliding scenarios	20
Coup scenarios	21
Suspension of a member state	21–22
Elections monitoring and external (in)validation prerogative of monitoring missions	23–25
Crisis follow-up and democracy promotion	26–27
Linkage between representative democracy and gender equality	28

Carried over from the Democracy Clause of the Declaration of Quebec City (2001), Article 19 formally acknowledged in diplomatic parlance the equally serious threats of coups (an "unconstitutional interruption") and authoritarian backsliding (an "unconstitutional alteration"). It stated that both scenarios would be grounds for barring a member state from participation in the OAS and the inter-American system. By extension, Article 19 codified the "conditionalizing" of sovereignty in the inter-American system (Van Klaveren 2001). Contrary to the Latin American tradition of upholding sovereign prerogatives of member states in an absolute sense, it clearly reserved the sovereign right of international recognition to states that were representative democracies. In short, the OAS was a club restricted to democratic membership.

In the spirit of Resolution 1080, Article 20 provided a mechanism against unconstitutional alterations (authoritarian backsliding). In the event of a threat to a country's constitutional order, any member state or the secretary-general could request an immediate meeting of the Permanent Council. If the Permanent Council's efforts were unsuccessful or if the urgency of the situation merited it, the Permanent Council could convene a special General Assembly wherein member states' foreign ministers would consider the situation. As in the case of Resolution 1080, Article 20 contained within it the potential for a wide range of responses by the member states to a crisis with democracy, including any measures deemed appropriate by the special General Assembly.

Where Article 20 articulated measures against unconstitutional alterations, Article 21 targeted unconstitutional interruptions or coups. Echoing the Protocol of Washington, it provided for the suspension of the membership of an undemocratic state by a special General Assembly. Interestingly, the suspension would be triggered by a vote with the support of a minimum two-thirds of the member states. OAS custom, however, has long been for member states to arrive at decisions via consensus. Article 21 nonetheless also emphasized the continuation of diplomatic initiatives in the event of the suspension of a member state.

Articles 23, 24, and 25 established the parameters for OAS elections monitoring. Importantly, Article 25 set out a clear authorization for observation missions to perform an external validation role, instructing them to inform the secretary-general and the Permanent Council whether "the necessary conditions for free and fair elections do not exist." Accordingly, Article 25 established a clear prerogative for OAS monitoring missions potentially to invalidate member states' electoral processes.

Articles 26 and 27 established a follow-up function for the OAS in strengthening democracy. The OAS could point to these articles potentially as the basis for staying on the ground after a crisis to ensure democracy's longer-term viability.

Finally, for the day-to-day operations of the various agencies and institutions of the inter-American system, the Democratic Charter provided a crucial linkage between democracy and other issue areas in a way that furnished instant legitimacy to their mandates.[7] The document linked the strengthening and consolidation of democracy with the concurrent reduction of poverty and inequality (Articles 11–16) as well as concrete improvements in human rights (Articles 7–10) and gender equality (Article 28).

In sum, the Democratic Charter contains provisions for dealing potentially with both coup and noncoup threats to democracy, using a variety of different measures, from nonthreatening to punitive ones. It encompasses crisis prevention and response. Not unlike the "ratcheting up" of security provisions in Chapters 6 and 7 of the UN Charter, it provides the basis for a graduated, flexible response in accordance with the severity of the problem, from constructive, preventive, and proactive measures to more severe, punitive ones. It allows for creative diplomacy rather than a single, "cookie-cutter" approach to defending democracy.

The Use, Misuse, and Disuse of the Democratic Charter

The new Inter-American Democratic Charter was soon put to test. Since 2001, there have been at least five political crises where grounds existed for applying the Democratic Charter: Haiti, Venezuela, Bolivia, Ecuador, and

Nicaragua. How the Democratic Charter was used or not used in these instances reveals a lot about its shortcomings as well as the overall difficulty of converting its noble principles into collective action in defense of democracy.

The first thing that is highly noticeable is the failure to use the Democratic Charter's preventive mechanisms contained in Articles 17 and 18.[8] Jean-Bertrand Aristide did not invoke the self-help clause contained in Article 17 following an armed attack on the presidential palace in December 2001, nor did he use it in the weeks leading up to his ouster by an armed rebellion on February 29, 2004. Despite months of heightening tensions in Venezuela prior to the April 2002 coup, Hugo Chávez did not turn to Article 17 either. In Bolivia, President Gonzalo Sánchez de Lozada (2003) and his successor Carlos Mesa (2005) also failed to invoke the self-help clause as their respective presidencies were threatened by mass demonstrations demanding their resignation.

Article 18, the community watch clause, has only been invoked in two of the five aforementioned country cases. On April 22, 2005, Article 18 was finally invoked. In Permanent Council Resolution 880 (OAS 2005b), Article 18 made its debut as the grounding for a high-level mission to Ecuador led by Acting Secretary-General Luigi Einaudi to explore ways to strengthen democracy in that country. It is worth noting that Article 18 made its appearance only *after* President Lucio Gutierrez had resigned in the midst of a full-blown political crisis. Neither Article 18 nor any other Democratic Charter measures were invoked in December 2004 when Gutierrez unconstitutionally undermined the separation of powers between the executive and the judiciary in Ecuador, nor in the weeks prior to Gutierrez's demise.

Article 18 was used for only the second time some six weeks later, at the annual OAS General Assembly in Fort Lauderdale, Florida. In a declaration entitled *Support to Nicaragua,* the General Assembly made reference to Article 18 in the preamble as the basis of authorization for sending a mission headed by Secretary-General José Miguel Insulza to Nicaragua for the purposes of establishing a dialogue among the polarized elites in that country's political crisis (OAS 2005c). Importantly, that marked the first use of Article 18 and the Inter-American Democratic Charter as they were meant to be used: as preventive tools of diplomacy. In contrast to the previous reluctance by threatened governments in the region to consent to Article 18, undoubtedly the impulse for Article 18 came largely from the Bolaños government itself. It found itself obliged to turn abroad for assistance in a political battle in which it was pitted against an unholy alliance of very powerful enemies: former Liberal Constitutionalist president Arnoldo Alemán and former Sandinista president Daniel Ortega.

Article 19, the heart of the Democratic Charter, has also never been invoked, despite ample grounds in both Haiti and Venezuela for doing so.

In Haiti, state-sponsored violence against political opposition was one possible justification; armed rebellion against an elected president was another. In Venezuela, in what Maxwell Cameron (2003b) calls a "slow-motion constitutional coup," the Chávez government has eroded the separation of powers in the country, including "judicial reform" that has stacked the judiciary with Chávez's appointments.

Article 20, the rough equivalent of Resolution 1080, is the only other operative clause that has been invoked. First, in a declaration issued from San José, Costa Rica, at its annual meeting of heads of state, the Rio Group referred to Article 20 to instruct the secretary-general to convene an emergency meeting of the Permanent Council to consider the situation in Venezuela.[9] Subsequently, Permanent Council Resolution 811 authorized a special mission of the secretary-general to Caracas as well as to convene a special General Assembly on April 18, 2002, to consider the crisis in Venezuela (OAS 2002b). The OAS's preference for using Article 20 was controversial; at the height of the crisis, Venezuelan ambassador Jorge Valero demanded that the Permanent Council invoke Article 21 to suspend Venezuela from the OAS in response to the coup d'état orchestrated by Pedro Carmona against Hugo Chávez.

The other instance where Article 20 was used was on June 8, 2004, in General Assembly Resolution 2058 on the situation in Haiti (OAS 2004d). Article 20 was cited among diplomatic measures to help restore democracy to Haiti, long *after* Aristide had been ousted. Surprisingly, neither Article 20 nor Resolution 1080 was invoked in response to the use of force to overthrow Jean-Bertrand Aristide in February 2004. Indeed, Resolution 862, passed by the Permanent Council just days before the forced departure of Aristide on February 29, contained not a single reference to the Democratic Charter (OAS 2004c).

In the final days of the Sánchez de Lozada presidency in Bolivia in November 2003, the OAS also failed to invoke the Democratic Charter, despite reiterating its support for the president. Most peculiar, well before Sánchez's demise, both Permanent Council Resolutions 838 and 849 underlined the OAS's "firm resolve" to apply and enforce the mechanisms set out in the Democratic Charter (OAS 2003b, 2003c). In spite of this rhetoric, both Sánchez and other Permanent Council member states failed to invoke the preventive clauses of the Democratic Charter in the midst of massive popular protests demanding his resignation.

By far the greatest number of references has not been by way of its operational clauses but rather in the more general spirit of the Democratic Charter. These references have also concentrated heavily on the resolutions' preamble sections rather than the operative clauses. Most resolutions or declarations concerning Haiti, Venezuela, Bolivia, Ecuador, and Nicaragua have contained mention of the right to democracy in Article 1, the essential elements of democracy contained in Articles 3 and 4, or even more vague references to the "context" or "framework" of the Democratic Charter.[10]

The Impasse over the Democratic Charter: Searching for Answers

As the previous section underscored, the Democratic Charter, although an admirable document on paper, has been formally invoked in defense of democracy only sparingly. Crisis prevention remains a glaring deficiency. Pro-democracy multilateral diplomacy failed to prevent the coup against Venezuelan president Chávez or the deepening crisis that eventually toppled Haitian president Aristide. Countering authoritarian backsliding also continues to be an elusive aim. In 2004, clear instances of unconstitutional alterations (Chávez and Ecuadorian president Gutierrez meddling with their respective countries' supreme courts) did not trigger responses by the OAS. Indeed, in the Ecuadorian case, the OAS did not really enter the picture until *after* Gutierrez was ousted months later in April 2005.

The OAS faces an ongoing challenge in putting the Democratic Charter into practice in a timely and effective manner. The lack of use of the charter may be attributable to the confusing and fluid situation on the ground within countries under crisis. For example, in Venezuela in April 2002, evidence subsequently suggested that *both* a coup *and* authoritarian backsliding were occurring concurrently. During the actual moments of the coup itself, the lack of reliable information made it difficult for the Permanent Council to determine immediately whether a coup had occurred or if Chávez had resigned.[11] Similarly, in Haiti, antidemocratic actions by forces linked with Aristide coincided with an armed insurgency to oust him.

In a related fashion, the regional democracy problematic has gradually changed over time since the charter was created in 2001, requiring the OAS to respond accordingly.[12] Where coups, self-coups, and authoritarian backsliding were prime concerns of the OAS during the 1980s and 1990s, with the onset of the new millennium, new threats or challenges have surfaced that demand innovative responses. One has been the advent of the "civil society coup" or "impeachment coup."[13] In Argentina (2001–2002), Bolivia (2003, 2005), Ecuador (2000, 2005), and Venezuela (2002), the ousting of incumbent elected presidents occurred through mass, mobilized outpourings of popular discontent demanding their resignation.

Another recent threat to democracy has come to the fore in Ecuador and Nicaragua. Divided government has led to instances of executive-legislative gridlock. Where Guillermo O'Donnell (1994) and others identified presidents during the 1990s as the principal culprits in undemocratic efforts to circumvent elected legislatures à la "delegative democracy," in

Ecuador and Nicaragua, powerful legislative alliances intentionally sought to weaken presidents for questionable ends, contributing to a governability crisis. In Ecuador, three consecutively elected presidents were each impeached by formidable congressional opponents. In Nicaragua, President Enrique Bolaños found himself locked in a bitter battle with a Liberal Constitutionalist–Sandinista legislative alliance led by former presidents Alemán and Ortega. All the above-mentioned scenarios, from confusion to new threats, have made it very challenging for the OAS to come to the immediate defense of representative democracy.

It is also tempting to see the overarching problem as one of design flaws within the Democratic Charter itself. Experience since 2001 has revealed that there are holes in the Democratic Charter text and the broader collective-defense-of-democracy regime that create problems for its implementation. For instance, the OAS lacks an accompanying early warning system as well as a monitoring or peer review mechanism for promoting Democratic Charter compliance (Cameron 2003b). Moreover, the definition of what constitutes "constitutional interruptions" versus "constitutional alterations" in Article 19 of the Democratic Charter is unclear (Cameron 2003b; Carter 2005). The Democratic Charter lacks a clear set of benchmarks to serve as a threshold for determining precisely at what point the OAS should intervene according to the main action clauses in Articles 17–21.

Indeed, there is an important magnitude issue at play. That is, it is unclear what antidemocratic measures are serious enough violations of the Democratic Charter to warrant OAS action (Ayala and Nikken 2006; Legler and Levitt 2006). Were the OAS to respond to every minor infraction of the Democratic Charter, it would need to intervene constantly in its member states' internal affairs to defend democracy. Yet by choosing not to respond to minor transgressions and to focus only on major threats, the OAS runs the risk of allowing the incremental erosion of democracy, or its "death-by-a-thousand-cuts," as in Peru during the 1990s under Fujimori, where by the time the OAS took action to defend democracy, the country had long since slipped into authoritarianism.

The Real Problem:
Normative and Geopolitical Constraints

Even if the Inter-American Democratic Charter's design flaws were corrected, the question remains whether the OAS's thirty-four member states could put its principles effectively into practice. At the June 2005 OAS General Assembly in Fort Lauderdale, a proposal by the US government to create a new democracy-monitoring mechanism with civil society participation was resoundingly rejected by Latin American and Caribbean member states. Developments at Fort Lauderdale crystallized the twin constraints that persistently hamper collective efforts to strengthen the Democratic Charter and its implementation: an ongoing clash of norms and a challenging geopolitical context. In turn, these obstacles are reflected in a chronic leadership deficit and the OAS's current financial woes.

The Normative Impasse

Under the surface of OAS efforts to defend democracy, there has been an ongoing clash between new pro-democracy norms and more established sovereignty norms.[14] In short, collective actions in support of democracy, which are in effect forms of intervention, run up against existing regional sovereignty norms of territorial inviolability, nonintervention, and self-determination, which are enshrined in the OAS Charter as well as the UN Charter. Indeed, the tension is apparent in Article 2(b) of the OAS Charter, which sets out the following potentially contradictory purpose of the OAS: "To promote and consolidate representative democracy, with due respect for the principle of nonintervention" (OAS 1997). This article is reiterated in the preamble of the Democratic Charter.

The still-tenuous nature of new intervention norms to defend democracy is further captured in the fact that the Democratic Charter itself lacks the status of an international treaty. An international treaty or convention carries with it a much heavier weight in international law and therefore a greater obligation on the part of signatories to uphold it. Article 1 of the Democratic Charter, for instance, states that the peoples of the Americas have a right to democracy and that their governments have an obligation to defend it. Given the frequency of democratic crises in the region, in treaty form the Democratic Charter would potentially strengthen new intervention norms at the expense of state sovereignty rights, as citizens whose right to democracy had been threatened would put added legal pressure on the OAS to defend democracy. It would appear that the OAS member states have been reluctant to conditionalize and constrain their sovereign prerogatives in such a way.

The newer democracy norms and the more established sovereignty ones have merged into a new hybrid "by invitation only" operative norm, potentially creating perverse scenarios. As hinted above, key operative clauses of the Democratic Charter and by extension the possibility of pro-democracy interventions require the explicit consent of the target government. Although this condition may protect member states from the threat of deceitful interventions disguised as defending democracy, in situations of authoritarian backsliding the OAS's intent to intervene to defend democracy must first obtain a pariah government's invitation.

The practical implication of the juxtaposition of democracy and sovereignty norms in the inter-American system is that the OAS's scope for action is largely limited to elections monitoring and soft forms of intervention, such as dialogue facilitation, that obtain the consent of the host government. Effectively, the still-strong sovereign constraints in place narrow the type of democracy that the OAS can promote to "electoralism" (Schmitter and Karl 1996). That is, the OAS has a significant role to play surrounding electoral processes, but member states impede its ability to do very much in between elections on sovereignty grounds. The OAS's abilities to prevent democratic crisis from occurring or to deal effectively with authoritarian backsliding are therefore severely constrained.

To complicate matters even further, the clash of democracy and sovereignty norms unfolds against a backdrop of evolving norms of multilateralism in tension. Traditionally, member states have upheld an interstate multilateral matrix characterized by "executive sovereignty," that is, the externally recognized supreme authority of heads of state and government, as well as their diplomatic representatives. Executive sovereignty has long reinforced a "club mentality" in inter-American multilateralism, one in which state leaders and their handpicked representatives follow a strict set of diplomatic rules, such as mutual respect and recognition of executive prerogatives, as privileges of membership in their exclusive club.[15]

Consistent with a more general global trend toward increasingly "complex" or "networked" multilateralism, the democracy issue area threatens to open up traditional multilateralism at the OAS to the participation and influence of nonstate actors.[16] Just as the sovereignty of the ruler has yielded historically to democratic, popular sovereignty in many countries, state-centric club multilateralism is under pressure to become more inclusive. Issues such as authoritarian backsliding by incumbent elected leaders, the very leaders privileged by executive sovereignty, threaten to transform diplomacy in a more complex, networked direction, as the citizens whose democratic rights are threatened turn abroad for support in a "boomerang effect" in their struggles against antidemocratic leaders.[17] Already, civil society groups throughout the Americas participated in the discussions that led to the Inter-American Democratic Charter in 2001. During 2002–2004, the Carter Center was a key pillar of the tripartite mission to defend democracy in Venezuela, alongside the OAS and the United Nations Development Programme. No doubt many classically trained diplomats are wary of opening their club to new nonstate membership.

The General Assembly in Fort Lauderdale underscored the genuine clash of newer and older multilateral norms occurring concurrently with the tension between democracy and sovereignty norms. In the months leading up to the June 2005 General Assembly, a new transnational coalition called the Friends of the Democratic Charter lobbied OAS member states to support reforms to strengthen the Democratic Charter, including a clearer definition of "unconstitutional alteration," as well as a mechanism for greater civil society involvement in monitoring Democratic Charter compliance among member states.[18]

In a rebuke to the United States, OAS member states largely rejected the proposals of the Friends of the Democratic Charter. On one level, the proposals might have been criticized for putting unnecessary constraints on OAS diplomatic flexibility and creativity, characteristics of time-tested inter-American and UN multilateral diplomacy. The idea of establishing benchmarks for Democratic Charter violations that trigger automatic diplomatic responses simply ran against the grain of traditional inter-American diplomacy.

On a deeper level, had they been accepted, the proposals would ultimately have weakened the prerogatives of the state-centric Permanent Council and its member states. Indeed, despite the clear need to find improved means to defend democracy, Secretary-General Insulza remarked that he did not support the idea of a semi-autonomous group of experts evaluating member states on their democratic records and that the Permanent Council should do so (Oppenheimer 2005). Voicing the sentiments of Latin American member states, Insulza (2005a) was opposed to the OAS converting itself into a "democracy watchdog." The secretary-general was determined to defend club multilateralism, even if it meant that Democratic Charter compliance remained at the mercy of many members who were potentially guilty themselves of not honoring their charter obligations. In sum, consistent with Andrew Moravscik's thesis (2000), Latin American leaders gave impulse to the creation of a collective-defense-of-democracy regime to ensure their political survival in the face of antidemocratic threats, but on their terms and by their consent, and not to challenge their authority, either at home or in the OAS.

The Geopolitical Impasse

What happened in Fort Lauderdale was illustrative not only of the current normative impasse; in a connected way it was also a clear reflection of the powerful geopolitical strains that impede the strengthening of the Democratic Charter and its application. Fort Lauderdale brought to the fore an ongoing struggle for influence in the OAS and the inter-American system, in which the Inter-American Democratic Charter was only the latest battleground. The US proposal had the effect of reinforcing the age-old cleavage between a US vision of the OAS as a multilateral forum for advancing its interests in the region and a rival Latin American vision where the OAS was perceived as a body to engage the United States multilaterally (instead of bilaterally) while containing its imperial ambitions (see Mace and Thérien 1996; Mace and Bélanger 1999). Following the US government's failure to get its chosen candidate elected as the new OAS secretary-general in 2005, Fort Lauderdale was yet another defeat for US interests.

US credibility in the region is in crisis, especially on the democracy front.[19] First, the Bush administration's immediate response to the coup against Chávez in April 2002 suggested that it had supported, or at least condoned, the unconstitutional and antidemocratic actions of the Venezuelan opposition at the same time that the Rio Group and individual Latin American leaders almost unanimously condemned the coup. In 2003, many Latin American states refused to endorse the US invasion of Iraq, which was ostensibly done to bring democracy to that country. In February 2004, the US government once again ignited controversy in the region for what many consider, especially among members of the Caribbean Community, the armed insurrection and coup that it engineered against President Aristide. The US government has also drawn criticism for its efforts to dissuade voters in Bolivia (2003, 2005) and Nicaragua (2005) from voting for leftist candidates Evo Morales and Daniel Ortega. As democracy was undermined in Ecuador during late 2004 and early 2005, US authorities also impeded the OAS from taking action against the culprit, President Lucio Gutierrez.

When President George W. Bush met with Venezuelan opposition figure Maria Corina Machado at the White House shortly before the OAS General Assembly in Fort Lauderdale, without ever previously having received a senior Chávez government official, few Latin American governments believed that the US government's democracy agenda was driven by noble intentions or principles. The incident fueled suspicions for many that the United States would attempt to manipulate any democracy peer review mechanism with civil society participation as a weapon against its enemies, like Venezuela, not necessarily to promote democracy. In the eyes of Latin American officials, such a mechanism could provide controversial organizations, such as Maria Corina Machado's group Súmate, with a forum for discrediting their governments. Accordingly, the US proposal met with near-unanimous rejection from Latin American member states, especially in Venezuela, Brazil, and the Southern Cone. The US proposal was widely perceived to be aimed at its adversary, Hugo Chávez, and not as a sincere effort to strengthen the OAS's collective-defense-of-democracy regime. Therefore, the Democratic Charter and its implementation will not improve so long as OAS member states do not trust the United States.

The crisis in US credibility and the Latin American wariness of US power have some serious implications for OAS efforts to promote and defend democracy. First, Latin American states have created multilateral forums where the United States has been intentionally left out. These include the Rio Group, Mercosur, the Ibero-American Summit and Secretariat, and the South American Community of Nations. Although these organizations may ultimately divide the labor of defending democracy with the OAS, they should also be recognized for what they are: potential rivals to the OAS in regional governance. Countries such as Brazil, Argentina, and Venezuela are helping to create a new, US-free South American axis (FOCAL 2003; Mace 2004).

These international institutions potentially provide alternative response mechanisms for political crises in the region. Cuba is a member of the Ibero-American Summit and Secretariat. That organization provides a channel for engaging Cuba on the democracy question. The aforementioned institutions are also embodiments of Brazil's regional power. Symptomatic of an important geopolitical shift in the works, it is instructive that during the political crisis that resulted in President Carlos Mesa's resignation in June 2005, Bolivian diplomats turned to their Brazilian counterparts first and not US officials (Hester 2005).

The downturn in US–Latin American relations may also have a negative impact on the OAS's already pressing financial situation. First, it is unlikely that many Latin American and Caribbean member states will support an increase in member quotas or paying their dues in arrears, prerequisites for helping the OAS out of its financial crisis, so long as they remain suspicious of US actions in the organization. Accordingly, the democracy issue area in the OAS (like most other issue areas) will continue to suffer from chronic underfunding. Ultimately, a financially weak OAS serves the interests of member states concerned with that organization being manipulated by the United States in pursuit of its own objectives. Conversely, the United States will continue to be reluctant to increase its financial support for the OAS as long as a moral hazard exists by doing so for member states in arrears and as long as it perceives member states to be unsympathetic to its multilateral agenda. That is, were the United States to increase its support for the OAS without a corresponding effort by member states to pay their back dues, those states would feel little obligation to pay up what they owed. A vicious funding circle therefore exists that traps the OAS in persistent financial difficulty.

The creation of new multilateral groupings mentioned above will also potentially exacerbate the OAS's funding problems. In particular, the new Ibero-American Summit and Secretariat, with its links through member states Spain and Portugal to the European Union, threatens to compete with the OAS for funding for special earmarked funds, a mainstay for underwriting OAS pro-democracy activity.[20]

US–Latin American tensions further contribute to an ongoing leadership deficit in the OAS on the democracy front. The lack of determined, sustained pro-democracy initiative and activism with respect to democracy defense and promotion has long been a problem in the inter-American system. Individual small and medium-sized states, such as Argentina, Chile, Venezuela, and Peru, have all at one point or another made important contributions to the strengthening of the inter-American collective-defense-of-democracy regime. Unfortunately, they could not sustain their leadership because of resource constraints or because of the diverting impact of economic and political problems on the home front. Larger states, such as the United States, Brazil, and Mexico, have generally been less significant in terms of their overall contribution to building the OAS's capacity in the area of democratic governance (Cooper and Legler 2001b). We can almost speak of an inverse relationship between countries' structural power in the hemisphere and their commitment to enhancing the OAS's diplomatic toolkit for defending democracy. This ongoing leadership deficit is exacerbated by the US–Latin American divide, which results in a more general reluctance to strengthen the OAS, the locus of recurring geopolitical tensions between the two.

The geopolitical context compounds any attempts to strengthen the Democratic Charter in another important way. That is, the paradigm of representative democracy itself enshrined in the Democratic Charter may be under threat from a rival vision. Following his successful consolidation of power in the wake of his victory in the August 15, 2004, presidential recall referendum, President Hugo Chávez began serious attempts to export his Bolivarian revolution, with its contempt for representative democracy, throughout the region. Venezuela's oil bonanza provides him with impressive resources to compete for hearts and minds in the region at a time when US foreign aid disbursements have been disappointingly small. According to some estimates, congressional legislation in 2005 gave him direct access to more than $1 billion per month in oil revenues, much of it earmarked for foreign policy priorities (Webb-Vidal 2005). This effectively dwarfs US official development assistance in the hemisphere.

Backed by petrodollars, Chávez's proposal for a Social Charter may eventually directly challenge the Democratic Charter. Although Chávez's commitment through the Social Charter to fighting poverty and inequality in the region is timely and commendable, the erosion of the independence of judicial and electoral authorities in Venezuela raises questions about his commitment to democracy. Yet, given repeated frustrations among the regions' leaders with US actions as well as ongoing US neglect of the hemisphere, many countries are choosing to approach Venezuela pragmatically rather than critically.

Conclusion: The Need for Normative and Geopolitical Alignment

It is tempting to see the Inter-American Democratic Charter impasse as a problem of design flaws. Indeed, as related above, the Democratic Charter does contain omissions, such as the lack of benchmarks for authoritarian backsliding. Nonetheless, as I have stressed in this chapter, textual improvements will not of themselves guarantee that OAS member states will invoke the Democratic Charter when democracy is threatened.

There are two interconnected sets of constraints that hamper the use of the Democratic Charter as it was originally envisioned. On the one hand, there is an ongoing clash of democracy, multilateralism, and sovereignty norms that effectively limits the OAS's scope for pro-democracy action. On the other hand, the OAS has been held hostage, so to speak, by geopolitical tensions between the United States and Latin American and Caribbean member states. As long as Latin American and Caribbean leaders are distrustful of US intentions in the region, the charter and its implementation will not be strengthened, and the OAS will continue to be hampered by financial difficulties and an ongoing leadership deficit. For these countries, therefore, a relatively weak OAS remains in their interest. The further internalization of collective-defense-of-democracy norms and the geopolitical interests of many OAS member states are thus presently at loggerheads.

It is not impossible that a more conducive environment for putting the Democratic Charter's principles into practice could reemerge in the future. After all, in the pioneering period from the Protocol of Cartagena de Indias in 1985 until the Democratic Charter in 2001, a widespread consensus propelled the development of the inter-American collective-defense-of-democracy regime forward. The United States and the countries of the Americas enjoyed strong relations and found it in their mutual interests to construct the regime. Until norms and national interests are once again favorably aligned, making the Democratic Charter a "living document" will continue to be an elusive goal.

Notes

1. The best existing treatment of the Inter-American Democratic Charter is found in a special issue of *Canadian Foreign Policy* (Cameron 2003a), edited by Maxwell Cameron.

2. For recent works on the evolution of the emerging OAS collective-defense-of-democracy regime, see Cooper and Legler (2001a, 2006), Boniface (2002, 2007), and Perina (2005).

3. On the 2000 Peruvian elections, see Santa-Cruz (2005). On the 2000 legislative elections in Haiti, see Maguire (2002).

4. The Vladivideo scandal refers to the broadcast on national television on September 14, 2000, of video footage showing President Fujimori's national security chief, Vladimiro Montesinos, bribing opposition congressman Alberto Kourito to switch his allegiance to Fujimori in Congress. The incident precipitated Fujimori's announcement a day later that he would step down from power the following spring. On the OAS role in the Peruvian political crisis of 2000, see Cooper and Legler (2001b) and Legler (2003).

5. For a detailed account of the origins of the Democratic Charter, see Cooper and Legler (2006).

6. The idea of the right to democracy also circulated in the UN system. See, for example, United Nations Commission on Human Rights (1999).

7. I am grateful to Jacqueline Deslauriers, executive coordinator of the Department for the Promotion of Democracy, for this insight.

8. I am grateful to Helen Barnes for the opportunity to consult her detailed work at the Carter Center on the applications of the Inter-American Democratic Charter.

9. The Rio Group is a multilateral grouping of Latin American and Caribbean states that arose during the Cold War in 1986 as an alternative regional governance body to the OAS. It contrasts with the OAS in terms of its lack of a permanent secretariat and the intentional exclusion of the United States from its membership.

10. There is some indication that the apparent lack of Democratic Charter use, especially of its main action-oriented clauses, should not be taken to mean that it has not performed a valuable function. John Graham, for example, observes that the charter has value as a credible deterrent. According to Graham (2002, 8), the OAS was able to use the prospect of invoking the Democratic Charter as a ploy to get Haitian authorities to concede to the establishment of a special OAS mission for strengthening democracy in 2002. Nonetheless, it is unlikely that the Democratic Charter was originally conceived as a diplomatic tool to stigmatize recalcitrant states.

11. This episode is discussed in detail in Cooper and Legler (2006).

12. For more detailed accounts of the evolving regional democracy problematic, see Legler, Lean, and Boniface (forthcoming) and McCoy (forthcoming).

13. The idea of civil society coup comes from Encarnación (2002). For the notion of impeachment coup, see Dexter Boniface (forthcoming).

14. Norms have been defined as standards of expected behavior among actors of a given identity (Finnemore and Sikkink 1998: 891).

15. On executive sovereignty and club multilateralism, see Cooper and Legler (2006).

16. On complex multilateralism, see O'Brien, Goetz, Scholte, and Williams (2000). On networked multilateralism, see Cooper and Legler (2006).

17. Keck and Sikkink (1998) call this outward thrust for political support by domestic civil society actors the "boomerang effect."

18. The Friends of the Democratic Charter comprise a network of former heads of state and high-ranking public officials advised by a group of senior academics. The Carter Center serves as the coordinating group. For a sample of the Friends' views, see Friends of the Democratic Charter (2005).

19. On the US credibility crisis, see Peter Hakim (2006) and Shifter and Jawahar (2006).

20. I am indebted to John Graham and Eduardo del Buey for these insights. On the OAS's financial woes, see FOCAL (2004) and Graham (2005b).

8

Protecting Human Rights: Recent Achievements and Challenges

Bernard Duhaime

A s attested by the contemporary history of the Americas, the international protection of human rights is firmly rooted in the inter-American project. The Organization of American States (OAS) and its norms and institutions have developed and provided the region's population with a dynamic system that has adapted itself to the realities of the hemisphere. In recent years, the inter-American human rights system (the system) has been marked by a series of advances that have permeated the development of international human rights law. In this chapter I first provide an overview of the main norms and institutions of this regime. I then assess some of its achievements and address a few of the challenges that it will face in the coming years.

Human Rights and the OAS

The system can be said to consist of the various legal instruments and mechanisms provided for by the OAS to ensure the protection and promotion of these rights.

The Normative Framework

At its very beginning, the OAS affirmed the importance of protecting human rights in the region. By becoming members of the organization, the states of the Americas undertook to respect the precepts stated in this regard in the OAS Charter (the charter) (for example, Preamble, Art. 2, 3, 17, 45, 49, 53). These principles were developed further in the American Declaration of the Rights and Duties of Man (the declaration), which lists the main human rights (Art. I–XXVI) governed by the system and constitutes its cornerstone.

131

Although a simple resolution, not a treaty within the meaning of international law, part of this declaration has certainly gained a binding character for member states today. Indeed, significant portions of this instrument are now considered part of customary international law (IACHR 2002: 39). Moreover, the OAS General Assembly (GA) has recognized on repeated occasions its obligatory nature—for example, AG/RES. 314 (VII-0/77), 370 (VIII-0/78) and 1829 (XXXI-0/01)—as reaffirmed by the Inter-American Commission on Human Rights (IACHR) (*IACHR Roach and Pinkerton Case* 1987, par. 46–49; *IACHR Edwards et al. Case* 2000, par. 107) as well as by the Inter-American Court of Human Rights (IACourt, the court), which has specified that the declaration contains and defines the human rights set down in the charter, to which all OAS member states have subscribed (*IACourt OC-10/89,* par. 29–47).[1]

In addition to these two instruments, the OAS member states adopted in 1969 the American Convention on Human Rights (the convention), which has been in force since 1978 and enshrines numerous rights listed in the declaration (Art. 1–26). This convention also stipulates that certain guarantees can be suspended in times of war, public danger, or other similar situations (Art. 27) and contains some provisions that limit or restrict the application of specific rights under certain conditions. Last, it provides for means and institutions to ensure the protection of human rights (Art. 33–73), including the IACHR and the court.

Beyond the convention, the OAS member states have also adopted various inter-American human rights treaties and other types of instruments in specific areas (including the Additional Protocol to the American Convention on Human Rights in the Area of Economic, Social and Cultural Rights, or the San Salvador Protocol; Protocol to the Convention to Abolish the Death Penalty; Inter-American Convention to Prevent and Punish Torture; Inter-American Convention on the Forced Disappearance of Persons; and the Inter-American Convention on the Prevention, Punishment, and Eradication of Violence against Women, or the Convention of Belem Do Para).

Inter-American Human Rights Institutions and Mechanisms

The system includes various institutions responsible for ensuring the protection and promotion of human rights. Within the OAS, the Inter-American Commission on Human Rights is the principal body entrusted with this mandate in the Americas and serves as the consultative organ of the organization in this area (Charter, Art. 106). It is made up of seven experts elected by the GA in their individual capacity. Accordingly, commissioners do not represent any particular state but, rather, all OAS members. The IACHR is therefore not a political body like the United Nations Human Rights Council. It meets two to three times a year and is assisted by a secretariat that includes approximately twenty attorneys. The IACHR ensures the observance of the declaration and the convention, as well as other inter-American human rights instruments. The IACHR has numerous functions that allow it to carry out its mandate based on different types of interventions, both legal and political in nature. For example, it conducts promotion and training activities, formulates recommendations to states regarding—among other things—progressive measures to implement the treaties referred to above, and observes the situation of human rights in the countries, in particular by formulating requests for information and carrying out on-site visits. Moreover, the IACHR receives and investigates individual petitions alleging inter alia violations of the declaration or the convention (in order to be able to present to the commission a petition against a member state, a person or a group must have first exhausted all domestic remedies or be unable to do so). The commission also approves and publishes reports on individual cases, on the general situation of human rights in some member states, and on specific themes, which it generally presents to the GA. Furthermore, the IACHR can adopt precautionary measures in serious and urgent cases that may cause irreparable harm to persons. It can also submit individual cases to the court and consult the latter on questions regarding the interpretation of the convention or any other treaty related to the protection of human rights in the Americas (Convention, Art. 34–51; *IACHR Statute,* Art. 18–20; *IACHR Rules of Procedure,* Art. 25).

The Inter-American Court of Human Rights, the creation of which was provided for in the convention, consists of seven judges, nationals of the member states and elected in their individual capacity by the GA. It is assisted by a secretariat and meets a few times a year. Unlike the IACHR, the court performs essentially jurisdictional functions since it is responsible for deciding contentious cases between the commission and the states relating to observance of the convention or any other instrument that grants it such jurisdiction. To be subject to the court's jurisdiction, a state must have first ratified the convention and made an express declaration to that effect. Concerning a case, the court can issue an order, or judgment, that is binding for states under international law. Moreover, at the request of the commission or any member state, the court can issue advisory opinions regarding the interpretation of the convention or any other instrument related to human rights in the Americas. A state can also consult it on the compatibility of one of its laws with the convention. Last, the court can also adopt provisional measures in serious and urgent cases. It reports to the GA (Convention, Art. 52–73).

In addition to the commission and the court, the OAS includes various specialized agencies that contribute directly or indirectly to the protection of human rights. They include the Inter-American Children's Institute, the

Inter-American Institute of Human Rights (IIHR) and the Inter-American Commission of Women (CIM).[2] Among the inter-American institutions responsible for promoting and protecting human rights, the commission and the court have played a predominant role, which will be examined more closely in the following sections.

Assessment of Some Achievements of the System

Since it was created, the system has sought to respond to the particularities of human rights issues specific to the Americas. In many countries of the region, this regime enjoys considerable credibility, very often greater than that enjoyed by its UN equivalent (González 2001: 14), owing, among other things, to the initiatives undertaken by its institutions to increase access to the system for victims.

Thus, the very development of the commission—from a body essentially destined to advise on and promote human rights to a true authority ensuring the protection of these rights—is in itself remarkable progress. The IACHR was able to bring about some of these changes by interpreting in a liberal manner its general mandate in favor of victims and the system. Indeed, during its first years, the commission, although authorized to formulate recommendations on the general situation of human rights in member states, did not have express jurisdiction to examine the situation of specific victims. However, by using its prerogative authorizing it to request information in this regard from member states, by carrying out on-site visits, but especially through its general reports, the IACHR was able to address issues related to specific claims and thus indirectly process individual communications that it received (González 2001: 5–6; González 1998: 497). Developing its own mandate related to petitions, the commission paved the way for subsequent reforms of its statute and then for the adoption of the convention, which reaffirmed its competence in this field (Rescia and Seitles 2000: 598–602). Similarly, the court amended its own rules of procedure, increasing victims' direct access to the system, first regarding reparations pleadings (1996–1997) and then regarding the entire procedure (2001). Indeed, now, although victims or their representatives are not authorized to directly submit a matter to the court—as that is still reserved for the commission or the states (Convention, Art. 61.1)—they can nevertheless make their own representations directly to the court once their case has been referred to the latter (*IACourt Rules of Procedure,* Art. 23; González 2001: 76; Cançado Trindade 2000: 40 ff.).

Moreover, the clear-cut positions adopted by the commission relating to mass and systematic violations committed by several Latin American authoritarian regimes in the 1970s and 1980s, at a time when many states and organizations kept silent, have strengthened the IACHR's credibility (González 2001: 5–14; González 1998: 496; King-Hopkins 2000: 424; Shelton 1988: 327). Since the 1980s, the system, now equipped with a court, has been able to develop and adjust to the new realities of a changing continent. Starting out as a regime essentially focused on these mass and systematic violations, it has gone on to tackle other problems emblematic of the region and support the continent in its reforms and transitions. The rest of this section, although not making an exhaustive list or analysis of them, will examine some major achievements of the system in recent years, in particular in the context of the struggle against impunity, of armed conflicts and the fight against terrorism, as well as regarding democracy, the right to freedom of expression, and the administration of justice.

The Struggle Against Impunity

A major contribution of the system is unequivocally the developments that it brought about in the struggle against impunity, an unfortunately common problem in the region for many years. These innovations led to the establishment of jurisprudential bases that still serve today as indicators regarding the administration of justice in the continent and elsewhere. First, it should be pointed out that the commission had already played a decisive role in denouncing the phenomenon of forced disappearances in the late 1970s (for example, during its on-site visit in Argentina and its subsequent report). Several of these actions helped to stop or reduce this phenomenon in some countries (González 2001: 12–14).

However, it was in 1988 that the court issued the emblematic *Vélasquez Rodríguez* ruling, concerning allegations of abduction, arbitrary detention, and torture. In addition to being an important precedent regarding procedural and evidentiary issues, as well as the rule of exhaustion of local remedies (*IACourt Vélasquez Rodríguez Case* 1988: 35–36, 41, 52; Shelton 1989–1990: 7–10), this decision consecrated the principles governing states' obligation to respect and ensure human rights while guaranteeing the right to judicial guarantees and to judicial protection, as required by the convention (Art. 1, 8, 25). In this case, the court concluded that the state was responsible for the victim's disappearance—even though it was not necessarily directly carried out by state agents—because of its failure to fulfill the obligation to prevent this disappearance or to punish those responsible, thus contravening the convention (*IACourt Vélasquez Rodríguez Case* 1988: 66 and par. 174–177; Shelton 1989–1990: 10). This decision influenced the subsequent developments of inter-American jurisprudence related to extrajudicial executions committed by state agents or private individuals, as well as regarding investigations that are to be conducted by the authorities in relation to allegations of human rights violations (for example, *IACHR*

Bolaños Case 1996, par. 32–34; *IACHR Abella et al. Case* 1997, par. 413–424; *IACHR Ejido Morelia Case* 1997, par. 109–112). Ten years later, the Inter-American Court reaffirmed its position, specifying that impunity represents the total lack of investigation, prosecution, capture, trial, and conviction of those responsible for human rights violations and that it fosters chronic repetition of such violations and leaves the victims defenseless (*IACourt Paniagua Morales et al. Case* 1998, par. 173).[3] Accordingly, states have the obligation to resort to all legal means at their disposal to combat that situation. Similarly, the commission and the court later reaffirmed the victims' successors' "right to the truth," or right to know the fate of their loved ones (*IACHR Velásquez et al. Case* 2000, par. 80; *IACHR Extrajudicial Executions Case* 2000, par. 269; *IACourt Barrios Altos Case* 2001, par. 48; *IACourt Bámaca Velásquez Case* 2000, par. 199 ff.).

The system has also led to important advances in contesting the legality of laws or judicial measures taken by the states that enable or encourage impunity in the contexts of conflicts or transitions. For example, the commission condemned the laws that granted amnesty to all those possibly responsible for human rights violations (IACHR 1999; IACHR 2000a). It specified that states have the obligation to investigate and punish such violations, that this obligation cannot be renounced, and that situations of impunity arising from de facto or de jure amnesties contravene the convention (IACHR 2000a, par. 215–230). Similarly, in the *Barrios Altos* case (2001), the court reaffirmed that this type of law is incompatible with Articles 1.1, 8, and 25 of the convention because it precludes the identification of perpetrators, obstructs the investigation, limits access to justice, and prevents victims and their next of kin from knowing the truth and receiving the corresponding reparations (par. 43 ff.).

Similarly, the inter-American bodies also considered that regimes contravened the declaration and the convention when they insisted that human rights violations perpetrated by members of the armed forces be brought to trial before military rather than civil tribunals. The commission stated, for example, that these tribunals could not be considered to have the independence required to judge violations perpetrated by the armed forces and specified that this type of case should be heard by civil tribunals (IACHR 1999; *IACHR Lindo et al. Case* 2000).

In addition to jurisprudential developments related to impunity, the system equipped itself with an Inter-American Convention on the Forced Disappearance of Persons, which has been in force since 1996, and which stipulates not only special obligations for the states regarding cooperation and sanctions but also an additional expeditious procedure that allows the IACHR to request information related to allegations of forced disappearances (Art. 14).

Armed Conflicts and the Fight Against Terrorism

The system has also contributed to the protection of human rights in the context of armed conflicts, in particular internal conflicts, a scourge that has unfortunately plagued the recent history of the Americas. While dealing with allegations of human rights violations in this context, the commission and the court adopted a particular approach, using norms of international humanitarian law (or IHL) as *lex specialis* to interpret alleged violations that fall under international human rights law, in particular regarding the right to life, the right to physical integrity, and other guarantees that cannot be suspended in time of war or similar public danger (Convention, Art. 27; IACHR 2002, par. 29). This approach aims at using the laws of war—a more specific body of rules that is better adapted to situations of armed conflicts—to appropriately interpret the scope of human rights norms in this context. Although this type of reference to IHL as *lex specialis* was contested by some (*IACHR Coard et al. Case* 1999; *IACourt Las Palmeras Case* 2000),[4] it was also used by other international adjudicative bodies, including the United Nations International Court of Justice.[5]

Thus, the IACHR used the law of international armed conflicts to interpret certain guarantees applicable in the context of the invasion of Grenada by the United States (*IACHR Coard et al. Case* 1999, par. 37–42). Similarly, it interpreted a number of provisions of the convention in light of the law of noninternational armed conflicts, to assess the legality of the use of lethal force by the authorities during military operations in the Colombian conflict (*IACHR Ribón Avilan Case* 1997), as well as the assault on La Tablada barracks in Argentina (*IACHR Abella Case* 1997, par. 161).

However, the court changed this approach somewhat in 2000, specifying that it was competent to declare violations only regarding the treaties that specifically granted it this power, which, in this case, excluded the IHL conventions (*IACourt Las Palmeras Case* 2000).[6] Finally, in 2001, in a ruling on allegations of torture committed during the Guatemalan civil war, the court specified that, although it was not competent to declare that a state was internationally responsible for having violated IHL norms, it was nevertheless competent to *observe* that some acts contravened these latter norms and *declare* that the same acts also violated the American convention (*IACourt Bámaca Velásquez Case* 2000, par. 207–209). As enigmatic as this nuance may be, the court's prudence may be explained by the fact that some IHL violations can also constitute war crimes and thus involve the criminal responsibility of certain individuals, which, under the circumstances, might have proved to be a delicate issue to deal with.

This approach of referring to *lex specialis* is highly pertinent nowadays, for example, in the analysis of antiterrorist measures since, as pointed out by the commission, terrorist acts and the measures adopted to deal with them sometimes fall within the context of an armed conflict or can give rise to such a conflict (IACHR 2002, par. 29). The system has been able to respond to the issues raised by this problem in a particular way. For example, in 2002 the OAS adopted the Inter-American Convention Against Terrorism, which aims at preventing, punishing, and eliminating terrorism (AG/RES. 1840 [XXXII-0/02]), providing in particular for various obligations for the states, notably in the area of cooperation. This treaty explicitly stipulates that measures carried out to combat terrorism must be compatible with international human rights law and IHL (Art. 15). Soon after this convention was adopted, the IACHR published the *Report on Terrorism and Human Rights* (IACHR 2002), which presented an assessment of the progress made by inter-American law in this area, particularly regarding the rights to life, personal liberty and security, physical integrity, judicial guarantees, freedom of expression, and equality, among others.

It must be said that the system had already established a series of principles applicable to this reality. For example, in two advisory opinions (*IACourt OC-8/87, IACourt OC-9/87*), the court examined the capacity of a state to suspend the right to liberty (Convention, Art. 7) and the right to judicial guarantees (Art. 8) in emergency situations (Art. 27), measures that, in principle, could be examples of counter-terrorist measures. Although these rights are not listed in the convention as nonderogable rights, the court specified that certain aspects of these rights cannot be suspended since they guarantee the respect and effectiveness of other nonderogable rights. Thus, according to the court, it is impossible, in these situations, to suspend all the judicial guarantees of an individual (*IACourt OC-8/87*, par. 21 ff.) or to prevent extraordinary remedies aimed at ensuring the respect of fundamental rights, for example those aimed at determining the lawfulness of the detention of an individual or those aimed at determining whether or not the exceptional measure is properly implemented (*IACourt OC-8/87*, par. 40-42; *IACourt OC-9/87*, par. 38).[7]

The commission found that the use by the Peruvian and Colombian governments of masked or "faceless" witnesses or judges to prosecute presumed terrorists or insurgents was incompatible with the convention (IACHR 1999; IACHR 2000a). It did, however, point out the need to adopt, in certain cases, measures to ensure the security of these persons while not compromising the rights of the accused (IACHR 2002, par. 251 ff.).

More recently, the IACHR has had to refer to some of these principles in examining certain counter-terrorist measures put forward by the US government since September 11, 2001. Thus, concerning the precautionary measures that it adopted in March 2002 regarding the detainees in Guantánamo Bay, the IACHR used IHL as *lex specialis* to interpret the provisions of the declaration in the context of an armed conflict. It reiterated that certain aspects of the right to personal liberty and security, as well as to judicial guarantees, cannot be suspended even in times of war; and it urged the United States to ensure the determination of the status of detainees, given that it was fundamental to assessing the scope of the applicable guarantees and avoiding the latter's violation.[8]

Democracy, Freedom of Expression, and the Administration of Justice

Although the strengthening of democracy is not part of the principal mandate of inter-American human rights institutions but rather depends mainly on the OAS political bodies and a number of its specialized agencies, including the Secretariat for Political Affairs, the system has contributed to the consolidation of democracy in the region in various ways. It should first be noted that the interdependence between the protection of human rights and democracy was reaffirmed by various inter-American instruments, including the OAS Charter (Art. 3f, 47) and the convention (Preamble) (see also AG/RES. 1840 [XXXII-0/02], Preamble). This principle was nevertheless expressly set out in the 2001 Inter-American Democratic Charter (Preamble, Art. 7).[9]

This interdependence has, to some extent, been illustrated through the history of the commission. Some of its reports on human rights in specific states, which were presented and discussed by members in OAS political bodies, certainly contributed to bringing about political changes in the region (regarding Nicaragua, for example, see Rescia and Seitles 2000: 606 ff.; González 2001: 14; Dykmann 2003: 143). However, this practice has decreased, partly because of pressure exerted in some quarters (Rescia and Seitles 2000: 606; González 2001: 13). Today, unfortunately, the annual reports of the commission and the court are barely addressed by the GA and thus rarely discussed by the states, since little time is devoted to this subject.

The system has been able to clarify the importance of human rights in the consolidation of institutions and democratic processes by developing norms and jurisprudence on various issues intrinsically linked to them, such as the right to freedom of expression. It must first be specified that the system has developed norms that are in principle more favorable to this right than are other international standards (*IACourt OC-5/85,* par. 50; Ubeda de Torres 2003; Bertoni 2000: 20). Moreover, in 2000, the commission adopted the Declaration of Principles on Freedom of Expression, which contains a more precise interpretation of Article 13 of the convention (guaranteeing the right to freedom of expression). It emphasizes that this right is inextricably linked to the democratic order and is indispensable to the very existence of democratic societies (principles 1, 4, 12).

Similarly, in 1994, the IACHR had specified that laws that penalize criticisms made against the state or its public officials (*desacato* laws) were not only incompatible with the convention but also prevented open and rigorous debate on public policies, which is essential to the existence of democratic societies (IACHR 1995: 197; González 2001: 29). Likewise, the court specified that respect for the right to freedom of expression is a sine qua non condition for the effective functioning of a free and democratic society and constitutes its cornerstone (*IACourt OC-5/85,* par. 70; *IACourt Palamara Iribarne Case,* par. 112; *IACourt Canese Case* 2005, par. 86–88).

Both institutions developed jurisprudence on this right, more specifically relating to (1) violence perpetrated against journalists or in retaliation for a form of expression, (2) the prohibition of prior censorship, (3) subsequent penalties—in particular during electoral campaigns, (4) indirect restrictions, and (5) the dual character of the right (the right to express ideas and the right to receive information), as well as the obligation to belong to professional corporations (UNAM 2000; Grossman 2000–2001; Ubeda de Torres 2003; Bertoni 2000, 2004).[10] Moreover, the IACHR created in 1997 the Office of the Special Rapporteur for Freedom of Expression, which, in addition to its involvement in the development of jurisprudence on the subject, has issued reports, analyses, and recommendations related to the situation of this right in member states, as well as to specific themes.[11]

Last, it should be noted that the system has also developed other important human rights standards that can be used as indicators for ensuring the consolidation of democracy in the region, in particular regarding the administration of justice. The commission and the court have indicated to the states the limits authorized by the charter, the declaration, and the convention related to the measures that can be adopted to preserve their own security or protect democracy. Thus, the commission and the court have systematically reiterated that the right to judicial guarantees and to judicial protection, which are inextricably linked with the effective administration of justice, are rights that must be guaranteed under all circumstances (*IACourt OC-8/87; IACourt OC-9/87;* IACHR 2002). Both institutions have thus pointed out that to exceed these limits in the name of democracy is to compromise the very survival of the democratic order. These indicators have gained in importance since September 11, 2001, when viewed in the light of abuses committed in the name of security by some regimes in the region from the 1960s to the late 1990s.

From this perspective, the example of Peru under Fujimori is quite revealing. Although the commission and the court repeatedly condemned the violations committed by this regime in the name of security and the preservation of democracy (IACHR 2000b, notes 2 and 3), the Peruvian government of the time not only rejected these decisions and publicly refused to respect them, but also attempted to denounce the jurisdiction of the court in judging Peruvian affairs.[12] The IACHR and the court denounced that government's attempts to bypass the effective administration of justice in different ways (laying off judges, deploying faceless judges, holding military tribunals, pressuring justice officials, etc.), notably for reasons of national security. Furthermore, in its important report on the situation of human rights in Peru, published during the 2000 General Assembly in Windsor, Canada, the IACHR reiterated all these condemnations, denouncing in particular the government's manipulation of the judiciary. However, the commission went much further and denounced the process and the results of the Peruvian elections of the time, specifying that there had been a flagrant violation of political rights guaranteed by the convention (Art. 23), which attested to the total lack of rule of law and democracy in Peru (IACHR 2000a: 134). Although it is difficult to accurately identify the factors that led to Fujimori's withdrawal at the end of 2000, it goes without saying that this IACHR report and all the denunciations made by both the court and the IACHR against the government of the time contributed to promoting awareness of the issue among member states, as well as to the process of transition that subsequently led the country to democracy. In this respect, it should be noted that the high-level mission sent to Peru by the OAS following the Windsor General Assembly made every effort to implement reforms aimed at improving the electoral process, the protection of human rights, the effective administration of justice, and freedom of the press—all issues that had been previously identified by the IACHR and the court (AG/RES. 1753 [XXX-0/00]; OAS 2000c; OAS 2000d; IACHR 2000a).[13]

Although these themes will not be developed here, it should be mentioned that the system has also been able to bring about significant normative and institutional developments regarding the rights of indigenous peoples,[14] women,[15] children,[16] and migrant workers,[17] and the issue of the death penalty,[18] among others.

Challenges Facing the System

Although the system has developed in remarkable ways and has contributed in a constructive way to the protection of human rights in the Americas, numerous important challenges still lie ahead. The inter-American human rights institutions have repeatedly expressed concerns regarding specific problems, urging member states to intervene in order to ensure the universalization of the system, to improve respect for and the effective implementation of the decisions of the commission and the court by member states, to broaden victims' access to the system, and to grant institutions the resources needed to perform their mandates (OASGA 2005: 170–178). These concerns were reflected in positions formulated by many civil society actors (Coalición 2005a: 3; 2005b). Unfortunately, the Summits of the Americas process has not led to significant progress in this regard. The declarations and action plans that flowed from the Miami summit (1994) to that of Mar del Plata (2005) announced some priorities of the states related to public policies in the region. Although, on the one hand, they dealt with some human rights issues (in either a very general way or a thematic, highly compartmentalized way) and, on the other hand, promised that the system would be strengthened, few concrete measures were put forward to remedy the previously mentioned problems. At most, these declarations and action plans merely took note of these obstacles, without announcing effective solutions or adopting a strong position in this regard (Lamarche 2000; Lessard 2000).

First, it should be acknowledged that universalization of the system is far from having been achieved, considering that its normative and institutional framework has not been fully integrated into the region. In fact, only twenty-five of the thirty-five OAS members have ratified the convention, despite repeated invitations from the IACHR and the court to do so.[19] The United States and Canada, two economic and political powers with great influence in the hemisphere, and most of the states in the English-speaking Caribbean, the heart of the Caribbean Community, are still not heeding the call. Similarly, only twenty-two states have, to date, recognized the obligatory jurisdiction of the court. The summits do not appear to have led to a significant breakthrough on this point, despite the declarations of principles formulated by the states in this regard. Indeed, it is alarming to observe that, since December 1994, no state has ratified the American convention and only six member states have recognized the obligatory jurisdiction of the court since that date.[20] Without drawing any hasty conclusions, it should be noted that the summit process has unfortunately not reduced the impact of a two-tier system consisting of, on the one hand, states bound by the convention and subject to the control of the court (mainly Latin American states with a civilist legal tradition) and, on the other hand, states bound uniquely by the declaration and subject only to the control of the commission (mainly English-speaking states with a common-law legal tradition) (González 2001: 66). From Yellowknife to Ushuaia, not all states of the Americas have the same obligations in this regard, and citizens do not have the same rights and recourses. Is this not an inconsistency that is incompatible with any project of true continental integration (Lamarche 2000; Bronson and Lamarche 2001)? The summit process could have made human rights protection a sine qua non condition for states' participation in the hemispheric project. A firm commitment to this goal could have required, for example, that all states ratify the principal inter-American human rights instruments, or at least the convention, and recognize the obligatory jurisdiction of the court, as advocated, for example, in the European model (Amnesty 2005: 2; Lamarche 2000: 53; Bronson and Lamarche 2001; Casal n.d.: 4 ff.).

Another formidable challenge for the system will be to ensure greater respect for and more effective implementation of commission and court decisions by the member states concerned. Thus, it should be pointed out that the latter have the obligation under international law to respect judgments and orders of the court (Convention Art. 68.3; *IACourt Castillo-Petruzzi et al. Case* 1999) and should adopt in good faith measures to implement the commission's recommendations (Art. 41 and 51; IACHR 2001, par. 71–72; *IACHR Garza Case* 2000, par. 117; AG/RES. 2128 [XXXV-0/05]; AG/RES. 2075 [XXXV-0/05]). Although most states have no specific mechanism to this end and prefer to act on a case-by-case basis, others, including Costa Rica, have adopted legislative measures to allow for the direct implementation of such decisions by the national judicial authorities (CEJIL 1997). Both the IACHR and the court, which are competent to assess the performance of states in this regard and report to the GA (*IACourt OC-13/93; IACourt Baena-Ricardo et al. Case* 2003), have repeatedly expressed concerns about the limited implementation of their decisions by the states involved (OASGA 2005: 170–178). There is no formal OAS procedure, however, that leads the political bodies of the organization to adopt more severe measures to force an uncooperative state to abide by OAS decisions, as in the European system. Although the summit process has been able, at least symbolically, to increase political support for the system to this end, thus encouraging some states to adopt a more constructive approach (Guatemala, for example), the challenge remains formidable since some states have publicly declared that they disagree with the positions of the inter-American institutions and refuse to implement some of their decisions (Venezuela, for example). Beyond the question of political will, to which a political process such as that of the summit can bring some pressure, the fact remains that other states that are grappling with major conflicts (Colombia), or are quasi-failed states (Haiti), face considerable institutional problems that, at least in the short term, will restrict their capacity to implement the system's directives (Duhaime 2005: 139).

It goes without saying that for victims and civil society, one of the main challenges for the coming years will be accessing the system. As we have seen, the commission and the court have, in the past, adopted measures to deal with this problem. Despite these reforms, victims' access remains limited for various reasons (distance of institutions, complexity of the processed cases, fees associated with litigation, etc.). Many stakeholders have suggested that a legal aid fund be set up or that equivalent mechanisms be implemented, similar to those in force in the European system (CEJIL 2004: 2; Cançado Trindade 2000: 45; Coalición 2005b). This type of solution is certainly most desirable theoretically, but its implementation seems unlikely in the short term, given the OAS's current budgetary crisis. However, access is also limited due to delays in the processing of cases by the commission and the court. In this respect, it can be said that the system is, to some extent, a victim of its own success, since its initiatives of promotion and outreach, as well as the relative visibility of inter-American recourses—which has grown in recent years through the information revolution—have considerably increased the number of complaints presented. That has generated backlogs and delays in the analysis of files. Indeed, the full processing of a complaint by the IACHR can take more than five years, to which could be added a similar period when the case is subsequently brought before the court. These delays only exacerbate the violations experienced by victims who, in many cases, have already spent many years exhausting domestic remedies, when it was possible for them to do so. Under these circumstances, the IACHR and the court simply do not have enough staff to process the cases within a reasonable time frame (Tittemore 2004–2005). Various procedural solutions have been envisaged to control this phenomenon (pro forma processing of complaints, preparing summary reports, use of friendly settlements, and so on; see Cançado Trindade 2000; CEJIL 1999). Given the nature of the complaints procedure, which requires exhausting domestic remedies, it is submitted that the system should aim first and foremost at strengthening the national justice systems, in both normative and institutional terms, rather than providing for a substitute remedy.

The real problem is nonetheless one of resources (Tittemore 2004–2005): the IACHR has seen the number of petitions received annually increase by approximately 170 percent since 1997, while its resources have not been increased accordingly. On the contrary, its budget was reduced despite the fact that the OAS entrusted it with new mandates (Duhaime 2005: 139; OASGA 2005: 170–178; Feinberg 2004: 7, 32–35; Amnesty 2005: 2). To offset the shortfalls, the IACHR must often resort to voluntary contributions from member states or to external resources to fund some activities. In addition to being a short-term solution that limits the institutional and operational latitude of the IACHR, this alternative could, at least in principle, taint the appearance of impartiality and independence of this institution with quasi-judicial functions. Nevertheless, despite repeated calls from the IACHR and the court (OASGA 2005: 170–178), as well as the General Assembly resolutions that reiterate the importance of strengthening the system, including from a financial perspective (AG/RES. 2075 [XXXV-0/05]), there is no indication the OAS's budget will increase funding dedicated to the IACHR and the court in the short term (Feinberg 2005: 10). In this context of crisis within the OAS, the remaining question is first and foremost one of political will: that is, members will have to decide, as they should have done so many years ago, whether or not protecting human rights is a real priority for the region and within the OAS.[21]

* * *

With regard to the system's norms and institutions, the summit process has certainly resulted in some progress worth mentioning. It has, for example, led to the adoption of the Inter-American Democratic Charter and to the establishment of the Unit for Human Rights Defenders (AG/RES. 1818 [XXXI-0/01], adopted following the 1998 and 2001 summits). It also provided political support to the activities of the Rapporteurs for Freedom of Expression (Declaration de Santiago) and on migrant workers and their families (AG/RES. 1480 [XXVII-0/97], adopted following the 1994 summit). Moreover, it certainly opened up new political spaces for civil society within the Americas and the OAS (Gaudet and Sarrasin 2005; Lessard 2000), thus allowing important debates on human rights and free trade.

However, it should be noted that the discussion surrounding the adoption of an eventual pan-American free trade agreement did not effectively deal, from a normative and institutional perspective, with the possible spillover impact of such economic integration (in particular in the area of deregulation and privatization) on the respect for human rights (Lessard 2000: 11–12; Bronson and Lamarche 2001), a concern that has been repeatedly expressed by civil society (Centro de Derechos Humanos 2005; Amnesty 2005: 2–3; Allmand 2001; Coalición 2005a: 3 ff.). This issue continues to be debated within inter-American institutions (Centro de Derechos Humanos 2005). However, many questions have, as yet, not been answered, such as the hierarchy of norms and the primacy of international human rights law, as well as the decisionmaking bodies competent in this regard (Bronson and Lamarche 2001; Centro de Derechos Humanos 2005; Coalición 2005a). Although the idea of a pan-American free trade agreement seems to have gone back to the drawing board, the recent adoption of bilateral treaties reaffirms the importance of addressing these questions. For example, what would happen if a state was forced to adopt measures in accordance with such an agreement that would restrict the enjoyment of certain rights, or was forced to adopt regressive measures related to economic, social, and cultural rights (in fields such as health, education, the environment, or access to drinking water), thus contravening the treaties applicable in this regard (Convention, Art. 26)? Which international obligation would take priority? Which institution would be competent to assess the compatibility of such measures with international law? The principles stated in the framework of the summit process could, in my view, have reiterated the primacy of international human rights law (in particular relating to imperative norms of international law) and referred to the foundations of inter-American human rights law laid out in the OAS Charter (Allmand 2001).[22] Moreover, the current proliferation of international jurisdictional institutions in various fields, as well as the confusion that it has generated, aptly demonstrate the obvious importance of clarifying the institutional question (as illustrated by the recent softwood lumber dispute, which pitted Canada against the United States before NAFTA and WTO bodies). It goes without saying that a process that was more firmly rooted in the institutional structure of the OAS would certainly have facilitated the identification of normative and jurisdictional solutions on this issue. Indeed, would it not have been better to integrate the inter-American human rights system into the regime as envisaged and to reiterate the primacy of its norms and institutions in this dynamic (Lessard 2000: 11–12; Allmand 2001; Bronson and Lamarche 2001; Centro de Derechos Humanos 2005; Coalición 2005a; Coalición 2005b)?

The highly topical nature of the issues related to the impact of free trade on human rights brings to the fore what, in my view, constitutes the principal challenge to the system at the substantive level, that is, respect for economic, social, and cultural rights (or ESCRs, guaranteed by Art. 26 of the convention and by the San Salvador Protocol) in a region where poverty and exclusion continue to encumber the lives of the majority of the population. Although the commission and the court have until now dealt with these matters in a rather cautious way, they do not appear to have a clearly defined position regarding the implementation of these rights, in particular the capacity of said institutions to recognize violations of ESCRs in individual cases. Thus, on the issue of the *justiciability* of ESCRs, the IACHR and the court declared that it was impossible for them to conclude that a state had violated Article 26 of the convention, because the latter provides for a state obligation of realizing these rights in a progressive manner (*IACourt Five Pensioners Case* 2003, par. 147–148; *IACHR Pivaral Case* 2005). However, the commission has also recognized violations of the said article (*IACHR García Fajardo Case* 2000) or considered admissible petitions alleging such violations (*IACHR San Mateo du Huanchor Case* 2004; *IACHR Cardenas et al Case* 2004—relating to facts similar to those of the *Five Pensioners Case; IACHR Odir Miranda Cortez Case* 2000—relating to facts similar to those of the *Pivaral Case*). The court, however, does not seem to have completely excluded the possibility of recognizing violations of this provision (*IACourt Panchito López Case* 2004, par. 255). Moreover, both institutions have also recognized that the violation of certain civil and political rights could also lead to violations of the social, economic, and cultural dimensions of these rights (*IACourt Baena-Ricardo et al. Case* 1999 and 2001). For example, the commission and the court seem to be prepared to declare violations of the economic, social, and cultural rights of children (*IACourt Villagran Morales Case* 1999; *IACourt Panchito López Case* 2004) and indigenous peoples (*IACourt Awas Tingni Case* 2001, par. 149–151; *IACHR Maya Indigenous Community of the Toledo District Case* 2004, par. 150; *IACourt Yakye Axa Case* 2005, par. 162–163; *IACourt Moiwana Case* 2005) placed in situations of extreme vulnerability.

Moreover, it should be noted that Article 19 of the San Salvador Protocol specifies that member states must submit periodical reports to the OAS secretary-general, the IACHR, and other OAS specialized agencies (see also Convention, Art. 42). Resolution AG/RES. 2074 (XXXV-0/05) provides for standards that must be used to evaluate these reports and calls for the creation of a working group to conduct this assessment. It also asks the commission to develop, in collaboration with the Inter-American Institute of Human Rights, indicators of progress for evaluating reports. Rather than a new complaint mechanism, this procedure aims at evaluating the general progress made in the area of ESCRs in the states. During its regular period of sessions of October 2005, the IACHR conducted a closed seminar with some nongovernmental organizations, member states, and experts to discuss possible paths to pursue on this issue. These developments, simultaneous to the negotiations aimed at the adoption of a proposed Social Charter (AG/RES. 2139 [XXXV-0/05]), should be closely monitored.

Finally, two specific institutional issues draw our attention. First, given the active role played by the inter-American institutions regarding human rights and democracy, it is crucial that the independence and autonomy of these institutions be maintained vis-à-vis the states and the OAS political debates. These prerogatives are essential for them to perform judicial or quasi-judicial functions. The restructuring projects proposed by former secretary-general Miguel Angel Rodríguez provoked strong reactions, which subsequently led then acting secretary-general Luigi R. Einaudi to make some adjustments to ensure the institutional independence of the IACHR (Duhaime 2005: 139–140).

Furthermore, the proliferation of mandates, mechanisms, and procedures entrusted to various inter-American bodies will inevitably generate overlaps of initiatives directly or indirectly related to human rights. For example, the IACHR intervenes with the IIHR regarding human rights promotion, with the Inter-American Committee Against Terrorism regarding human rights and terrorism, with the CIM regarding the monitoring of the Convention of Belem Do Para, and with several OAS agencies regarding that of the San Salvador Protocol. The challenge is thus considerable: not only will close coordination be necessary, but these various entities will have to operate in compliance with their respective jurisdictions, without compromising the independence and autonomy of the commission and the court.

Conclusion

The norms and institutions that comprise the system have been marked by noticeable developments throughout the latter's recent history and have permitted the OAS to address with a great deal of adequacy various issues of particular concern for the Americas in the field. While norms and jurisprudence have evolved to strengthen the member states' human rights obligations, they have also permitted the consolidation of a dynamic institutional framework of supervision, composed mainly of the commission and the court.

The latter have undertaken noteworthy initiatives to broaden access to the system for victims of human rights violations. In addition, they have contributed significantly to the development of international human rights law standards with regard to major problems affecting the hemisphere. The system has defined with greater specificity the scope of member states' obligation to eradicate impunity, in particular in the context of transition processes. It has deepened the understanding of state obligations during armed conflicts and counter-terrorism initiatives, including with regard to the use of lethal force and to due process guarantees. The system has also reaffirmed the intimate links between human rights and democracy and has contributed to the strengthening of some aspects of democratic development, in particular with regard to the necessity of the right to freedom of expression and of a sound administration of justice for the consolidation of democratic institutions.

As the American Declaration of the Rights and Duties of Man approaches its sixtieth anniversary, the inter-American system still faces major challenges regarding the universalization of the normative and institutional framework, the implementation of decisions of the commission and the court, and victims' access to the system. The summit process certainly constituted an opportunity to address some of the challenges the system faces, but it has brought very few concrete results so far. It has, however, provided greater visibility to the contemporary human rights concerns of civil society within the debates surrounding continental integration.

Notes

The author would like to thank his collaborator, Évelyne Jean-Bouchard.

1. These institutions are examined below. See *infra,* section I(2). Cases of the commission are referred to as *IACHR, name of the case, year of publication,* and are accessible at www.cidh.org/casos.eng.htm. Cases of the court are referred to as *IACourt, name of the case, year of publication;* advisory opinions of the court are referred to as *IACourt, OC—number of the opinion/year of publication;* court cases and opinions are accessible at www.corteidh.or.cr/juris_ing/index.html.

2. See, in general, www.oas.org/OASpage/humanrights.html.

3. On the general subject of impunity, see also IACHR 1999; IACHR 2000a; IACHR 2001a; IACHR 2001b.

4. See also the pleadings related to the IACHR precautionary measures regarding Guantánamo Bay detainees: www.ccr-ny.org/v2/legal/september_11th/sept11Article.asp?ObjID=7lt0qaX 9CP&Content=134.

5. Advisory Opinion on the Legality of the Threat or Use of Nuclear Weapons, July 8, 1996, ICJ Reports 1996, www.icj-cij.org/cijwww/ccases/cunan/cUNAN judgment/ cunan_cjudgment_19960708_Advisory%20Opinion.htm, par. 25.

6. In this sense, this approach was different from that used by the commission three years earlier in the above-cited *Ribón Avilan Case,* where it had not only referred to IHL to interpret the American convention but also concluded that IHL

had been violated. The court's approach in the *Las Palmeras Case* seems to be irreconcilable with the approach that it adopted in the 1999 *Villagran Morales Case,* where it concluded that Guatemala had in fact violated the 1989 UN Convention on the Rights of the Child, despite the fact that the latter convention did not expressly grant it jurisdiction to do so (par. 196).

7. According to the IACHR, certain aspects of these rights, related to the publicity or rapidity of judicial proceedings, for example, could be subject to certain derogations (IACHR 2002, par. 249 ff.).

8. See also supra note 4.

9. But see Chapter 7 of this book: Thomas Legler, "'Empty Pieces of Paper' or a 'Living Document'? The Inter-American Democratic Charter."

10. See, in general, Office of the Special Rapporteur for Freedom of Expression, Topical Index on Freedom of Expression, http://www.cidh.oas.org/relatoria/showarticle.asp?artID=149&lID=2.

11. See, in general, Office of the Special Rapporteur for Freedom of Expression Reports, http://www.cidh.oas.org/relatoria/showarticle.asp?artID=159&lID=2.

12. Many observers criticized the OAS's feeble reaction to this matter; see González 2001: 57.

13. See also www.oas.org/main/main.asp?sLang=E&sLink=http://www.upd.oas.org and www.oas.org/main/main.asp?sLang=E&sLink=http://www.upd.oas.org.

14. See, for example, OAS/Ser.L/V/II.108, Doc. 62; OAS/Ser.L/V/II.95, Doc. 7 rev. Chap. IV; OAS/Ser.K/XVI GT/DADIN/doc.260/06; *IACourt Awas Tigni Case* 2001; *IACHR Dann Case* 2002; *IACHR Maya indigenous community of the Toledo District Case* 2004; *IACourt Yakye Axa Case* 2005.

15. See, for example, Convention of Belem Do Para; OAS/Ser./L/V/II.114, Doc. 5 rev. Chap. VIb; OAS/Ser.L/V/II.100, Doc. 17 Chap. VIc; OAS/Ser.L/V/II.117, Doc. 44; *IACHR Raquel Martín de Mejía Case* 1995; *IACHR Ana, Beatriz and Celia Gonzalez Perez Case* 2001; *IACHR X & Y Case* 1996; *IACHR Morales de Sierra Case* 2000.

16. See, for example, *IACourt OC-17/2002; IACourt Villagran Morales Case* 1999.

17. See, for example, *IACourt OC-18/200;* OEA/Ser./L/V/II.111 Doc. 20 rev. Chap. VI.

18. See, for example, *IACourt OC-3/83; IACHR Andrews Case* 1996; *IACHR Baptiste Case* 2000; *IACHR McKenzie et al. Case* 2000; *IACourt Hilaire et al. Case* 2002; *IACHR Domingues Case* 2002; *IACHR Villareal Case* 2002; Tittemore 2004–2005.

19. Although only thirty-four countries participate actively, the OAS is made up of thirty-five member states. The government of Cuba, a member state, has been suspended from participation since 1962.

20. Moreover, less than 50 percent of members have ratified the other inter-American instruments for the protection of human rights, except for the Convention of Belem Do Para, which has been ratified by 91 percent of members since it was adopted in June 1994.

21. On this subject, see the Declaration of Québec (2001), which specifically asked the thirty-first OAS GA to envisage increasing the system's resources, while that at Mar Del Plata (2005) affirmed instead the need to strengthen and improve the system's *efficiency.*

22. Which includes, according to the Inter-American Court, the right to equality *(IACourt OC-18/2003).*

9

Insiders, Outsiders, and the Politics of Civil Society

William C. Smith and
Roberto Patricio Korzeniewicz

The vertiginous globalization of production, trade, and finance and the restructuring of collapsed state-centric models of development have been accompanied by new patterns of participation and representation in civil society in the Americas. In this chapter, we build upon our previous work, focusing on the Summits of the Americas process and the embattled negotiations for a Free Trade Area of the Americas (FTAA).[1] We argue that regional advocacy networks and coalitions and, in a few instances, transnational social movements have acquired the capacity to deploy strategies, sometimes simultaneous, sometimes sequential, that range from participation within existing national and regional institutional arrangements to radical contestation of the basic forces and logic of globalization.

These patterns of contestation and collaboration are emblematic of what Karl Polanyi (1957) identified as a "double movement," in which the global expansion of markets has been accompanied by pressures for the social and political regulation of those same markets. "From above," political and economic elites and governmental bureaucracies have attempted to construct a patchwork quilt of old and new supranational institutional arrangements favorable to the expansion and globalization of markets. Concomitantly, "from below," a less coordinated array of projects has emerged from a diverse ensemble of actors in civil society, resisting corporate-led globalization and, in some cases, actively promoting alternative paths to globalization.

We contend that in the 1990s there emerged an increasingly polarized pattern of collaboration and contestation, differentiating "insider" and "outsider" transnational civil society actors in the hemisphere.[2] Indeed, in the new post–Cold War environment, a few "enlightened" state actors, together with some technocrats in multilateral agencies, actively engaged civil society in promoting summitry and market integration. Drawing upon a neoliberal vision, some civil society actors—conceptualized in terms of the "third sector"—played key roles in the provision of certain types of "global public goods" with benefits that are "quasi universal in terms of countries, peoples, and generations," including safeguarding human rights, implementing judicial reform, supporting market-friendly forms of environmental protection, ensuring gender equality, and reconciling the rights of indigenous peoples with the rules of the new globalized economy (Kaul, Grunberg, and Stern 1999: 2–3 and passim). By contrast, most governments in the region embarked upon projects of neoliberal economic restructuring and were extremely reluctant to run the risk that civil society participation might derail market reform.

Hence, a clear and growing polarization occurred as civil society organizations adopted increasingly divergent paths. Following an "insider" strategy, some civil society networks and coalitions privileged the development of collaboration with governments, the Organization of American States (OAS), and international financial institutions, such as the World Bank and the Inter-American Development Bank (IDB), and pursued repertoires of collective action centered on official agendas and gradual reform. Other transnational networks and coalitions followed an "outsider" strategy, privileging ties to grassroots social movements and organized labor, deploying oppositional identities and confrontational strategies vis-à-vis globalization and regional economic integration schemes, and pursuing repertoires of collective action centered on contestation and mobilization. The "insider" strategy met relative success in influencing the rhetoric built around the summitry process, whereas the "outsider" strategy fell short of the utopian visions motivating many of its defenders but did successfully mobilize considerable grassroots support and played a role in expanding opposition to the FTAA negotiations throughout the region.

Following September 11, 2001, the constellation of factors shaping transnational activism changed significantly. The September 11 attacks and the Bush administration's response had the initial effect of demobilizing and delegitimating many civil society organizations, particularly those that had relied on more confrontational collective action repertoires. Simultaneously, the policies of the Bush administration dramatically downgraded the previous priority Clinton officials had placed on promoting greater civil society participation in multilateral governance. Instead, the current administration in Washington has advanced a more single-minded preoccupation with "democracy promotion" linked with a narrowly focused unilateral posture aimed at combating what were perceived as new, nontraditional security threats in the region.

US power has not been free to work its will completely unopposed, however. The election of Ricardo Lagos and Michelle Bachelet in Chile, Luiz Inácio Lula da Silva in Brazil, Néstor Kirchner in Argentina, and, more recently, Tabaré Vásquez in Uruguay brought to power "modern," pragmatic, center-left governments that have been cautiously supportive of greater multilateralism and more autonomy from the foreign and security policies advanced so single-mindedly by the Bush administration. These governments also have been more critical than their predecessors of the technocratic governance procedures frequently associated with the more dogmatic versions of the Washington consensus. They proved more open to public discussions with relevant national publics, including sectors of civil society, on behalf of tougher bargaining strategies vis-à-vis the FTAA and US designs for regional economic governance. With their own peculiarities, the irruption of indigenous movements in the Andes, symbolized by the election of Evo Morales in Bolivia in 2005; the "revolutionary" project advanced since 1998 by Hugo Chávez in Venezuela; and even the center-right Vicente Fox government in post-2000 Mexico also represent different challenges to US-sponsored visions for hemispheric governance. Our contention is that the concatenation of these various changes transformed prevailing patterns of civil society participation.

Shaping Transnational Activism in the Americas

A stylized view of the institutional structures and strategies of collective action that distinguished "insider" and "outsider" patterns of participation in the Summits of the Americas and the FTAA negotiations is presented in Table 9.1.

In fact, as Table 9.1 indicates, virtually from the outset, the summits and the FTAA proceeded on two separate and independent tracks. From the Miami summit (1994) forward, the "insiders" dedicated considerable effort to transnational coordination among moderate civil society groups and the channeling of their policy recommendations into the official summit process. By and large, the "outsider" organizations did not take part in these consultations. Initially, in fact, the two groups were largely unaware of each other's activities. Over time, some of the networks active in one or the other track began to play both games. Soon, however, the "outsider" networks became disenchanted with the summitry process, and their involvement in the FTAA rapidly became increasingly contestatory, focusing on mobilizing support for parallel or alternative "Peoples' Summits."

This pattern of transnational activism in the Americas has been shaped primarily by the interaction between shifting configurations of domestic and international political opportunity structures and more enduring characteristics of specific issue areas—basically the provision of "global public goods" vis-à-vis "private goods" rooted in distributive conflict, with strong externalities among states, regions, social classes, firms, or individuals. The manifestations of these dynamics differ significantly, as sketched in Table 9.2.

Table 9.1 Polarization of Transnational Civil Society Actors in the Americas

	Insider Networks/Movements	Outsider Networks/Movements
Institutional structures and organizational path dependence	Privilege close links with governments and multilateral agencies (e.g., World Bank, IMF, WTO, IDB, OAS, USAID, etc.) and global corporations and banks. Open domestic political opportunity structures facilitate participation by NGOs and advocacy groups regarding the provision of public goods leading to transnational network formation. Strategies of cooperation and collaboration; working the media and behind-the-scenes lobbying activities.	Privilege ties to grassroots social movements and organized labor. Deployment of oppositional identities and confrontational strategies vis-à-vis globalization. Closed/blocked domestic political opportunity structures (sometimes by authoritarian regimes) and strong distributional externalities lead groups to seek transnational alliances and to form networks and coalitions with counterparts in other countries. Strategies of confrontation, contestation, and mobilization; street protests, mass demonstrations, teach-ins, etc.
Strategies and collective action repertoires	Policy-oriented research, policy papers addressed to influential political and private sector elites. Consultations focused on official agendas do not lead beyond the formation of networks, and eventual transborder coalitions tend to be rather weak; no social movement formation. Priority on gradual reform ("fix it, don't nix it") of the existing global system by improving corporate governance and strengthening global institutions.	Action-oriented research, critical manifestos, and policy proposals addressed to key activists and broad mass publics simultaneously in various countries. Intense informational exchange, cooperation, and joint issue campaigns with counterparts promote transborder networks, coalitions to carry out joint campaigns, and, in some cases, the emergence of transnational social movements. Priority on accumulation of forces and "anti-hegemonic" politics ("nix it, don't fix it") of systemic transformation of corporate-led globalization.
Impacts on global and regional political and economic agendas	Relative success in mobilizing grassroots sectors and constructing new "alternative identities," but only indirect and long-term influence in shaping policy agendas and the construction of "alternative frames"—"Another World Is Possible!"	Relative success in influencing the rhetoric of national and multilateral policy elites via the politics of expertise, with little emphasis on generating broad public support. Corporate-led globalization is inevitable so make it more accountable and transparent.

Table 9.2 Shaping Transnational Civic Activism in the Americas: Political Opportunity Structures (POS), Global Public Goods, and Distributive Conflict

	Closed International POS	Open International POS
Closed domestic POS	Repression, exclusion, and closed "technocratic" decisionmaking structures Little domestic mobilization Little transnational activism Authoritarianism or low-quality electoral democracies No norm change; elite projects prevail over weak civil societies	Summit agenda "Global public goods"—human rights, gender rights, indigenous rights, judicial reform, environment, etc. Logics of delegation, self-regulation, monitoring, and strategic positioning "Insiders" Transnational networks (information exchange) and transnational campaigns (coordinated action) Boomerang + spiral effects = norms cascade → gradual, long-term, international and domestic policy and norm change
Open domestic POS	FTAA agenda State- and corporate-led projects of globalization/regional integration Logic of exclusion + high levels of distributive conflict "Outsiders" Defensive transnationalization and transnational networks, coalitions, and (infrequently) social movements Confrontation, mobilization, and demands on states to exercise sovereignty, protect domestic interests, and advocate policy and norm change vis-à-vis global institutions	Combination of domestic and transnational activism (domestic democratic participation gradually replaces boomerang/spiral effects as predominant mode of activism) Rapid and more far-reaching institutionalization of norms of democratic participation and social and economic justice Progressive, multilevel global governance involving states, supranational institutions, epistemic communities, and transnational civil society actors "Another World Is Possible!"

In Table 9.2, we map these interactions and indicate their probable consequences in terms of "insider" and "outsider" strategies of transnational activism and the implications of multilevel opportunity structures relative to changes in international norms and attendant modes of regional governance. The next sections elaborate on these alternative modes of transnational activism. Finally, we offer a preliminary analysis of the contemporary conjuncture.

The "Insiders" and Summitry: From Collaboration to Disenchantment

When both domestic and international opportunity structures are closed to civil society participation, as depicted in the upper-left quadrant of Table 9.2, elite projects for hemispheric integration and globalization will prevail over weak civil societies, and civic activism will confront virtually insurmountable obstacles. In contrast, the upper-right quadrant of the table captures in stylized fashion the fundamental characteristics of the period spanning from the Miami (1994) to Quebec summits (2001). These years were marked by relatively open international opportunity structures coexisting with more highly constrained domestic opportunities in which fragile Latin American democracies were engaged in the implementation of divisive market reforms by means of executive-led "delegative" strategies of governability.

The Clinton administration, acting in loose concert with the Chilean, Canadian, and Costa Rican governments and the Organization of American States, was interested, for its own purposes to be sure, in promoting certain select forms of civil society participation. As governments and multilateral organizations deployed incentives to promote greater involvement by civil society organizations and networks, many "insiders" benefited from these enhanced opportunities for participation. This particular opportunity structure encouraged national nongovernmental organizations (NGOs) and advocacy groups to "go transnational" and to engage in activities of self-regulation and monitoring with regard to innovation and implementation in specific policy domains.

These logics of *delegation, self-regulation,* and *monitoring* were particularly relevant with regard to the global public goods agenda and to collective action by civil society actors generally supportive of globalization and regional integration. Many "insiders" possess specific professional expertise and specialized knowledge that can facilitate the solution of coordination problems across multiple issue domains involving a diverse array of governmental and social actors. Rather than confronting the informational and transaction costs themselves, national leaders and international functionaries frequently find that cooperation with transnational social actors can provide more effective and efficient "private" solutions for implementing and monitoring the impacts of politically sensitive policies.

In addition to these logics, state functionaries and technocrats at multilateral institutions such as the OAS and the IDB may be motivated by objectives rooted in a logic of *strategic positioning,* deployed to neutralize or co-opt potentially antisystemic movements or to forestall lobbying efforts and mobilization in opposition to important strategic initiatives or specific policy preferences. Moreover, by allowing the selective participation of more moderate civil society actors, powerful governments such as the United States may see their leverage over weaker governments strengthened.[3]

In the process, favored civil society activists can achieve limited participation in decisionmaking arenas. The dominant modality of collective action in these transnational networks is information exchange, with relatively limited capacity for the deployment of coordinated strategy and tactics and little capacity to mobilize a popular social base.[4] In the period analyzed (1994–2001), these "insider" actors operating in this collaborative mode practiced the politics of credibility and information and coalition formation and brokerage to trigger the well-known "boomerang" and "spiral" effects that frequently foreshadow "norms cascades" (Risse 2000) that may facilitate the emergence and institutionalization of international norms supportive of human rights, social justice, and democratic deepening.

Many of the organizations involved in hemispheric negotiations from Miami to the Mar del Plata summit in 2005 were long established and simply decided to make the summits an important part of an expanding agenda of concerns. The leading organizations at the core of the various "insider" networks included the Esquel Group Foundation (EGF), the Canadian Foundation for the Americas (FOCAL), the North-South Center (NSC), and Corporación PARTICIPA.[5] The final documents of the first Miami summit bore "the imprint of an unprecedented participation by non-governmental actors," with some of the official initiatives drawing "word for word" from the documents submitted by the leading "insider" organizations (Rosenberg and Stein 1995: vi).

By the same token, even some of the more mainstream organizations were dismayed not only by their own internal division but also by their scant influence, which was underscored by the fact that their recommendations on everything from human rights and collective action in defense of democracy to the link between trade and the environment were either watered down or simply eliminated during the official consultations. Most important, the Miami summit failed to create any institutional framework to monitor and to ensure accountability of governments charged with implementing the summit action plans in areas such as human rights or failed to provide effective channels for public participation in crucial areas such as macroeconomic policymaking (EGF 1999a).

These modest beginnings in Miami led to redoubled efforts to use indirect means to overcome the collective action problems limiting the more active participation of the "insiders." Several examples of these indirect efforts merit brief mention, beginning with the Civil Society Task Force, which was created by USAID and coordinated by EGF to function "as a clearinghouse as well as a vehicle to coordinate civil society input and monitoring action" on the summits (EGF 1999a: 386). Over 400 groups were participating in this network by the late 1990s (EGF 1999b: 1).

In similar fashion, USAID funded the Red Interamericana para la Democracia, a network that included, among others, the Compañeros de las Américas (United States), Asociación Conciencia (Argentina), Fundación Poder Ciudadano (Argentina), and Corporación PARTICIPA (Chile) (Guiñazú 2003). The Leadership Council for Inter-American Summitry, created by the North-South Center, represented another initiative along similar lines to provide the summit process with an institutional memory. Converging with these efforts, another network, Citizen Participation: From the Santiago Summit to the Canada Summit, linked FOCAL, EGF, and Corporación PARTICIPA to promote "constructive dialogue" between governmental and nongovernmental sectors in support of the summit mandates. Finally, although its track record has been exceedingly modest, the OAS also became directly involved with the creation of its own networked arena organized under the guise of the Inter-American Strategy for Public Participation (ISP) (EGF 1999b: 386; OAS 2000b).

The relative success of the "insider" organizations at the Miami and Santiago summits stands in stark contrast to their failure to gain access to and influence in the FTAA negotiations. Troubled by the deepening alienation on the part of many civil society groups, USAID asked EGF to organize an FTAA consultation process. The EGF-led working group brought together a diverse group of some two dozen organizations, including some of the "outsider" groups (for example, the National Wildlife Federation, Women's Edge, and some research and advocacy groups such as the Development Gap), to hammer out a broad consensus on a number of proposals and recommendations. However, without strong US support, the FTAA Committee of Government Representatives on Civil Society failed to adopt any of their recommendations (Pagés 2000).[6]

From the perspective of civil society groups, the failure of the ministerial meetings strengthened the perception that most of the region's governments were not serious about civil society participation in the FTAA and that they had no intention of backing off from their intransigent refusal to provide real information about the negotiations to the public or even to their own national parliaments. Moreover, in the eyes of the critics, the exclusion of civil society input (with the partial exception of business and financial interests) from official FTAA channels confirmed that the "insiders" had no power, little autonomy, and were hardly more than agents of their home country governments.

In response to these criticisms, the Canadian government made a concerted effort to heal the breach that had opened with civil society activists. Miami was called the "Trade Summit," and Chile hosted the "Education Summit." What would be the theme for the Canadian summit, scheduled for Quebec in early 2001? The Canadians were determined to host a summit with a substantive legacy, rather than merely a photo opportunity. There was reason for concern, particularly given that momentum toward the completion of the FTAA by 2005 had badly stalled. In response, the Canadians decided to make Quebec the "Democracy Summit," in an attempt to shift the focus from a trade-driven agenda and to attenuate opposition from grassroots antitrade and environmental activists (Cooper 2001; Dymond 2001).

The Canadians made a deliberate effort to broaden discussions to include three baskets of interrelated issues: (1) strengthening democracy, (2) creating prosperity, and (3) realizing human potential. In addition, human security and connectivity issues were placed on the agenda. The hope was that "promoting democracy" could be linked directly in the same negotiating track with the objective of "creating prosperity" (the focus of the FTAA agenda). Moreover, in this regard, the inclusion of labor and environmental standards in the main body of the preliminary text, instead of in separate "side agreements," raised expectations that civil society participation in the summit process and the FTAA negotiations might be put back on track (Cooper 2001).

In these relatively promising circumstances, the "insiders" carefully prepared for the Quebec summit. Corporación PARTICIPA, together with FOCAL and EGF, coordinated an elaborate series of national and regional civil society consultations, culminating with a final hemispheric meeting in Miami in early 2001. The product of these consultations was a final report containing a wide range of specific recommendations on human rights, corruption, education, gender issues, indigenous rights, sustainable development, and trade and micro enterprises (Corporación PARTICIPA 2001).

The meeting in April 2001 of the thirty-four presidents and heads of state proved rather anticlimactic. Hewing to the precedents set in Miami and Santiago, the Canadian summiteers issued a long Final Declaration, with accompanying documents and dozens of action items. The Quebec summit made only modest progress, creating limited momentum toward getting the FTAA back on track. Beyond the rhetoric, the Final Declaration was predictable—the "Democracy Summit" turned out to be principally about free trade after all.

The postmortems of the progress made in Quebec hinged essentially on preestablished views of the FTAA. For pro-business advocates of the FTAA, the Quebec summit was disappointing and was criticized for advancing too slowly toward a kind of "NAFTA lite." Nonetheless, for many supporters in the policy community, merely keeping the trade talks going was a significant achievement, while special praise was given for the inclusion of the "democracy clause" that limited participation in the FTAA process to countries with democratic governments. For civil society, however, Quebec was deeply disheartening—even many of the "insiders" were critical of the weak endorsements of labor rights and environmental protection, together with lip service paid to the rest of the social agenda defended by most activists.

The accomplishments achieved at the Fourth Summit of the Americas, in Mar del Plata, were at best "modest and innocuous" (Tokatlián 2006) and, in fact, signified a major setback for the US-sponsored project of hemispheric integration. For its part, the Bush administration demonstrated little flexibility vis-à-vis Latin American concerns regarding agricultural subsidies, nontariff trade barriers, and other related asymmetries. In this context, encouraging North American Free Trade Agreement (NAFTA) partners Canada and Mexico to push the FTAA to the forefront of the agenda reflected a strategic political miscalculation by the Bush administration. In addition to the predictable anti-imperialist diatribes of Venezuela's president Hugo Chávez, several of the more progressive but fiscally conservative governments—such as Brazil under Lula, Uruguay under Tabaré Vásquez, and Argentina under Kirchner—were openly critical of US unilateralism on security issues and less willing than in the past to accept passively the "usual nostrums" (Bumiller and Rohter 2005) about free trade, open markets, privatization, and the rest of the neoliberal agenda.

The resulting impasse, with twenty-nine governments in favor of advancing the FTAA versus five governments opposed, belied claims that the NAFTA bloc, the Caribbean Community (CARICOM), the Central American Free Trade Agreement (CAFTA), and the Andean countries represented a true consensus, when the dissenters, including the Argentine host, its Mercosur partners (Brazil, Uruguay, and Paraguay), and Venezuela together account for 75 percent of South America's total gross domestic product (GDP). The schizophrenic statement on trade in the Final Declaration, recognizing the two contradictory postures, underscored the reality that the summit and the FTAA were no longer the key arena for free trade negotiations, and that instead it would fall to the World Trade Organization's Doha Round to decide upon the scope and timing of trade liberalization.[7]

In this negative context for advocates and supporters of the US project for regional governance and integration, the trend toward disenchantment regarding civil society participation evident in Quebec continued at Mar del Plata. In fact, compared with previous summits, the "insiders" were virtually absent from the public eye as active participants in shaping the hemispheric agenda.

The Outsiders and the FTAA:
Mobilization and Mounting Contestation

To understand the dynamics of the "outsiders" and their strategies vis-à-vis regional integration and governance issues, we return our attention to Table 9.2. Here we find that trade negotiations are very different from summitry and that transnational activists operate in a context of movement from the upper-left quadrant toward the lower-left quadrant—closed opportunity structures at the international level and somewhat more open domestic institutional arrangements in the region's electoral democracies. Although generally not supportive of autonomous civil society mobilization, elected governments by and large have avoided overt repression, making organization and mobilization more feasible than under previous authoritarian regimes. Nevertheless, the logics of delegation, self-regulation, monitoring, and strategic positioning obviously play little role in these circumstances. Rather, the FTAA negotiations operated along a highly centralized track largely monopolized by regional governments acting through executive branch agencies.

Functionaries in finance and trade ministries charged with overseeing the FTAA negotiations are confident they possess the requisite professional knowledge and reject the need for outside expertise. In addition, and again in contrast to education and democracy, which were the centerpieces of the Santiago and Quebec summits, the most contentious FTAA issues have significant distributional consequences and major externalities for third parties, including other governments, firms, workers, peasants, women, indigenous groups, and others. Consequently, the FTAA track is shaped by a dominant logic of *exclusion.*

Faced by closed international FTAA negotiations, "outsider" activists opposed to state and corporate-led schemes of regional integration and globalization adopt strategies of "defensive transnationalization."[8] Accordingly, they sought to overcome their collective action problems by strengthening ties with organized labor and grassroots constituencies in their own countries and by forming coalitions with like-minded groups throughout the hemisphere. Depending on the specific context, their collective action repertoires range widely from protest and mobilization to lobbying their governments to exercise national sovereignty to protect domestic interests from the negative impacts of trade liberalization. These diverse actions all imply demands for policy and norm changes, frequently including proposals for greater transparency, popular consultations, and expanded regulatory schemes based on strengthened multilateral governance.

Also, in contrast with "insider" groups whose activities focus on information exchange, "outsider" actors have greater potential to give birth to broader transnational social movements, whose dominant form of collective action goes beyond information exchange to mount joint mobilization across national boundaries and attract activists committed to more comprehensive goals of challenging the prevailing social order. Their deployment of strategies of disruption and sustained mobilization require higher levels of collective identity and solidarity compared with networks and coalitions, as well as more sophisticated forms of governance and organization. These propositions have been largely confirmed by events since the first Miami summit.

A variety of groups supported a critical declaration registering strong dissent from the official Miami summit Plan of Action (see CCSOO 1995). Organized labor's position in the early years of summitry was similarly complicated. Some leaders in the American Federation of Labor–Congress of Industrial Organizations (AFL-CIO) and Organización Regional Interamericana de Trabajadores (ORIT) desired to avoid an open break with the Clinton administration and the more moderate "insiders," whereas others pushed for a more critical position. This was particularly evident in labor's demands for a more comprehensive inclusion of labor issues, including higher standards than NAFTA's on labor and environmental issues (AFL-CIO/ORIT 1995: 363).[9]

The trade ministerial meetings held in 1997 in Belo Horizonte, Brazil, and in early 1998 in San José, Costa Rica, were catalytic events triggering a notable advance in the formation of an "outsider" network. With the backing of the largest labor confederation in Latin America, the Brazilian Central Única dos Trabalhadores (CUT), and several large Brazilian multisectoral NGOs, progressive groups from throughout the hemisphere had much greater participation in Belo Horizonte than in Miami three years earlier. Highly critical of neoliberalism, social exclusion, and corporate-led globalization, these groups advocated an alternative model of economic integration that would be more democratic, participatory, egalitarian, and environmentally sustainable.[10]

The San José trade ministerial meeting represented a significant setback for the "insiders" and for governmental attempts to muster broader civil society support for the FTAA. Their exclusion from the meetings and the absence of opportunities for debate (Rosenberg 2000) were crucial in leading to the formal constitution of a new network, the Alianza Social Continental (ASC), which would soon become the most influential "outsider" movement operating throughout the hemisphere.[11]

The ASC emerged as a broad and heterogeneous mega-network, a "movement of movements." It currently comprises a stable core group of sixteen national multisectoral networked affiliates (composed of local and national NGO networks and grassroots groups) and ten regional sectoral networks. From the early 1990s, the three most active and well-organized national networks have been the US-based Alliance for Responsible Trade (ART), the Red Mexicana de Acción Frente al Libre Comercio (RMALC), and Common Frontiers (a multisectoral Canadian network). Although more recently formed, and initially weak institutionally, the strength of organized labor in Brazil—and the 2002 election of Lula's Workers' Party (Partido dos Trabalhadores, PT)—resulted in the rapid emergence of a fourth core member—the Rede Brasileira pela Integração dos Povos (REBRIP), which recently succeeded RMALC as the ASC's coordinating secretariat.[12]

The Santiago summit in 1998 represented a further critical transformation for the "outsiders." Held in conjunction with the official meetings, a so-called Peoples' Summit mobilized approximately 1,000 delegates, including union representatives, environmentalists, women's groups, human rights organizations, indigenous peoples, academics, and others. Their debates energized the formation of an oppositional identity and strategy on the part of groups gradually aligning themselves with the incipient ASC network. The Final Declaration proclaimed that civil society organizations and social movements in the Americas

> reject the anti-democratic character of agreements such as the FTAA. Organizations that represent distinct segments of civil society in our continents are excluded from the process. We do not accept that any more of these kinds of agreements, which have negative repercussions for the populations as a whole, be signed at the cost of our peoples. (ASC 1999e: 589–590)

Following the Santiago Peoples' Summit, the ASC released the first version of its "living document," *Alternatives for the Americas: Building a Peoples' Hemispheric Agreement* (ASC 1999b). This document set forth the basic programmatic platform of the still relatively new but increasingly well-organized "outsiders'" network:

> Civil society representatives want to be heard in this debate [on the FTAA] because the very essence of democratic self-determination is at stake. Governments must maintain the right to set rules for foreign investors, to settle investment disputes under national law and to control fly-by-night, speculative capital if economic integration is to be environmentally sound and beneficial to all the citizens of the Americas, especially historically marginalized groups including women, indigenous peoples and people of color. (ASC 1999b: 15)

Although Latin American activists sometimes harbored grievances that their US and Canadian counterparts took advantage of their greater access to governments and the media to advance their own sectoral or national interests and to tilt the ASC's positions in their own favor, these differences were secondary compared with their strong agreement on core issues. The closure of channels of access in the FTAA negotiations thus facilitated the acceleration of network activities and strengthened a common social movement identity among "outsider" groups. The constant updating of the Alianza's *Alternatives for the Americas* documents the consolidation of this identity and the deepening convergence between "northern" and "southern" perspectives, particularly regarding the democratic deficit characterizing summitry and trade negotiations.

The trade ministerial meeting held in late 1999 in Toronto, Canada, was another watershed. Initially, the Canadian government's apparent interest in developing an "alternative" foreign policy distinct from Washington's preferences, plus its provision of financial and logistical support to a parallel Civil Society Forum of the Americas, seemed likely to entice the "outsiders" to moderate contestation in favor of dialogue with their "insider" counterparts and more positively disposed government officials.[13] However, the trade ministers' complete disregard for the recommendations of the Civil Society Forum was the last straw. The ASC responded by escalating its opposition to the FTAA agenda and provoking a major rupture of relations with the "insider" civil society groups, which were denounced as government proxies.

This growing polarization went public at the mid-2000 meeting of the OAS in Windsor, Canada. Coming in the wake of the "Battle of Seattle" against the World Trade Organization and the protests against the International Monetary Fund (IMF) and the World Bank in Washington, D.C., the protests and overtones of violence at Windsor led even those diplomats and summiteers, like the Canadians, who had previously advocated greater participation (at least of the "insiders") to adopt an exasperated attitude toward what they labeled as the "intolerance" of "uncivil society" (Rosenberg 2000).

Despite this negative turn of events, the Canadian government attempted a rapprochement with civil society representatives at the so-called Democracy Summit in Quebec in 2001. A poisonous atmosphere was created, however, due to the deployment of a massive security operation by the Canadians (with the assistance of US agencies) to protect the summiteers. The ASC, spearheaded by its Canadian affiliates, Common Frontiers and the Réseau Québécois sur l'Intégration continentale, made street protests, marches, and teach-ins a major priority and warned activists "not to fall for the game of simulation" represented, in its view, by plans to attract civil society groups to the officially sponsored Peoples' Summit (Cueva 2001; ASC 2001).

Emphasis on mobilization did not entail abandoning policy debates. For example, the Alliance for Responsible Trade prepared a comprehensive document entitled "America's Plan for the Americas: A Critical Analysis of the US Negotiating Positions on the FTAA" (Anderson and Hansen-Kuhn 2001). The ASC also hammered home one of its central demands, namely the public "liberation" of the FTAA negotiating documents. As Héctor de la Cueva of RMALC, at the time the ASC's general secretary, put it, "Year after year, one after one, we give them our documents, our resolutions, our proposals . . . and up to now we have no answer to any of these documents." Numerous Canadian legislators and Latin American parliamentarians also decried the lack of transparency and participation and echoed this demand for access to the FTAA negotiating documents (*Globe and Mail* 2001).

Events during the summit were surrealistic. Dignitaries gave speeches that were broadcast on television, while in the lower part of the city, where the parallel Peoples' Summit took place, teach-ins, concerts, and crowds estimated at 30,000 peacefully marched in protest. In addition, more radical anarchist and revolutionary groups, referred to by some as the "Jurassic left," engaged in acts of provocative violence and threatened to breach the 3-meter-high, 4.5-kilometer-long security perimeter known as the "Wall of Shame."[14]

FTAA-related issues dominated the official agenda at Quebec. Moreover, while some "insiders" were partially placated by the endorsement of the "Democracy Clause" for the OAS, others were deeply disappointed that their social agenda had received so little official attention. But if the "insiders" felt ambivalent, there was no doubt about the reaction of the "outsiders" and organized labor, who were quite caustic in their condemnation of the Final Declaration, which they denounced as a project to create a "NAFTA clone" or a "NAFTA on steroids" for the hemisphere as a whole.

Consistent with the notion of "defensive transnationalization" (see Table 9.2), the US AFL-CIO strongly criticized President George W. Bush's equivocations on labor standards and the environment. Similarly, the Brussels-based International Confederation of Free Trade Unions (ICFTU) and ORIT issued a stinging condemnation of the Quebec summit's Final Declaration (see ICFTU-ORIT 2001).

The ASC supported labor's criticism. However, despite their rhetorical radicalism, the ASC's leaders were at pains to stress that they were not protectionists, anarchists, or idealistic "globophobes." Indeed, they stressed their own positive vision for regional integration, emphasizing that opposition to the neoliberal vision is widely shared across the hemisphere by citizens of various ideological persuasions. Acting on this premise, these groups redoubled efforts to organize broad grassroots constituencies for mass mobilizations throughout the Americas in opposition to the FTAA. Their watchword, of course, was "¡No al ALCA! ¡Otras Américas son posibles!" (No to the FTAA! Other Americas are possible!).

The most significant of the "outsider" mobilizations against the FTAA in the post-Quebec period occurred in Miami in November 2003. Coming on the heels of the failure of the World Trade Organization meeting held in Cancun, Mexico, the objective of the Miami ministerial meeting was to wrap up loose ends and prepare for the FTAA's formal implementation in January 2005. Instead, the negotiators failed to commit to a "single undertaking," which was rejected in favor of an "FTAA-lite"—a watered-down compromise involving a national opt-out provision on crucial rules favored by the United States. The "outsiders" arguably played a role in this outcome. The ASC and the other *movimentista* actors, bolstered by the strong presence of organized labor unions such as the AFL-CIO, were able to exert greater pressure for accountability than at past trade meetings.

To a considerable extent, this greater influence was made possible by a major shift in political opportunity structures in Brazilian domestic politics following the January 2003 inauguration of Lula's PT-led government, which had played a major role in organizing the first of several meetings of the World Social Forum, staged in Porto Alegre in southern Brazil. In fact, the long-standing linkages among the PT, the Brazilian organized labor movement, and global social justice networks significantly strengthened the political capacity of the "outsiders" in two ways. First, these ties made it easier for the "upward capacity of protest networks to introduce social movement values and positions into the strategic thinking and choices of policymakers," such as the Brazilian FTAA negotiating team. Second, these same linkages contributed to the "downward capacity of such policymakers to induce more radical protest networks to accept pragmatic political compromises such as weakening and delaying the FTAA rather than killing it" (Bennet 2005: 211). The augmented capacity of the "outsiders" to influence the regional agenda thus contributed to the deepening paralysis of the FTAA negotiations and made it more difficult to bridge the fundamental differences separating the US and Brazilian governments.

The regional stalemate was strikingly evident in the 2005 summit in Mar del Plata, Argentina. Returning to the lower-left quadrant of Table 9.2, it is clear that this outcome was largely predictable. In contrast with the "global public goods" agendas at previous encounters, the Mar del Plata summit's official theme, "Creating Jobs to Fight Poverty and Strengthen Democratic Governance," was guaranteed to generate controversy. Proposals linking "decent employment" and democracy catalyzed and brought to the fore the growing criticism among many governments—which was widely reflected in public opinion throughout the region—of some of the fundamental assumptions of the Washington consensus.

The trends in civil society participation discussed previously in relation to the "outsiders" were amply confirmed at Mar del Plata. The anti-FTAA posture of the "outsiders" represented by the Alianza Social Continental and similar groups dovetailed with the criticism of Washington's hegemony and promotion of "market fundamentalism" expressed by some governmental leaders, such as Argentina's Néstor Kirchner, but most notably by the polemical Hugo Chávez. Compared with previous summits, this partial convergence meant that the strategy of mass mobilization and oppositional discourse typical of "outsiders" now found greater resonance among more conventional political forces, including trade unions, human rights organizations, political parties of the left, and others. This, in turn, gave greater social legitimacy to government leaders challenging the FTAA and the Washington consensus. Although this political and discursive shift can be portrayed as a success by the "outsiders," it remains to be seen whether the latter might not have won a pyrrhic victory. By distancing themselves from more moderate center-left leaders such as Lula and the Brazilian PT or Ricardo Lagos and Michelle Bachelet of the Chilean Socialist Party, the "outsider" social movements may risk losing their autonomy to populist political leaders such as Venezuela's Hugo Chávez.

The Present Conjuncture: A Surprising Convergence?

The events of September 11, 2001, and Washington's launching of its "global struggle against violent extremism" had a profound impact on civil society mobilization. Indeed, at least in the short term, shifts in prevailing institutional arrangements increased the perceived relative costs of contestation, which had a temporary dampening effect on some of the more radical challenges by the "outsiders" to the summitry process and the FTAA negotiations. Moreover, the post-2001 period witnessed a change in posture on the part of the US government regarding civil society participation. Rather than broadly supporting the active participation of all "insiders," the Bush administration has sought to promote only those civil society groups identified with pro-US "democratic globalism."[15]

Returning to the patterns of civil society mobilization explored in Table 9.2, numerous sectors expressed an initial concern that citizens in the United States might trade off civil and political liberties for promises of "security." Similarly, it was initially thought that US unilateralism might result in strongly constrained international opportunity structures in the Americas, thus signaling a move from the right to the left side of Table 9.2. In these circumstances, had domestic opportunity structures in the south of the continent followed suit toward greater closure and exclusion, then a shift from the lower to the upper half of Table 9.2 also could have taken place. Had this double shift in fact actually occurred and become permanent, the possibilities for both domestic and transnational activism would have receded, if not disappeared. In such a scenario, bolstered by a strengthened security rationale, a reinvigorated free trade agenda might have prevailed, perhaps even leading to the scheduled 2005 implementation of the FTAA.

This scenario did not come to pass. Rather, strong tendencies toward closure and exclusion emanating from the United States collided with other national projects and social forces elsewhere in the Americas. Politics in several key countries of the region, particularly in South America, have moved toward significantly more open national opportunity structures. A number of elements have been at work in generating this domestic opening, ranging from a growing resistance by Latin American public opinion to the US war in Iraq to a widely shared perception by both elites and masses regarding the failure of Washington consensus policies to reverse worsening poverty and deepening social inequalities. There also has been a growing realization that, in addition to the need for economic policies more supportive of growth with equity, the "shallow" electoral democracies in the region have failed to address deepening social crises or to respond adequately to pervasive cynicism on the part of broad sectors of the public on issues of ethics, corruption, and demands for efficient government.

In this context, the elections of Ricardo Lagos in Chile, Lula da Silva in Brazil, Néstor Kirchner in Argentina, and, more recently, Tabaré Vásquez in Uruguay and Michelle Bachelet in Chile herald the transition of "modern" left parties from opposition to power. These pragmatic, center-left governments have generally been both more critical of the hegemon's foreign and security policies and simultaneously reluctant to accept the perceived negative effects of the US preferred version of economic integration via the FTAA. In response to corruption, crises of political representation, and a desire to strengthen their own legitimacy, the leaders of these center-left governments frequently have shown more willingness than their neoliberal predecessors to work with "insiders'" groups in civil society. Moreover, these governments have also demonstrated a greater opening and desire to engage "outsider" organizations and networks as key political constituencies in support of their own projects of social and economic reform.

Representing a strand of left politics quite distinct from the governments headed by Lagos, Lula, Kirchner, Vázquez, or Bachelet, the emergence of powerful indigenous social and political movements in Bolivia and Ecuador—and the larger crisis of governability in the Andes—present a different set of political opportunities for radical groups and their international allies. In this regard, the proclamation by President Hugo Chávez of Venezuela of his own anti-imperialist Bolivarian Alternative for the Americas as a rival to the neoliberalism represented by the FTAA, plus the Venezuelan president's strategic use of Venezuela's petroleum wealth, certainly exacerbates geopolitical tensions and uncertainties and thus opens possible new political opportunities for antisystemic movements in the region.

The result of these changing constellations of domestic and international opportunities and attendant patterns of civil society mobilization has been a partial shift affecting both the summit agenda and the FTAA track. Might this shift eventually lead to the "utopian" scenario depicted in the lower-right quadrant of Table 9.2? In such a scenario, the more open domestic structures created by both "modern" and more "populist" govern-ment and political movements would motivate "insiders" to push for more rapid and far-reaching changes in national politics and policies. Capitaliz-ing on their previous successes in forging transborder networks and coali-tions, "insiders" could be expected to continue to deploy "boomerang" and "spiral" tactics when necessary to complement and reinforce their primary focus on domestic politics. If successful, this combination could lead to more rapid and extensive institutionalization of democratic norms of rep-resentation and participation, at least regarding issues such as human rights, gender equity, indigenous rights, and the less conflictive aspects of pro-environmental issues.[16]

But regardless of future developments, what changes in strategies can we expect from the "outsiders" in the current new conjuncture? Given elec-toral contingencies and continuing economic vulnerability, it would be fool-hardy to adventure firm predictions regarding the future relations between Kirchner and the *piqueteros,* for example, or between Lula's PT govern-ment and the Landless Workers Movement (MST), or the prospects that Chávez might one day organize a more coherent party structure in support of his project of "socialism for the twenty-first century." Despite these ob-vious uncertainties, however, we believe the tentative convergence between the "outsiders" and official Brazilian FTAA negotiators evidenced at the Miami 2003 ministerial meeting, for example, provides a glimpse of a pos-sible trajectory in which some "outsiders" moderate their traditional strat-egy of popular mobilization toward more "conventional" forms of lobbying government agencies and carrying their message to public opinion in ways less reliant on confrontation.

Were this reorientation to occur, strategies of popular mobilization would not necessarily be abandoned. On the contrary, continuing mobilizations prove essential to advancing beyond "defensive transnationalization" (e.g., urging governments to protect citizens against the undesirable aspects of NAFTA, the FTAA, or the WTO) to articulate a more assertive and forward-looking alter-native vision of regional integration and globalization actively promoting equity and social inclusion. Combining contestation and mobilization with a willingness to work "within the system" via elections, political parties, and judicial institutions cannot be discounted. Nevertheless, in this case, the "out-siders" might undergo some fragmentation as some choose to follow a more "insider" track while others remain in a more contestatory posture.

Conclusion

Whether new political developments signified by the emergence of both "modern" and "populist" leftist governments and movements are harbingers

of the optimistic scenario characterized by broadening opportunity structures at both the domestic and international level will be highly contingent
on innumerable factors, including, of course, the vicissitudes of international politics and economics. Within Latin America, the evolution of current political trends inaugurated by center-left reform governments will
hinge largely on the perceived success of their policies. The yardstick used
to measure this success will no doubt vary considerably from country to
country. The ability to generate both more rapid economic growth and
improvements in social welfare certainly will be crucial, but progress toward
greater transparency and less corruption, the expansion of human rights, and
improvements in public safety will also be fundamental for the social and
electoral consolidation of modern leftist government. Success on these
measures could facilitate a reversal of the polarization of the 1990s and create the possibilities for new forms of convergence and cooperation between
"insiders" and "outsiders," strengthening the influence of a broader and
more united social justice movement.

By the same token, significant failures in achieving these goals might
exacerbate the polarization between "insiders" and "outsiders" and deepen
the backlash against political parties in the region, thus contributing to a
deepening crisis of representation and a further deterioration of democratic
practices and institutions. But a return to the neoliberal regimes of the
1990s is improbable. Rather, the failure of reformist governments of the
"modern" type could open the way for radical political forces and social
movements committed to more "revolutionary" strategies to transform
feckless electoral regimes and confront the pathologies of globalization. In
short, the current shift to the left in Latin American politics is likely to continue, although the current gradual pace of change could give way to a more
radical rupture, perhaps entailing (particularly in the Andes) the possibility
of considerable instability and repetitions of the "street coups" and the
ousters of presidents in Bolivia and in Ecuador.

In any probable scenario, however, rival political and economic projects of regional integration—regardless of their particular combination of
self-regulating globalized markets and supranational regulation through
political institutions—will have no choice but to contend with "insider" and
"outsider" advocacy networks and social movements representing the emergence in the Americas of new, sui generis transnational social and political
actors and identities.

Notes

Our research on transnational networks has been made possible by a grant from the
Ford Foundation for a project on mapping regional civil society networks in Latin

America. We also participated in another Ford-sponsored project conducted under the auspices of FLACSO-Argentina's Research Program on International Economic Institutions. Our publications related to these projects include Korzeniewicz and Smith 2000a, 2000b, 2003a, 2003b, 2003c, 2004, and 2005.

1. See Smith and Korzeniewicz (1997).

2. According to Marisol Pagés, "The 'insiders' are those that attempt to work closely with the official process, sometimes compromising their demands so as to make them more politically viable. The 'outsiders' are those that exercise external pressure, articulating their demands in a more explicit manner and often against governmental positions. Opening the process of the FTAA negotiations undoubtedly will require continuing both kinds of efforts—the 'outsiders' pressure and force openings or tendencies toward greater openness in the system, while the 'insiders' take advantage of these small opportunities—to push issues toward greater substance" (Pagés 2000: 172).

3. The opposite is also possible—weaker governments may be motivated to facilitate the formation and activities of transnational networks for the purpose of mobilizing public support in contentious negotiations with the United States or with multilateral financial institutions.

4. In drawing these distinctions among networks, coalitions, and movements, we follow Khagram, Riker, and Sikkink (2002).

5. These organizations (along with others space does not allow us to analyze) worked in close coordination with the officials in charge of the summit process, including the "Troika," composed of the Civil Society Task Force, the Summit Follow-up Office of the OAS, and the Summit Implementation Review Group (SIRG).

6. As some of the civil society people noted, the "government representatives in the FTAA process would *tomarnos el pelo* (take us as fools)," and the invitation to participate was "at best a *buzón* (a mailbox) and at worst a *lata de basura* (a trashcan)." See Pagés 2001, personal communication.

7. Perhaps the fairest postmortem was offered by Dean Foster (2005: 6), who observed that "beyond a flashy title and irrelevant comparisons to the European Union," the Mar del Plata impasse offered "little actual trade and liberalization to get excited about at the moment—for either free trade advocates or its opponents."

8. Sikkink astutely observes, "These activists have not sought out international organizations but rather have been forced to work internationally, because their governments have made international agreements that move significant decision-making power into international institutions. Because such activists operate in domestic opportunity structures that they perceive as open relative to international institutions, they organize transnationally to minimize losses rather than to seek gains" (Sikkink 2005: 163–164).

9. The political clout of the AFL-CIO in US domestic politics and ORIT's claim to represent over 40 million members bolstered labor's claims of broad-based grassroots opposition to free trade accords. It also strengthened the union movement's criticism of the legitimacy of many of the "insider" groups.

10. The pro-business character of the official ministerial negotiations deepened the cleavages separating the more mainstream "insider" organizations from the labor and grassroots progressive groups when the former decided to participate directly in the workshops and other events organized by business groups (see ASC 1999a).

11. The ASC's stated objectives included the following: (1) strengthening civil society within and between countries in the Americas; (2) being recognized as the legitimate interlocutor representing a dynamic movement; (3) implementing agreed-upon common strategies while, at the same time, respecting diversity; (4) supporting

and strengthening the efforts of the different sectors at the local, national, and regional levels; (5) promoting the enforcement of the basic standards approved by the International Labor Organization (ILO); and (6) campaigning on behalf of demands for the enforcement of all rights already recognized in the many international instruments, covenants, and declarations already signed (ASC 1999a).

12. For a complete list of affiliated groups (many themselves composed of national networks and belonging to a variety of regional and global networks), see http:www.asc-hsa.org.

13. The ASC's ability to play some aspects of an "insider" game based upon policy advocacy was evident in Toronto with the presentation of two programmatic documents for the consideration of public opinion as well as hemispheric governments: *Social Exclusion, Labor, and Poverty in the Americas* (ASC 1999c) and *Social Investment, Finances, and Debt in the Americas* (ASC 1999d).

14. The radicals included the Black Bloc affinity group, the CLAC (whose initials in French stand for Anti-Capitalist Convergence), and other direct-action groups waving red, black, and Cuban flags while confronting police, who were deployed in armored cars and used water cannons and tear gas.

15. See Barry (2005) for a brief analysis of US government initiatives to promote civil society groups favoring Washington's vision of "democratic globalism."

16. Sikkink (2005: 171) correctly observes that the "boomerang was never an optimum form of political activism. It was a particular set of tactics derived in less than desirable political circumstances: when activists faced repression or blockage in their home country. At least in many parts of Latin America, redemocratization has reopened previously closed domestic politics, and activists have understandably redirected their energies into the closer and more responsive process of domestic politics. This is a positive political development." For a similar analysis, see Korzeniewicz and Smith (2003c).

PART 4

Trade and Economic Development

10

Trade Institutions: An Intricate Web of Arrangements

Maryse Robert

Today, more than a decade after the First Summit of the Americas, which launched the Free Trade Area of the Americas (FTAA) process in 1994, increasing trade among countries of the hemisphere remains a top priority. For Latin America and the Caribbean, trade agreements, particularly with larger developed countries, create opportunities to expand markets, attract investment, and stimulate job creation. In the mid-1980s and early 1990s, these countries embraced reforms aimed at dismantling protectionist measures in their own markets and at promoting a more open and dynamic pattern of integration into the world economy. They began to liberalize their trade and investment regimes and negotiated numerous trade agreements, some of which go beyond the elimination of tariffs and nontariff barriers, whereas others are limited to trade in goods. They also entered into deeper forms of integration at the subregional level, which explains why the hemispheric trade regime is made up of a number of overlapping bilateral and subregional trade agreements.

In contrast with the optimism of the early 1990s characterized by the return to democracy in the region and the implementation of economic and political reforms, and despite the great strides and progress achieved, the first decade of the new millennium brought new anxieties and concerns. There is a growing perception among citizens in Latin America and the Caribbean that economic reforms, and trade agreements in particular, have not entirely fulfilled the promise of delivering the benefits of democracy, namely reducing poverty, unemployment, and inequality. Although these economies have experienced an upsurge in economic activity during the current decade, due in large part to high commodity prices and a robust demand from the United States and China, massive inequalities still exist and poverty rates are excessively high at 40 percent.

Countries of the region are increasingly aware that signing trade agreements and having access to markets, while necessary, are not sufficient. They know that they need to implement a "complementary" policy agenda to help their economic agents become more competitive and reap the benefits of these trade agreements. In recognition of this fact, several newly negotiated trade agreements, starting with the multilateral trade agreement among the Central American countries, the Dominican Republic, and the United States (CAFTA-DR), include a formal mechanism aimed at addressing trade-related capacity-building needs during the negotiating and implementing phases of the agreement, as well as during the transition to free trade, with the objective of improving these countries and their firms' competitiveness.

After assessing the early efforts to negotiate trade agreements in the Americas, I discuss the revitalization of subregional trade institutions in the 1990s, the motivations behind regional trade agreements, and the developments since 1990 on the hemispheric trade front, from the Enterprise for the Americas Initiative (EAI) to the FTAA project and the newly signed free trade agreements (FTAs) that have proliferated in recent years, in part as an alternative to the FTAA. I then reflect on the difficulties that overlapping agreements may pose, particularly with respect to rules of origin, dispute settlement, or incorporating by reference provisions from another agreement. Finally, I highlight potential options that might help reduce the distortions created by these overlapping trade agreements and increase the transparency related to these instruments.

Early Efforts to Negotiate Trade: In Search of Institutions

Two visions have been at play in inter-American trade relations since the nineteenth century (Hurrell 1995). One calls for the negotiation of a hemisphere-wide agreement, whereas the other favors agreements at the subregional level. When Simón Bolívar, the leader of the Latin American wars of independence, organized the Congress of Panama in 1826, his aim was to foster closer hemispheric cooperation through the creation of a union of Spanish-speaking Latin American republics, with a common military, a mutual defense pact, and a supranational parliamentary assembly. Bolívar's dream never came to fruition, however, as civil wars imploded in those countries.

The United States was the first to propose a specific plan for a hemisphere-wide trade agreement. In 1889 US Secretary of State James G. Blaine convened the First International Conference of American States and called for the expansion of commercial cooperation between Latin American countries and the United States. Blaine had two main objectives: the establishment of a customs union among countries of the Americas and the adoption of a mechanism for the peaceful settlement of disputes (Mace 1999). The Americans were in search of trade institutions, a set of rules by which countries in the hemisphere would interact on the trade front. The

Chilean Francisco Bilbao had also suggested, a few decades earlier, the elimination of duties among countries of the hemisphere, as well as a federal union and a common citizenship, whereas Henry Clay, the speaker of the US House of Representatives in the early 1820s, had championed closer relations with Latin American countries.

By the end of the nineteenth century, an increasing number of countries in Latin America were embracing the view that free trade was a necessary step to promote economic growth and development. But efforts to negotiate a trade agreement did not succeed because several Latin American states were reluctant to open up their market to the United States only, for fear of losing access to the European markets. The United States also lacked enthusiasm for free trade, as illustrated by the McKinley Tariff Act of 1890, under which Congress raised duties on numerous imports to substantially higher levels.

The collapse of the commodity and capital markets in the early 1930s marked another turning point. Latin America abandoned economic liberalism altogether and sought to reduce its dependence on exports of primary products and imports of manufactures. A new model based on import substitution, and formalized in the 1950s by Raúl Prebisch of the United Nations Economic Commission for Latin America (now known as the Economic Commission for Latin America and the Caribbean, or ECLAC), slowly emerged. Tariffs and nontariff barriers sheltered domestic products from foreign competition and were accompanied, in some cases, by the nationalization of multinational companies, exchange rate and capital controls, and a populist fiscal policy.

In the United States, the Great Depression of the 1930s led to a very different outcome. In 1934, Congress enacted Secretary of State Cordell Hull's Reciprocal Trade Agreements Program, aimed at expanding US exports abroad and at strengthening the foundations of world peace by improving trade relations with key countries. The United States espoused the "free trade idea" and ensured that it would be a pillar of the postwar institutions. Multilateralism and most-favored-nation (MFN) treatment became the core elements of the American approach to trade policy.[1]

On the hemispheric front, participating countries at the Ninth International Conference of American States, held in Bogotá in 1948, signed the charter creating the Organization of American States (OAS) and the American Declaration of the Rights and Duties of Man, the first international expression of human rights principles. Two trade-related treaties addressing the same key issues discussed in 1889–1890 suffered a different fate. The American Treaty on Pacific Settlement, known as the Pact of Bogotá, covering the peaceful settlement of disputes, and the Economic Agreement of Bogotá, which was meant as an impetus for the negotiation of a free trade area and also included rules on investment, were ratified by very few countries.[2]

The 1960s and 1970s were marked by the negotiation of preferential trade arrangements aimed at fostering domestic industrialization. Members of these trade schemes pledged to create customs unions, coordinate their policies in areas such as transport and communications, and establish a common market as their ultimate goal. The Central American Common Market (CACM, 1960),[3] the Andean Pact (1969; known since 1997 as the Andean Community), and the Caribbean Community (CARICOM, 1973)[4] were established with those objectives in mind. The MFN principle was rejected as an inadequate instrument to level the playing field between developed and developing countries. With the exception of the CACM, which was largely successful in its early years, the integration movement failed to cover more than a few sectors. In fact, the industrialization and liberalization programs experienced a number of setbacks. Low levels of intraregional trade, tension between governments and private-sector coalitions opposed to any form of trade liberalization, and disputes on the distribution of the costs and benefits of the preferential trade schemes led to very poor results. At the Latin American level, in 1960 Mexico and six South American countries established the Latin American Free Trade Association (LAFTA), which sought to eliminate the barriers to trade among its members by 1972. LAFTA did succeed in increasing its membership, as eleven countries had joined its ranks by 1967, but its liberalizing exercise never amounted to more than bilateral tariff-cutting negotiations in mostly unimportant sectors.[5]

The 1990s: A New Beginning for Subregional Trade Institutions

In the mid-1980s and early 1990s, following the severe effects of the debt crisis, Latin American and Caribbean countries embarked on a series of ambitious economic reforms. They began to dismantle protectionist measures in their own markets and embraced market-focused and outward-oriented policies. To gain credibility and to benefit from the signaling effects that modern trade agreements generate, these countries also revitalized their "old" trade institutions, eliminating tariffs among themselves, agreeing on a common external tariff, and adding, in some cases, provisions on services, intellectual property, and investment. Although integration gained strength in the 1990s, by the new millennium several subregional trade arrangements were experiencing a few setbacks in their long journey toward deeper integration.[6]

Central America

With the return of democracy and the end of political tensions, Central America made a significant shift toward economic openness in the early

1990s. A presidential summit convened in Antigua, Guatemala, in June 1990 led to the adoption of a plan to reactivate economic integration. The new Central American Integration System (SICA) set up a legal and institutional structure for regional integration through the Tegucigalpa Protocol, which was signed in 1991 and later ratified by the congresses of all five countries (Costa Rica, El Salvador, Guatemala, Honduras, and Nicaragua) and Panama (a CACM observer). In 1993, these six countries signed the Guatemala Protocol, which amended the 1960 General Treaty on Central American Economic Integration, with a view to reviving economic integration. Agreements on rules of origin, unfair business practices, safeguards, standardization measures, metrology and authorization procedures, and sanitary and phytosanitary measures were adopted in the 1990s, whereas the agreement on dispute settlement entered into force in 2003 and was amended in 2006.

In 2000, El Salvador and Guatemala ratified the Acuerdo de Guatemala, signed in 1992, to establish a customs union. Honduras and Nicaragua expressed interest in joining the union. Two years later, in 2002, in a meeting held in Managua, the presidents of the five Central American countries amended the Guatemala Protocol to design an action plan to implement the customs union. By 2005, El Salvador, Guatemala, Honduras, and Nicaragua (known as CA-4) had already simplified their procedures to facilitate the cross-border movement of merchandise, which means that merchandise en route from Nicaragua to Guatemala, passing through Honduras and El Salvador, will only be registered in Guatemala.

Andean Community

The 1990s also marked a new beginning for Andean trade institutions, with the establishment in 1993 of a free trade area comprising Bolivia, Colombia, Ecuador, and Venezuela. Peru negotiated an agreement with these four countries for its gradual incorporation into the Andean Free Trade Area in 2006. In fact, at their presidential summit held in the Galapagos Islands in December 1989, the Andean nations set aside the import-substitution model that had dominated their development strategy and hindered their integration and agreed to establish a free trade area by 1993 and a customs union by 1997.

Efforts to implement a common external tariff (CET), which had failed in the 1970s, led to an agreement by February 1995, when the Andean Customs Union took effect. The CET was approved by Colombia, Ecuador, and Venezuela at the basic levels of 5, 10, 15, and 20 percent and entered into force. Bolivia enjoyed preferential treatment and only applied levels of 5 and 10 percent, whereas Peru did not sign the agreement.

The decision to deepen the customs union was taken by all five members in the 2002 Declaration of Santa Cruz de la Sierra. In October of the same year, the Andean Community members agreed to a new CET, the application of which has now been postponed several times. The ultimate goal of the Andean Community members, as approved in May 1999 at the eleventh Andean Presidential Council, was to establish, by the end of 2005, the Andean Single Market, a common market providing for the free movement of capital and persons, in addition to the free circulation of goods and services.

The attempt to create a single market by 2005 failed. The Andean Community had, however, succeeded in making significant progress with the establishment of a framework for the progressive liberalization of trade in services, the harmonization of national regulatory regimes in sectors such as telecom and tourism, and greater integration in energy and transport. Countries had negotiated an open skies agreement and agreed on a regime covering issues such as intellectual property, investment (albeit in a limited fashion), competition policy, rules of origin, technical barriers to trade, sanitary and phytosanitary measures, and disputes among members through the Quito-based Court of Justice.

Andean members began to grow apart in the new millennium, and the year 2006 confirmed this new trend. On April 22, Venezuela (which had joined in 1973) formally notified the Andean Community Secretariat of its decision to withdraw from the group. President Hugo Chávez denounced the free trade agreement the United States had signed with Peru on April 12 and the agreement being finalized with Colombia (later signed on November 22). In September 2006, Chile, which had left the bloc in 1976, announced its return as an associate member.

CARICOM

New impetus was injected into the CARICOM integration process when Caribbean leaders met in Grenada in 1989.[7] Having to compete with larger and more developed markets and recognizing the need for a unified Caribbean community, they agreed to move toward a deeper level of economic integration, the Caribbean Single Market and Economy (CSME). This new initiative revolves around the free movement of goods, services, capital, and skilled labor; the freedom of CARICOM nationals to establish enterprises anywhere in the community; the completion of the application of the common external tariff; more comprehensive harmonization of laws affecting commerce and regulation of economic activities; the reform of the institutions of the community; and more intensive coordination of macroeconomic policy and planning, external trade, and economic relations. Preparations for the CSME included the negotiation of nine protocols amending the Treaty of Chaguaramas, which had established the Caribbean Community in 1973. Protocol 1, providing for the restructuring of the organs and institutions of the community and redefining their functional relationship, entered into force provisionally on July 4, 1997. On July 5, 2001, at their meeting in the Bahamas, CARICOM leaders signed the Revised Treaty of Chaguaramas, and by 2002, most states had ratified the treaty, giving it full force in their respective countries. The CSME has also led to the establishment of the Caribbean Court of Justice (CCJ), which has replaced the London-based Privy Council as the region's final court of appeal. It is charged with the interpretation and application of the revised treaty, and it exercises exclusive jurisdiction with respect to dispute settlement, mediation, conciliation, and arbitration.

The first phase of the CSME took effect on January 1, 2006, and was formalized at the launch of the Caribbean Single Market (CSM) on January 30, 2006, in Kingston, Jamaica. The CSM removes barriers to trade in goods, services, and several labor categories. The second phase of the process is the implementation of the CARICOM single economy by the end of 2008.

The Commonwealth of the Bahamas joined the Caribbean Community, though not the Common Market, in 1983, and announced in July 2005 that it would not become a member of the CSME. Members of the Organization of Eastern Caribbean States (OECS),[8] which have achieved a significant level of integration among themselves, as reflected by their common monetary policy and common currency, have been particularly vocal in highlighting their difficulties in implementing the CSME and in promoting the Regional Development Fund, a mechanism proposed in the revised treaty to assist disadvantaged countries, regions, and sectors in competing effectively in the CSME.

Like the Andean Community, CARICOM members have prepared a list of measures restricting trade in services, which will be progressively eliminated. Moreover, although the ultimate goal of CARICOM countries is free movement for all, the implementation is proceeding in a phased approach. The categories of persons allowed free movement for work purposes now include university graduates, artists, athletes, musicians, and media workers. As is the case in Central America and the Andean Community, CARICOM member states have introduced a new passport using the common CARICOM format.

Mercosur

The return to democracy in Argentina and Brazil in the mid-1980s and the structural reforms that followed the debt crisis of the mid-1980s led to the establishment of Mercosur in March 1991, when Argentina, Brazil, Paraguay, and Uruguay signed the Treaty of Asunción. Their objective was to create a common market and ensure the free circulation of goods, services, capital, and labor among member countries through the elimination of tariffs and nontariff barriers, the adoption of a common external tariff and a common trade policy, the coordination of macroeconomic and sectoral policies, and the harmonization of the members' legislation in relevant areas. Chile, which had at the time an external tariff of 11 percent, lower than the CET set by Mercosur members, did not sign the treaty but became an associate member of Mercosur in 1996 after signing a trade agreement with the group under the framework of the Latin American Integration Association (LAIA), the successor organization to LAFTA.[9] Bolivia followed in 1997. The other members of the Andean Community have also become associate members of Mercosur after concluding a partial-scope agreement under LAIA.[10] Also in 2005, the four Mercosur members became associate members of the Andean Community. In 2006, Venezuela joined Mercosur as a full member after leaving the Andean Community.

Mercosur made considerable progress in its early years. On January 1, 1995, intra-Mercosur trade benefiting from duty-free rates accounted for some 85 percent of trade. In addition, because the automotive sector and products originating in free zones, two sectors along with sugar not covered by the free trade area, already receive preferences in the context of LAIA's bilateral agreements signed by Mercosur members, it is estimated that 95 percent of intra-Mercosur trade is duty-free. But as is the case in other subregional agreements in the Americas, the implementation of the CET proved to be challenging. A number of country- and sector-specific exceptions (capital, informatics, and telecommunication goods, as well as the automotive and sugar sectors) remained. Moreover, the CET ceiling increased by three percentage points to 23 percent in November 1997. The temporary increase was then lowered to 2.5 percent in 2001, 1.5 percent in 2002, and eliminated at the end of December 2003. The CET was scheduled to be fully implemented by 2001 in Argentina and Brazil and by 2006 in Paraguay and Uruguay. In 2003, however, under Mercosur Decision Nos. 31/03 and 34/03, Uruguay and Paraguay were given an extension until 2010.

In addition to market access for goods and related issues, Mercosur agreements cover issues such as dispute settlement, environment, competition policy, services, investment, and government procurement. Mercosur has two dispute settlement mechanisms. The 1995 Protocol of Ouro Preto, which established the organizational structure of Mercosur, provides for a longer procedure, whereas the Protocol of Olivos, which entered into force on January 1, 2004, is automatic and of an expedited nature. It includes a choice of forum (Mercosur or WTO), recourse to mediation, and the establishment of a Permanent Review Court of five arbitrators, which sits in Asunción. Moreover, the Mercosur Framework Agreement on the Environment, which came into effect in all four countries on June 27, 2004, provides for the application of Mercosur dispute settlement procedures in case of disputes under that agreement. The 1997 Protocol of Montevideo, which aims to liberalize trade in services over a ten-year period, came into force on December 7, 2005.

Mercosur is still facing numerous challenges with respect to implementing intra-Mercosur negotiated agreements. At the Twenty-Eighth Mercosur Summit, held in Asunción in June 2005, President Luiz Inácio Lula da Silva (Lula) of Brazil acknowledged that Mercosur "failed to put into practice decisions it has reached and agreements it has signed" (*Latin News Daily* 2005). At the time of his declaration, the 1996 Mercosur Competition Protocol had been ratified by only two countries, that is, Brazil and Paraguay. Moreover, the 1994 rules on investment from member countries (Protocol of Colonia) and nonmember countries (Protocol of Buenos Aires) had not entered into force, and the 2003 Protocol on Government Procurement was also awaiting ratification by member countries.

As a way to foster trade among member countries, in 2005 Mercosur members created a US$100 million structural convergence fund aimed at developing infrastructure, fighting poverty, and promoting competitiveness. Brazil's contribution accounts for 70 percent of funds to the scheme, Argentina's 27 percent, Uruguay's 2 percent, and Paraguay's 1 percent. Paraguay is slated to receive 48 percent of the funds, Uruguay 32 percent, and Argentina and Brazil 10 percent each to pay for development projects in needy areas. Mercosur members also agreed on the establishment of a parliament where Brazil would have thirty-six seats and Argentina thirty-one, whereas Paraguay and Uruguay would receive sixteen each.

In addition, Mercosur countries have agreed to create a temporary "Mercosur visa" in order to facilitate the entry and stay of natural persons, and a framework agreement has been drawn up to facilitate the mutual recognition of professional licenses.

The Motivations Behind Regional Trade Agreements

Preferential liberalization has been flourishing in the Americas, as illustrated by the revitalization of the "old-type" subregional trade arrangements in the early 1990s and the numerous free trade agreements negotiated between countries of the region since then. The new regionalism represents a break with history. Instead of sector-specific tariff concessions, most recent trade agreements signed by Latin American countries include a universal, automatic, and across-the-board elimination of tariff barriers (da Motta Veiga 2004), as well as new disciplines. In fact, these agreements respond to a new economic logic, which is investment-driven (Lawrence 1997; Ethier 1998). This is particularly true for smaller economies, for whom the signaling effects of a free trade agreement (especially with a developed country) not only lock in domestic reforms but also help them attract investment, serve as an export platform for goods and services to larger markets, and, in so doing, contribute to fostering growth and development (Salazar-Xirinachs 2004). This explains why free trade agreements that have entered into force since the mid-1990s contain disciplines calling for deeper integration in "new" areas such as trade in services, investment, and intellectual property.

But the motivation of most countries in signing trade agreements goes beyond economic factors. For the United States, a number of geostrategic objectives were front and center in negotiating CAFTA-DR, including strengthening efforts to control drug traffic, reducing immigration, and promoting political stability and democracy in the region (Salazar-Xirinachs and Granados 2004: 230). Political and strategic objectives were also among the core objectives that led to the establishment of most subregional groupings in the Americas. For example, fostering better relations between Argentina and Brazil played a significant role in the creation of Mercosur, whereas deepening ties—beyond trade—among Caribbean countries was one of the key factors leading to the establishment of CARICOM. The efforts to unite the economies of the Western Hemisphere into a single free trade agreement, the Free Trade Area of the Americas, were also from the outset part of a broader agenda.

From the Enterprise of the Americas Initiative to the FTAA Project

At the end of the 1980s, securing their market access to the United States and, most importantly, attracting foreign investment were the driving force behind the quest of Latin American countries for a closer relationship with the United States. A mini-summit on the control of illicit drug trafficking, held in Cartagena in February 1990 with the presidents of Colombia, Bolivia, and Peru, helped convince the administration of President George H. W. Bush that market-friendly reforms were being implemented in the region and that a post–Cold War policy was greatly needed to support those efforts. The response of the US government came in the form of the Enterprise for the Americas Initiative, announced by President Bush on June 27, 1990. Trade was the most ambitious of the EAI's three pillars since its ultimate goal was the establishment of a hemisphere-wide agreement. The new US initiative also envisaged the creation of a multilateral fund within the Inter-American Development Bank (IDB) to foster investment. Easing the debt burden through bilateral debt relief to increase incentives for reform was the third EAI pillar. Although the EAI took a backseat to the negotiation of the North American Free Trade Agreement (NAFTA), the new administration of Bill Clinton, which took office in 1993, supported the negotiation of a hemisphere-wide trade agreement and called for a summit of heads of state and government of the thirty-four democratically elected governments of the region, held in Miami in December 1994.

The FTAA Process: The Miami Summit Vision

From the very beginning, the FTAA was part of the broader summit agenda, which aims to preserve and strengthen the community of democracies in the Americas, to promote prosperity through economic integration and free trade, to eradicate poverty and discrimination from the hemisphere, to guarantee sustainable development, and also to fight corruption and drug trafficking, as well as to develop infrastructure. In fact, when the leaders agreed on the target date of 2005 for the completion of the FTAA negotiations, they clearly made the link among free trade, growth, jobs, social progress, and democratic stability (Feinberg 1997). When President George W. Bush announced the desire of his administration to explore the negotiation of a free trade agreement with Central America at the OAS on January 16, 2002, he reiterated the Summits of the Americas vision that "the future of this hemisphere depends on the strength of three commitments: democracy, security, and market-based development." He added that "these commitments are inseparable" (Salazar-Xirinachs and Granados 2004).

The launching of the negotiations took place at the second summit, held in Santiago, Chile, in April 1998. The ministers responsible for trade had met a month earlier in San José, Costa Rica, to recommend the initiation of the negotiations. By November 2003, when the ministers met in Miami, FTAA participating countries had completed four negotiating phases and three drafts of the agreement. The position of chair of the negotiations had been held by Canada (May 1998–October 1999), Argentina (November 1999–April 2001), Ecuador (May 2001–October 2002), and Brazil and the United States jointly (since November 2002). In addition to ministers, the Trade Negotiations Committee (TNC), which is composed of the deputy ministers responsible for trade, was guiding the work of the negotiating groups (market access, investment, services, government procurement, dispute settlement, agriculture, intellectual property rights, subsidies, antidumping and countervailing duties, and competition policy) and other committees and groups (the Technical Committee on Institutional Issues [TCI], the Consultative Group on Smaller Economies [CGSE], and the Committee of Government Representatives on the Participation of Civil Society [SOC]). The Tripartite Committee, consisting of the IDB, OAS, and ECLAC, was providing technical, analytical, and financial support to the FTAA process, and the FTAA Administrative Secretariat was attending to the administrative and logistical aspects of the negotiations.

Four results (agreement on business facilitation measures, release of the draft agreements, dialogue with civil society, and creation of the Hemispheric Cooperation Program) are of particular importance. In Toronto in

November 1999, the ministers agreed on a number of business facilitation measures, eight of which were customs-related, whereas ten others addressed transparency issues, amounting to the publication and dissemination of inventories and databases. The release of the draft agreements at the Quebec summit, following the ministers' decision at the Buenos Aires ministerial meeting in April 2001, was a pioneer event in the history of trade negotiations. It was a clear demonstration of the leaders' collective commitment to transparency and to increasing and sustained communication with civil society in response to the call by nongovernmental organizations (NGOs) for more transparency and for the publication of the draft FTAA text. The dialogue with civil society took different forms, one of which was the input received by SOC, a group established at the outset of the negotiations and a unique feature of the FTAA. Finally, the Hemispheric Cooperation Program (HCP) approved at the Quito ministerial in November 2002 was set up to ensure that FTAA countries would strengthen their capacities to participate in the negotiations, implement their trade commitments, and, most importantly, address the challenges and maximize the benefits of hemispheric integration through increased competitiveness. National and subregional strategies were prepared by FTAA countries, with the support of the Tripartite Committee, to identify their trade-capacity-building needs. A first meeting between potential donors and those requesting assistance for the implementation of the HCP took place in Washington, D.C., on October 14–15, 2003.

The FTAA Process: The Turning Point

The election of Lula as president of Brazil in the fall of 2002 marked a turning point for the FTAA. Representing the Partido de Trabajadores, Lula committed himself to broadly maintaining the macroeconomic policies pursued by the government of Fernando Henrique Cardoso, namely fiscal discipline, a floating exchange rate, and inflation targeting, in short the orthodox policy platform that broadened his support among voters. On the trade front, however, Brazil made clear that its main priorities were the multilateral negotiations at the World Trade Organization (WTO), where prospects for a meaningful reduction in agricultural tariffs and subsidies—a key Brazilian demand in the FTAA—were more promising, and the consolidation of the Mercosur integration as well as that of the South American continent. These goals led Brazil to call for a new framework for the FTAA negotiations, one that would depart from the Miami summit vision and focus first and foremost on market access (elimination of tariffs and other related barriers) rather than on a comprehensive FTA also containing trade rules. Brazil's political desire was first to deepen Mercosur, which did not have a common regime in place on intellectual property, investment, and government procurement and services, as rules on these issues were either inexistent or not in force at the time.

Brazil was also concerned that the FTAA had to meet the seventeen objectives set out by the US Congress in the US Trade Act of 2002, signed into law on August 6, 2002. Congress had on the same occasion renewed the fast track authority (now known as trade promotion authority [TPA]), which grants the administration the authority to negotiate trade agreements for congressional approval on an up-or-down vote within a specified time frame.

The appointment by President George W. Bush in 2001 of Robert B. Zoellick as US trade representative had also marked a key turning point for the FTAA. Zoellick complained that the United States was falling behind the rest of the world when it came to trade liberalization. He noted that out of 130 FTAs existing in 2001, the United States was party only to two— NAFTA, with Canada and Mexico, and a bilateral agreement with Israel— whereas the European Union had free trade or special customs agreements with twenty-seven countries, twenty of which it had completed in the previous ten years. With Zoellick, the Bush administration decided to move on multiple fronts (multilateral, regional, and bilateral) and to advocate "competitive liberalization," with the main objective of increasing US leverage and promoting open markets at the bilateral level, in the hemisphere and around the world. In a statement before the US House of Representatives on May 8, 2001, US Trade Representative Zoellick mentioned that "leaders from many . . . nations in this Hemisphere have now told us they want to pursue free trade agreements with the United States. We will consider each of these offers seriously, while focusing on the FTAA."[11] The United States was clearly signaling to all that bilateral and regional trade deals would be used to press countries to make concessions in the WTO negotiations and that bilateral deals were a real alternative to the FTAA.

The FTAA Process: The Miami Ministerial Vision

Two different visions were at play when FTAA countries met again at the eighth FTAA ministerial, held in Miami in November 2003. The two co-chairs, the United States and Brazil, had different interests. Brazil's objective was to negotiate greater market access on goods and agriculture, in particular, and to leave the discussion on rules for the WTO negotiations, whereas the United States wanted a comprehensive agreement but was ready to move on the bilateral front with countries of the region, should the hemispheric talks slow down. To demonstrate that it was serious about bilateral negotiations, the United States announced two days prior to the ministerial that it would launch bilateral negotiations with the Dominican Republic and Panama, respectively. Moreover, in Miami, the United States made public its intent to pursue free trade agreements with four Andean countries, Bolivia, Colombia, Ecuador, and Peru.

Unable to agree on how to move ahead in their negotiations, FTAA countries took "a new approach" in Miami—different from the single-undertaking principle—allowing "all nations to buy into—and benefit from—a common set of rights and obligations in a two track approach, while a path remains open, for the nations that want to be more ambitious, to do so within the FTAA" (Zoellick 2004).

The ministers responsible for trade agreed on a two-tiered approach for the FTAA. They instructed the Trade Negotiations Committee to develop a common and balanced set of rights and obligations applicable to all countries and affirmed that interested parties "may choose to develop additional liberalization and disciplines." The TNC was tasked to establish procedures for these negotiations. During the first week of February 2004, the TNC met in Puebla, Mexico, to carry out the instructions of the Miami ministerial. After a week of intensive work, TNC members needed more time to consult in capitals and among delegations. To facilitate this process, the cochairs agreed to recess the TNC and to reconvene this same meeting tentatively during the first week of March 2004 in Puebla. Consultations were undertaken in Buenos Aires on March 31 and April 1, 2004, but did not lead to progress. The meeting between Brazilian foreign minister Celso Amorim and US trade representative Robert Zoellick in Davos, Switzerland, on January 30, 2005, and the meeting of the TNC co-chairs on February 23–24, 2005, in Washington, D.C., also did not move the process forward, leaving the negotiations at a standstill.

The FTAA was front and center again at the Fourth Summit of the Americas, held in Mar del Plata, Argentina, in November 2005. It remained until the very end the main stumbling block to having a final declaration. Even though job creation was the official theme of the summit, it is the FTAA that captured the leaders' attention and time, as they argued on how (and whether) the summit declaration should refer to this issue. They finally agreed on two paragraphs. The first paragraph (Paragraph 19a of Mar del Plata Declaration) expressed the views of the vast majority of countries attending the summit, which were prepared to resume their FTAA meetings and negotiations, whereas the second paragraph (Paragraph 19b of Mar del Plata Declaration) represented the position of the other countries, stating "that the necessary conditions [were] not yet in place for achieving a balanced and equitable free trade agreement with effective access to markets free from subsidies and trade-distorting practices." In view of both positions, the government of Colombia was asked to undertake consultations, after the WTO ministerial conference held in Hong Kong in December 2005, with a view to bringing together the officials responsible for trade negotiations.

Challenges Posed by the
Proliferation of Trade Agreements

Although it has proved difficult, concluding a hemisphere-wide trade agreement establishing one set of rules or bringing under the same umbrella all the free trade agreements in the Americas would contribute to eliminating the distortions created by the proliferation of trade agreements at the bilateral and regional levels in the region. In addition to customs unions and free trade agreements, several "new generation" partial-scope agreements negotiated under the LAIA framework, and known in Spanish as *acuerdo de complementación económica* (ACE), also provide for the automatic elimination of tariffs but do not cover new issues such as trade in services, intellectual property, investment, and government procurement in any substantive manner. Moreover, a number of nonreciprocal trade agreements, such as the Andean Trade Promotion and Drug Eradication Act (ATPDEA), the US–Caribbean Basin Trade Partnership Act (CBTPA), and the Caribbean-Canada Trade Agreement (CARIBCAN, which gives preferential duty-free access on goods from the countries of the Commonwealth Caribbean to the Canadian market), are one-way concessions providing for the elimination or reduction of tariffs and other barriers on a selected group of products originating in beneficiary countries.

Overlapping trade agreements are particularly burdensome for businesses and governments when rules and market access differ from agreement to agreement, as is the case with tariff schedules and rules of origin. Businesses must devote resources applying these rules and governments must spend money enforcing them. Preferential rules of origin aim at preventing trade deflection, whereby imported commodities would enter the free trade area through the country with the lowest tariff. This explains why rules of origin become much less relevant when free trade partners deepen their relationship and adopt a common external tariff. Rules of origin also specify criteria determining which goods not entirely produced within the free area qualify for duty-free treatment.

Proliferation of bilateral and subregional agreements may also create problems of judicial cohesion with respect to dispute settlement. Let's assume that country A has entered into a trade agreement with country B and a similar agreement with country C, and that B and C bring the same claim against A, based on the same discipline in their respective agreement. It is not entirely implausible to think of a situation where the AB panel finds that A has violated the AB agreement, whereas the AC panel decides that A has not violated the AC agreement. Moreover, should both agreements include a choice of forum provision, thereby allowing the complaining party to bring its claim either under the FTA or the WTO, and assuming that the alleged breach violates a WTO obligation, and that one of the parties (B, for example) decides to bring its claim to the WTO dispute settlement mechanism (known as the Dispute Settlement Understanding, or DSU), the same "alleged breach" may theoretically lead to different results. Now, the matter could be further complicated if both B and C bring a claim against A under their respective FTA and later C decides to bring the same claim under the DSU, regardless of the fact that this would be a breach of the choice of forum provision in its FTA with A (Salazar-Xirinachs 2004).

A similar problem could arise if a trade agreement incorporates by reference a provision from another agreement such as the WTO, or the text of a provision from another agreement verbatim, be it with respect to intellectual property rights, services, antidumping, or any other issue. The AB and AC panels and the DSU panel could theoretically reach a different decision. The investor-state dispute settlement mechanism contained in the investment chapter of most FTAs in the Americas has dealt with the issue of judicial cohesion by including a consolidation provision, which provides that claims against a party, submitted to arbitration by investors of other parties, that have a question of law or fact in common may, under certain conditions, be heard or determined together.

The proliferation of bilateral and subregional trade agreements is in general less of a problem for disciplines on services, as their provisions and exceptions (list of nonconforming measures) are the same—or very similar—in most FTAs, with the exception of financial services.

The coexistence of bilateral and subregional agreements may also bring challenges of its own. CAFTA-DR is a prime example of this, as it is a multilateral trade agreement among seven parties, the United States, the Dominican Republic, and the five Central American countries that are subject to preferential rules under the CACM. CAFTA-DR governs, as a general rule, trading relations among Central American countries. The agreement is very clear, though, that "nothing . . . prevent[s] the Central American parties from maintaining their existing legal instruments for Central American integration, adopting new legal instruments of integration, or adopting measures to strengthen and deepen these instruments, provided such instruments and measures are not inconsistent with th[e] Agreement" (Article 1.3.2). CAFTA-DR allows Central American countries to deepen their agreement, as long as the CAFTA-DR disciplines are not eroded. Except in a few cases, Central American producers will have the choice between the CAFTA-DR rules of origin and the Central American rules of origin. If the CAFTA-DR rules are invoked, this means that a good originating in one Central American country and going to another Central American country will be given the same tariff treatment that the importing country grants the United States. In contrast, if the producer chooses to use the Central American rules of origin, the good will be exempt from customs tariff, with the exception of sugar and coffee (González 2005). CAFTA-DR also takes into account the 1998 free trade agreement between Central America and the Dominican Republic and allows for three exceptions in the multilateral application of the CAFTA-DR with respect to rules of origin.

Proliferation of Trade Agreements in the Americas: The Way Forward

The proliferation of trade agreements in the Americas—and indeed worldwide—is a phenomenon that is unlikely to fade away soon. In fact, it is in part because of the slow pace of multilateral liberalization at the WTO and hemispheric level that countries of the region, including the United States, are now concluding bilateral and subregional agreements (Goldfarb 2005). The simplest way to reduce the distortions created by overlapping agreements would be to make progress in reducing multilateral trade barriers and in negotiating a rules-based hemisphere-wide trade agreement. Another, albeit related, option would be to eliminate the need for preferential rules of origin. This could be achieved by lowering MFN tariffs or abolishing them altogether. An MFN rate of zero percent means that there is no need to determine whether a good not entirely produced within the free trade area is entitled to duty-free treatment since the tariff is the same for free trade and non–free trade partners. If the MFN rate is very low and the preferential rules of origin very restrictive, businesses may decide that it is more economical to pay the tariff than to be subject to the rules of origin (Crawford and Fiorentino 2005).

The proliferation of trade agreements in the Americas is a relatively recent occurrence, which might explain why very few claims have been brought under bilateral or regional instruments. In fact, most countries of the region have preferred to bring and pursue claims against their trading partners at the WTO level. Therefore, the problems that the proliferation of trade agreements may engender with respect to dispute settlement remain for the time being more theoretical than a matter of historical record (Salazar-Xirinachs 2004).

Improving transparency on tariffs, regulations, and rules of origin in a user-friendly fashion would also contribute to easing the burden on businesses. Another option to improve transparency with respect to the proliferation of trade agreements in the region would be to have a peer review of each agreement on a regular basis, for example every two or three years. This would require countries of the hemisphere to meet two or three times a year to discuss the main issues covered in the agreements being reviewed, based on a report prepared by the parties to each agreement and/or hemispheric or regional organizations. The peer review would essentially be an exercise in transparency that would encourage participants to enforce their own rules. Moreover, it would also provide an excellent opportunity for countries of the region to share best practices—concrete examples—of how to reap the benefits of these agreements, as, in addition to having high poverty rates and income inequality levels, the hemisphere confronts unemployment rates that are almost double what they were in the mid-1990s, distressing levels of crime and violence, and democracy that remains fragile.

Notes

1. A notable exception was the decision of the United States and Canada to negotiate, in 1965, a "free trade" agreement in the automotive sector. See Robert (2000: 170–176).

2. The original OAS member states are Brazil, Haiti, the United States, and the Spanish-speaking countries of the Western Hemisphere. All other sovereign countries of the region subsequently joined the Organization, Canada (1990), Belize, and Guyana (1991) being the most recent members.

3. The General Treaty was signed on December 13, 1960, by El Salvador, Guatemala, Honduras, and Nicaragua. Costa Rica acceded on July 23, 1962. For more on the CACM, see SIECA (2005).

4. The Treaty of Chaguaramas created a juridical hybrid consisting of the Caribbean Community as a separate legal entity from the Common Market, which had its own discrete legal personality. The legal separation of these two institutions was emphasized by the elaboration of two discrete legal instruments: the Treaty establishing the Caribbean Community and the Agreement establishing the Common Market (which was later annexed to the Treaty and designated the Common Market Annex). This institutional arrangement facilitated states joining the Community without being parties to the Common Market regime. For more info, see http://www.caricom.org/jsp/community/original_treaty.jsp?menu=community.

5. LAFTA members: Argentina, Bolivia, Brazil, Chile, Colombia, Ecuador, Mexico, Paraguay, Peru, Uruguay, and Venezuela.

6. This section does not cover the North American Free Trade Agreement, as it is only a free trade agreement with no intention on the part of NAFTA parties (Canada, the United States, and Mexico) of becoming a customs union or a common market. Moreover, NAFTA is covered in great detail in Chapter 11.

7. CARICOM members are as follows: Antigua and Barbuda, the Bahamas, Barbados, Belize, the Commonwealth of Dominica, Grenada, Guyana, Haiti, Jamaica, Montserrat, St. Lucia, St. Kitts and Nevis, St. Vincent and the Grenadines, Suriname, and Trinidad and Tobago. Barbados, Guyana, Jamaica, Suriname, and Trinidad and Tobago are designated as "more developed countries." All other member states, other than the Bahamas, are designated as "less developed countries." The five associate members are Anguilla, Bermuda, British Virgin Islands, Cayman Islands, and Turks and Caicos Islands. See www.caricom.org.

8. The OECS counts nine members, two of whom are associate members (Anguilla and the British Virgin Islands). Antigua and Barbuda, the Commonwealth of Dominica, Grenada, Montserrat, St. Kitts and Nevis, St. Lucia, and St. Vincent and the Grenadines are the other OECS members. See www.oecs.org.

9. LAIA offers a framework to its members for negotiating among themselves partial trade liberalization agreements in the goods sector.

10. A country can become a Mercosur associate member upon fulfillment of two conditions: being an LAIA member and concluding a free trade agreement with Mercosur.

11. See the prepared Statement of Robert B. Zoellick, US Trade Representative, before the Subcommittee on Trade of the Committee on Ways and Means of the US House of Representatives. Washington, D.C., May 8, 2001: 7.

11

NAFTA: An Unsustainable Institutional Design

Louis Bélanger

Entered into force in 1994, the trilateral North American Free Trade Agreement (NAFTA) was greeted as, by far, the most ambitious and comprehensive trade deal ever to have been signed. Built itself on the 1989 Canada–United States Trade Agreement (CUSTA), which Mexico was in a sense invited to join, NAFTA has since served as a paragon for a flurry of bilateral and subregional free trade agreements in the hemisphere and was used as a blueprint for most of the negotiation of the Free Trade Area of the Americas (FTAA) (see Chapter 10 in this book). In the meantime, however, a growing number of NAFTA's supporters inside North America began to view it as unfinished business. Over the last few years, numerous scholars and practitioners have put forward detailed proposals to tackle areas of liberalization that remained unaddressed by the original deal and to correct how others were originally handled by negotiators (Goldfarb 2003). The most recent of these proposals are also the most comprehensive (e.g., Hufbauer and Schott 2005; Council on Foreign Relations 2005; Schwanen 2004). Among many improvements, they call for the abolition of the "rules of origin" system, limitations on the use of trade remedies, and harmonization of standards. At the heart of the ongoing discussion on the relative merit of all these proposals, one fundamental problem arises, that is, the problem of governance. First, demands for improvements raise the simple questions of why NAFTA is seemingly so difficult to amend and why even small and reasonable suggestions for adaptation necessarily imply a dramatic "reopening" of the deal. Second, many of the proposed improvements would require, in order to be implemented effectively, doses of the political coordination that the drafters of the original treaty so carefully managed to avoid. In both cases, we, in fact, face a very specific governance problem— the problem of decisionmaking delegation in trade agreements.

This chapter is not about the institutions that NAFTA would need in order to become something else, such as a "North American Community" or a "New Partnership" that would extend its scope to nontrade issues like immigration, security, or development (Pastor 2001). It is about the institutions that NAFTA lacks to be sustained as it is and to be true to its own original goals, which were to establish a free trade area and to create a framework for further cooperation so as to expand and enhance its benefits (NAFTA 1993: Art. 102). There are good reasons that NAFTA was designed the way it was. Power differentials among the three countries, constitutional constraints, and political sensitivities have all helped to restrict to homeopathic proportions the infusion of decisionmaking delegation in NAFTA. In many ways, this rejection of political delegation has had a structural impact on the whole architecture of the agreement. To reverse this state of affairs, even modestly, implies in a sense changing the nature of NAFTA institutions. Is such a change politically unrealistic? Maybe. But if the following analysis is right, without a change NAFTA will quite rapidly reveal itself to be an unsustainable agreement. So, thinking about reforming it, if only to determine if it is "redesignable" or not and at what cost, is certainly worth a try. Moreover, NAFTA is not the only free trade agreement for which political delegation represents or will represent a challenge in this hemisphere. As multilateral as well as commercial institutions evolve from primitive reciprocal trade-and-tariff agreements to sophisticated organizations aimed at regulating complex issues like investments, subsidies, standards, or intellectual property rights, the self-implementing model of trade governance that we find in NAFTA shows its limits. The need to think creatively about these limits and how to overcome them is crucial for the future of international trade governance in the Americas.

Incompleteness and Delegation in International Cooperation

In order to understand the current institutional features of NAFTA and to reflect systematically on how they could evolve, this chapter makes use of the theoretical tools provided by the rational institutionalist program of research in political science (Weingast 2002) and international relations (Koremenos et al. 2001). This program, as well as works in the new microeconomics of organizations from which it takes much of its inspiration, offers or suggests some interesting hypotheses about how states bargain over governance issues and delegation when they negotiate international agreements, and how their relations are, afterward, constrained by the institutions they have created.

According to rational institutionalism, the need for delegation emerges primarily from the interlinked but distinct problems of enforcement and incomplete contracting. The problem of enforcement (or compliance) is widely discussed in the general literature on international cooperation, as well as in the more topical writings on NAFTA and other trade agreements (see Yarbrough and Yarbrough 1992; McCall Smith 1998, 2000). Here, delegation is mainly designed by states in order to limit opportunistic interpretations of their respective obligations and rights under the agreements they have signed. In the case of NAFTA, this judicial role of "saying the law" in an impartial manner is delegated to ad hoc "panels" or "tribunals" made up of independent experts. The problem of incompleteness arises, for its part, from the inescapable fact that, like any contract, all international agreements are incomplete (Hart 1995; Williamson 1985). As a contract, an international treaty always "contains gaps or missing provisions; that is [it] will specify some actions the parties must take but not others; it will mention what should happen in some states of the world, but not in others" (Hart 1988: 123). Incompleteness has two broad sources (Scott 2003). One is exogenous, or a given, to the contracting parties: even if they would like to write a perfect contract, they cannot do so because they cannot anticipate all future states of the world and because the costs of even trying to write such a perfect contract would be infinite. Another source of incompleteness is endogenous to the contract: parties to a contract may choose for different reasons to deliberately leave certain terms of their agreement unspecified. So, even if there is some incompleteness that is inevitable and incompressible in an international agreement, incompleteness remains elastic in the sense that states choose or bargain over the level of relative completeness that a certain treaty will achieve.

Incompleteness implies that parties will face ex post situations that cannot be adequately handled by simple conformity to the letter of the contract. Being aware of this, states negotiating a treaty have a choice: they can decide ex ante that they will deal with incompleteness outside of the treaty, by negotiating emerging issues anew, or they can provide the treaty with mechanisms for dealing cooperatively with unspecified states of the world. In the latter case, it means that they will create one form of decisionmaking delegation or another (Fearon 1998: 274–275).

These governance structures are fundamentally different from dispute settlement mechanisms (DSMs) or other tribunal-like forms of judicial delegation. Theoretically, we can say that what fundamentally distinguishes political delegation from judicial delegation is their respective relation to incompleteness: judicial delegation belongs to the realm of what has been completed by the treaty and must be enforced, but political delegation is usually associated with what has been left incomplete and thus cannot and should not be decided by judges but by politicians or their representatives. A good illustration of the distinction between judicial and political delegations in an international institution can, of course, be found in the United Nations system. Here, the International Court of Justice is the body to which member states delegate the resolution of interpretational disputes among themselves, and the Security Council is the political body to which member states have delegated the authority to make decisions on matters of war and peace.

Political delegation in treaties takes two general forms, depending on the function they perform. First, most international agreements include provisions for their own endogenous modification, and some do it by putting in place rules that go beyond the primitive process of simply renegotiating a new contract or a new amending protocol. For example, in the trade area, the World Trade Organization (WTO) agreements can be amended by the General Council or the Ministerial Conference. Theoretically, this can be done by a qualified majority vote, even if practically WTO members still apply the rule of consensus inherited from the General Agreement on Tariffs and Trade (GATT) (Davey 2005). Second, international agreements can delegate to the parties themselves or their delegates the authority to decide on secondary rules to make operational the general obligations originally contained in the treaty, thus permitting it to evolve without rising to amending it. Mercosur (Mercado Común del Sur), for example, essentially put in motion the work of a council of the common market responsible for implementing the very vague principles and commitments contained in the Treaty of Asunción (Treaty of Asunción 1991, Art. 10). All these different forms of political delegation create rules for *modifying* the original rights and obligations contained in the treaty by redefining, specifying, or rewriting what was first written down. In contrast, judicial delegation creates rules for *arbitrating* disputes over the exact significance of the reciprocal rights and obligations. Thus, political delegation aims at "completing" incomplete contracts, whereas judicial delegation aims at enforcing relatively complete contracts (Abbott and Snidal 2000: 433; Goldstein et al. 2000).

Thus states negotiating an international agreement like NAFTA can choose between different combinations of delegation and incompleteness, even if they know that completeness is unachievable. Powerful states like the United States hesitate to abandon discretionary power in favor of any form of contractual arrangements, simply because they then lose some of the advantage from which they benefit when power relations are unobstructed by rules. But when they decide that it is in their interest to nevertheless negotiate a treaty, and particularly in cases of deep cooperation, powerful states prefer relative completeness—and the hard judicial delegation that is often a byproduct of precision—rather than political delegation (Abbott and Snidal 2000: 448–449). They can use completeness as bargaining counters for low levels of governance structures because less powerful states, even if they lose a lot when completeness is acquired at the price of an atrophy of delegation, would often prefer it to nothing. As we will see below, in the case of NAFTA, the trenchant asymmetry of power and economic dependency between the

United States and its two neighbors has correspondingly produced an institutional arrangement that is rich in completeness and judicial delegation but poor in political delegation.

In an asymmetrical relation, we can also anticipate that the costs and benefits of the chosen combination of completeness and delegation will vary for each state. For example, the lack of adequate delegation to adapt the agreement to new states of the world will probably be felt more strongly by the more dependent partners. Canada and Mexico will be meeting relatively higher costs, not only because they will suffer more economically from the growing loss of efficiency provided by an aging NAFTA that is difficult to adapt, but also because they will suffer politically from having to deal with the United States on a growing set of trade issues that fall outside the ruled-base legal coverage provided by the agreement. This means that the adoption, for NAFTA, of a specific institutional design has set in motion a political dynamic that should be understood if one wants to assess the general economy of the agreement, its performance, and its future prospects.

Relative Completeness and Delegation in NAFTA

NAFTA's institutional design is characterized by a combination of extraordinarily high levels of precision and comprehensiveness in the treaty itself with a quasi-absence of secondary ruling mechanisms. This specific equilibrium (or disequilibrium) between completeness and judicial and political delegation has been highlighted by many specialists:

> We know no other free trade agreement of NAFTA's magnitude. In fact, very little was excluded from the negotiation of this agreement, which contains some 295 articles and 90 annexes (often themselves supplemented with appendices), as well as explanatory notes. . . . Not only is NAFTA very broad in scope . . . it is also extremely precise and comprehensive. In addition to a chapter titled "General Definitions," each chapter contains one or more articles . . . providing definitions specific to the chapter in question. In all, some three hundred definitions are spread throughout the agreement in an effort to dispel any ambiguity as to the meaning of the terms and expressions used. . . . This same degree of precision is demonstrated in the repeated use of often long and technical annexes and appendices. (Bernier and Roy 1999: 72)

The counterpart of this relatively high level of completeness is a quasi-absence of political delegation aimed at ensuring the coordination and the future of cooperation. No future mandatory round of negotiation is scheduled or envisaged. Almost nothing is left for trinational bodies to decide. This is what led Frederick Abbott (2000) to notice the discrepancy one finds in NAFTA between a fairly well-developed system of judicial delegation and a quasi-absence of political or decisionmaking delegation. Delegation in NAFTA takes two forms: some political delegation is vested in the Free Trade Commission, and some judicial but also indirect administrative delegation is vested in four dispute settlement mechanisms. This section analyzes the limitations and constraints imposed by the agreement in both instances.

The Free Trade Commission

The essential political body created by NAFTA is the Free Trade Commission. Composed of the trade ministers of each of the three countries, the commission meets at least once a year and has almost no power of its own. It monitors the implementation of the agreement and can settle interpretive disputes with the possible help of a panel system. Thus, NAFTA gives the commission limited *political interpretive authority*. The commission has no real mandate to modify the agreement in the future; the clause on modifications in the last chapter of the agreement makes no mention of it (NAFTA 1993, Art. 2202). This basically means that NAFTA does not provide for *endogenous modifications:* additions or amendments to the agreement would have to be processed from outside the agreement's framework, through the same diplomatic channels and domestic ratification procedures required for brand-new agreements. It is thus not surprising that such modifications have never occurred. There are two specific instances in which alterations to the agreement require actions from the commission: it has a role to play in negotiating eventual accession of other states (Art. 2204) and in authorizing technical and limited—*tacit*—amendments, as in the case of modifications to rules of origin or customs regulations (Art. 414 and 512).

These interpretive and decisionmaking capacities granted to the commission are extremely constrained. An early illustration of the limitation of the commission's capacity to enforce actions aimed at facilitating the implementation of NAFTA was its failed attempt at establishing a permanent North American Trade Secretariat (NATS). At its first meeting in January 1994, the commission decided to create such a permanent secretariat that would be responsible, among other things, for coordinating the work of the national secretariats to be established by each country. Because Canada and the United States inherited, from the two parallel agreements, an environmental and a labor secretariat, respectively, the NATS was to be established in Mexico City. However, since there are no provisions for this administrative body in the text of NAFTA, the US Congress never voted the money necessary for its implementation (Grijalva and Brewer 1994: 5). The commission never took other decisions of this kind after this episode.

The commission used its interpretive authority in 2001 when it attempted to clarify some provisions pertaining to the operation of Chapter 11's arbitration tribunals (Canada 2001). In the end, tribunals have operated according to the commission's interpretive note, but this move has not gone unchallenged. One panel's ruling indicated clearly that such clarifications could not, in any circumstances, be interpreted as modifications of the original text of the agreement, thus setting clear limits to the use of interpretations to indirectly amend the agreement (Arbitration Tribunal 2002: 23). As for the commission's authority to modify such technical provisions as the classification of products for origin determination or the schedule for tariff elimination, it is subject to each nation's implementation procedures. In Mexico, such modifications must be ratified by the Senate. In the United States, they require a presidential proclamation, preceded by consultations with the Committee on Ways and Means of the House of Representatives and the Senate Committee on Finance (US House of Representatives 1993a: Sec. 103 and 202). Thus, these modifications are not directly enacted by the commission.

As mentioned, the only clear instance in which the commission may have a role in substantially modifying the agreement is in the case of an accession. Here, the commission is mandated to conduct the negotiation with the third country or group of countries seeking a NAFTA membership. However, the agreement clearly states that the result of such negotiation would be subjected to the agreement of each government and the necessary ratification procedures in each country, and the US implementing legislation is quite clear on this (US House of Representatives 1993b: 463). Therefore, the commission could hardly even begin negotiating eventual accessions before the US president has successfully sought advance congressional approval.

This analysis of the delegation of authority vested in the commission reveals three striking facts. First, NAFTA has been carefully crafted to ensure that, even in its most technical and trivial aspects, absolutely no measures or rulings coming out of the work of its institutions could be conceived as self-executing. That is, no decisions are enforceable without appropriate domestic legislative (in the US and Mexican cases) or executive actions. Second, the domain of what can be amended without being subject to full ratification procedures, the equivalent to negotiating another agreement, is extremely limited. Third, the commission has limited political interpretive authority but no mandate to propose or process modifications and has not yet initiated such a proposition or process, which indicates that modifications are to be decided outside of the NAFTA framework.

The Dispute Settlement Mechanisms

As already mentioned, this extraordinarily low level of political delegation corresponds to the institutionalization of relatively strong dispute settlement mechanisms. This can be seen as a direct by-product of precision; the concern for writing the most definitive treaty possible requires mechanisms that are able to autonomously take charge of the need for ex post interpretation (McCall Smith 2000). However, in spite of its high level of precision and its evident ambition to accomplish deep cooperation or completeness, NAFTA has not institutionalized the ultimate delegation mechanism for interpretation and precision, which would be the kind of permanent tribunal observers like Robert Pastor are advocating today (Pastor 2001). The judicial delegation system NAFTA offers is limited to the formation of ad hoc panels mandated for each dispute, which do not have the authority of a standing tribunal since only panel rulings that take place under Chapter 19 (antidumping and countervailing measures) are binding.

If we leave aside the DSMs included in the labor and environment side agreements, NAFTA itself contains four different systems of panels, which can only be described briefly here. Chapter 20 provides a general arbitration mechanism for disputes over the interpretation of the agreement or on the consistency with the agreement of measures taken by one party. The purpose of this mechanism is clearly to enforce the agreement itself, and it echoes in large measure the WTO dispute settlement system. Panels cannot impose compliance with the agreement but can authorize retaliation through suspension of concessions. Although some commentators may, at first, have seen the DSM provisions of Chapter 20 as being hopeful in terms of policy coordination, they were soon disappointed (see Weintraub 1994; Morales 1999: 46).

The DSM established under Chapter 11 has the very narrow mandate of hearing reclamations from investors alleging that their rights under NAFTA have been violated. Chapter 11 arbitration panels cannot remand decisions from domestic agencies; they have the authority only to award compensation. Because it has never been used, Chapter 14's DSM is rarely mentioned. It offers a procedure for settling disputes in the financial sector through the use of Chapter 20's arbitration mechanism (Hufbauer and Schott 2005: chap. 4).

The functioning of Chapter 19's DSM is of particular interest to us. This is the case not only because it has been the most widely used of the four NAFTA DSMs but, more fundamentally, because it is the only one that is binding, in the sense that it has the power to order the reconsideration of a decision taken by a national administrative agency. It opens the possibility of indirect delegation of administrative authority since a NAFTA body that is itself deprived of administrative authority has the power to monitor the work of domestic agencies. How this possibility has been constrained by the creation of Chapter 19 and its implementation is a direct product of the tension between relative completeness and political delegation that structures the whole agreement. When they first discussed how to handle trade remedy laws during the CUSTA negotiation, Canadians and Americans brought very different solutions to the table. Canada's solution was that the two countries would exempt each other from the application of their respective antidumping (AD) and countervailing duties (CVD) laws. Public as well as private distorting trade practices would then have been subjected to a common system of competition rules and policies. Logically, such a system not only would have necessitated enforcement through a binational dispute settlement authority; it also would have required the delegation of administrative authority to take actions against dumping and other distorting practices, like subsidies. In other words, it would have meant not only the "binationalization" of the appeals functions otherwise performed by national courts, but also the "binationalization" of the administrative and more political functions otherwise performed at the national level by the US Commerce Department and the US International Trade Commission on the one hand, and Revenue Canada and the Canadian International Trade Tribunal on the other (Hart 1994: 170–172).

This proposition was rejected by the United States, and the remedy laws issue came close to killing the deal (Hart 1994, chap. 15). The Chapter 19 finally adopted was a last-minute compromise. Under CUSTA and NAFTA, each country maintains its own trade remedy laws and AD/CVD determination procedures, but actions by national agencies are subject to challenge and review by a binational panel system that substitutes for domestic recourse through courts of appeal. Here, completeness is obtained by, in a sense, incorporating the three countries' bodies of remedy law into the orbit of the agreement, and that was clearly chosen as a substitute for politico-administrative delegation. This raises the question of whether this panel system of review is mandated to conduct strictly judicial appeals of the legality of agencies' decisions (judicial delegation), or is it also mandated to make pronouncements on the fairness and appropriateness of these decisions beyond the strict question of their legality (political/administrative delegation)? This question has been at the center of the debate over Chapter 19 since its negotiation. In the legal jargon that has dominated in this debate, the problem is one of deference: if the nature of the delegation authority vested in the panels was purely judicial, they should defer to the political discretion and technical competence of administrative agencies, therefore limiting their action at judging if the administrative agencies have violated the law or their own statutes in reaching a particular decision; if, to the contrary, this delegation authority was extended to judge the impartiality of the agencies' usage of their political discretion, then the panels should handle cases with more scrutiny and render more intrusive decisions. From the beginning, Americans have defended the first conception, interpreting the panel system as nothing more than a more expeditious substitute for domestic courts of appeal. For their part, Canadians have defended the second conception, arguing, for example, that since panelists were, at least originally, to be international trade experts rather than judges, the intention was clearly to replace court adjudication by a more aggressive intervention in the agencies' decisionmaking process (Feldman 2004).

The history of Chapter 19 implementation shows that its albeit limited potential for nonjudicial delegation has been systematically pressured. One meticulous analysis of the decisions by Chapter 19 panels under CUSTA found that even if they operated within the limits of what domestic judicial reviews could reasonably do, binational panelists were often more intrusive than domestic courts in their evaluation of the economic and legal analysis produced by the agencies in support of the contested determinations (Davey 1996). The United States has constantly tried to curb the panels' use of the leeway provided by the agreement by requesting extraordinary challenges under the pretext that panels have shown insufficient deference to the domestic agencies (Feldman 2004). They have also taken advantage of the NAFTA negotiation to introduce two changes into Chapter 19 that favor their conception of the review system: (1) the judiciary character of the panels has been reinforced by the insertion of a new provision stating that lists of potential panelists should "include judges or former judges to the fullest extent practicable" (NAFTA 1993: Annex 1901.2); (2) the use of the extraordinary challenge procedure to contest insufficient deference to the government agencies has been facilitated by clarifying that "failing to apply the appropriate standard of review" can be considered as a panel's manifest abuse of its power, authority, or jurisdiction (NAFTA 1993: Art. 1904.13) (Feldman 2004). These changes did not suffice to impose the US view on the nature of the authority delegated to the panels. For example, a recent extraordinary challenge committee explicitly expressed the opinion that the panels' authority cannot be constrained to judge the legality of the agency's decision; it also has to determine its overall "rationality" (ECC 2005: 27–28). Nevertheless, the main point here is that delegation in NAFTA is so severely limited to judicial functions that even minimal delegation of administrative authority of the sort we find in the Chapter 19 DSM is forcefully and systematically challenged.

NAFTA Put to the Test of Time

Despite all the efforts made by its creators, NAFTA necessarily remains an incomplete contract. Moreover, because of the zeal of the same creators, it is badly equipped to face its incompleteness. As the future unfolds, its lack of provisions for endogenous modification will undoubtedly lead to a growing obsolescence, and its lack of coordination devices will lead to costly inefficiencies.

Inadaptability and Erosion

One immediate evolving "state of the world" that NAFTA is ignoring is the web of free trade agreements negotiated by each of the three North American countries with other states *after* the entry into force of NAFTA. Since 1994, Mexico City, Ottawa, and Washington have signed bilateral or regional trade agreements with a fair number of partners.[1] They could have expanded their privileged trade relations as a bloc, using the agreement's accession clause. At first, in the case of Chile, that is what was foreseen. But, due primarily to President Clinton's failure to obtain the necessary "fast track" trade authority from Congress, thus revealing the quasi-inoperability of Article 2204, the three countries rapidly abandoned the idea of synchronizing their trade policies. The result is that in negotiating with third parties, the North American partners, partly because they draw lessons from their NAFTA experience, innovated and sought more "advanced" trade agreements. But they did so separately, without harmonizing their own trinational arrangement. Thus, even if most of the trade deals signed afterward by the three took NAFTA as their template, these new agreements have created rights and obligations from which, due to the 1994 agreement's unadaptability, the North American free trade zone does not benefit.

One good illustration of this evolution is given by the chapters on investment in the trade agreements that the United States recently signed with Chile and the Central American countries. One of the most contested provisions of NAFTA is the article of Chapter 11 that authorizes foreign investors to seek financial compensation in cases of "indirect" expropriation. Many commentators consider that the broad language used in the agreement to define what is an indirect expropriation opened the door to excessive claims and could have a chilling effect on governments' rightful intentions to regulate the private sector in the general interest (see Hufbauer and Schott 2005: 224–235). Accordingly, NAFTA partners have reviewed the language used in later trade agreements. Thus, the United States–Chile Free Trade Agreement (FTA) and CAFTA specify that a nondiscriminatory governmental measure, conceived and implemented with the legitimate objective of protecting the public, for example for health and environmental protection or for security reasons, should not be considered an indirect expropriation.[2] Moreover, the United States, like Canada, modified its general foreign investment protection model agreement accordingly. However, even though the terms of the contractual relations of all three North American countries developed with non-NAFTA trade partners have improved, NAFTA rules remain untouched.

Unpredicted states of the world can emerge from the outside, but they also often emerge from enforcing the contract itself. In other words, the institution's design can produce outcomes other than the ones originally anticipated, therefore creating the need for adjustments. One sensitive area where the rules established by NAFTA have not led to the performance initially expected is the dispute resolution mechanism established by Chapter 19. As we have seen above, the lack of a common standard of review of antidumping and countervailing decisions has fueled many extraordinary challenges characterized by prolonged, costly disputes. Other factors have plagued the panel system, with delays far exceeding the limits stated in the agreement. The result is that even if Article 1904 establishes a 315-day limit for the completion of panel proceedings, Feldman calculated that the average length for the completion of cases so far has been 613 days (Feldman 2004: Annex 2). This underperformance is important since the access to expeditious and thus cheap reviews of American AD and CVD measures was certainly the "crown jewel" and the "deal breaker" of the negotiation as far as Canada, and probably Mexico, were concerned.

Such an erosion of one of the key benefits provided by NAFTA would normally require some maintenance work. Some quite simple adjustments that would not necessitate amending the agreement have been suggested, like increasing the funding and administrative independence of the national sections of the NAFTA secretariat, creating a better-paid, more permanent, and collegial roster of panelists, or simply enforcing the time frame originally established in Annex 1901. However, given the unavailability of an appropriate monitoring mechanism, a renegotiation would be necessary to implement other suggested improvements. Thus, clarifying the procedures for the selection of substitute panelists when replacement is necessary during the proceedings of a case, or addressing the delicate problem of the text's lack of an agreed-on standard for review, would definitely require the "completion" of the existing provisions (Feldman 2004; Hufbauer and Schott 2005: 249–252).

The Costs of Completeness over Coordination

NAFTA not only has been designed in a way to avoid delegating any authority for endogenous modification; it has also been designed in a way to keep to a miniature level the delegation of low-level secondary ruling authority. As we have seen in the first section of this chapter, the difference between the two kinds of political delegation is important: the first, more "constitutional," one is aimed at modifying the text of the contract, whereas the second, more "administrative," one is aimed at regulating a domain of cooperation that was left unspecified in the first place because the drafters preferred this solution or because the nature of this domain makes it particularly difficult to anticipate the future. Illustrations of this type of delegation authority can be found in both boards of governors of the World Bank and the International Monetary Fund. Here again, in the case of NAFTA, completeness has been used as a substitute for delegation. The best example is certainly the "rules of origin" system.

Having created preferential treatment for their respective products in each other's markets, countries that enter into a free trade partnership must address the problem of how to prevent imports from other countries from benefiting from this preferential treatment. Basically, there are two mechanisms available. One mechanism is to coordinate a common external tariff, therefore making sure that exporters from third countries cannot exploit differences between members in tariffs or nontariff barriers simply because there are no differences to exploit. The other mechanism is to discriminate at the borders between, on the one hand, products that truly originate from the trade zone members or that have been sufficiently transformed inside it and are thus entitled to a preferential treatment, and, on the other hand, products that are simply imported from a third country. In the first case, the one we find in customs unions, the objective of creating an effective free trade zone is pursued by permanent coordination of trade policies and, thus, delegation of trade policymaking. In the second case, the one we find in NAFTA and other FTAs, the objective is pursued by ex ante creating an extensive system of rules of origin, involving precise methodologies like "regional value content" determination or "change in tariff classification," to determine levels of transformation in the member countries that a specific product has to go through to qualify as "originating." Rules of origin are a means to achieve through completeness what would otherwise be obtained by delegation of authority and, thus, the abandonment of independent external trade policies (Kunimoto and Sawchuck 2004: 3).

But choosing completeness as a substitute for delegation comes with a price. Rules of origin are costly for governments to administer and for business to comply with. A recent study estimates the compliance costs (what it costs to have certified the origin of a product) assumed by Canadian firms exporting to the US at more than 1 percent of the value of all exports (Kunimoto and Sawchuck 2005: 8). Rules of origin, especially if they are restrictive (i.e., if they impose high levels of "regional content"), can be used to undo what the FTA was supposed to achieve. They can also be conceived as fairly protectionist measures vis-à-vis extraregional imports, which distort sourcing or purchasing decisions. Hence, Madanmohan Ghosh and Someshwar Rao have calculated that the elimination of the NAFTA rules of origin system would increase Canada's gross domestic product (GDP) by 1.04 percent (2004: 34).

Two observations are particularly worrying in the case of NAFTA's rules of origin. First, they are significantly more restrictive than those contained in other free trade agreements signed by the United States (Kunimoto and Sawchuck 2004: 11). This means that the other beneficiaries of these agreements have greater access to the American market than do

Canada and Mexico. Second, since 1998, the use of the rules of origin system by Canadian firms exporting in the United States has regularly declined (Kunimoto and Sawchuck 2005: 19). This can be explained by the mere fact that businesses are discouraged by the costs of compliance, especially when the non-NAFTA tariffs—most-favored-nation (MFN) tariffs under the WTO—are low. The costly and restrictive NAFTA rules of origin system clearly contributes to the erosion of the agreement's efficiency.

To get rid of this system, NAFTA would have to replace relative completeness by political delegation, because a common external tariff cannot be achieved by simply enforcing a set of ex ante rules. The essential reason is that the external tariff of a nation is more the product of many political and evolving actions than of fixed economic interests. There is often a misperception of the political implications of a common external tariff, or a customs union. The harmonization of external tariffs may seem to be a rather technical operation, but in fact it implies a coordination of each of the members' trade policies (Huelsemeyer 2004). Among other elements, according to William Dymond and Michael Hart (2005), a "simple" customs union between Canada and the United States would involve a joint trade policy for the conduct of trade relations and negotiations with third countries at the multilateral and bilateral levels, a common approach for the selection of trade partners, and an integrated trade remedy system to address third country trade and to participate as joint plaintiffs or joint respondents in dispute settlement cases. Conscious of the radicalism of such an evolution of the NAFTA framework, proponents of a common external tariff tend to downplay this political dimension. Hence, Dymond and Hart's proposal for a bilateral customs union foresees the creation of several "joint Canada-US commissions" (2005: 25–26), but they remain extremely vague when it comes to how they would operate and under what kind of delegation of authority, leaving the reader with the impression that conducting a joint trade policy is more "technically challenging" than politically demanding.

One important lesson highlighted by the examination of the rules of origin system is that international agreements that trade completeness for delegation not only pose a problem of adaptability and efficiency due to their *lack of delegation;* they may also make cooperation costly because of the *extent of completeness.* Indeed, the more complicated and precise the rules are, as with NAFTA rules of origin, the more resources will be needed to administer them, to comply with them, and to litigate them. As contract theorist Eric Rasmusen put it: "contract-reading costs matter as much as contract-writing costs" (2001: 32); delegation may appear a more attractive alternative when one considers the often hidden costs of completeness.

The other evident case where NAFTA negotiators have traded completeness for delegation, as we have seen, relates to competition policies and trade remedies. The enforcement of Chapter 19 is costly, not only economically but also politically, as the Canada–United States softwood lumber dispute has shown. The obvious alternative to the dispute settlement system established by Chapter 19 is to create a unified trade remedy regime, making the mutual exemption from each other's remedy laws possible (Dymond and Hart 2005: 20–21). But again, doing so would require delegation. It would imply not only the delegation to an international body of the authorities currently held by federal agencies responsible for deciding on antidumping and countervailing cases in each of the countries, but presumably also the authorities vested in domestic antitrust agencies (Council on Foreign Relations 2005: 22). It may be possible to obtain a significant improvement of the NAFTA treatment of remedy laws without going this far. However, the bottom line is that here, as in the case of the rules of origin system, crossing the limit drawn in 1994 implies going beyond the point where completeness alone can bring trade liberalization. It necessarily requires bringing in at least some political delegation.

Conclusion: Political Implications

The specific structure of NAFTA's institutional design has political as well as economic implications. We have seen in the first pages of this chapter why, when asymmetrical powers like the three North American countries negotiate an institution like NAFTA, a combination of high relative completeness and quasi-absence of political delegation is a likely outcome. Now, the question is, What happens once the agreement is in place? How will asymmetrical states conduct themselves in such an institutional environment? Is it politically sustainable?

The theory of incomplete contracting suggests that, in the absence of adequate governance mechanisms, an incomplete contract will necessarily lose its efficiency as time goes by and unforeseen and unspecified states of the world unfold. In the economic universe of private transactions, matters that are left out of the contract are settled by residual rights, like property rights (Hart 1995). In the universe of international relations, however, they are settled by power politics. This means that the less powerful NAFTA partners, Canada and Mexico, are the ones most likely to suffer from the agreement's incompleteness and lack of efficiency. Accordingly, they will most probably translate their growing frustration into demands for "completing" NAFTA with some form of political delegation. That would be coherent with Joseph Grieco's theory of voice opportunities, inspired by Albert O. Hirschmann (Grieco 1995, 1996a; Hirschmann 1970). Less powerful states, Grieco argues, often fear that institutionalized economic integration, even if it proves to be advantageous for everyone, would increase their dependence on a dominant and potentially hegemonic neighbor. For

this reason, they usually try to compensate by negotiating "voice opportunities." He describes these as "institutional characteristics whereby the views
of partners (including relatively weaker partners) are not just expressed but
reliably have a material impact on the operations of the collaborative
arrangement" (Grieco 1996a: 288). Thus, the more the "NAFTA era" pro-
gresses, the more Canada and Mexico will attach relative values to gains in
voice opportunities, or delegation.

Although the "NAFTA era" may still be in its infancy, political frustration over the limits and the rigidity of the agreement has mounted in
Mexico and Canada. In the face of important domestic pressures, the Mexican government has repeatedly expressed its discontent with the liberalization of its agriculture sector under NAFTA and, given US intransigence,
threatened to use the agreement's escape clause if that was the only means
available to renegotiate certain provisions of the deal. On sugar, Mexico
has since the beginning been involved in an incredible controversy over the
status of "side letters" exchanged during the ratification process in the US
Congress, which were intended to modify some provisions of the agreement
(Hufbauer and Schott 2005: 320–323). Mexico, in the cross-border trucking
case, and Canada, in the softwood lumber case, have experienced enormous
political frustration when American agencies, subject to pressures from
domestic interest groups, proved unwilling to enforce NAFTA panel decisions. Faced with these politically embarrassing shortcomings, right after
his 2000 election, President Vicente Fox proposed the creation of a North
American common market, if not a European-style economic community,
that would graft political decisionmaking institutions onto NAFTA and
expand its scope.

In Canada, despite growing concerns about the limits of NAFTA, the
government's official position has long been that it was satisfied with the
new status quo (Canada 2003). Still, in 2002, the Canadian Parliament completed a long exercise of consultation on the future of North American relations in the aftermath of September 11. It was concluded that NAFTA
should evolve from a mainly self-implementing and self-enforcing agreement to one that includes significant governance structures: a common
competition policy, a North American summit process, interparliamentary
cooperation, and, eventually, a standing court of justice (Canada, House of
Commons 2002). The former ambassador to the United States, Allan
Gotlieb, aptly summed up the growing sentiment of his fellow Canadians
when he stated: "We must try to build . . . a North American community that
substitutes enforceable rights and obligations for political arbitrariness and
the muscle of special interests. The reward of success in such an endeavour
is the securing of our political sovereignty; the price of failure is continuing
dependency and a diminishing sense of national self-confidence" (Gotlieb

2004: 39). The Canadian government cannot ignore the important domestic forces that are pushing in the direction of a redesigned NAFTA. For example, in 2003, the Canadian Council of Chief Executives made public a proposal for a new "all-encompassing agreement" based on the model of the Canada–United States International Joint Commission (CCCE 2003: 5) and is asking that "the NAFTA partners should consider taking additional institutional steps, starting with an annual summit meeting of the NAFTA leaders and creation of a permanent NAFTA secretariat" (CCCE 2004: 29). The Canadian Chamber of Commerce, for its part, is calling for a common competition policy. In the language of the chamber, "We will need to tackle this 'unfinished business' at some point" (CCC 2004). In fact, the Canadian Conservative Party, which won the last federal election, has already signaled its interest for a deepening of NAFTA, which would include harmonized external tariffs, the elimination of the rules of origin, and the adoption of common regulatory standards (Conservative Party of Canada 2004: 39).

The political game over NAFTA's institutional design is already being played, as we have seen in the case of the legal debate on the nature of the authority vested in Chapter 19 panels. But the more the post-1994 NAFTA era advances, the more the incompleteness of the original deal will attract political attention, particularly in Canada and Mexico. Beyond economic inefficiencies, it is the lack of an adequate rules-based mechanism to deal with the agreement's aging and shortcomings that risks undermining its sustainability. Simply because the economic and political costs of incompleteness are so asymmetrically shared, Canada and Mexico are much less powerful and much more dependent on their trade with the United States than vice versa. Without a structural change to its institutional design, growing inefficiencies and a decline in political support in Canada and Mexico will probably lead to NAFTA's erosion and decline. Such a result would not be without consequence for the prospect of a hemispheric-wide FTAA that has been until now conceived, in terms of institutional design, on the NAFTA model.

Notes

I would like to thank the Woodrow Wilson Center for Scholars, where I was a public policy scholar at the time this chapter was written. Claude Barfield, Robin King, Maryse Robert, Sidney Weintraub, Bob Wolfe, and the three editors of this book have provided useful comments on an earlier draft. I thank them, but remain solely responsible for the content of this chapter.

1. Canada has since signed FTAs with Chile, Costa Rica, and Israel; Mexico with Bolivia, Chile, Costa Rica, Colombia, the European Free Trade Association, the European Community, Israel, Japan, Nicaragua, Uruguay, and Venezuela; and

the United States with Australia, Bahrain, the Dominican Republic, El Salvador, Guatemala, Honduras, Jordan, Morocco, Nicaragua, and Singapore.

2. See *United States–Chile Free Trade Agreement* (2003), Annex 10-D, and *Dominican Republic–Central America–United States Free Trade Agreement* (2004), Annex 10-C.

12

Attacking Poverty: The Institutional Base

Albert Berry

The Americas include countries with average incomes ranging from very high (the United States and Canada) to very low (Haiti, Honduras, Bolivia, and a few others), making the region unusual in the degree of income inequality between countries. Most Latin American countries are also famous for their high level of internal inequality. As a result, poverty tends to be high even where average income is not particularly low—Brazil is the outstanding case. As with all regions, there are significant differences across countries, and the exceptions to the "extreme inequality" label pinned on Latin America as a region have, at one time or another, included Argentina, Uruguay, Costa Rica, and Chile. Currently, however, only Costa Rica and Uruguay might be described this way, and their share of the region's population is minuscule. The roots of inequality in Latin American countries go deep, both in time and in the fabric of most of these societies. Of historical importance has been the cleavage between the conquerors and the indigenous groups (in spite of the considerable racial mixing over the nearly five centuries since the conquests), the predemocratic state of the Iberian countries at the time of the conquest, and inertia. The United States and Canada have poverty as well, but it is based on much higher poverty lines than the other countries and has a different socioeconomic connotation. The main focus of regional poverty concerns is thus naturally the region minus Canada and the United States.

Since the 1950s or a bit longer, inequality has not been brought down in Latin America, either by policy or through normal growth mechanisms. On the policy front, the efforts in most countries have been far too modest and/or ill-designed to have any chance to reduce inequality significantly. And hopes that the growth process itself would eventually perform that function—as proposed by Simon Kuznets (1955)—have also not been borne out. But a solid growth performance of 5.5 percent per year between the end

213

of World War II and 1980 did raise per capita income by about 3 percent per year and by 190 percent over the period. Based on a poverty line suggested by Oscar Altimir (1982), its incidence fell from about 65 percent in 1950 to about 25 percent in 1980.

Progress then came to an abrupt halt with the debt crisis of the 1980s, as per capita income fell and poverty climbed back to about 35 percent. By the early 1990s, the economic reforms introduced in the wake of the economic crisis were being implemented among the high hopes of their proponents. Since that time, however, growth has remained sluggish, averaging just 2.8 percent over the period from 1990 to 2004 and about 1 percent in per capita terms (somewhat less on a per worker basis since the rate of participation has been rising), and the level of inequality has worsened in a number of countries without, it seems, improving significantly in any. As a result, the incidence of poverty, though down from its peak of the early 1980s, is still near precrisis levels. In short, Latin America has had a bad twenty-five years since 1980, after a successful thirty-five years before then. Accordingly, poverty remains a serious concern and continues to present a major policy challenge, mainly to the countries themselves but also to the region, including the two rich countries that are part of it.

Since the early 1980s, inequality has increased in the Americas as a region, with the United States, Canada, and to a lesser extent Chile outperforming the other countries, because of the 1980s debt crisis that resulted from the spin-off effects of price hikes by the Organization of Petroleum-Exporting Countries (OPEC) in the 1970s, the resulting inflation, and the policy response to it in the United States and the United Kingdom. Although this causal process leading to the debacle did not have its roots in the developing countries generally or in Latin America more particularly, the price was paid there. The debt crisis also opened the door for increased external pressure on the Latin American countries to open up their doors to trade and foreign investment. The industrial countries were substantially responsible both for the debt crisis itself and for the unsatisfactory after-effects.

What role have institutions—national, regional, bilateral, or international, and including nongovernmental as well as governmental—played in the poverty/inequality drama of Latin America over this period and especially since the 1980s, when the region fell into crisis and then partially recovered? What trends show up in the patterns of behavior and influence of those institutions? What might they have done better, and what roles might and should they play in the future?

In the second section of this chapter, I briefly review the current understanding of the determinants of poverty and inequality in Latin America, including selected aspects of public policy. Then I discuss what policies appear best suited to deal with these challenges as they currently manifest themselves in the region. In the next section, I consider how the current institutional base has influenced poverty and inequality outcomes. I look briefly at the sort of reforms or changes that could lead to better outcomes and then conclude the chapter.

Poverty, Inequality, and Growth

Under the usual definition (inability to pay for a minimum physical standard of living), changes in poverty depend on both the rate of growth of per capita income and any change in the pattern of income distribution. When poverty is defined also with reference to relative income, the role of inequality becomes still more important as a determinant of poverty. Another aspect of poverty is income and job insecurity. According to Latino-barometer's public opinion survey, 85 percent of Latin Americans as of 1996–1997 were either unemployed or worried about losing their jobs (IDB 2003). The comparable number for European countries was 32 percent. It is speculated that the absence of widespread social insurance in Latin America may account for much of the difference, since the rates of job rotation are similar in the two regions. Even in Latin countries with quite low unemployment rates, this ratio is at least 65 percent, whereas the highest figure for Europe (Spain) is under 50 percent and the lowest (Denmark) is under 15 percent.

The experience of the last twenty-five years in Latin America, with respect to each of the four proximate determinants of poverty, may be summarized as follows:

1. The rate of growth has been slow, even in the postcrisis years since 1990, hence making poverty reduction difficult.
2. Where it has changed, the inequality of primary income has usually worsened.
3. Income and job instability appear to have increased, and traditional job protection and related benefits have shrunk, such that for many people life has become more precarious.[1]
4. Poverty redressal policies like old-age pensions (e.g., Brazil) or subsidies to induce lower-income families to keep their children in school longer (e.g., Mexico) are becoming more frequent, and public health systems have also tended to improve their capacities over time, partly as the population shifts from rural to urban settings.

On the first two counts the experience has been much poorer than might have been hoped for, on the basis of either the experience of the previous thirty-five years or the hopes of the neoliberal policy reformers. On the last front, the record gives modest grounds for hope that Latin America is moving haltingly and under difficult circumstances toward better social safety nets of the sort that industrialized countries typically have. Some other indicators of human welfare also look better than the growth and distribution numbers. Life expectancy, for example, has continued to rise.

The proximate determinants of growth are the level and the effectiveness of investment, with effectiveness related to technological change and the degree of resource utilization. Performance on these fronts is affected by some public policies, including those in the areas of trade, capital flows, and migration, that are heavily influenced by decisions and stances taken in other countries and/or the international agencies. Other presumed determinants of growth, such as investment in education and policy support for small and medium-sized enterprise, are more the domain of the countries themselves. Aid conditionality and the more general perception that stability matters to a country's international economic relationships have shifted macroeconomic management, previously mainly the preserve of national policy, toward the gray area where international factors play an increasing role.

The historical record, here and in other parts of the world, shows that inequality is very resistant to change. This, together with our understanding of the determinants of inequality, suggests that it will be no easy task to lower it significantly. There are thus few, if any, grounds for hope that poverty can be rapidly reduced in the absence of robust economic growth.

Interpretations of why growth has been slow and distributional trends unsatisfactory since the 1980s inevitably include comparisons with the previous thirty-five years, the so-called import substitution industrialization (ISI) period, during which regional growth hit its historical peak. The level of inequality changed little during this fast growth period, but poverty was greatly reduced. The positive momentum ended around 1980, as real interest rates rose dramatically and countries that had borrowed heavily during the easy-money 1970s found themselves unable to service their debts. The ensuing debt crisis led in Latin America to a decade of stagnation and helped to foster a major policy shift away from the interventionist trade and other policies of the ISI period toward a more "market-friendly" or neoliberal approach. Many in the international financial institutions (IFIs) saw the crisis as the natural result of a flawed economic strategy. By the early 1990s, reforms were being put in place and international capital was returning to the region. But performance since then has, as noted, been mediocre at best.

What went wrong? Proponents tend to say that the reforms have not been pushed far enough to yield their full potential benefits. Critics are understandably doubtful about going farther down a path that has thus far yielded no obvious fruit. Several hypotheses have been advanced to explain the weak performance under the new economic model:

1. After the liberalization of capital flows, freer capital movement led to financial and economic crises during the 1990s, with serious negative impacts on growth.

2. The trade reforms went too far, precluding the sort of arguably efficient protection carried out earlier in East Asia and in such Latin America countries as Brazil, Mexico, and Colombia.

3. Just as the region was turning outward, so were China and India, with their huge low-wage labor forces, thus both limiting export markets overall and undercutting the chance for a boom in labor-intensive exports from Latin America.[2]

4. The main source of indifferent performance since 1990 has been the negative inertial effects of the 1980s crisis. In this view the whole unhappy story of the post-1990 period is due to the loss of the pre-1980s momentum. Inertia may matter more than policy.

5. Perhaps the new model only works well when implemented with unusual skill. Chile's successes since 1982 might be in part interpreted this way. Most countries might take quite a while to get the implementation right.

It will probably take another decade or so of research for economists to get the story fairly clear on what went wrong. Empirical analysis of the trade–capital flows–growth relationship has turned out to be difficult. Probably the most important link, and certainly the least understood, is that from trade and capital flows to investment, a variable that has failed to recover its peaks of the ISI years. What stands out dramatically in retrospect is the weak intellectual underpinning of the market-friendly reforms. Even if the reforms eventually bear considerable fruit, it is clear that as of 1980, no one knew whether they would or not. What is now clear in retrospect (and no doubt was to many observers at the time) is that an adequate approach to the debt crisis had to involve a substantial bailout of the debtor nations. But the creditors and the IFIs took too long to edge toward this conclusion. Two countries that emerged relatively well from their respective crises were Chile and Korea; both happened, for different reasons, to benefit from huge capital inflows when they needed it.

Partially competing interpretations of why inequality has risen in Latin America are the labor-saving character of technological change and the increases in trade and capital flows. In Latin America the effect of the former may have been accentuated by increasing openness, especially to foreign direct investment, which introduces capital-intensive technologies. The timing of the increases in inequality in Latin America, which have been spaced out from the mid-1970s on, tends to match the timing of trade openings and of liberalization more generally (Berry 1997). Giovanni Cornia (2004), Francisco Rodriguez (2004), and others have argued that financial liberalization has played an important role. Privatization, especially when carried out in settings rife with corruption, is also likely to increase inequality, as it appears to have done in Argentina (Margheritis 1999).[3] Whatever the precise impact of the reforms on inequality, it appears unlikely to have been positive, given that the final outcomes have gone in the opposite direction.

Where to Go from Here to Reduce Inequality and Poverty

The lack of a credible consensus either on why economic growth has been slow, even in the postcrisis period since 1990, or on why inequality has tended to increase has, as the other side of the same coin, a lack of clarity as to what policies would now produce fast growth and improved distribution. Virtually everyone agrees that a higher investment rate and more rapid productivity growth will be needed.[4] Better education, especially for children of lower-income families, is also universally cited as part of the package of desirable policies. A stronger demand for labor leading to better employment opportunities is recognized as a key mechanism, and a small and medium-sized enterprise (SME) sector that is both growing and raising its productivity is a near-universal inclusion. But such mantras do not get us far, since either they border on the tautological (better employment opportunities) or it is not very clear how to achieve them (the rest). The desirability of macroeconomic stability is part tautology (of course, it is better than its opposite, other things being equal) and partly questionable— it is not at all clear that countries should strive for very low rates of inflation, since this may come at the expense of both growth and flexibility.

At the level of serious policy detail, we know very little with confidence about how to create enough satisfactory (i.e., well-paying, stable, and otherwise decent) jobs. My own judgments run along the following lines.

1. The importance of a coherent employment strategy and of effective public-private cooperation in its implementation cannot be over-emphasized.
2. Raising exports is usually desirable from a growth point of view, but getting rid of all import barriers is usually not, especially for large countries like Brazil, Mexico, Argentina, and Colombia, three of which fared well under their earlier ISI regimes. Although the distributional impact of more trade depends on the case, there appears to be little hope for the large employment-creating effects seen earlier in the East Asian tigers and now in Vietnam. Empirically speaking, trade liberalization in developing countries tends to go with falling real wages (Rama 2003), though this may be in part

or in whole because trade liberalization sometimes occurs when countries are in difficulties and real wages are destined to fall anyway.

3. Using the exchange rate to aid international competitiveness can be the best tool to this end; it has been a nearly standard component of policy packages that have generated economic takeoffs though exports (Berry 2005).

4. There is little or no evidence that price stability by itself will trigger growth, as some optimists have believed.

5. Some degree of control over international capital movements is desirable where there is otherwise too great a risk of the sort of financial and currency crises that have plagued nearly all Latin American countries at some point since 1990, leaving a legacy of severely negative growth effects. The need is to deter short-term capital movements, from which countries seem to benefit little even in the best of cases.

6. Foreign direct investment (FDI) can be beneficial (as when it facilitates a big increase in exports) but is sometimes harmful to employment or in other ways, so the optimal strategy involves selection and attraction of the desirable types of investment.

7. Continued efforts to improve education and training should with luck and good management be beneficial to both growth and equality, but such benefits cannot be counted on to arrive quickly and may not be nearly as great as sometimes hoped. If education does turn out to be an important piece of the puzzle, then quality at the primary and secondary school levels will probably be pivotal, together with better training of specific, important groups of workers.

8. An integrated "industrial policy" of some sort may be necessary to provide the policy coherence and the level of certainty required by private agents in order to invest at needed levels (Carnegie Council on Ethics and International Affairs 2005; Rodrik 2004).

9. Supporting small and medium-sized enterprise may be important to the achievement of good employment outcomes and hence poverty alleviation, as well as to growth.

10. Wage policy, and labor market policy, more generally, are unlikely to produce significantly positive effects on the poor. Pushing legislated minimum wages very high runs the risk of backfiring on the poor by discouraging employment creation. Eradicating many of the existing labor market interventions on the grounds that they lower efficiency and/or increase inequality may not help much either, and certainly cannot be counted on for a big boost by itself.

11. The budget, and more specifically pensions, public health systems, and public education, are of increasing importance in the battle

against poverty and inequality. Some targeted poverty alleviation programs seem to have yielded considerable benefits (Coady and Grosh 2004).

Only the unfolding empirical record will tell, but there appear at present to be few grounds for optimism that income inequality in Latin America will fall quickly. Those hopes embodied in the liberalization processes (trade, capital flows, privatization, labor markets) either appear to have backfired (trade, capital flows) or to be question marks (most of the others).[5] Eventually the distribution of human capital is likely to narrow, if only because educational attainment at the bottom will be rising, whereas at the top it cannot rise much. Population growth is slowing and labor force growth with it, which takes some pressure off the labor market. Welfare systems and societal safety nets will ultimately strengthen. But since each of these effects tends to occur slowly, it would be optimistic to expect much poverty alleviation as a result of falling inequality over the next decade or so.[6] The unrealistic hopes placed in the reforms have been accompanied by the natural reluctance to reverse or even refine their major elements and have led to a somewhat desperate search for solutions to the employment and distribution problems in other areas (education, microcredit, and SME policy). None of these approaches to inequality and poverty has a clear track record; some may be hamstrung until some of the more rigid elements of the Washington consensus approach are dropped. For example, it is possible that the widening earnings gaps by level of education or human capital interface with international trade and capital flows in such a way that they cannot be reversed until those flows are modified.

Although the pattern of growth does matter, the main mechanism of poverty reduction will no doubt continue to be growth of per capita income, so it is important to ask how the existing institutions will affect that growth. With a bad pattern of growth—perhaps not unlike the one we have recently seen—the rate might have to reach 5 percent to effect significant poverty reduction, a daunting challenge based on recent experience. But achieving a pro-poor pattern of growth will also be daunting.

Policies Affecting Poverty and Inequality:
The Clash Between Needs and Existing Institutions

The institutional framework within which Latin American economies evolve reflects their own specific historical legacies, the large direct influence of the United States and the lesser impacts of other industrial countries, and the relevant international institutions, most of which are also heavily influenced by the United States and the other rich countries. Noteworthy elements of the Iberian legacy include a tendency toward authoritarian government, a high level of inequality, and an ethnic cleavage between the conquerors and the indigenous peoples. This heritage contributed to the rather slow progress of democracy in the region and to the continuing very high levels of social and economic inequality.

Notable features of the hemispheric setting in recent times have been the heavy influence of the United States in both political and economic affairs, the absence of institutions capable of warding off or alleviating the damage from the crisis of international debt, and the increasing emphasis on market-friendly policies during recent decades.

Judged in retrospect against the events of the last twenty-five years, the combination of national, regional, world, and nongovernmental institutions that have helped to determine the social and economic outcomes in Latin America must be judged rather harshly. No major identifiable challenge has been met impressively (see the summaries in Table 12.1), unless one includes price stability as such a challenge, but such stability is less an end in itself than a means to other ends (such as real growth). Some bases for future successes may have been laid, but that is harder to judge. Although it is not clear exactly what sort of institutions would have been optimal, since it is not clear what policies would have been optimal, the institutions in some areas can be judged to have failed, and some reasonably safe surmises are possible as to what a good institutional framework would have looked like in certain areas.

Like their international counterparts, most national institutions and governments have fallen well short of the challenge posed to them by the debt crisis and its aftermath. It was natural that, during the heart of the crisis, efforts and thinking should be dedicated mainly to survival rather than to longer-run strategies. Attention to the latter was also curtailed, no doubt, by the strong pressure from outside to follow the recommendations of the IFIs, with which some economists and technocrats in each country in any case agreed. It was a lot to expect countries themselves to evolve a superior development strategy in the midst of crisis, under pressure from external institutions and usually with little capacity to look quickly and deeply at policy alternatives. Macroeconomics, narrowly defined, came to dominate policymaking, to the detriment of forging strong microeconomic and sectoral policies.

A source of optimism among the pro-market reformers was the hope that increased democracy, less government, and open markets would bring a detectable decline in political corruption, which has long been blamed as a contributor to inequality in Latin America. But Joseph Tulchin and Ralph Espach (2000) note that, here too, events have failed to conform to hopes. The reforms, especially the privatization component, were seldom carried out in a transparent way and were notably corrupt in Brazil under Fernando

Table 12.1 The Major Challenges, Relevant Institutions, and Their Responses in Key Policy Areas

Challenges	Institutions	Responses
1. Macroeconomic stabilization	IMF, key governments to deal with debt crisis and later financial crises	Insufficient capital inflow to achieve stabilization; pressure for greater trade and capital market openness may have backfired; strengthening of financial systems may be a plus for the future
2. Effective exchange rate management	IMF, key governments	Insufficient recognition of the damage from overvaluation and from exchange rate volatility
3. Effective international economic integration	IFIs, FTAs; subregional common markets; FTAA	Excessively free market approach with little nuance or policy space for countries; Washington consensus approach in the context of WTO and FTAA
4. Finding or recovering motors of fast growth; especially understanding what generates high levels of investment	IDB; World Bank; key governments; specialized agencies	Based too much on the simplistic pro-market approach with too little attention or expertise with respect to other elements, such as support for smaller enterprise, education, and training
5. Automatic provision of assistance to lower-income members of the region, as in the European Union	None	Absent
6. Effective learning about what policies work	World Bank, IDB, ECLAC; UNDP, key governments (epistemic communities)	Given little attention, partly because it was presumed that a large part of the answer was known (in the form of the pro-market policies)
7. Focus on employment and income distribution in a coherent way	ILO; ECLAC; World Bank, IDB, UNDP	ILO less strong than the IFIs and in any case has not always been on target; lack of persuasive ideas

Collor de Mello and in Argentina under Carlos Menem.[7] Whether in the economic or the political aspect of Latin American development, a common thread of reformist thinking was this sort of oversimplification of reality.

The Institutions

National and IFI Roles

The United States has long taken a close interest in the affairs of Latin America, with the weight between economic and political motives varying over time. The fear of communist uprisings in the region has no doubt been at times exaggerated in the US discourse, and the economic importance to the United States of what happens in Latin America is almost certainly greatly exaggerated in US political thinking.[8] Its economic ties with Latin America probably have only a minimal impact on US gross domestic product (GDP) per capita, perhaps 1–2 percent. The United States is a country with a wide range of resources, and there is a great deal of substitutability between Latin America and other parts of the Third World as sources of raw materials and destinations of exports.[9]

The key features of US involvement and concern over the last few decades may be summarized as follows:

1. During the Cold War, an extreme (and uniquely American) preoccupation with the threat of communism in the region, a concern that trumped the inclination to support democratic processes (as evidenced by the experiences in Guatemala, Chile, and Venezuela).
2. A more general concern with social unrest in the region and a fear that high levels of poverty would be politically explosive in ways damaging to the United States, manifesting itself, for example, in the Alliance for Progress with the Peace Corps, low-level agrarian reform, and so on.
3. A growing tendency to push for market-oriented economic policies since the 1970s, facilitated by the debt crisis and the associated shift of power and influence to the creditor countries and the IFIs that they dominate. Throughout the postwar period, the United States (and Canada) have generally presumed that their economic interaction with the rest of the region was beneficial to it (as well as to themselves). The focus on trade and foreign investment (both foreign direct investment and portfolio capital), rather than aid as the key way to promote growth and poverty reduction, was enshrined in the Washington consensus of the early 1980s, with the US Treasury, the World Bank, and the International Monetary Fund (IMF) agreeing

that market-friendly economic reforms, among which freer trade would be central, held the greatest promise for healthy development in the region.

4. A large and increasing role of big business and big finance (Pauly 2003) in the design of US policy, as globalization proceeds with the United States as its leading exponent. The populist thread of US history, typified by the belief in the small family farm and in the need to control the depredations of large firms, has been largely replaced by the neoliberal doctrine of recent times, and there has hence been little chance for the salutary messages of that earlier phase to be passed on to Latin America.

5. A recent focus on the "drug problem" and a strategy of dealing with it at the point of origin in other countries rather than in the US market itself. This goal leads to (tacit) support for the paramilitaries in Colombia, to concern with the incoming Morales regime in Bolivia, and to conflicts with human rights groups in the region and in the United States.

Despite the dominant role of the United States in the region's institutional responses to poverty and the threats it is seen to create, a substantial part, in fact probably the bulk, of the involvement of international institutions in ways related to poverty has taken place through supraregional institutions like the World Bank, the IMF, and the UN specialized agencies. Apart from the international institutions whose scope is the world, the regional ones whose activities are most likely to be relevant to policy are the Inter-American Development Bank.(IDB), whose role as lender naturally makes it important; the Economic Commission for Latin America and the Caribbean (ECLAC); the Pan-American Health Organization (PAHO), important because health issues are so closely linked to poverty (or better, may be considered as part of the definition of poverty); the Food and Agriculture Organization (FAO) (poverty is also closely related to agriculture); the Organization of American States (OAS); and the regional branches of UN agencies like the United Nations Development Programme (UNDP) and the International Labor Organization (ILO). The most powerful of these institutions, the IMF and the World Bank, are most influenced by the United States and, more generally, by the conservative forces of the industrial countries. Some others, like ECLAC, provide greater scope for Latin American, or more generally "developing country," thinking.

Though regional growth has been good in the last couple of years, US policy on Latin America currently faces a challenge arising from the perceived failure of the neoliberal economic policies it has championed for the region, the associated combination of social unrest and the election of left-leaning governments, the historically low esteem with which US policy is held, and the fact that US attention is focused elsewhere at this time. The favored policy, the Free Trade Area of the Americas (FTAA), is, for the time being, on hold, and alternative socioeconomic arrangements are receiving more discussion than before. The tools of direct US intervention may have been weakened somewhat. More genuine elections in countries that, although suffering great inequality, are also more urbanized, more educated, and more anxious to vote tend to bring more leftist parties and presidents to power, a natural outcome of growing democratic participation.

The Fixation on Economic Integration: How Big Are the Potential Benefits?

A major presumption of both the Washington consensus and the FTAA (the raison d'être of the First Summit of the Americas, in 1994) was that Latin America would benefit both from more trade in general and from more within the hemisphere. This idea, together with the other components of the pro-market strategy, thus took center stage in thinking about how to raise economic growth and lower poverty in the region. It was related to the proposition that economic integration leads to income convergence among the participating countries or regions. How valid are these presumptions?

A reasonable guess is that more trade could be quite beneficial to most of the region, but not necessarily if based on the sort of "free trade" structure that would result from a US-dominated or Washington consensus process, as opposed to something more in tune with the needs of Latin America. A really positive outcome seems unlikely, since it would probably require a design process characterized by both a high level of competence in identifying what would be best for the region and a willingness on the part of the United States (and Canada) to be more generous than is typical in such negotiations. Trade negotiations are not carried out primarily by people either interested in or knowledgeable about the mechanisms of development. The focus of those from the industrial-country side is almost exclusively to get a good deal for themselves.

The idea that facilitating increased trade and capital flows could be the best thing the United States and Canada could do for Latin America has its theoretical roots in simple international trade and finance theory and an interesting empirical base in the history of income convergence within most large countries or regions with few internal barriers to economic transactions. Although not particularly fast, income convergence across regions of a country or a region like the European Union is the norm rather than the exception, and many economists predicted that globalization and economic integration would have a similar impact across countries as well. But the postcrisis period since about 1990, during which the Washington consensus model has been increasingly implemented in Latin American countries, has not seen this expectation borne out, but rather some widening of the gap between the United States and Canada and the rest. There are several reasons to doubt that an FTA would foster income convergence within the hemisphere. The most obvious is the very mixed results thus far from the liberalizing reforms, in contrast with the impressive records established earlier under the combination of ISI with export promotion in East Asian and some Latin American countries. An increasingly popular and more middle-of-the-road view accepts that industrial policy can contribute to growth in low-income countries, and hence that developing countries should be conceded special privileges in this respect, whether in the form of the right to use tariff protection or of other ways to encourage specific sectors.

Also relevant is recent evidence that international borders matter a lot, even in such trade-friendly settings as Canada and the United States, the world's largest bilateral trading partners, with low levels of protection against each other, the same majority language, and other similarities.[10] This implies that even totally free movement of goods and services between countries may not produce the levels of trade that do contribute to income convergence within countries. It is possible that key factors in intracountry income convergence are the unrestricted freedom to migrate from region to region and the absence of currency risk. If so, as long as these features are missing in an integration process (as they would be in an FTAA), income convergence might be absent or small.

Better access to foreign markets is of greatest benefit to the low-income people in poor countries when it creates opportunities to sell labor-intensive goods, as in the Asian Tigers in the 1960s–1970s and currently in China, Vietnam, Bangladesh, and elsewhere. But although many Latin American economies still suffer considerable levels of poverty, their marginal (i.e., new) exports are for the most part not intensive in unskilled labor but rather in natural resources and/or skilled labor. This post-Washington consensus surprise (at least for some analysts) has no doubt played a role in those increases in income inequality that have accompanied economic integration in the region. The high level of inequality in Latin America goes with an unusually high range of technological heterogeneity, and whenever a policy change, such as liberalization, gives further impetus to capital-intensive technologies (as trade liberalization seems to have done), the impact on employment and on income distribution may be negative. Without a better understanding of trade-growth links, especially those operating through the level and direction of investment, no one can be sure whether the impact of further trade liberalization on growth and poverty in Latin America will be positive or negative.

Although they involve very simple assumptions, widely circulated World Bank estimates of the one-shot benefits from full global World Trade Organization (WTO) liberalization are of some interest. In the most recent revision, Kim Anderson and Will Martin (2005: 1319) put the benefits at US$287 billion, with developing country gains at $90 billion. Scaled down from full worldwide liberalization to a more realistic Doha round scenario, the total gains were estimated at $96 billion, with $16 billion going to developing countries, and with 6.2 million people raised above the poverty line. Such one-shot gains, when distributed over a 2001–2015 phasing-in period, fade into virtual insignificance; developing world GDP would be raised by only one one-hundredth of 1 percent per year. Some figures are higher (e.g., Cline 2004), but few reach a total gain of 1 percent of developing country GDP (Ackerman 2005). Although these figures refer to the world as a whole, the main message—that estimated gross benefits are very small in relation to GDP—is applicable to Latin America. Estimated net benefits would be even smaller, if positive at all; Kevin P. Gallagher (2005) points out that the administrative costs alone of implementing the new rules and the welfare losses from those rules are large in relation to the estimated benefits. Large tariff revenues would also be lost, with corresponding damage to the always fragile fiscal condition of most developing countries.

In short, getting or not getting the benefits identified in these exercises is unimportant relative to the identification of a generally good growth strategy. If increases in trade and capital flows could in fact produce sizable gains, the mechanisms whereby they would do so are obviously not contained in the models currently used by the World Bank and are usually hard to identify with any precision. Meanwhile, the possible losses associated with the greater difficulty of implementing an effective industrial policy could certainly be large. Judging by the difference in growth performance between the big success stories of recent decades and the mediocre performers, this inability could slow growth by a couple of percent per year or more, an impact that dwarfs all the other effects identified. The impact of any given trade liberalization on the effectiveness of overall economic strategy is thus the big question that countries need to sort out.

In the meantime, even if they did not jeopardize growth potential, the estimated static benefits from further liberalization are too small for countries to go out of their way to get. If the industrial countries make better market access available without costly quid pro quos, the deal could then become a good one for Latin America and other developing countries. Experience to date provides few grounds for optimism. The Uruguay round of General Agreement on Tariffs and Trade (GATT) negotiations was seen as a watershed; Organization for Economic Cooperation and Development (OECD) markets for agriculture and labor-intensive manufactures, especially textiles and clothing, were ceded to the developing countries in exchange for the inclusion of services, intellectual property, and investment in the trading system. But, as Sylvia Ostry (2005: 3) puts it, this "Grand Bargain turned into a Bum Deal," with much less opening in agricultural markets than expected and major institutional upgrading required of the countries of the South.

The trade-poverty reduction link, always weaker in Latin America than in those Asian countries specializing in labor-intensive exports, is probably the more so now, given the increased presence of multinational corporations using modern technology.

Challenges and the Existing Institutions

The debt crisis debacle. The biggest institutional failure of the last quarter century, mainly attributable to the international institutions, was the inability to ward off the disastrous effects of the 1980s debt crisis that followed the oil price shocks. These events plunged the region into a decade of recession. Capital market liberalization then led to a series of financial and currency crises in the 1990s that retarded recovery. A major bailout should have been undertaken to alleviate the impact of the debt crisis, and the shift to capital mobility was, if not wrong, at least premature. The institutional structure was one in which macroeconomic fluctuations generated elsewhere in the world brought severe shock effects to Latin America, and the region was not adequately assisted in dealing with those shocks. Major blame rests on the IMF and the industrial country governments.

Exchange rate management. As national capital markets have increasingly integrated into the world market, the movement of short-term speculative capital has become a problem, leading to financial and currency crises preceded by overvalued exchange rates that discourage the production of tradeables.

Imperfectly designed outward orientation. The region's international economic integration has increased, but in probably nonoptimal ways, because of a too simplistic adherence to the goal of openness for Latin America and to the failure of the United States and other OECD countries to open their own markets completely. The most likely explanation for the fact that the increased trade and other shifts toward liberalization did not produce the anticipated results is that the sort of industrial policy (implemented in part through trade interventions) that worked so successfully in East Asia and at times in some Latin American countries was superior to the freer trade strategy currently pushed on the region. Outside pressure from the IFIs and the industrial country governments was substantially responsible for this probably damaging policy change. The preference against the use of industrial policy was too simplistic.

Failure to find a pro-poor growth pattern. Too little serious attention and effort has been directed toward promotion of pro-poor growth, partly for lack of knowledge and partly because the rigid pro-market ideology tends to crowd out alternative ideas that might conflict with it. Even less serious attention has been directed to the development of an employment strategy, the main key to poverty alleviation and improved income distribution. Support for microcredit, favored by the IDB and other institutions as a way to foster microenterprise, has been both meritorious and moderately successful (Westley 2001), but its effects have not been potent enough to counteract negative trends in the relative productivity of firms by size (Stallings and Perez 2000). Microeconomic and sectoral policy tended to get short shrift during the phase when (a simplistic version of) "getting the prices right" was seen as the "be all and end all" for economic success. Partly through overconfidence in the results forthcoming from the market-friendly reforms and perhaps partly from inertia or unconcern, the regional and international institutions did not make support for SMEs or for education and training policy strong enough to contribute importantly to pro-poor growth. Overall, policy learning has been slow. No single international agency has responsibility in this area; those with the general clout to have made a difference have not done so.

The investment challenge. The second macroeconomic failing of the last quarter century has been the inability to get the rate of investment back up to the level needed to sustain strong growth. The debt crisis ushered in a new period in which risk factors were high and investment was increasingly left to the private sector. One of the risks of a market system with very little public sector involvement is the inherent volatility of this key determinant of growth and the difficulty of controlling it through policy variables. The unwillingness or inability to take vigorous steps to promote private and public investment may condemn a country to stagnation. In this area the blame is shared by the IFIs and the national governments that have simply not focused enough on investment.

Emigration as palliative. Emigration did remain a useful safety valve for excessive pressure on the labor markets or for the strains of civil wars in Mexico, several Central American countries, and recently Colombia, but also it had a pernicious side in that, as with other developing countries, the US and Canadian systems of immigrant selection contributed strongly to the brain drain from the rest of the region. The main benefits in terms of poverty alleviation are the result of the lower-skilled migrants entering the United States, many illegally, from Mexico and Central America. Large flows of this sort do have social costs, as is apparent in both the United States and Canada.

From an overall perspective, the institutional response to the challenges of the last quarter century has thus been ideological, rigid, and weak. There is a need to attack those challenges both from a general perspective of what determines growth, distribution, and hence poverty, including what seems to have contributed to the rather widespread increases in inequality over the last several decades in Latin America, and from the perspective of what is beneficial and what is not about the existing economic and political interfaces between the rich countries of the region and the rest.

Thinking Ahead: Institutions to Support an Attack on Poverty and Inequality in the Region

Fortunately, the weaknesses and errors of the past do not doom policy for the future. It is risky, however, to approach the future without a decent understanding of what has gone right and wrong in the past, and here we are much less well placed than would be desirable.

Since the most dramatic failure occurred in the area of macroeconomics and stabilization, where the IMF and rich country governments played the key roles, the biggest challenge now is to avoid another 1980s debt crisis debacle or financial and currency crises like those of the 1990s, usually involving overvalued exchange rates and ultimately due to the free flow of short-term capital. Recognition of the failings of international institutions in these areas (in particular the IMF and the rich country governments that control/influence it) has been slow to emerge, with a general tendency to place blame for financial crises on the developing countries themselves (Stiglitz 2000). Powerful vested interests in the financial sectors of the United States and other industrial countries weigh against a system friendly to developing countries (Pauly 2003). Unlike the World Bank, the technical competence of the IMF does not lie in the broad area of development economics, firm convictions on a variety of issues notwithstanding. The modest and delayed attention given to Tobin-tax type suggestions to curtail the flow of speculative capital reflects these problems.[11] If international institutions do not step forward, the main responsibility for fending off future crises will continue to rest with the Latin American countries. One danger is that the process of making domestic financial systems less vulnerable to crisis—which is desirable in itself—can (perhaps already did) make them less agile as tools of development. If access to credit becomes increasingly focused on large (safe) firms and on microenterprise (through microfinance), it is possible that the significant growth potential and the even greater employment-creating potential of the SME sector will be weakened. Inadequacy in this area is probably one factor underlying the weak employment and distributional outcomes in some countries of the region thus far.

Even though international macroeconomic management has been an area of failure, and the world economy has become a more dangerous place for Latin American countries, economic interactions with the industrial countries continue to bring very significant benefits in the areas of trade, foreign investment, migration, and technological transfer. Whether the policy changes of the last quarter century have increased or decreased those benefits is debatable, but it is unlikely that present patterns are close to optimal. There is little doubt that the countries of the region need more policy space to find the right balance in their policies relating to these international economic processes.

In more "domestic" policy areas like labor markets, education, and support for small enterprise, the potential contribution of other countries and international institutions lies primarily in the technical advice area. It could be substantial were the effort significant, but so far it has been quite modest.

What sort of institutional realignment could deliver better policies and outcomes? One obvious hypothesis is that Latin America would be better off with more decisionmaking power lodged closer to home. A regional IMF-type institution endowed with some independence would probably handle things differently from and arguably better than the IMF has done. To begin with, it would give less weight to the views of the US financial lobby, which abjures capital controls and constitutes one of the more pernicious influences on the macroeconomic stability front. On trade issues and other components of the Washington consensus package of reforms, more regional institutions would probably be less hard-line, closer to the sensible center with respect to the roles of markets and of governments. Getting the SME sector moving, whether by hooking it effectively onto export- and import-competing activities or through other means, may be the main key to equitable growth and may require more policy support and intervention than can easily pass muster under the eye of the existing IFIs and other international actors.

At the same time that the region needs more policy independence to search for better responses to the social and economic challenges it faces, some countries run the risk of falling off the tightrope on the other side. In the face of widespread poverty and great inequality together with economic stagnation, many ideas are touted as "better ways" to manage an economy. Most such ideas turn out to be impracticable for one reason or another; many incorporate wishful thinking induced by the perceived failure of the existing apparatus but do not reflect sufficiently in-depth understanding of economics to provide the basis for a solid critique of that apparatus. Although achieving an effective synthesis of market principles and the rules of effective resource allocation with a wider range of complementary ideas is the key to identifying modifications that will really help, it is not an easy task. The best institutional combination would involve considerably more policy space for experimentation in a number of policy domains, matched by a reasonable level of tolerance and support from outside governments and international institutions, and by a great dose of prudence and analytical professionalism on all sides. Latin Americans operating out of regional institutions could, arguably, produce the needed combination of prudence and open-mindedness.

Unlike the European Union, which has mechanisms aimed at providing special assistance to the lower-income members, trade arrangements involving Latin American countries and the United States, Canada, or both (like NAFTA) do not. The need for an equalization fund of the sort available within the European Union has been mooted in the context of NAFTA but does not appear to be on the horizon in a serious way.[12]

Do the facts that US prestige in the region is currently low, that US attention is directed elsewhere, and that there is a high urgency to come up with solutions open any doors to increased independence of the region in dealing with its own problems? That is a matter of degree. Though the United States will continue to exert a powerful influence on the region, using the great bargaining power provided by its market, its influence vis-à-vis the regional heavyweight, Brazil, is modest; the importance of rising markets like China's and India's is recognized; and an increasing degree of policy coherence could be evolving among some countries of the region at this time.

Conclusion

Latin America appears unlikely to recover the rapid poverty-reducing performance of the 1945–1980 period without some changes in its approach, given the unsatisfactory record over the last quarter century. Since no one has a very good handle on the precise policy package best suited to bring down poverty and inequality under current circumstances, what those changes should be is hard to say. Assuming that reductions of inequality in the primary distribution of income remain very hard to achieve, growth will be the key to poverty reduction. A higher investment rate is the single key to faster growth, but the determinants of the increasingly dominant private sector component of investment are not well enough understood for countries to be able to quickly raise its level to what would be needed for fast growth.

In spite of the fact that trade and foreign investment can clearly bring benefits, the evidence to date casts many doubts on whether the single-minded Washington consensus strategy that has dominated policy for a couple of decades now is the best bet for the future. Increased economic integration that is not guided by a more general strategy may fail to deliver the goods. As long as the United States and the IFIs put their confidence in relatively simplistic pro-market policies, they are unlikely to be good partners as Latin America searches for the best way to go. When their views are more flexible and their proposed framework includes the sort of development fund that has been used in the European Union, the time may be ripe for fully effective collaboration. In the meantime, Latin American countries need a reasonable amount of policy space and deserve support to build revised policies around a serious analysis of the events of the last twenty-five years.

Notes

1. ECLAC surveys toward the end of the 1990s revealed that "growing percentages of the population . . . felt that they were living in conditions of risk, insecurity and defencelessness" (ECLAC 2000: 16).

2. Against this trade-limiting factor must be placed the fact that the huge US balance-of-payments deficit in recent years has made it easier for developing countries to export.

3. Like trade reforms, privatization has the potential to raise efficiency and improve income distribution if carried out wisely and honestly. An interesting number of cases where these positive outcomes have emerged can also be identified (Jones 2003).

4. Though if the productivity increase does not take place in smaller firms as well as in larger ones, its impact may simply be to worsen income distribution. Many discussions of productivity are dangerously loose in their failure to recognize this; they present data on productivity growth in the large firm sector or among registered firms as indicative of overall success in this area (e.g., Winters et al. 2004).

5. Labor market reforms have gone less far than others, according to most observers, although measurement is much harder here.

6. The only policy that in its day probably could have quickly reduced income inequality in Latin American countries was an equalizing land reform (i.e., land reform that produced a relatively equitable distribution of land). With the reduced relative size of the agricultural sectors today, its potential impact is now much less than, say, fifty or more years ago.

7. Whitehead (2000) discusses why the optimistic theories did not bear out well, and Rose-Ackerman (2000) presents an interesting interpretation of the outcome.

8. There has been a widely noted tendency for the US State Department to frequently have good information and understanding on the societies and events in Latin America, but for its views to be overridden by less informed and/or more ideological members of the administration.

9. Those American firms and regions with closer links to Latin America naturally articulate a different view, since for them Latin America may matter a great deal. Businesspeople systematically underestimate substitutabilities in the economies of which they are a part, and affected voices always speak louder than unaffected ones on policy issues.

10. McCallum (1995) reported that in 1988, Canadian provinces traded more than twenty times as intensely with each other as with US states of the same size and distance, and Helliwell (1998) took a broad look at the economic meaning of borders.

11. The "Tobin tax," proposed by Nobel Prize–winning economist James Tobin, would impose a penalty on short-term speculation in currencies through a United Nations–managed tax of 0.1 percent to 0.25 percent on all trade of currencies across borders (Tobin 1978).

12. Representative Robert Menendez (Democrat) of New Jersey recently proposed a $500 million social investment and economic development fund to be matched by Latin American countries, to help with democratization and poverty reduction. Such a narrowly defined objective with limited funding cannot be taken to signal interest in an important equalization fund more akin to that in Europe.

PART 5

Conclusion

13

Institutions in the Americas: Theoretical Reflections

Kenneth W. Abbott

This chapter reflects a different perspective from the others in this volume: not that of an expert on the inter-American system (IAS), but of one interested generally in the role of institutions in global governance (Abbott and Snidal 1998) and in theories of institutions (e.g., Abbott 1999, 2005). From this perspective, my goal is to suggest how theories of international institutions help us understand the institutions of the Americas. Many chapters already apply, explicitly or implicitly, some theory of institutions; in those cases I aim to reinforce the analysis by systematically presenting relevant theoretical frameworks. I also identify additional theoretical insights and areas where developments in the Americas suggest extensions to current theory, and I highlight areas for further research.

The concept of an "institution" is one of the most protean in social science. Many disciplines—including sociology, economics, political science, and organization theory—study institutions, all applying their own definitions. Yet virtually all treat as institutions a wide range of explicit and implicit rules and practices that order behavior. "Institutions," in other words, is a broader category than "organizations," although organizations are visible and important institutions. This volume focuses mainly on organizations—such as the Organization of American States (OAS), Summits of the Americas (SOA) process, and Inter-American Development Bank (IDB)—and I do so as well. However, a few inchoate institutions enter the analysis, including the norm of nonintervention and the idea of "the Americas."

I draw primarily on international relations (IR) theory. IR is obviously appropriate for the study of international institutions, but it is also valuable for another reason. IR is famously divided among contending theoretical "paradigms" (Abbott 1999; Slaughter 2000). This fractionation complicates the field, and sometimes diverts analytical energy into "paradigm wars." Yet fractionation enriches the field as well: the very multiplicity of approaches helps scholars identify and analyze diverse elements of social situations, responses to problems, and features of institutions. This range of theoretical approaches produces a fuller picture of complex institutions.

Theories of International Relations

IR includes four major theoretical paradigms: realism, institutionalism, liberalism, and constructivism. These differ primarily along two dimensions: the *actors* whose behavior is seen as central to political outcomes and the *factors and processes*—causal, constitutive and normative—that influence actor behavior and therefore outcomes.

Realist theory views states as the principal actors. States may be treated as abstract unitary entities or as governments making coordinated, high-level decisions and acting in unitary fashion. Realism focuses particularly on great powers and other major states and on security issues. In this realm, states' principal concern is survival; because they interact in anarchy, their guiding principle is self-help. Since states are functionally similar and share a common goal and strategy, power differentials explain significant outcomes. Realists do not argue that institutions will never be created or will always be meaningless: alliances, arms control regimes, and confidence-building measures can all enhance security. However, powerful states generally set the terms of cooperation (although they may provide incentives for cooperation by others, and the weak may combine to "balance" the strong), and institutions survive only so long as powerful states see them as serving their interests.

Institutionalist theory also treats states as the principal actors. Institutionalists observe, however, that states pursue many interests beyond security and power: trade and investment, clean air, health, and numerous other goals, most of which require cooperation.[1] Drawing on economics and game theory, institutionalism focuses on impediments to welfare-enhancing cooperation (e.g., uncertainty, transaction costs, and collective action problems such as incentives to free-ride and to defect from cooperative agreements) and on the ways institutions help overcome them (e.g., producing and disseminating unbiased information, reducing negotiating costs, publicizing reputations, monitoring compliance, and lengthening the "shadow of the future"). Institutions that are neither powerful nor coercive can perform these functions.

Liberal theorists view individuals, nongovernmental organizations (NGOs), civil society organizations (CSOs), business firms, and other non-state actors (NSAs) as the principal political actors. States may be primary on the international stage, but their preferences are shaped by contestation among individuals and groups within domestic politics (Moravcsik 1997).

By decomposing the unitary state, liberal theory opens important avenues of analysis:

1. If domestic politics determine state preferences, domestic governance structures—from constitutions to electoral practices—can be major determinants of international action. Scholars have principally explored the differences between liberal democracies and authoritarian states on issues such as war and compliance with obligations. Conversely, activities of international institutions aimed at modifying or reinforcing domestic political structures, such as election monitoring, can have international as well as domestic consequences.

2. If states are not unitary, government agencies and officials can affect international outcomes and participate in international regimes. For example, "transgovernmental" networks of financial regulators, law enforcement agencies, and other officials have become increasingly prominent. Proponents argue that these arrangements are fast and flexible, expand national regulatory reach, allow advanced agencies to assist others, and remain subject to democratic control (Slaughter 2004).

3. Similarly, officials of intergovernmental organizations (IGOs), if granted some autonomy, can influence international outcomes, even creating greater autonomy for themselves. Many institutionalist and liberal scholars emphasize the role of states in creating and managing IGOs. However, a growing body of literature treats IGO leaders and bureaucracies as significant in their own right (Barnett and Finnemore 1999, 2004).

4. Interactions between domestic and international politics become significant. For example, in the "two-level game" metaphor, heads of government play simultaneously on two chessboards: international negotiations and domestic politics (Putnam 1988). In the "boomerang" strategy—cited by Thomas Legler in Chapter 7 and by William C. Smith and Roberto Patricio Korzeniewicz in Chapter 9 of this volume—human rights activists responding to local abuses, unable to obtain redress domestically, reach out internationally, enlisting IGOs and liberal states to pressure their governments (Keck and Sikkink 1998). International institutions also draw on the capabilities of domestic NGOs, for example to produce information and monitor behavior.

5. NSAs operate transnationally as well as domestically. Individuals, CSOs, and firms act as advocates, provide information, take the lead in operations such as disaster relief, participate in international negotiations, promulgate norms, monitor state compliance, activate "fire alarms" in response to violations, and even enforce commitments

through techniques such as "shaming." Liberal scholars (especially those influenced by constructivist theory, discussed below) emphasize the role of "norm entrepreneurs": NSAs that call attention to issues, "frame" them for maximum political impact, persuade states and IGOs to adopt and implement appropriate norms, and monitor and enforce those norms.

Although these three paradigms identify different causal factors, they all emphasize predominantly rationalist causal processes.[2] All three view actors as behaving purposively, calculating how to further their interests given material and political constraints, and acting strategically when interactions with others affect payoffs. In short, actors in all three theories make decisions primarily according to a "logic of consequences" (March and Olsen 1989). As a corollary, institutions that hope to modify actor behavior must alter incentives, constraints, and other determinants of consequences.

Constructivist theory, the fourth paradigm, considers the entire range of domestic and international actors and differs dramatically from rationalist paradigms in terms of its central factors and processes. Constructivism rejects the assumption that actors have interests and preferences that can be objectively determined; indeed it denies that many international actors objectively exist. Instead, states, IGOs and NGOs, interests and preferences, self-images and identities (e.g., as part of "the Americas"), values, norms, and other politically significant features of the world are "constructed"— given life and meaning—through shared social understandings. Some understandings arise slowly, crystallizing as elements of culture, philosophical principles, or civilizational perspectives (Finnemore 1996: 2; Ruggie 1998). Others, however, are purposively created—by individual norm entrepreneurs, CSOs, states, or IGOs—through techniques of "strategic social construction" (Finnemore and Sikkink 1998: 910–911).

Once ideas, norms, identities, and other social understandings are established, they become determining factors in international life.[3] Actors typically behave in accordance with understandings they have internalized or to which they have been socialized. They do not "calculate" the most rewarding actions; they "deliberate" as to the most appropriate actions in given situations, using a "logic of appropriateness." Social understandings even "constitute" actors with particular capacities (Barnett and Duval 2005). Neither process is strictly causal. As a corollary, institutions that seek to modify behavior must alter ideas, norms, identities, or other subjective constructs. For example, a constructivist might argue that the conflictual features of anarchy in realism are not inherent but constructed and learned (Wendt 1992); they can therefore be relearned, as in the European and North American "security communities" (Adler and Barnett 1998). Even materially weak IGOs can use their perceived expertise and neutrality to shape ideas, norms, and preferences (Barnett and Finnemore 2004).

Until recently, most IR scholars treated these perspectives as mutually exclusive. Scholars would adopt a particular approach, assert that it explains the major features of international politics, and study issue areas where it has explanatory power. This approach produced competing "images" of international governance based on the identification of primary actors (Pollack and Shaffer 2001):[4]

- an interstate or intergovernmental image (with realist, institutionalist, and even liberal[5] variants and with constructivist critiques and alternatives);
- a transgovernmental image (liberal) that focuses on collaboration among state officials and agencies;
- a bureaucratic image (combining institutionalist, liberal, and constructivist elements) that focuses on the autonomous influence of IGOs;
- a transnational image (liberal and constructivist) that focuses on activities of NSAs.

Increasingly, however, scholars have come to view these approaches as valuable complements, even if at some level and in some forms rationalist and constructivist accounts may be ontologically or epistemologically inconsistent (e.g., Fearon and Wendt 2002). I argue elsewhere that institutionalism, prima facie the most relevant approach for studying international institutions, should be taken beyond its inherited state-centric, rationalist-functionalist form by "enriching" it with insights from realism, liberalism, and the more purposive forms of constructivism (Abbott 2005). Although pure neoliberal institutionalism produces important insights into interstate relations, a more inclusive institutionalist theory would help scholars and policymakers analyze and design complex governance arrangements.

Although I do not undertake such theory building here, I do apply all four strands of theory to the institutions of the IAS. I organize the remainder of this chapter around the four "images" of governance.

States as Actors: The Intergovernmental Image

The intergovernmental image provides the dominant perspective in this volume: as L. Ronald Scheman states in Chapter 2 of this volume, international cooperation is "no more effective than the underlying political relations among the participating nations." In this view, states create IGOs and other institutions to perform particular functions on their behalf, design them with those aims—and their own control—in mind, and direct their operations.

For institutionalists, at least, states often grant institutions some autonomy. To be sure, states can achieve many benefits of cooperation—administrative support, exchange of information, and pooling of resources and risks—merely by centralizing interactions in dependent institutions. Further benefits, however, require some autonomy. An independent IGO can mediate and resolve disputes, produce unbiased information, "launder" state actions to make them more acceptable, and perform other valuable functions (Abbott and Snidal 1998). Still, the focus of institutionalism remains on states.

Power Differentials: Realism

Several chapters emphasize the enormous power differentials that exist in the Americas, above all between the United States and other states, but also between major powers like Brazil and Mexico and smaller states (e.g., Chapter 6 in this volume). Given these differentials, realist theory would make several predictions, most of which appear to be fulfilled.

Above all, realism would predict that the United States will exercise dominant influence over the existence and shape of regional institutions and will use them to further its interests. This seems to be borne out in practice. On the positive side, when the United States calls for regional action, the forms of cooperation it seeks usually result; the United States has also used the OAS and other regional institutions to justify its actions. On the negative side, the United States has repeatedly reneged on cooperative understandings when its interests called for unilateral action, even military intervention; these actions have contributed to the periodic stagnation of regional cooperation (see Chapter 3 in this volume).

More interestingly, the mere likelihood that the United States will exercise a predominant, egoistic influence appears to inhibit valuable cooperation. Although other American states have accepted considerable centralization (e.g., OAS structures, specialized agencies, SOA process), they have been very reluctant to grant IAS institutions meaningful independence, at least in part out of concern that the United States could still manipulate them for its own purposes.[6] Even the North American Free Trade Agreement (NAFTA) has not been granted decisionmaking authority (see Chapter 11 in this volume). Ironically, the United States also resists IGO independence: as a hegemon with disproportionate influence in decentralized bargaining, the biggest risk of international cooperation for the United States lies in delegation to autonomous institutions (Abbott and Snidal 2001). In the IAS, then, power differentials lead both the strong and the weak to resist strong institutionalization, including adequate funding (see Chapter 7 in this volume).

Realist theory would also predict that smaller states might join forces to "balance" the dominant state.[7] Because of the enormous power disparity in the Americas, balancing would be expected to take softer political forms, not more threatening (and fruitless) military forms. Refusing to create strong institutions the United States might control can be seen as one form of balancing. More affirmatively, American states have established numerous subregional arrangements for economic integration (e.g., Mercosur, South American Community of Nations) and political cooperation (e.g., Rio Group, Ibero-American Summit). These groupings exclude the United States, creating independent bases of political and economic power (again, see Chapter 7).

Balancing also relates to the concept of "voice opportunities" (Grieco 1996), introduced in Chapter 11. On its own, balancing is more akin to exit than to voice (Hirschman 1970). However, exit from regimes dominated by a hegemon can be risky. Seeking voice within those regimes can be more beneficial, reducing conflict, maintaining engagement with the hegemon, and turning institutional decisions in favor of the smaller states. However, small states need leverage to achieve voice, and soft balancing helps create it.

The flip side of dominance is leadership. Although a hegemon may act to further purely private interests, it may also advance interests with public-good characteristics, benefiting others. On issues of that sort—just which issues they are may be controversial—hegemonic leadership is often essential to collective action (Olson 1965). As Gordon Mace and Jean-Philippe Thérien note in Chapter 3, US leadership has been a major factor in periods of American regime building, most recently the launch of the SOA process.

Since the attacks of September 11, 2001, however, the United States has been distracted, diminishing its leadership in the region, with adverse consequences for cooperation on issues such as the Inter-American Democratic Charter (adopted the same day as the attacks). Episodes like this suggest a modification for regional regimes to theories of hegemonic dominance. A hegemon is typically involved in global activities far more than smaller states in its region. As a result, it often views regional developments as minor adjuncts of global phenomena, whereas its regional partners see them as important and unique. This structural asymmetry produces divergent priorities, hampers leadership, and leads to suboptimal regional outcomes.

The converse of this phenomenon is also significant. With the hegemon drawn to global issues and regimes, it is in smaller states' interest to keep the hegemon engaged in the region. Engagement produces benefits wherever hegemonic activity creates public goods: regional security, deterring external interference, investment and trade, economic assistance, even prestige (see Chapter 2 in this volume). Operating in the shadow of a hegemon, then, is complex. Small states need "Goldilocks" institutions: not too strong, not too weak. They must keep the hegemon engaged but not give it or institutions it controls too much influence. Even so, the tendency of the hegemon to view regional issues through a global lens is likely to produce continuing frustration.

Interests and Incentives: Institutionalism

A wide range of common interests underlies cooperation and governance in the Americas, as institutionalist theory would predict. Common (though not entirely harmonious) interests are apparent in areas such as health (the Pan-American Health Organization, or PAHO); other "low politics" issues (specialized agencies and commissions, discussed in Chapter 2); security (the Declaration on Security in the Americas, arms control, confidence-building measures, discussed in Chapters 5 and 6); human rights (a highly developed legal regime, discussed in Chapter 8); and democracy (the Inter-American Democratic Charter, discussed in Chapter 7), in spite of weaknesses in many of these institutions.

Yet many chapters also highlight divergent interests on particular issues, including most of those just mentioned, that hamper cooperation. These chapters reveal multiple fault lines reflecting the heterogeneity of the hemisphere: not only between North and South or the United States and smaller states, but also among South America, Central America, the English-speaking Caribbean, and other groupings.

In these circumstances it is tempting to call for political will (see Chapters 2, 3, and 5). However, if the interests of states are strongly opposed, such calls are unlikely to be fruitful. In analyzing cooperation in the Americas, then, it would be valuable to chart the patterns of interests in particular issue areas using basic game theory.

If state interests are diametrically opposed, as in the deadlock game, cooperation and the exercise of political will are highly unlikely, whatever the institutional framework. If interests are mixed, as in prisoner's dilemma, states will face collective action problems in achieving and maintaining cooperation, but cooperation will be possible, often with the help of institutions. If interests are harmonious, as in coordination, cooperation is likely; here too, if interests are somewhat mixed, as in battle of the sexes, institutions can help, and actors may be amenable to the exercise of political will.

Divergent interests often lead to weak institutions, which serve as an element of political compromise: *demandeurs* are granted rhetorical commitments to appease their constituents; resisters are granted weak institutions to ensure that the commitments remain rhetorical. This pattern emerges frequently in the Americas. For example, many commitments in the IAS are weakly legalized.[8] Legalization requires not only legally binding obligations but also precise commitments (or procedures for making them precise in particular cases) to limit auto-interpretation and avoidance, and the delegation of authority to independent institutions to interpret and apply obligations (Goldstein et al. 2000; Abbott and Snidal 2001). To be sure, some IAS commitments are strong on one or more of these dimensions: IGO charters, the human rights system, and arms control and corruption conventions. But significant instruments are soft on multiple dimensions: SOA declarations and action plans, the Democratic Charter, the Declaration on Security, and most specialized agency actions. Soft legalization is an important tool for managing divergent interests, yet it reduces the effectiveness of commitments (Abbott and Snidal 2001).

Similarly, several chapters note that the institutions responsible for the SOA process are not effectively "nested" (Aggarwal 1998). Nesting is especially important in rule-based regimes, to avoid rule conflicts, forum shopping, and disputes (Alter and Meunier 2006). The SOA process is not strongly rule-based, but it produces commitments with enough normative content to make nesting significant. In theory, ministerials are nested under summits, whereas the OAS, IDB, specialized agencies, and governments are nested under ministerials, with responsibility for implementation (see Chapters 3 and 4). In practice, however, nesting is weak: ministerials are not integrated with summits; the IDB has resisted nesting; slippage continues in national implementation; and powerful subregionals remain outside the system.

Institutionalist theory can explain some of these features: the international system as a whole remains weakly institutionalized, so effective nesting is hard to accomplish; nesting is typically incomplete when new institutions are grafted onto continuing ones; the subregionals have different memberships, making them difficult to nest. The fundamental explanation, however, may be broader. With divergent interests, states cannot be expected to produce optimally engineered regimes; they will produce regimes that are functional in other ways, in particular by embodying political compromises, such as combining rhetorical strength with institutional weakness. Institutionalism has taught us much about institutional design (Koremenos, Lipson, and Snidal 2004; Mitchell 1994), and scholars should use this knowledge to critique institutions poorly designed to achieve their substantive goals (see Chapters 4 and 6 in this volume). But states also have more political goals, which they pursue rationally and purposively, including through institutional design.

Perhaps the most remarkable feature of cooperation in the Americas is its cyclical nature. As several chapters describe, cooperation has proceeded in fits and starts for over a century, with periods of apparent harmony and institutional creation followed by periods of discord and stagnation. In Chapter 3, Mace and Thérien describe the compromises forged in cooperative periods as "ambiguous," based on misperception and divergent expectations, and leading to inevitable breakdowns. What accounts for this pattern? Institutionalist theory suggests some likely explanatory factors. But none appears to fully explain the pattern, leaving this an attractive area for research.

Two causal factors have already been suggested. First, large power differentials among states lead to unstable compromises. Powerful states push agendas driven by global concerns, while weak states pursue a "Goldilocks" strategy, engaging the hegemon but keeping institutions weak; the combination produces awkward compromises. As cooperation unfolds, powerful states respond to global incentives and freely exercise their power, while weak states resist strengthening the regime, weakening cooperation.

Second, divergent interests also produce unstable compromises. In the Americas, interests are almost always mixed; they may even be opposed, overcome by short-term incentives long enough to reach agreement, but not long enough to maintain it. Defection follows naturally. Institutionalist theory teaches that substantively deep, highly institutionalized agreements can "screen out" states not sincerely interested in cooperation (Downs, Rocke, and Barsoom 1996).[9] Yet American states have often felt it necessary to pursue regionwide agreements, encompassing states with noncooperative interests; such agreements are likely to be shallow and weakly institutionalized. In this sense, the growth in subregional agreements, better able to screen participants, could be beneficial.

Even with divergent interests, it is surprising that states in the Americas—which have interacted for decades—appear so often to misperceive one another's preferences. One hypothesis might be that transaction costs and subjective preconceptions lead to inadequate efforts at understanding. Another might be that changes in preferences, not misperception of stable preferences, are responsible for cycling. Still, it would be reasonable for the IAS to incorporate intensive dialogue, disclosure, screening, and other forms of preference revelation in future efforts at regional cooperation.

Domestic Politics and State Preferences: Liberalism

Even if states remain the primary international actors, in liberal theory state preferences are determined by domestic politics, not by objective characteristics. Domestic politics are shaped by national constitutions and political structures, the strength of civil society, and other local factors.

In the Americas, changes in domestic politics have led directly to regional cooperation in several areas. For example, as democracy spread throughout the region, the preferences of newly democratized states changed, leading them to support the SOA process and the democracy protection regime centered on the Democratic Charter (see Chapter 7). New democratic leaders used the charter to lock in reforms, especially the legitimacy of their own elections. Even with its weaknesses, the charter process is a major development and a prime example of positive interaction between domestic and international politics.

Unfortunately, some governments' commitment to democracy has proven rather shallow. Their resistance to strong charter processes, justified as avoiding intervention in domestic affairs, has limited the institution to relatively modest activities, such as election monitoring at government invitation. As liberal theory would suggest, government leaders seeking to protect their own positions, not "states," seem to be the primary actors here. Although liberal scholars frequently compare democracies with authoritarian states, this example suggests the value of extending the comparison across varying levels of democratic commitment and various democratic forms. One might also inquire why the commitment to human rights has proven more durable than that to democracy.

Changes in national civil-military relations have also animated regional cooperation. As democratic governments replaced authoritarian regimes, civil-military relations took a marked turn toward civilian control. This changed national preferences, leading to numerous domestic reforms and laying the groundwork for remarkable progress on security issues (see Chapters 5 and 6 in this volume).

Domestic politics may also bear on the questions of misperception and cycling. Domestic politics are rarely transparent or easy for outsiders to comprehend. If domestic developments rather than objective "foreign policy" considerations determine state preferences, it is easier to understand repeated misperceptions. Institutional devices that render domestic interests and preferences more transparent should facilitate international cooperation. Domestic politics may also be more changeable than objective state interests, perhaps even moving in cycles. Domestic changes might then account for changes in state preferences and the cycling of cooperation.

Ideas and Norms at the Intergovernmental Level: Constructivism

Constructivists argue that ideas, beliefs, norms, identities, and other shared understandings are the major determinants of behavior by states and other international actors. Ideas can even constitute new actors or grant actors new authority. At the same time, actor behavior creates and modifies understandings—intentionally or otherwise—in an ongoing process of mutual construction. A number of subjective understandings are relevant to cooperation in the Americas.

The idea of the Americas as a political entity has been in existence since 1889. It may have been a strategic social construction even then, and conscious efforts to maintain it continue (see Chapter 4). This understanding has helped constitute the actors in the region: without an American identity, there would be little reason to predict the emergence of a highly institutionalized IAS. The American identity has never been strong enough to overcome divergent national interests (see Chapter 7), but it may help explain the resilience of the IAS in the face of repeated periods of stagnation. More recently, stronger identities have been forming around subregional and ethnic groupings, suggesting further decline for the IAS.

Common norms of human rights and more recently of democracy and human security (reflected in the Declaration on Security in the Americas) have emerged in the hemisphere. These norms have legitimated particular forms of government and supported institutionalized cooperation in a range of issue areas. In turn, states have used regional institutions to disseminate and reinforce those norms. However, all three sets of norms appear to have shallow roots in much of the hemisphere.

The norm of nonintervention has been a major element in all the uneasy "grand compromises" of hemispheric cooperation. However, nonintervention remains a broad, imprecise norm unsupported by institutions authorized to interpret and apply it in specific situations. Although the norm may have a high level of legal obligation, in other words, it has low levels of precision and delegation, and thus remains relatively soft. Since the United States has been able to justify acts of intervention under the current norm, it would presumably not agree to harden it, especially through stronger delegation.

Even for constructivists, ideas and norms rarely fit together neatly. They are frequently in conflict, and political deliberations must try to reconcile the tensions. The norm of nonintervention provides an excellent example. The norm itself is widely supported. In many areas, however, it stands in the way of effective cooperation. The clearest example in this volume is the "normative impasse" between nonintervention and democracy protection: as Thomas Legler describes in Chapter 7, even new democracies have been reluctant to invoke strong Democratic Charter mechanisms for fear of opening the door to intervention. In the Americas, nonintervention typically trumps other norms, not infrequently with adverse consequences.[10]

Ideas, identities, and other understandings may also be relevant to the perplexing question of cycling. To the hypotheses already advanced, one might add the cycling of ideas. For example, ideas favoring free markets and ideas supporting government intervention appear to rotate in and out of favor, although it is not clear if they do so on any regular schedule, or on the same schedule as economic integration. Even the American identity may cycle over time.

Officials and Agencies as Actors: The Transgovernmental Image

Treating officials and agencies along with states as meaningful actors in international politics, as liberal theory suggests, provides significant insights into cooperation in the Americas. Long-standing agencies and commissions such as PAHO, the Inter-American Telecommunications Commission (CITEL), Latin American Organization for Energy Development (OLADE), and Inter-American Juridical Committee, as well as more recent creations such as the Inter-American Drug Abuse Control Commission (CICAD) and Inter-American Committee Against Terrorism (CICTE), are built on networks of expert agencies, not on treaties and diplomatic exchanges among states. Similar arrangements have been created outside the OAS system, notably the Inter-American Center for Tax Administration (CIAT) and Council of Securities Regulators of the Americas (COSRA). These institutions are increasingly assigned the mundane technical tasks of international cooperation (see Chapter 2), and seem well suited for them. At higher levels, SOA ministerials create cooperative links among department heads. Even summits can be viewed as transgovernmental, as they create working relationships among heads of state.

Hemispheric security relationships are also structured transgovernmentally. The defense ministerials of the Americas have created valuable working relationships, advancing civilian control of the military and the security cooperation agenda. More challenging is the Inter-American Defense Board, a transgovernmental organization of military forces, created in an earlier era and still not integrated into the evolving security architecture (see Chapter 5).

Yet most transgovernmental arrangements in the Americas remain weak and underfunded. There is little evidence to support now largely discredited theories of "functionalism," which argued that cooperation on technical matters would gradually "spill over" into political cooperation and ultimately deep integration, as in Europe. Collaboration within specialized agencies has not apparently strengthened trust, common identity, or common interests across the region. It remains to be seen whether the SOA process and other recent initiatives will provide fresh impetus, but the current stagnation suggests otherwise. Perhaps the best hope for functionalism in the Americas lies in Mercosur and other subregionals, with their increasingly strong identities.

In other respects, however, it is helpful to view cooperation in the Americas as driven by national ministries rather than by "states." As the chapters in this book make clear, particular ministries dominate particular institutions: foreign ministries the OAS, finance ministries the IDB, defense ministries the security institutions, and so on.

Richard Feinberg and Paul Haslam's comparison in Chapter 4 of OAS and IDB responses to the SOA process reveals substantial "siloing" of relationships: expertise, interests, preferences, and organizational culture run vertically between national ministries and "their" IGOs. Since the SOA and OAS are both dominated by foreign ministries, the OAS responded positively to summit initiatives; since finance ministries played little role in the SOA, the IDB responded more negatively. Silo relationships also run in the other direction: since IGO initiatives are primarily implemented by their linked ministries, ministerial power, culture, and preferences determine how states respond. Consider PAHO: its close relationship with health ministries provides both advantages (e.g., specialized expertise) and disadvantages (weakness in domestic bureaucratic infighting) and introduces attitudes that may support or hinder collaboration with other organizations (a focus on medical interventions). As transgovernmental arrangements proliferate, siloing could become a significant problem.

IGOs as Autonomous Actors

IGOs possess bureaucracies, procedures, and cultures that influence international cooperation. Feinberg and Haslam's comparison of the OAS and IDB makes the point clearly. The OAS has a broad, weakly defined political mission. For years it pursued narrow organizational goals, avoiding strong action that might alienate member states; it linked with undynamic elements of member governments. The IDB, in contrast, has a clearly defined economic mission, ample resources, and well-established, technically oriented procedures. It linked with more powerful government agencies and focused on the needs of borrowers. It is not surprising that the two organizations responded so differently to the political shock of the SOA.

At the same time, the aggressive OAS response is noteworthy. Secretary-General César Gaviria acted autonomously and effectively to change the direction of the organization. Under his leadership, the OAS adopted new missions, reorganized, and modified internal incentives. It was all done in order to "nest" the organization more deeply within the SOA process, with the goals of increased authority, resources, and prestige. The OAS did receive a prominent role in the SOA process, and the initiatives in which it participates—such as the Joint Working Group, the Summit Implementation Review Group (SIRG), and the summit secretariat (see Chapter 3)—have significantly strengthened institutional support for the SOA.

In general, however, the institutions of the Americas have very limited autonomy. As forums, instead of steering negotiations toward clear mandates, they have produced "empty rhetoric," logrolling deals, and diffuse declarations (see Chapter 4). As norm implementers, they have limited monitoring and enforcement authority, exemplified by the failure to create a monitoring system under the Inter-American Democratic Charter.[11] IAS institutions may still have an impact, through information, rhetorical shaping of identities and ideas, cautious steering of negotiations, and the like, but their techniques and impact will remain relatively subtle.

Nonstate Actors on the International Stage: The Transnational Image

The rapid expansion of liberal IR theory, with its emphasis on individuals, NGOs, firms, and other CSOs, has barely kept pace with real-world developments.

NSAs, acting singly and in transnational coalitions (Keck and Sikkink 1998), have become a prominent part of global governance. Based on the chapters in this volume, however, it is striking how little the NSA revolution has penetrated the Americas. Smith and Korzeniewicz's study of "insider" and "outsider" CSOs in Chapter 9 makes clear that NSAs cannot be considered the primary actors in the IAS, although both groups have influence in particular areas.

Before the 1990s, the IAS largely ignored civil society (see Chapter 3 in this volume). The SOA process marked a turning point. It came as the spread of democracy enabled CSO formation, USAID provided financial support, and the Clinton administration pressed for CSO involvement in international regimes. President Bill Clinton and other leaders brought CSOs into the planning for the early summits, and they had significant influence on summit rhetoric. Yet as CSOs pressed for more concrete commitments, leaders backed down, turning aside or watering down proposals from the very groups they had brought into the process.

The OAS, again responding to the SOA process, reorganized to promote CSO participation. As Mace and Thérien recount in Chapter 3, from 1999 to 2004 the organization adopted guidelines for participation by CSOs, created a committee to facilitate participation, tasked the summit secretariat to coordinate participation, adopted a strategy to increase participation, and established a fund for CSO projects. But CSOs did not aggressively take up the OAS invitation, perhaps suspicious of its sincerity, and the rebuff of CSO proposals at the summits cast a pall on civil society relations. Participation in the Democratic Charter process has followed a parallel course, with the backlash against the Friends of the Charter revealing how strongly American governments resist CSO involvement (and how shallow their commitment to major IAS norms remains).

The Free Trade Area of the Americas (FTAA) negotiations have been far more closed than either of these processes (see Chapter 10). That is not surprising: the World Trade Organization (WTO) remains among the most closed IGOs. There may be good reasons for closure: Judith Goldstein and Lisa Martin argue that transparency in trade negotiations, including CSO participation, reveals the likely winners and losers, motivating and empowering interest groups to lobby, and particularly advantaging protectionist groups (Goldstein and Martin 2001). Yet Smith and Korzeniewicz reveal the political costs of closure in Chapter 9: CSOs excluded from the FTAA have become "outsiders," turning to oppositional ideologies, mobilization, and resistance.

Normatively, several chapters note the dangers of a "democratic deficit" in the IAS. They suggest that the exclusion of CSOs damages the legitimacy of the system. Even apart from legitimacy, CSO participation can provide important practical benefits. In most areas, at least, it seems a matter of some urgency to reconcile civil society with the IAS.

It would be illuminating to look across issue areas and ask why the inter-American human rights system has been as successful as it has, given the general hemispheric resistance to CSO participation. Human rights NGOs have long been active in the Americas: their activities inspired the "boomerang process," and they have been the principal advocates for the system. At the same time, human rights norms protect and empower NSAs, and the inter-American system incorporates them to a remarkable degree. The Inter-American Commission on Human Rights is made up of experts serving in their individual capacities; it operates in highly independent fashion. The judges of the Inter-American Court of Human Rights also serve in their individual capacities and can be considered NSAs (see Chapter 8). Both institutions rely on NGOs to provide information and prepare cases. How has this system, even with its weaknesses, been able to survive, when CSO participation in cognate areas like democracy has been turned back?

Conclusion

The institutions of the IAS are understudied in IR. The chapters in this book reveal how intricate and interesting those institutions are and what a valuable laboratory they provide for developing and testing theories of institutions. The chapters also reveal the difficulty of relying on a single theoretical paradigm to explain complex political arrangements. I have tried to suggest that, although a single theoretical approach like realism or transgovernmental liberalism may provide good analytical purchase on particular issues or institutions, a regime as complex as the IAS can only be fully explored with a multifaceted theoretical approach. Finally, since the regime is so understudied, I have tried to identify interesting and fruitful questions for future research. Outside of the European Union, IR has focused most of its attention on multilateral regimes. It could reap substantial benefits from studying other complex regional regimes, like those in the Americas.

Notes

1. There are "institutionalist" theories in many disciplines (Hall and Taylor 1996). I utilize what is sometimes called "neoliberal institutionalism," the best-developed theory of institutions in IR (Pevehouse 2002: 518).

2. However, liberal theorists in particular recognize that some individuals and groups are motivated by normative and other nonrationalist influences.

3. Constructivism is part of the school of "sociological institutionalism," which emphasizes the influence of social structures, including ideational structures, on agents.

4. Pollack and Shaffer do not discuss the bureaucratic image.

5. Liberal theory is intergovernmental to the extent it views states or heads of government as the principal actors in international arenas, pursuing preferences established domestically (Moravcsik 1997).

6. A few institutions do have significant autonomy, notably the IDB and the IACHR and Inter-American Court of Human Rights.

7. In some circumstances, small states rally around the dominant state for protection and other advantages, a process realists call "bandwagoning." When bandwagoning rather than balancing occurs has not been fully established.

8. Legalization is an institution in its own right.

9. They can also screen out states that lack capacity to implement commitments.

10. An alternative, liberal explanation might be that newly elected democratic governments prefer a democracy regime that is strong enough to reinforce their elections, but not strong enough to interfere with their less democratic postelection behavior.

11. The human rights institutions are a partial exception.

14

Assessing Hemispheric Institution Building

Gordon Mace, Jean-Philippe Thérien, and Paul Haslam

When it comes to grasping the nature of inter-American institutions, Craig Murphy's comparison of the building of international organizations to the construction of cathedrals in medieval Europe is particularly instructive (Murphy 1994: 33). Contemporary hemispheric institutions do not derive from an ideal model established over a hundred years ago. They are, rather, the complex result of various designs applied at different periods during the last century, with each new design modifying the preceding institutional layout.

The First Summit of the Americas in 1994 undoubtedly represented one such reorientation of hemispheric regionalism. The principal innovation of this third phase of institution building was the introduction of a two-level structure for governing the Americas. At the executive level, the summits of heads of state, supported by a dozen ministerial conferences and a Summit Implementation Review Group (SIRG), sought to enhance the legitimacy of inter-American governance and to give it a renewed sense of direction. Existing regional bodies such as the Organization of American States (OAS) and the Inter-American Development Bank (IDB) took on an administrative role, ensuring follow-up to the mandates formulated at the summits and the ministerials.

There are, of course, several factors explaining the shift that occurred in 1994 after more than twenty-five years of relative paralysis in inter-American cooperation. Some factors were external to the region and had to do with the end of the Cold War and the rise of what was then perceived as competitive trade blocs. But certain factors, perhaps more important than the external ones, were at work within the region itself. The most salient of these was the external debt crisis of the early 1980s, which produced a change of mentality among Latin American elites and was responsible in many ways for the turn toward democracy and market-based economic

255

policies. These changes in political and economic orientation were seen by policymakers in the United States as evidence of a real convergence of values between the United States and the rest of the Americas. The "historical moment" had to be seized so as to usher in a climate propitious to a new era in inter-American politics.

The renaissance that took place in the mid-1990s demonstrated the remarkable resilience of hemispheric institutions and their ability to overcome moments of crisis as well as long periods of stagnation. It also held out significant promise for the future of inter-American relations, inasmuch as it showed a capacity to accommodate the various, sometimes opposing, interests and aspirations of the governments of the region. After giving rise to vast expectations, however, the institutional renovation of the inter-American system has, in the final analysis, produced only limited results. Although it is true that the decade since 1994 has witnessed some progress, hemispheric cooperation continues to encounter stubborn obstacles. This ambiguous situation is inherent to each of the four issues that now comprise the core of the hemispheric agenda: governance, democracy, security, and the economy.

Governance

The institutional reorganization of the 1990s did breathe new life into the governance of regionalism in the Americas. By making it possible for heads of state to engage in a direct dialogue, the regular holding of summits invested the inter-American system with greater political meaning. The establishment of ministerials in a number of sectors resulted in a higher degree of cooperation among ministers and government officials from all countries of the hemisphere. The creation of a Joint Summit Working Group, assembling all the major agencies involved in regional cooperation, has, moreover, provided a useful instrument for improving the circulation of information and raising the efficacy of hemispheric governance. In addition to allowing better coordination of national policies, the multiplication of diplomatic communication channels has fostered the emergence of a common hemispheric agenda. And by facilitating the negotiation of new agreements, this common agenda has contributed to a notable broadening of the inter-American normative order.

It should also be pointed out that the new architecture of regional institutions has made it possible for nongovernmental actors to participate more extensively in hemispheric politics. Although William Smith and Roberto Patricio Korzeniewicz's distinction between "insiders" and "outsiders" in Chapter 9 of this book must be kept in mind, it is clear that inter-American diplomacy has today become more receptive to the views expressed by civil society and the business community. Through its efforts to become more inclusive, regional cooperation has furthered the empowerment and networking of social groups that had traditionally been left on the periphery of hemispheric public debate. In the long run, this innovation may turn out to be the main benefit accruing from the recent reform of the functioning of regionalism in the Americas.

Notwithstanding the progress described above, inter-American governance continues to confront a number of barriers. All in all, the advances have fallen well short of the hopes that seemed altogether justified in 1994. For one thing, summit diplomacy has not succeeded in gaining the momentum that many had predicted. Instead of being held annually or biannually, as had been proposed initially, the Summits of the Americas have taken place every three or four years. And, despite four years of preparation, the latest of these high-level meetings at the time of writing—the Mar del Plata Summit of 2005—has generally been deemed a failure. At the operational level, the inter-American system of governance has been incapable of clearly identifying priorities for action. The Plans of Action produced by the summits, which enumerate hundreds of objectives, have not been able to impart a specific direction to hemispheric diplomacy. Ironically, the most publicized item of this multifarious agenda, the Free Trade Area of the Americas (FTAA), currently finds itself in a stalemate. Moreover, the division of labor among the principal actors concerned—the OAS, other regional institutions, and national governments—has proven to be a constant source of confusion.

A tangible expression of the gap between the rhetoric and the reality of hemispheric governance is the underfunding of inter-American bodies. Despite its recent increase, the OAS budget remains altogether inadequate for the political, economic, social, and cultural mandates of the organization. Of course, the situation would improve somewhat if member states agreed to make their quota payments on time, but the fundamental problem of regional cooperation financing cannot be resolved without a considerable infusion of political imagination. One avenue to explore would certainly be the pooling of the resources made available to the inter-American institutions as a whole. In this perspective, some observers have noted that a transfer to the OAS of only 1 percent of the annual loan disbursements of the IDB would double the OAS budget.

Finally, inter-American governance remains permanently confronted with the difficulty of enforcing collective decisions. The summit process and the OAS can "encourage" and "urge" members to behave in a certain way, but they cannot constrain them. The source of this institutional weakness is well-known: founded on intergovernmentalism and the sovereign equality of states, the political architecture of the inter-American system does not recognize any supranational authority. As a consequence, hemispheric governance suffers from a flagrant lack of legitimacy. Under current conditions, it is difficult to imagine that a renewal of the legitimacy of inter-American governance could result from a spontaneous change of attitude among the governments of the region. In the short or medium term, if such a change in attitude were to materialize, it would more likely be the product of political pressure from regional nonstate actors or from those inter-American institutions, such as the Inter-American Commission on Human Rights, that are not state-dominated.

Democracy

There is no question that the institutional shift of 1994 advanced the cause of democracy in the Americas. Many diplomats and observers agree that the strengthening of democracy is henceforth the primary mission of the OAS. Although the ongoing consolidation of democracy in Latin America is by all accounts due more to domestic than to external factors, inter-American norms and practices have had a real impact on this process.

With respect to norms, the most important development of the last decade was certainly the adoption in 2001 of the Inter-American Democratic Charter. This agreement made it possible, in particular, to advocate the idea that only democratic governments may participate in hemispheric affairs. In a region historically subject to authoritarianism and coups d'état, the consensus achieved on this norm represents a substantial change in attitude. It should be stressed as well that the Democratic Charter proposes an innovative definition of democracy. It recognizes, specifically, that the peoples of the Americas have a right to democracy and that, beyond the mere holding of elections, democratic values must include justice and the transparency of the political system.

With regard to practices, the OAS now plays a key role in electoral processes. Since 1990, the organization has been invited to observe more than eighty elections throughout the hemisphere. Between elections, the OAS promotes dialogue among parliamentarians, political parties, and members of civil society. Over the past fifteen years, the OAS has furthermore intervened in a number of domestic crises. Until 2001 these interventions usually took place within the framework of Resolution 1080, adopted in 1991; since 2001, most interventions have been carried out under the Democratic Charter. Reference to the charter in dealing with the conflicts in Venezuela (2002), Nicaragua (2005), and Ecuador (2005) has sent a clear signal that the fate of democracy in the Americas can no longer be determined solely through the principle of national sovereignty.

Yet, despite all these positive developments, the state of democracy in the hemisphere remains fragile. The inter-American system apparently lacks the political and financial resources to ensure the achievement of the ambitious goals outlined in the Democratic Charter. The charter could not avert, for example, recent outbursts of political violence in Haiti and Bolivia. This is one of the factors that has prompted Tom Legler to ask, in Chapter 7, whether the Democratic Charter is ultimately no more than an "empty piece of paper."

The inter-American democratic regime does, in fact, suffer from a long list of shortcomings. First, noble intentions aside, its vision of democracy is centered essentially on the electoral process. The Democratic Charter's statement on the interdependence between democracy and social and economic rights—the importance of which was emphasized by Bernard Duhaime in Chapter 8—amounts to hardly more than a rhetorical turn of phrase. In addition, if something of a consensus does exist as to the appropriate attitude to adopt toward a coup d'état, the inter-American community continues to be divided with regard to the threat an "unconstitutional alteration" of the democratic order might pose. No criteria have been provided for defining such an alteration. Furthermore, the denunciation of an alteration of the democratic order remains an intergovernmental procedure from which civil society is completely excluded.

From a broader perspective, the punitive approach far outweighs prevention in the inter-American doctrine on democracy. This tendency has spawned distrust among certain Latin American states that are afraid the promotion of democracy could be used as a political pretext justifying US intervention in the region. One of the effects of this prevailing climate of distrust is that the conditions for accessing democracy remain ambiguous. The secretary-general of the OAS, José Miguel Insulza, aptly expressed this ambiguity when he declared that although the Democratic Charter "must be adhered to unconditionally . . . there are different paths for achieving our objectives" (Insulza 2005, 2). Ultimately, the inter-American democratic regime rests on a set of ever more sophisticated norms; however, this codification has not prevented a multiplicity of interpretations as to what the "right to democracy" actually means.

Security

Security issues have long dominated the inter-American agenda and its cycles of institution building and decline. By 1994, many of the traditional hemispheric security institutions were viewed as vitiated (the Rio Treaty), obsolete (the Inter-American Defense Board and College), or ineffective and irrelevant (the Pact of Bogotá). The end of the Cold War, which had caused so much conflict between Washington and Latin America, represented a new opportunity for cooperation, as did the emergence of new nontraditional security threats. As a result, the summit era witnessed the development of (1) a new agenda, (2) new institutions, and (3) the participation of new actors.

The agenda moved from a traditional military perspective focused on external threats or internal subversion to an approach broadly based on the concept of human security. This movement has been institutionalized in the Declaration on Multidimensional Security adopted in 2003. The declaration codified the "new security agenda," identifying as security issues civil-military relations, terrorism, drug trafficking, money laundering, and environmental and health threats, among others.

The declaration is only the culmination of broader post–Cold War institution building and cooperation. The OAS Committee on Hemispheric Security has met since 1991 as a working group to discuss common security problems. Since 1995, the hemisphere's ministers of defense have held ministerials intended to improve the coordination of regional security institutions. OAS organs have also been created, such as the Secretariat for Multidimensional Security and the Inter-American Committee Against Terrorism (CICTE). In addition, one may point to the proliferation of formal and informal confidence- and security-building measures (CSBMs), particularly at the subregional level, but also endorsed by the summit process.

Although the management of military and potentially militarized disputes in the Americas has become increasingly institutionalized, perhaps most importantly, the summit era has also implicated new actors in security matters. Indeed, one fundamental change in recent inter-American affairs has been the subordination of military and security issues in general to civilian authority. This is in marked contrast to Cold War practices in which a "club of generals" atmosphere pervaded the Inter-American Defense Board (IADB) and kept this institution stubbornly autonomous from the democratic structures of the OAS.

More than ever, the Western Hemisphere conforms to Arthur Whitaker's ideal of a hemisphere of peace, where the peaceful settlement of disputes is the norm rather than the exception (Whitaker 1954). Nonetheless, the apparent agreement on the concept of "multidimensional security," as David Mares points out in Chapter 6, actually represents the lowest common denominator of agreement on priorities and institutional reform. Above all, discussions in the Committee on Hemispheric Security have failed to develop an integrated framework among security institutions that relates the Rio Treaty and the IADB to the new institutional developments. A lack of coordination persists between the foreign ministers responsible for summit objectives and the ministers of defense. Also in Latin America, suspicion continues to exist between the military and civilian authorities, contributing to a lack of leadership on security issues. Furthermore, the limited application of new norms to a number of resilient cases of conflict (Haitian instability, Colombian civil war, the Bolivia-Chile border dispute) tends to undermine the consolidation of common hemispheric security. As Margaret Daly Hayes puts it in Chapter 5, "It is time to end the debate and begin action toward a more secure hemisphere."

The institutional consequence of the post-1994 period is, therefore, a proliferation of new institutions that overlap with existing ones—each set with a different raison d'être. The summit process has encouraged dialogue, contributed to the adoption of a new agenda, and strengthened civilian control of the military. In the final analysis, however, hemispheric security is still dominated by bilateral relationships, illustrated by the ample US funding for its military assistance programs (Plan Colombia being the most obvious example). In this sense, over a decade of reform has failed to change the underlying structure of hemispheric security relations.

Economy

The difficulties faced in the post-1994 round of institution building are most evident in the area of economic governance. Although the summits addressed a number of regional issues, the promised Free Trade Area of the Americas was the economic linchpin of the summit process. It was the mirage of access to the US market that brought Latin America to the table to discuss a broader range of cooperative strategies. Following the Miami ministerial of November 2003, the unraveling of this option undoubtedly contributed to the polarization and failure of the Mar del Plata Summit.

The importance of this ephemeral idea of an FTAA should not be underestimated. Because 1994 marked the first time since 1889–1890 that hemispheric free trade found itself on the inter-American agenda, it constituted an advance over past practices. Participants agreed on the desirability of free trade, the issues to be negotiated, and a time frame that envisioned completion by 2005. Although progress on the FTAA text had ground to a halt by 2004, the process had been accompanied by the significant development of support institutions. The Trade Unit (later OAS Trade Section) of the OAS was charged with disseminating information on trade and investment and the state of negotiations of FTAA. It also sought to build negotiating capacity in small economies through training workshops and related activities. As Richard Feinberg and Paul Haslam noted in Chapter 4, the FTAA process also strengthened the Trade Unit of the OAS.

Furthermore, the growing acceptance of the free trade idea was confirmed by the proliferation of bilateral free trade agreements (FTAs), bilateral investment treaties (BITs), and subregional and extraregional trade agreements. In fact, Maryse Robert's analysis in Chapter 10 reveals a dynamic process at the subregional level, where policy coordination and harmonization pushed economic integration and institutional development forward despite stalemate at the regionwide FTAA negotiations. These agreements are investment-driven; aim to deepen economic integration; and cover new issues such as intellectual property, investment, and services.

Ultimately, however, efforts to institutionalize a single hemispheric regime in trade and investment have reached an impasse. Despite broad support for the free trade ideal, subregional agreements are sufficiently incompatible in terms of disciplines and legal style to complicate their harmonization in an FTAA. As Louis Bélanger pointed out in Chapter 11, the precise legalized style of the North American Free Trade Agreement (NAFTA) limits its ability to evolve. But more fundamentally, the US penchant for legalization is at odds with the greater flexibility of intra–Latin American trade agreements, which allow for an evolution over time that is in keeping with the changing political priorities of member governments. The Mar del Plata Declaration illustrated this North-South divide on the FTAA between a US-led vision of NAFTA-plus and a South American vision reflecting the interests of Brazil and its allies. The United States and twenty-eight other countries signed a statement affirming their will to "advance the negotiations within the framework adopted in Miami in November 2003." In contrast, Mercosur plus Venezuela asserted that "the necessary conditions are not yet in place for achieving a balanced and equitable free trade agreement with effective access to markets free from subsidies and trade-distorting practices, and that takes into account the needs and sensitivities of all partners, as well as the differences in the levels of development and size of the economies" (Summit Declaration 2005: par. 19a, b).

The North-South divide over trade is also applicable to other areas of economic governance, particularly economic development. Here also, there is an absence of consensus, especially on the fundamental questions of how to address poverty, inequality, and the availability of decent work. Albert Berry argued in Chapter 12 that the current institutional framework is inappropriate to the particular challenge of development in Latin America. Institutions such as the IDB, International Monetary Fund, and World Bank adopted without question or empirical evidence the policy prescriptions of the Washington consensus. The relative lack of success of almost two decades of neoliberal economic reform has further underlined this divide.

The rigidity of the North American attitude toward state intervention in a region where market forces alone have been unable to ensure growth with equity complicates the march to hemispheric economic integration. In this respect, the institutions of economic governance in the Americas reflect divergent foundational ideas regarding the relationship between state and society.

A Mixed Picture

The preceding assessment of the post-1994 phase of institution building in the Americas bespeaks the altogether mixed record of hemispheric regionalism. On the one hand, inter-American institutions have displayed an unmistakable robustness through their proven ability to address problems of collective action, to reduce transaction and information costs, and to facilitate agreements. But on the other hand, regional institutions have often remained ineffective, failing to resolve many of the issues deemed important by participating governments. This in turn has generated a high level of dissatisfaction due to unfulfilled expectations. The dichotomy between the robustness and the effectiveness of inter-American institutions is an old and recurring problem caused by a number of structural characteristics of the inter-American system, a very complex regime, as Kenneth W. Abbott reminded us in Chapter 13. Among the major obstacles to improved performance are those associated with asymmetry, inequality, and identity.

Asymmetry, or the uneven distribution of power, has always been a central feature of inter-American relations, not only at the hemispheric level but also at the subregional level. Each subregion of the Americas faces a situation of asymmetry that governments have addressed, but never to the complete satisfaction of all the countries involved. Certain integration schemes did achieve some success in dealing with an asymmetric situation. The Andean Group of the early years, for instance, adopted various measures in favor of Bolivia and Ecuador: longer time periods for imposing tariffs, special treatment in the context of the common industrial policy, more money from the regional bank, and so on. However, other integration projects, such as the Latin American Free Trade Association, failed precisely because of asymmetry.

Of course, it is at the hemispheric level that asymmetry in the Americas is the most problematic. The Western Hemisphere is the only region in the world where a superpower on the scale of the United States coexists with an array of small and middle powers. The asymmetry of this situation makes cooperation much more complicated because the imbalance in overall capacity makes it difficult for weaker parties to have a significant impact on the regional agenda. The effectiveness of the institutions in dealing with the specific problems of the low-capacity countries depends heavily on the attitudes of the larger countries, particularly the largest of all.

Another structural characteristic of the region concerns the unequal distribution of wealth. Latin America and the Caribbean is the region of the world where inequality is the most acute. Poverty and inequality are complex phenomena that must be tackled chiefly at the national level. But regional institutions have a strategic supporting role in helping governments and local communities in the fight against poverty and inequality. Unfortunately, inter-American institutions have a poor record in reducing inequality in the region, despite the progress registered at the macroeconomic level. Lack of consensus concerning the most appropriate strategies explains why, in spite of the large amounts of money spent over the years, results have been limited.

Regional institutions, however, can do only so much in the fight against inequality, and the resulting North-South cleavage is never absent from the dynamics of hemispheric integration. A more fundamental way of dealing with this problem would be to design a free trade area project involving measures that take into account the enormous economic disparities between the large and small economies of the region.

If hemispheric regionalism fails to address the problem of inequality, it will not succeed in instilling a widespread sense of belonging and loyalty. Gordon Mace and Jean-Philippe Thérien reminded us in Chapter 3 that this eventuality is entertained even by hemispheric elites, who have echoed former OAS secretary-general César Gaviria's "final question," formulated in his farewell report: "Do we really want to unite our peoples in a common destiny?" (Gaviria 2004: 361–362). Gaviria's reflection was made only one year before Enrique Iglesias, a respected figure of inter-American cooperation and longtime head of the Inter-American Development Bank, left the IDB to take charge of the secretariat of the Ibero-American Summits. The symbolic significance of Iglesias's move cannot be ignored. Along with Gaviria's statement, it illustrates a loss of faith in the Western Hemisphere Idea and in hemispheric regionalism as an integral part of the identity of most citizens of the region.

The Americas are a region where multiple and competing loyalties exist. To date, inter-American institutions have not been able to generate a strong sense of identity among their participating communities. The ensuing dearth of legitimacy may be the fundamental reason why national governments lack the political will to sustain hemispheric integration by making the compromises needed to further the process.

Thus, with hemispheric regionalism once again experiencing a phase of stagnation, we may well ask what lies ahead for inter-American cooperation in general and hemispheric region building in particular. Basically, there are two possible attitudes when considering the limited results of the current phase of hemispheric regionalism. The pessimistic attitude would lead one to entirely lose faith in the system and to conclude that region building is not possible in the Americas, given the opposing interests of the major actors and their unwillingness to work together toward a community of the Americas. A more optimistic approach would be to see region building—whether in the Americas or elsewhere—as a learning process and to acknowledge that more time will be needed to reach the level of confidence required to sustain a robust cooperative endeavor. The ghosts of the past must make way for new, more open-minded attitudes on the part of the United States and its Latin American neighbors. Newcomers to the inter-American system, such as Canada and the Caribbean countries, could make a useful contribution in this regard.

One question thus becomes central: how to stop the current period of stagnation and relaunch inter-American cooperation. Surely, what is at stake here involves attitude and vision more than bargaining and short-term gains. If hemispheric regionalism is to survive as a relevant channel for collective, legitimate action, it will need to address much more seriously the issue of inequality. This implies policy initiatives in at least two important and related areas. One is development assistance, multilateral and bilateral, which must be made more efficient, as suggested by L. Ronald Scheman in Chapter 2. The other concerns trade and economic relations in general, which also have a direct and probably more important bearing on everyday life in the hemisphere. Governments of the larger economies must display more flexibility in negotiating regional trade rules so as to provide developing countries with an adequate policy space to reduce poverty and inequality. In this connection, the social cohesion fund put in place in the European Union could serve as a useful model for the Americas.

In order to coexist with other spaces for collective action, hemispheric regionalism and its institutions must be perceived as producing added-value benefits that the communities cannot find at the national or subregional level. And this can only be achieved if inter-American cooperation truly takes into account the interests and preferences of all the societies involved. In the nineteenth century, Simón Bolívar and Thomas Jefferson each envisioned a community of nations of the Americas. The visions differed, but they could very well coexist (Mace and Thérien 1996: 3–7). Today's challenge is to create an integrated space for cooperation in the hemisphere. It remains to be seen whether inter-American regionalism will become that space or ultimately prove to be nothing more than a chimera.

Acronyms

ACE	*acuerdo de complementación económica*
AD	antidumping
ALADI	Latin American Integration Association
AMIA	Argentinian-Israelite Mutual Association
ART	Alliance for Responsible Trade
ASPA	American Servicemen's Protection Act
BLADEX	Latin American Export Bank
CABEI	Central American Bank for Economic Integration
CACM	Central American Common Market
CAF	Andean Development Corporation
CAFTA-DR	Central American–Dominican Republic Free Trade Agreement
CARIBCAN	Caribbean-Canada Trade Agreement
CARICOM	Caribbean Community (1973)
CCC	Canadian Chamber of Commerce
CCCE	Canadian Council of Chief Executives
CCJ	Caribbean Court of Justice
CCSOO	Concerned Civil Society Organizations Office
CDB	Caribbean Development Bank
CEAL	Latin American Business Council
CECLA	Special Commission for Latin American Coordination
CECON	Special Committee on Trade Consultation and Negotiation
CET	common external tariff
CFAC	Central American Conference of Armies
CHS	Committee on Hemispheric Security
CIAP	Inter-American Committee for the Alliance for Progress
CIAT	Inter-American Center for Tax Administration

CICAD	Inter-American Drug Abuse Control Commission
CICTE	Inter-American Committee Against Terrorism; Inter-American Convention Against Terrorism
CICYP	Inter-American Council for Commerce and Production
CIDA	Canadian International Development Agency
CIDI	Inter-American Council for Integral Development
CIFTA	Inter-American Convention Against the Illicit Manufacturing of and Trafficking in Firearms, Ammunition, Explosives, and Other Related Materials
CIM	Inter-American Commission of Women
CIP	Inter-American Ports Commission
CITEL	Inter-American Telecommunications Commission
COSRA	Council of Securities Regulators of the Americas
CRS	Congressional Research Service
CSBMs	confidence- and security-building measures
CSM	Caribbean Single Market (2006)
CSME	Caribbean Single Market and Economy
CSOs	civil society organizations
CUSTA	Canada–United States Trade Agreement
CUT	Central Única dos Trabalhadores
CVD	countervailing duties
DMA	Defense Ministerial of the Americas
DSM	dispute settlement mechanism
DSU	dispute settlement understanding
EAI	Enterprise for the Americas Initiative
ECC	Extraordinary Challenge Committee
ECLAC	Economic Commission for Latin America and the Caribbean
ECSC	European Coal and Steel Community
EGF	Esquel Group Foundation
ESCRs	economic, social, and cultural rights
FARC	Revolutionary Armed Forces of Colombia
FDI	foreign direct investment
FELABAN	Latin American Federation of Banks
FOCAL	Canadian Foundation for the Americas
FTAA	Free Trade Area of the Americas
FTAs	free trade agreements
GA	General Assembly
GATT	General Agreement on Tariffs and Trade
GDP	gross domestic product
HCP	Hemispheric Cooperation Program
IACD	Inter-American Agency for Cooperation and Development

IACHR	Inter-American Commission on Human Rights
IACNDR	Inter-American Committee on Disaster Reduction
IACourt	Inter-American Court of Human Rights
IADB	Inter-American Defense Board
IAJC	Inter-American Juridical Committee
IAS	inter-American system
ICFTU	International Confederation of Free Trade Unions
IDB	Inter-American Development Bank
IFIs	international financial institutions
IGOs	intergovernmental organizations
IHL	international humanitarian law
IICA	Inter-American Institute for Cooperation on Agriculture
IIHR	Inter-American Institute of Human Rights
III	Inter-American Indian Institute
IIN	Inter-American Children's Institute
ILO	International Labor Organization
IMF	International Monetary Fund
IR	international relations
ISI	import substitution industrialization
ISP	Inter-American Strategy for Public Participation
JSWG	Joint Summit Working Group (OAS, IDB, ECLAC, and PAHO)
LAFTA	Latin American Free Trade Association
LAIA	Latin American Integration Association (successor to LAFTA)
MDGs	Millennium Development Goals
Mercosur	Mercado Común del Sur
MFN	most-favored-nation
MIDs	militarized interstate disputes
MOS	Modernization of the State
MST	Landless Workers Movement
NAFTA	North American Free Trade Agreement
NATO	North Atlantic Treaty Organization
NATS	North American Trade Secretariat
NSA	nonstate actors
NSC	North-South Center
OAS	Organization of American States
OECS	Organization of Eastern Caribbean States
OLADE	Latin American Organization for Energy Development
ORIT	Organización Regional Interamericana de Trabajadores
OSCE	Organization for Security and Cooperation in Europe
OSFU	Office of Summit Follow-up (later became Summits of the Americas Secretariat)

PAHO	Pan-American Health Organization
PAIGH	Pan-American Institute of Geography and History
POS	political opportunity structure
PRI	Party of the Institutional Revolution
PT	Partido dos Trabalhadores
REBRIP	Rede Brasileira pela Integração dos Povos
RMALC	Red Mexicana de Acción Frente al Libre Comercio
RSS	Regional Security System
SELA	Latin American Economic System
SICA	Central American Integration System
SIECA	Central American Economic Integration Secretariat
SIRG	Summit Implementation Review Group
SMEs	small and medium-sized enterprises
SOA	Summits of the Americas
SPP	Security and Prosperity Partnership of North America
TNC	Trade Negotiations Committee
UNCTAD	United Nations Conference on Trade and Development
UNITAR	United Nations Institute of Training and Research
USAID	US Agency for International Development
USTR	US Trade Representative
WHO	World Health Organization
WTO	World Trade Organization

Bibliography

Abbott, Frederick M. 2000. "NAFTA and the Legalization of World Politics: A Case Study." *International Organization* 54(3): 519–547.

Abbott, Kenneth W. 1999. "International Relations Theory, International Law, and the Regime Governing Atrocities in Internal Conflicts." *American Journal of International Law* 93(2): 361–379.

———. 2005. "Toward a Richer Institutionalism for International Law and Policy." *Journal of International Law and International Relations* 1(1–2): 9–34.

Abbott, Kenneth W., Robert O. Keohane, Andrew Moravcsik, Anne-Marie Slaughter, and Duncan Snidal. 2001. "The Concept of Legalization." In Judith Goldstein et al., eds., *Legalization and World Politics.* Cambridge, MA: IO Foundation and Massachusetts Institute of Technology, 17–36.

Abbott, Kenneth W., and Duncan Snidal. 1998. "Why States Use Formal International Organizations." *Journal of Conflict Resolution* 42(1): 3–32.

———. 2000. "Hard Law and Soft Law in International Governance." *International Organization* 54(3): 421–456.

———. 2001. "Hard and Soft Law in International Governance." In Judith Goldstein et al., eds., *Legalization and World Politics.* Cambridge, MA: IO Foundation and Massachusetts Institute of Technology, 37–72.

Academic Roundtable. 2005. "Communiqué to the Ministers of Foreign Affairs, General Assembly of the OAS." Ft. Lauderdale, June 3.

Ackerman, Frank. 2005. "The Shrinking Gains from Trade: A Critical Assessment of Doha Round Projections." Medford: Tufts University, Global Development and Environment Institute, Working Paper No. 05-01.

Adler, Emanuel, and Michael Barnett. 1998. *Security Communities.* New York: Cambridge University Press.

AFL-CIO/ORIT (American Federation of Labor–Congress of Industrial Organizations/Organización Regional Interamericana de Trabajadores). 1995. "Declaration of Concern of the Inter-American Regional Organization of Workers." In Robin Rosenberg and Steve Stein, eds., *Advancing the Miami Process: Civil Society and the Summit of the Americas.* Coral Gables, FL: North-South Center Press at the University of Miami, 361–366.

Aggarwal, Vinod, ed. 1998. *Institutional Designs for a Complex World: Bargaining, Linkages and Nesting.* Ithaca, NY: Cornell University Press.

Aguilar, Alonso. 1965. *Pan-Americanism from Monroe to the Present: A View from the Other Side.* New York: Monthly Review Press.

Allmand, Warren. 2001. "Human Rights and the Free Trade Area of the Americas." http://www.ddrd.ca/site/publications/index.php?lang=en&subsection=catalogue&id=1269 (accessed July 19, 2005).

Alter, Karen J., and Sophie Meunier. 2006. "Nested and Overlapping Regimes in the Transatlantic Banana Trade Dispute." *Journal of European Public Policy* 13(3): 362–382.

Altimir, Oscar. 1982. *The Extent of Poverty in Latin America.* Washington, DC: World Bank staff working paper.

Amnesty International. 2005. "Summit of the Americas: Our Call for Human Rights: A Message from Amnesty International Members in Advance of the Fourth Summit of the Americas." IOR 62/005/2005.

Anderson, Kim, and Will Martin. 2005. "Agricultural Trade Reform and the Doha Development Agenda." *World Economy* 28(9): 1301–1327.

Anderson, Sarah, and Karen Hansen-Kuhn, eds. 2001. *America's Plan for the Americas: A Critical Analysis of the US Negotiating Positions on the FTAA.* Washington, DC: Alliance for Responsible Trade, February 12.

Arbitration Tribunal. 2002. *In the Matter of an Arbitration Under Chapter Eleven of the North American Free Trade Agreement Between Pope and Talbot Inc. and Government of Canada. Award in Respect of Damages,* May 31.

Aronson, Bernard W. 1996. "Our Vision of the Hemisphere." *US Department of State Dispatch,* October 15, 184–185.

ASC (Alianza Social Continental). 1999a. "Building a Hemispheric Social Alliance in the Americas." http://www.web.net/comfront/hems_main.htm (accessed March 10, 2005).

———. 1999b. "Alternatives for the Americas: Building a People's Hemispheric Agreement." http://www.web.net/comfront/forumdocs_socialex.html (accessed March 8, 2005).

———. 1999c. "Social Exclusion, Labor and Poverty in the Americas." http://www.web.net/comfront/forumdoc_socialex.html (accessed March 11, 2005).

———. 1999d. "Social Investment, Finances and Debt in the Americas." http://www.net/comfront/cf_doc_invest.htm (accessed March 10, 2005).

———. 1999e. "Final Declaration of the Summit: Peoples' Summit of the Americas." In Richard E. Feinberg and Robin L. Rosenberg, eds., *Civil Society and the Summit of the Americas: The 1998 Santiago Summit.* Boulder, CO: Lynne Rienner, 589–590.

———. 2001. "Informe sobre la semana de actividades de la Alianza Social Continental con ocasión del Lanzamiento público de la Segunda Cumbre de los Pueblos de las Américas a realizarse en la Ciudad de Québec, Canadá en april 2001." http://www.asc-hsa.org (accessed March 10, 2005).

Atkins, G. Pope. 1989. *Latin America in the International Political·System.* 2nd ed. Boulder, CO: Westview.

———. 1999. *Latin America and the Caribbean in the International Political System.* 4th ed. Boulder, CO: Westview.

Ayala Coroa, Carlos, and Pedro Nikken Bellshaw-Hógg. 2006. *Collective Defense of Democracy: Concepts and Procedures. Diffusion of the Inter-American Democratic Charter 5 (January).* Lima: Andean Commission of Jurists/Carter Center.

Bachelet, Pablo. 2005. "Diplomats Criticize US Resistance to OAS Human Rights Guidelines." *Miami Herald,* July 1 (accessed via Lexis/Nexis, August 7, 2005).

Bachelet Jeria, Michelle. 2003. "Fifth Conference of Ministers of Defense of the Americas. Report of the Outgoing Chair." Committee on Hemispheric Security, OEA/Ser. G. CP/CSH/INF.19/03 add. 1, February 25, 2003, p. 4.

Ball, Margaret M. 1969. *The OAS in Transition.* Durham, NC: Duke University Press.

Banega, Cyro, Björn Hettne, and Fredrik Söderbaum. 2001. "The New Regionalism in South America." In Michael Schultz, Fredrik Söderbaum, and Joakim Öjendal, eds., *Regionalization in a Globalizing World.* London: ZED Books, 234–249.

Barnett, Michael, and Raymond Duvall. 2005. "Power in International Politics." *International Organization* 59(1): 39–75.

Barnett, Michael, and Martha Finnemore. 1999. "The Power, Politics, and Pathologies of International Organizations." *International Organization* 53(4): 669–698.

———. 2004. *Rules for the World: International Organizations in World Politics.* Ithaca, NY: Cornell University Press.

Barry, Tom. 2005. "World Movement for Democracy Made in USA—the Crusade of the Democratic Globalists." Silver City, NM: Americas Program, July 14. http://americas.irc-online.org/am/161 (accessed January 10, 2006).

Bennet, W. Lance. 2005. "Social Movements Beyond Borders: Understanding Two Eras of Transnational Activism." In Donatella Della Porta and Sidney Tarrow, eds., *Transnational Protest and Global Activism.* Lanham: Rowman and Littlefield, 203–226.

Berenson, William, M. 2004. "Legal Opinion on the Relationship Between the Organization of American States and the Inter-American Defense Board: Legal Options for the Adoption of the Organization's Step-child." Organization of American States, Committee on Hemispheric Security, February 20. www.oas .org/csh/english/documents/CP11778E06.doc (accessed February 15, 2005).

Bernier, Ivan, and Martin Roy. 1999. "NAFTA and Mercosur: Two Competing Models?" In Gordon Mace and Louis Bélanger, eds., *The Americas in Transition: The Contours of Regionalism.* Boulder, CO: Lynne Rienner, 69–91.

Bernstein, Harry. 1961. *Making an Inter-American Mind.* Gainesville: University of Florida Press.

Berry, Albert. 1997. "The Inequality Threat in Latin America." *Latin American Research Review* 32(2): 3–40.

———. 2005. "From the Vicious Circles of Stagnation to High, Sustained, and Poverty-Reducing Growth: Are There General Recipes?" University of Toronto, draft.

Bertoni, Eduardo A. 2000. *Libertad de expresión en el estado de derecho—Doctrina y jurisprudencia nacional, extrajera e internacional.* Buenos Aires: Editores del Puerto.

———. 2004. *Libertad de expresión en las Américas, los cinco primeros informes de la relatoría para la libertad de expresión.* San José: IIDH.

Bhalla, Surjit. 2002. *Imagine There's No Country: Globalization and Its Consequences for Poverty, Inequality, and Growth.* Washington, DC: Institute for International Economics.

Bloomfield, Richard J. 1994. "Making the Western Hemisphere Safe for Democracy? The OAS Defense-of-Democracy Regime." In Carl Kaysen, Robert A. Pastor, and Laura W. Porter, eds., *Collective Responses to Regional Problems: The Case of Latin America and the Caribbean.* Cambridge, MA: American Academy of Arts and Sciences, 15–28.

Bloomfield, Richard J., and P. Lincoln. 2003. "Meeting of Experts on Confidence and Security Building Measures." Remarks to Organization of American States

Summit-Mandated Meeting of Experts on CSBMs, Miami, February 3. US Department of State. www.state.gov/t/pm/rls/rm/18529.htm (accessed July 19, 2005).

Bloomfield, Richard J., and Abraham Lowenthal. 1990. "Inter-American Institutions in a Time of Change." *International Journal* 45(4): 867–888.

Blume, Klaus. 2004. "Fear of Terrorist Attack Spreads in Central America." *Deutsche Presse-Agentur,* August 31 (accessed via Lexis/Nexis, August 8, 2005).

Boniface, Dexter. 2002. "Is There a Democratic Norm in the Americas? An Analysis of the Organization of American States." *Global Governance* 8(3): 365–381.

———. 2007. "The OAS's Mixed Record." In Thomas Legler, Sharon Lean, and Dexter Boniface, eds., *Promoting Democracy in the Americas.* Baltimore, MD: Johns Hopkins University Press.

Borner, Silvio, Frank Bodmer, and Markus Kobler. 2004. *Institutional Efficiency and Its Determinants.* Paris: OECD.

Bradley, Curtis A. 2002–2003. "International Delegations, the Structural Constitution, and Non-Self-Execution." *Stanford Law Review* 55: 1557–1596.

Brinkley, Joel. 2005. "US Proposal Draws Fire as an Attack on Venezuela." *New York Times,* May 22.

Brison, Scott. 2004. *Partners for Progress.* Joint Meeting of the Canadian Chamber of Commerce and US Chamber of Commerce, Washington, DC, March 31.

Bronson, Diane, and Lucie Lamarche. 2001. "A Human Rights Framework for Trade in the Americas." Rights and Democracy. http://www.ddrd.ca/site/_PDF/publications/globalization/frameworkFinal.pdf (accessed July 19, 2005).

Bruno, Michael. 2005. "Latin America Seen Posing Nontraditional Threats." *Aerospace Daily and Defense Report* 215(58): 4 (accessed via Lexis/Nexis, October 16, 2005).

Buergenthal, Thomas, Robert E. Norris, and Dinah Shelton. 1983. *Protecting Human Rights in the Americas.* 3rd ed. Arlington, VA: N. P. Engel.

Bumiller, Elisabeth, and Larry Rohter. 2005. "Bush, Replying to Chávez, Urges Latin Americans to Follow US." *New York Times,* November 6.

Bush, George. 1989. "Remarks to the Council of the Americas." *Public Papers of the President of the United States,* vol. 1. Washington, DC: Government Printing Office, 504–507.

Buzan, Barry. 2004. *From International to World Society? English School Theory and the Social Structure of Globalisation.* Cambridge: Cambridge University Press.

Cameron, Maxwell A. 2003a. Special Issue on the Inter-American Democratic Charter. *Canadian Foreign Policy* 10(3).

———. 2003b. "The Slow-Motion Constitutional Coup in Venezuela." *Informed* (UBC) 6.

Canada. 2003. *Partners in North America: Advancing Canada's Relations with the United States and Mexico—Government Response.* Ottawa.

Canada. Department of Foreign Affairs and International Trade. 2001. *M. Pettitgrew se félicite des interprétations adoptées à la réunion de la Commission de l'ALENA au sujet du chapitre 11.* Communiqué no. 116, August 1.

Canada. House of Commons. 2002. *Partenaires en Amérique du Nord: Cultiver des relations du Canada avec les Etats-Unis et le Mexique.* Rapport du Comité permanent des Affaires étrangères et du Commerce international, December.

Cancado Trindade, Antonio Augusto. 2000. "Current State and Perspectives of the Inter-American System of Human Rights Protection at the Dawn of the New Century." *Tulane Journal of International and Comparative Law* 8: 5–47.

Carnegie Council on Ethics and International Affairs. 2005. *The Americas at the Crossroads: Putting Decent Work Back on the Development Agenda.* New York: Carnegie Council, Globalization and Development Forum, White Paper 1.

Carnegie Endowment for International Peace. 1931. *The International Conferences of American States, 1889–1928.* New York: Oxford University Press.

Caro, Isaac. 1992. "Medidas de Confianza Mutua en America Latina." *FLACSO-Chile,* typescript, November 16.

Carter, Ashton B., William J. Perry, and John D. Steinbruner. 1992. *A New Concept of Cooperative Security.* Washington, DC: Brookings Institution.

Carter, Jimmy. 2005. "The Promise and Peril of Democracy." Keynote Speech to OAS Lecture Series of the Americas. Washington, DC, January 25.

Casal, Jesús María. n.d. "Desafíos de los procesos de integración respecto de los derechos humanos." Comisión andina de Juristas. http://www.cajpe.org.pe/NUEVODDHH/Integraci%F3nyDDHH1.pdf (accessed July 19, 2005).

CCC (Canadian Chamber of Commerce). 2004. *Closer Together: The Consequences of Greater Economic Integration.* Notes for an address by Nancy Hughes Anthony, president and CEO, Arthur Kroeger College of Public Affairs Leadership Forum, Ottawa, ON, February 10.

CCCE (Canadian Council of Chief Executives). 2003. *Security and Prosperity: The Dynamics of a New Canada–United States Partnership in North America.* January 14.

———. 2004. *New Frontiers: Building a Twenty-First-Century Canada–United States Partnership in North America.* April.

CCSOO (Concerned Civil Society Organizations Office). 1995. "Promises to Keep: The Unfinished Agenda for Human Rights and Economic Justice in the Americas." In Robin Rosenberg and Steve Stein, eds., *Advancing the Miami Process: Civil Society and the Summit of the Americas.* Coral Gables, FL: North-South Center Press at the University of Miami, 207–216.

CEJIL (Center for Justice and International Law). 1997. "La necesidad de mantener un debate abierto en la evaluacion del sistema interamericano." *Gaceta* 7.

———. 1999. "Una oportunidad para mejorar la protección de las victimas: La reforma del reglamento de la Comisión." *Gaceta* 11.

———. 2004. "Desafíos del sistema interamericano en la actualidad." *Gaceta* 19.

Central American Economic Integration Secretariat (SIECA). 2005. *Estado de situación de la integración económica centroamericana.* Guatemala City: SIECA.

Centro de Derechos Humanos "Miguel Augustin Pro Juárez—PRODH." 2005. "Impact of Economic Integration Processes on Human Rights in the Americas." Mexico. http://www.dd-rd.ca/site/_PDF/publications/americas/audienceIACHR.pdf (accessed March 15, 2005).

Cerna, Christina. 1987. "The Inter-American Commission on Human Rights." *Connecticut Journal of International Law* 2(2): 311–318.

———. 1992. "The Structure and Functioning of the Inter-American Court of Human Rights (1979–1992)." *British Year Book of International Law* 63: 135–229.

Cheyre Espinosa, Juan Emilio. 2000. *Medidas de confianza mutua: Casos de América Latina y el Mediterráneo.* Santiago, Chile: Centro de Estudios e Investigaciones Militares.

Chillier, Gaston, and Laurie Freeman. 2005. "Potential Threat: The New OAS Concept of Hemispheric Security." Washington, DC: Washington Office on Latin America, Special Report, July. http://www.wola.org/publications/security_lowres.pdf (accessed February 15, 2006).

Christopher, Warren. 1993. "A Bridge to a Better Future for the United States and the Hemisphere." *US Department of State Dispatch* 4(37): 625–626.

Cinotti, David N. 2003. "The New Isolationism: Non-Self-Execution Declarations and Treaties as the Supreme Law of the Land." *Georgetown Law Journal* 91(6): 1277–1301.

Cline, William R. 2004. *Trade Policy and Global Poverty*. Washington, DC: Centre for Global Development and Institute for International Economics.

Coady, David, and Margaret Grosh. 2004. *Targeting of Transfers in Developing Countries: Review of Lessons and Experience*. Washington, DC: World Bank.

Coalición Internacional de Organizaciones para los Derechos Humanos en las Américas. 2005a. "Pronunciamiento presentado con ocasión del proceso de preparación de la IV Cumbre de las Américas." GRIC del 8 y 9 de Septiembre, "Crear Trabajo para Enfrentar la Pobreza y Fortalecer la Gobernabilidad Democrática," Mar del Plata, Argentina 4 y 5 de noviembre de 2005. http://www.civilsociety.oas.org/Events/XL%20meeting/coalicion1.doc (accessed March 15, 2005).

———. 2005b. "Pronunciamiento presentado con ocasión del Trigésimo Quinto periodo ordinario de sesiones de la Asamblea General de la Organización de Estados Americanos." Coalición Internacional de Organizaciones para los Derechos Humanos en las Américas, 2005. http://www.cejil.org/asambleas.cfm?id=156 (accessed March 15, 2005).

Cole, Laurie. 2003. "Civil Society Participation in the Inter-American System: The Case of the Organization of American States." *The Summit of the Americas Follow-up Series*. Ottawa: FOCAL 2: 1–28.

Colombia. 2003. "Democratic Security and Defense Policy." Office of the President of the Republic and the Ministry of Defense, Bogotá. http://www.colombiaemb.org/opencms/opencms/system/galleries/download/defense/seguridad_democratica_eng.pdf.

Committee on Hemispheric Security (CHS). 2002a. "Concepts of Security in the Hemisphere: Questionnaire and Responses." Washington, DC: Organization of American States. http://www.oas.org/main/main.asp?sLang=E&sLink=documents/eng/oasissues.asp (accessed February 15, 2005).

———. 2002b. "Compendium of Replies of the Member States to the Questionnaire on New Approaches to Hemispheric Security." OEA/Ser. G, CP/CSH-430/02 rev. 1, October 1.

———. 2003. Presentation of the Rapporteur of the Special Conference on Security. Special Conference on Security, Report of Rapporteurs, CES/doc 14/03 add. 1. http://www.oas.org/main/main.asp?sLang=E&sLink=documents/eng/oasissues.asp (accessed February 17, 2005).

———. 2005. "Draft Resolution: Inter-American Convention on Transparency in Conventional Weapons Acquisitions." Approved May 9, 2005, OEA/Ser.G CP/CSH-682/05 rev. 1, May 13.

———. Miami Group of Experts. 2003. "Illustrative List of Confidence- and Security-Building Measures for Countries to Consider Adopting on the Bilateral, Sub-Regional, and Regional Level." February 3–4, 2003, OEA/Ser.G CP/CSH-535/03 rev. 1, January 28.

Congressional Research Service (CRS). 2001. *Treaties and Other International Agreements: The Role of the United States Senate*. Washington, DC: Library of Congress, January.

Connell-Smith, Gordon. 1966. *The Inter-American System*. London: Oxford University Press.

————. 1968. "The OAS and the Dominican Crisis." In Joseph S. Nye, ed., *International Regionalism: Readings*. Boston: Little, Brown, 97–105.

————. 1974. *The United States and Latin America: An Historical Analysis of Inter-American Relations*. London: Heinemann Educational Books.

Conservative Party of Canada. 2004. *Demanding Better: Platform 2004*. Ottawa: Conservative Party of Canada.

Cooper, Andrew F. 2001. "The Quebec City 'Democracy Summit'." *Washington Quarterly* 24(2): 159–171.

Cooper, Andrew F., and Thomas Legler. 2001a. "The OAS Democratic Solidarity Paradigm: Questions of Collective and National Leadership." *Latin American Politics and Society* 43(1): 103–126.

————. 2001b. "The OAS in Peru: A Model for the Future?" *Journal of Democracy* 12(4): 123–136.

————. 2006. *Intervention Without Intervening? The OAS Defense and Promotion of Democracy in the Americas*. New York: Palgrave Macmillan.

Cornia, Giovanni Andrea, ed. 2004. *Inequality, Growth, and Poverty in an Era of Liberalization and Globalization*. Oxford and New York: Oxford University Press.

Corporación PARTICIPA. 2001. *Resultado del Proceso de Consulta a Organizaciones de la Sociedad Civil en el marco de la III Cumbre de las Américas*. Santiago: Corporación PARTICIPA, FOCAL, and Esquel Group Foundation.

Corrales, Javier, and Richard E. Feinberg. 1999. "Regimes of Cooperation in the Western Hemisphere: Power, Interests, and Intellectual Traditions." *International Studies Quarterly* 43(1): 1–36.

Council on Foreign Relations. 2005. *Building a North American Community. Report of the Independent Task Force on the Future of North America*. New York: Council on Foreign Relations.

Crawford, Jo-Ann, and Roberto V. Fiorentino. 2005. *The Changing Landscape of Regional Trade Agreements*. Discussion Paper No. 8. Geneva: World Trade Organization.

Cueva, Héctor de la. 2001. Authors' interview of the leader of the Red Mexicana de Acción Frente al Libre Comercio and General Secretary of the Alianza Social Continental. Mexico City, February 5.

da Motta Veiga, Pedro. 2004. *Mercosur's Institutionalization Agenda: The Challenges of a Project in Crisis*. Buenos Aires: INTAL-ITD Working Paper-SITI-06E.

Davey, William J. 1996. *Pine and Swine: Canada–United States Trade Dispute Settlement: The FTA Experience and NAFTA Prospects*. Ottawa: Centre for Trade Policy and Law.

————. 2005. "Institutional Framework." In Patrick F. J. Macrory, Arthur E. Appleton, and Michael G. Plummer, eds., *The World Trade Organization: Legal, Economic, and Political Analysis*. New York: Springer, vol. 1: 51–87.

Dell, Sidney. 1972. *The Inter-American Bank*. New York: Praeger.

Department of Legal Affairs and Services. N.d. "A-66: Inter-American Convention Against Terrorism." www.oas.org/juridico/english/sigs/a-66.html (accessed July 10, 2005).

Desjardins, Marie-France. 1996. *Rethinking Confidence-Building Measures: Obstacles to Agreement and the Risks of Overselling the Process*. London: International Institute for Strategic Studies, Adelphi Paper 307.

Diamint, Rut. 2004. "Security Challenges in Latin America." *Bulletin of Latin American Research* 23(1): 43–62.

DMA (Defense Ministerial of the Americas). 1996. *Declaration of Bariloche and of the Working Groups.* http://www.fasoc.cl/files/articulo/ART4117e3668d7c9.pdf (accessed March 15, 2006).

———. 2002. "Declaration of Santiago." Declaration of the Fifth Conference of Ministers of Defense of the Americas, Santiago, Chile (November 18–22). See, especially, items 8–12. http://www.state.gov/p/wha/rls/71005.htm.

Domínguez, Jorge I., ed. 1998. *International Security and Democracy.* Pittsburgh: University of Pittsburgh Press.

Dominican Republic–Central America–United States Free Trade Agreement. Washington, DC, August 5, 2004.

Dorn, Edwin, et al. 2000. *American Military Culture in the Twenty-First Century.* Washington, DC: Center for International and Strategic Studies.

Downs, George W., David M. Rocke, and Peter N. Barsoom. 1996. "Is the Good News About Compliance Good News About Cooperation?" *International Organization* 50(3): 379–405.

Dreier, John C. 1968. "The Special Nature of Western Hemisphere Experience with International Organization." In Robert W. Gregg, ed., *International Organization in the Western Hemisphere.* Syracuse, NY: Syracuse University Press.

Duhaime, Bernard. 2005. "Commission interaméricaine des Droits de l'Homme en 2005: Enjeux." *Assymétries, analyses de l'actualité internationale* 1: 138.

Dykmann, Klaas. 2003. "The Policy of Human Rights of the Organization of American States in Latin America (1970–1991)." *Revista Complutense de Historia de América* 29: 133.

Dymond, William. 2001. "Canadian Objectives for the Quebec Summit of the Americas." Institute of the Americas. www.iamericas.org/publications/americas.html (accessed March 10, 2005).

Dymond, William, and Michael Hart. 2005. *Policy Implications of a Canada-US Customs Union.* North American Linkages series. Ottawa: Policy Research Initiative, June.

ECC (Extraordinary Challenge Committee). 2005. *In the Matter of Certain Softwood Lumber Products from Canada.* NAFTA Secretariat (ECC-2004-1904-01USA), August 10.

ECLAC (Economic Commission for Latin America and the Caribbean). 1992. *A Western Hemisphere Trade Area: An Overview of the Issues.* Santiago: ECLAC.

———. 1994. *Open Regionalism in Latin America and the Caribbean.* Santiago: ECLAC.

———. 2000. *Social Panorama of Latin America: 1999–2000.* Santiago: United Nations Publications.

———. 2002. "A Standardized Methodology for the Measurement of Defense Spending." United Nations, Economic Commission for Latin America and the Caribbean, Doc LC/L.1663-P.

Economist. 2005. "A Spectre Stalks the Americas: Hugo Chávez." The Americas section, US edition, February 26 (accessed via Lexis/Nexis, October 17, 2005).

EGF (Esquel Group Foundation). 1999a. "Establishing an Effective Government–Civil Society Dialogue." In Richard E. Feinberg and Robin L. Rosenberg, eds., *Civil Society and the Summit of the Americas: The 1998 Santiago Summit.* Boulder, CO: Lynne Rienner, 385–402.

———. 1999b. "Civil Society Task Force: Overview." Unpublished manuscript.

Einaudi, Luigi R. 2005. "Address by the Acting Secretary General of the Organization of American States, Luigi R. Einaudi, on the Status of the Reorganization of the General Secretariat, at the Regular Session of the Permanent Council." Washington, DC: Organization of American States, January 26.

Encarnación, Omar G. 2002. "Venezuela's 'Civil Society Coup.'" *World Policy Journal* 19(2): 38–48.

Escudé, Carlos, and Andrés Fontana. 1998. "Las políticas de seguridad de Argentina: Sus fundamentos y contexto regional." In Jorge Domínguez, ed., *Seguridad Internacional, Paz, y Democracia en el Cono Sur.* Santiago: FLACSO-Chile, 81–124.

Estevadeordal, Antoni. 1999. *Negotiating Preferential Market Access: The Case of NAFTA.* Buenos Aires: INTAL-IDB Working Paper 3.

Ethier, Wilfred J. 1998. "The New Regionalism." *Economic Journal* 108(449): 1149–1161.

Ezeta, Héctor Manuel. 1992. "La inevitable (pero difícil) transición de la OEA." *Revista Mexicana de Política Exterior* 35: 25–39.

Farer, Tom J., ed. 1988. *The Future of the Inter-American System.* New York: Praeger.

Fearon, James D. 1998. "Bargaining, Enforcement, and International Cooperation." *International Organization* 52(2): 269–305.

Fearon, James D., and Alexander Wendt. 2002. "Rationalism vs. Constructivism: A Skeptical View." In Walter Carlsnaes et al., eds., *Handbook of International Relations.* London: Sage Publications, 52–72.

Feaver, Peter D. 2003. *Armed Servants: Agency, Oversight, and Civil-Military Relations.* Cambridge, MA: Harvard University Press.

Feinberg, Richard E. 1997. *Summitry in the Americas: A Progress Report.* Washington, DC: Institute for International Economics.

———. 2000. "Comparing Regional Integration in Non-Identical Twins: APEC and the FTAA." *Integration and Trade* 4: 1.

———. 2004. *Unfunded Mandates in the Western Hemisphere: The OAS, IDB, and Summitry in the Americas.* Ottawa: FOCAL, Summit of the Americas Follow-up Series No. 3, January. http://www.focal.ca/pdf/Unfunded%20Mandates_sp .pdf (accessed March 15, 2005).

———. 2005. "Advancing Toward the Mar del Plata 4th Summit of the Americas." Centre d'Etudes Interaméricaines. http://www.cei.ulaval.ca/PDF/CEIRichard Feinberg%20.pdf (accessed March 15, 2006).

Feldman, Elliot J. 2004. *Duties and Dumping: What's Wrong with Chapter 19?* Background paper prepared for the Canadian-American Business Council and the Center for Strategic and International Studies by Baker and Hostetler, June.

Fenwick, Charles G. 1962. "The Issues of Punta del Este: Non-Intervention v. Collective Security." *American Journal of International Law* 56(2): 469–474.

———. 1963. *The Organization of American States: The Inter-American Regional System.* Washington, DC: Kaufman Printing.

Finnemore, Martha. 1996. *National Interests in International Society.* Ithaca, NY: Cornell University Press.

Finnemore, Martha, and Kathryn Sikkink. 1998. "International Norm Dynamics and Political Change." *International Organization* 52(4): 887–917.

FOCAL (Canadian Foundation for the Americas). 2002. *Access to Justice and Independence of the Judiciary in the Americas.* Ottawa: FOCAL, Summit of the Americas Follow-up Series No. 1, October.

———. 2003. "South America Looking Towards a 'Continental Axis.'" Editorial. *FOCAL Point* 2(5): 10–11.

———. 2004. *Unfunded Mandates in the Western Hemisphere: The Organization of American States (OAS), the Inter-American Development Bank (IDB), and Summitry in the Americas.* Summit of the Americas Follow-up Series, January.

Foster, Dean. 2005. "Twenty-Nine-Member FTAA: Nothing to Get Excited About." *FOCAL Point: Spotlight on the Americas* 4: 10.

Fourth Summit of the Americas. 2005. *Plan of Action: Creating Jobs to Fight Poverty and Strengthen Democratic Governance.* Summit of the Americas Information Network.

Franko, Patrice. 2000. *Toward a New Security Architecture in the Americas: The Strategic Implications of the FTAA.* Washington, DC: Center for Strategic and International Studies.

Friends of the Democratic Charter. 2005. "The Taboo of Democratic Defects." Editorial. *Miami Herald,* May 2.

Gallagher, Kevin P. 2005. *Putting Development First: The Importance of Policy Space in the WTO and the IFIs.* London: Zed Books.

Gannon, Francis X. 1984. "Will the OAS Live to Be 100? Does It Deserve To?" *Caribbean Review* 13(4): 12–15, 42–43.

Gaudet, Louis-Frédéric, and Rachel Sarrasin. 2005. "Retour sur le Sommet des Amériques de Mar del Plata: Quelles directions pour la société civile?" *La Chronique des Amériques, Observatoire des Amériques* 36.

Gaviria Trujillo, César. 1997. "The Future of the Hemisphere." *Journal of Interamerican Studies and World Affairs* 39(1): 5–10.

———. 2004a. *Una década de transformaciones: Del fin de la Guerra Fría a la globalización en la OEA.* Bogota: Editorial Planeta.

———. 2004b. *The OAS in Transition, 1994–2004.* Washington, DC: Organization of American States.

Ghosh, Madanmohan, and Someshwar Rao. 2004. "Répercussions économiques d'une éventuelle union douanière canado-américaine." *Horizons* 7(1): 32–34.

Gleijeses, Piero. 1991. *Shattered Hope: The Guatemalan Revolution and the United States, 1944–1954.* Princeton, NJ: Princeton University Press.

Globe and Mail. 2001. "Activists Reject Invitation Behind Fence." April 18.

Goldfarb, Danielle. 2003. *Beyond Labels: Comparing Proposals for Closer Canada-US Economic Relations.* Backgrounder No. 76. Toronto: C. D. Howe Institute.

———. 2005. *US Bilateral Free Trade Accords: Why Canada Should Be Cautious About Going the Same Route.* Toronto: C. D. Howe Institute.

Goldstein, Judith, Miles Kahler, Robert O. Keohane, and Anne-Marie Slaughter, eds. 2000. Special issue: "Legalization and World Politics." *International Organization* 54(3).

———, eds. 2001. *Legalization and World Politics.* Cambridge, MA: IO Foundation and Massachusetts Institute of Technology.

Goldstein, Judith, and Lisa Martin. 2001. "Legalization, Trade Liberalization, and Domestic Politics: A Cautionary Note." In Judith Goldstein et al., eds., *Legalization and World Politics.* Cambridge, MA: IO Foundation and Massachusetts Institute of Technology, 219–248.

González, Anabel. 2005. *The Application of the Dominican Republic–Central America–United States Free Trade Agreement.* Washington, DC: OAS.

González, Felipe. 1998. "Informes sobre Países, Protección y Promoción." In Juan E. Médez and Francisco Cox, eds., *El Futuro del Sistema Interamericano de los Derechos Humanos.* San José: IIDH.

———. 2001. "La OEA y los derechos humanos despues del advenimiento de los gobiernos civiles: Expectativas (in)satisfechas." *Cuaderno de Análisis Jurídicos Serie Publicaciones Especiales* special issue: Derechos Humanos e Interés Público 11.

Gore, Albert, Jr. 1994. "The OAS and the Summit of the Americas." *US Department of State Dispatch* 5(48): 785–789.

Gotlieb, Allan. 2004. *Romanticism and Realism in Canada's Foreign Policy.* Toronto: C. D. Howe Institute, Benefactors Lecture, November 3.

Graham, John W. 2002. "A Magna Carta for the Americas: The Inter-American Democratic Charter: Genesis, Challenges and Canadian Connections." Focal Policy Paper FPP-02-09, September.

———. 2005a. "Mar del Plata Post Mortem and New Challenges." *FOCAL Point: Spotlight on the Americas* 4(10): 14–16.

———. 2005b. "La OEA se hunde: ¿Merece ser salvada?" *Foreign Affairs en Español* 5(2): 3–98.

Grieco, Joseph M. 1995. "The Maastricht Treaty, Economic and Monetary Union and the Neo-realist Research Programme." *Review of International Studies* 21(1): 21–40.

———. 1996a. "State Interest and International Rule Trajectories: A Neorealist Interpretation of the Maastricht Treaty and European Economic and Monetary Union." In Benjamin Frankel, ed., *Realism: Restatement and Renewal.* London: Frank Cass, 261–306.

———. 1996b. "State Interests and International Rule Trajectories: A Neorealist Interpretation of the Maastricht Treaty and European Economic and Monetary Union." *Security Studies* 5(3): 261–305.

Grijalva, J. Ernesto, and Patrick T. Brewer. 1994. "The Administrative Bodies of the North American Free Trade Agreement." *San Diego Justice Journal* 2: 1–18.

Gros Espiell, Hector. 1986. *Conflictos Territoriales en Iberoamérica y Solución Pacífica de Controversias.* Madrid: Ediciones Cultura Hispánica.

Grossman, Claudio. 2000–2001. "Freedom of Expression in the Inter-American System for the Protection of Human Rights." *Nova Law Review* 25: 411–442.

Grugel, Jean. 2004. "Civil Society and Inclusion in New Regionalism: Can Civil Society Influence a Trade-led Agenda?" Paper prepared for the Second Annual Conference of the Euro-Latin Trade Network, Florence, Italy, October 29–30.

Guiñazú, María Clelia. 2003. "La sociedad civil en el proceso de integración comercial: El caso argentino." In Diana Tussie and Mercedes Botto, eds., *Sociedad civil y el proceso de Cumbres de las Américas ¿Nuevos o viejos patrones de participación y cooperación en América Latina?* Buenos Aires: Editorial Tema, 145–170.

Hakim, Peter. 2006. "Is Washington Losing Latin America?" *Foreign Affairs* 85(1): 39–53.

Hall, Peter A., and Rosemary C. R. Taylor. 1996. "Political Science and the Three New Institutionalisms." *Political Studies* 44(4): 936–957.

Harris, David J., and Stephen Livingstone, eds. 1998. *The Inter-American System of Human Rights.* Oxford: Clarendon Press.

Harrison, Lawrence E. 1997. *The Pan-American Dream.* New York: Basic Books.

Hart, Michael. 1994. *Decision at Midnight: Inside the Canada-US Free-Trade Negotiations.* Vancouver: University of British Columbia Press.

Hart, Oliver D. 1988. "Incomplete Contracts and the Theory of the Firm." *Journal of Law, Economics, and Organization* 4(1): 119–139.

———. 1995. *Firms, Contracts, and Financial Structures.* Oxford: Clarendon Press.

Hayes, Margaret Daly. 1983. "Collective Security and the Global Balance." In Viron P. Vaky, ed., *Governance in the Western Hemisphere.* New York: Praeger, 159–174.

————. 1984. *Latin America and the US National Interest: A Basis for Foreign Policy.* Boulder, CO: Westview.

————. 1986. "Security in the Western Hemisphere." In Keven Middlebrook and Carlos Rico, eds., *The United States and Latin America in the 1980s: Contending Perspectives on a Decade of Crisis.* Pittsburgh: University of Pittsburgh Press.

————. 1996. "Building the Hemispheric Community: Lessons from the Summit of the Americas Process." Washington, DC: Inter-American Dialogue.

Helliwell, John F. 1998. *How Much Do National Borders Matter?* Washington, DC: Brookings Institution.

Herdocia Sacasa, Mauricio. 2004. "Integración y modelo de seguridad democrática en Centroamérica: Su influencia dentro de la OEA." In *Security and Defense Studies Review* 4(1): 26–43. http://www3.ndu.edu/chds/Journal/PDF/2004/Herdocia_article-edited.pdf (accessed March 15, 2005).

Hester, Annette. 2005. "The Eagle's Talons Loosen." *Globe and Mail,* June 14.

Hirschman, Albert O. 1970. *Exit, Voice, and Loyalty: Responses to Decline in Firms, Organizations, and States.* Cambridge: Harvard University Press.

Howard-Jones, Norman. 1981. *The Pan American Health Organization: Origins and Evolution.* Geneva: World Health Organization.

Huelsemeyer, Axel. 2004. *Toward a Deeper North American Integration: A Customs Union?* Orono, ME: Canadian-American Center, Canadian-American Public Policy series No. 59, October.

Hufbauer, Gary C., and Jeffrey J. Schott. 2004. *The Prospects for Deeper North American Economic Integration: A US Perspective.* Commentary No. 195. Toronto: C. D. Howe Institute, January.

————. 2005. *NAFTA Revisited: Achievements and Challenges.* Washington, DC: Institute for International Economics.

Hurrell, Andrew. 1995. "Regionalism in the Americas." In L. Fawcett and A. Hurrell, eds., *Regionalism in World Politics: Regional Organization and International Order.* Oxford: Oxford University Press, 37–73.

Hurst, Lionel. 2003. "An Evaluation of the Conditions and Outcomes of Inter-Agency and International Security Coordination Among the Nations of the Caribbean and the Americas in 2003 and Beyond." Presentation to the Center for Hemispheric Defense Studies, National Defense University, March 25. http://www.caribvoice.org/Opinions/coordination.html (accessed March 10, 2006).

Huser, Herbert C. 2002. *Argentine Civil-Military Relations: From Alfonsin to Menem.* Washington, DC: National Defense University Press for the Center for Hemispheric Defense Studies.

IACHR (Inter-American Commission on Human Rights). 1995. *Annual Report of the Inter-American Commission on Human Rights 1994.* OEA/Ser. L/V.88 doc. 9 rev. 1, February 17.

————. 1999. *Third Report on the Situation of Human Rights in Colombia.* OEA/Ser.L/V/II.102 doc. 9 rev. 1, February 26.

————. 2000a. *Report on the Situation of Human Rights in Peru.* OEA/Ser.L/V/II.106, doc. 59 rev., June 2.

————. 2000b. Press release No. 18/00, December 8.

————. 2001a. *Fifth Report on the Situation of Human Rights in Guatemala.* OEA/Ser.L/V/II.111 doc. 21 rev., April 6.

————. 2001b. *Third Report on the Situation of Human Rights in Paraguay.* OEA/Ser.L/V/II.110 doc. 52, March 9.

————. 2002. *Report on Terrorism and Human Rights.* OEA/Ser.L/V/ll.116 doc. 5 rev. 1 corr.

————. 2003. Documentos Básicos en Materia de Derechos Humanos en el Sistema Interamericano, OEA/Ser.L/V/I.4 rev. 9, January 31, containing the IACHR and IACourt Statute and Rules of Procedure as well as the Charter of the OAS, Inter-American Democratic Charter, the Declaration of Principles on Freedom of Expression, and all the Inter-American Human Rights Instruments referred to in this chapter.

ICFTU-ORIT (International Confederation of Free Trade Unions and the Organización Regional Interamericana de Trabajadores). 2001. "Global Union Demands Stronger Labor Protection in the FTAA." April 24. http://www.icftu.org (accessed March 10, 2005).

IDB (Inter-American Development Bank). 1995–2001. *Annual Reports.* Washington, DC: Inter-American Development Bank.

————. 1996. "Agreement Establishing the Inter-American Development Bank." As amended. Washington, DC: IDB. Reprint.

————. 1999a. "Report of the Working Group on the Institutional Strategy." GN-2077-1, August 13.

————. 1999b. "Renewing the Commitment to Development: Report of the Working Group on the Institutional Strategy" (revised version). Memorandum to the Board of Executive Directors, August 24.

————. 2000. *Reforming Primary and Secondary Education in Latin America and the Caribbean: An IDB Strategy.* Sector Strategy and Policy Papers Series. Washington, DC: IDB.

————. 2001a. *40 Years: More Than a Bank.* Washington, DC: IDB.

————. 2001b. *Summit of the Americas Strategic Programs: The Agenda of the IDB.* Washington, DC: IDB.

————. 2002a. "Institutional Strategy Implementation: Progress Update." Memorandum to the Board of Executive Directors, February.

————. 2002b. "Mexico: Country Program Evaluation, 1990–2000." Office of Evaluation and Oversight, February 14.

————. 2002c. *One Year After Quebec: Summit of the Americas: The Agenda of the IDB.* Washington, DC: IDB.

————. 2002d. "Trade Capacity Building." Washington, DC: IDB. Internal Memorandum, November 1.

————. 2003. *Good Jobs Wanted. Labor Markets in Latin America.* Washington, DC: IDB.

————. 2005a. *The Labor Dimension in Central America and the Dominican Republic: Building on Progress, Strengthening Compliance, and Enhancing Capacity.* Washington, DC: IDB, White Paper.

————. 2005b. *The Millennium Development Goals in Latin America and the Caribbean: Progress, Priorities, and IDB Support for Their Implementation.* Washington, DC: IDB.

Ikenberry, G. John. 2001. *After Victory.* Princeton, NJ: Princeton University Press.

Immerman, Richard H. 1982. *The CIA in Guatemala: The Foreign Policy of Intervention.* Austin: University of Texas Press.

Inman, Samuel G. 1965. *Inter-American Conferences, 1826–1954: History and Problems.* Washington, DC: University Press of Washington, DC.

Insulza, José Miguel. 2005a. *Discurso del Dr. José Miguel Insulza en la VII Conferencia de la Cátedra de las Américas.* Lima: Universidad San Martín de Porres, July 15.

―――. 2005b. *Speech by the Secretary General of the OAS at the Inaugural Session of the Fourth Summit of the Americas,* Mar del Plata, Argentina, November 4.

Inter-American Defense Board. 1995. "Report of the Inter-American Defense Board on the Draft Inventory of Confidence-Building Measures of a Military Nature That Are Being Implemented in the Hemisphere." OEA/Ser.K/XXIX.2 COSEGRE/doc.10/95, October 30.

Inter-American Institute of International Legal Studies. 1966. *The Inter-American System: Its Development and Strengthening.* Dobbs Ferry, NY: Oceana Publications.

Jones, Leroy P. 2003. *Privatization and the Poor: Issues and Evidence.* Deliverable 18, USAID Pro-Poor Economic Growth Research Studies and Guidance Manual Activity. Bethesda, MD: Development Alternatives.

JSWG (Joint Summit Working Group). 2004. *The Fight Against Corruption.* Washington, DC: OAS, Summit of the Americas Secretariat, June.

Kacowicz, Arie. 1998. *Zones of Peace in the Third World: South America and West Africa in Comparative Perspective.* Albany: State University of New York.

Kaul, Inge, Isabelle Grunberg, and Marc A. Stern. 1999. "Public Global Goods." In Inge Kaul, Isabelle Grunberg, and Marc A. Stern, eds., *Global Public Goods: International Cooperation in the Twenty-First Century.* New York: United Nations Development Programme and Oxford University Press, 2–19.

Keck, Margaret, and Kathryn Sikkink. 1998. *Activists Beyond Borders: Transnational Advocacy Networks in International Politics.* Ithaca, NY: Cornell University Press.

Kessler, Glenn. 2005. "Rice Urges OAS to Back Democracy." *Washington Post,* June 6.

Khagram, Sanjeev, James V. Riker, and Kathryn Sikkink. 2002. "From Santiago to Seattle: Transnational Advocacy Groups Restructuring World Politics." In Sanjeev Khagram, James V. Riker, and Kathryn Sikkink, eds., *Restructuring World Politics: Transnational Social Movements, Networks, and Norms.* Minneapolis: University of Minnesota Press, 3–23.

King-Hopkins, Kimberly D. 2000. "Inter-American Commission on Human Rights: Is Its Bark Worse Than Its Bite in Resolving Human Rights Disputes?" *Tulsa Law Journal* 35: 421–441.

Koremenos, Barbara, Charles Lipson, and Duncan Snidal, eds. 2001. Special Issue: "The Rational Design of International Institutions." *International Organization* 55(4): 761–799.

―――. 2004. *Rational Design: Explaining the Form of International Institutions.* Cambridge: Cambridge University Press.

Korzeniewicz, Roberto Patricio, and William C. Smith. 2000a. "Poverty, Inequality, and Growth in Latin America: Searching for the High Road to Globalization." *Latin American Research Review* 35(3): 7–54.

―――. 2000b. "Los dos ejes de la Tercera Vía en América Latina." *América Latina Hoy—Revista de Ciencias Sociales* Special Issue on "Globalización y Sociedad," 26: 41–55.

―――. 2003a. "Protesta y colaboración: Redes transnacionales de la sociedad civil y su participación en las cumbres y el libre comercio en las Américas." In Diana Tussie and Mercedes Botto, eds., *Sociedad civil y el proceso de Cumbres de las Américas ¿Nuevos o viejos patrones de participación y cooperación en América Latina?* Buenos Aires: Editorial Tema, 47–78.

―――. 2003b. "Redes transnacionales, diplomacia ciudadana y proyectos de integración económica en América Latina." In Andrés Serbin, ed., *Entre la confrontación y el diálogo: Integración regional y diplomacia ciudadana.* Buenos Aires: Siglo 21, 119–176.

———. 2003c. "Mapping Regional Civil Society Networks in Latin America." Report for the Ford Foundation, 1000-1624.

———. 2004. "Coaliciones, redes, y movimientos sociales transnacionales en patrones emergentes de colaboración y conflicto en las Américas." *América Latina Hoy—Revista de Ciencias Sociales* 36: 101–139.

———. 2005. "Transnational Civil Society Actors and Regional Governance in the Americas: Elite Projects and Collective Action from Below." In Louise Fawcett and Móncia Serrano, eds., *Regionalism and Governance in the Americas: Forms of a Continental Drift.* London: Palgrave, 135–157.

Kunimoto, Robert, and Gary Sawchuck. 2004. "Moving Toward a Customs Union: A Review of the Evidence." *Horizons* 7(1): 23–31.

Kuznets, Simon. 1955. "Economic Growth and Income Inequality." *American Economic Review* 45(1): 1–28.

Kydd, Andrew. 2001. "Trust Building, Trust Breaking: The Dilemma of NATO Enlargement." *International Organization* 55(4): 801–828.

Lachowski, Zdzislaw. 2004. *Confidence and Security-Building in the New Europe.* SIPRI Research Report No. 18.

Lagos, Enrique, and Timothy Rudy. 2002. "The Third Summit of the Americas and the Thirty-First Session of the OAS General Assembly." *American Journal of International Law* 96(1): 173–181.

Lamarche, Lucie. 2000. "L'exigence du respect des droits de la personne dans le processus d'intégration économique continentale." *Intégration Hémisphérique et Démocratie dans les Amériques, Citoyenneté, Participation, Responsabilité, Droits et Démocratie.* Presentation in a symposium organized by Droits et Démocratie, 51–55.

Landmine Monitor. 2003. http://www.icbl.org/lm/2003/chile.html (accessed November 29, 2005).

———. 2004. "Chile." http://www.icbl.org/lm/2004/chile (accessed November 29, 2005).

Latin News Daily. 2005. "Infighting at Mercosur Summit." June 21.

Lawrence, Robert. 1997. "Preferential Trading Agreements: The Traditional and the New." In Ahmed Galal and Bernard Hoekman, eds., *Regional Partners in Global Markets: Limits and Possibilities of the Euro-Med Agreements.* London: Centre for Economic Policy Research, 13–34.

Leadership Council for Inter-American Summitry. 1999. *Mastering Summitry: An Evaluation of the Santiago Summit of the Americas and Its Aftermath.* Coral Gables: North-South Center Press.

———. 2001. *Advancing Toward Quebec City and Beyond.* Coral Gables: North-South Center Press.

Legler, Thomas. 2003. "Peru Then and Now: The Inter-American Democratic Charter and Peruvian Democratization." *Canadian Foreign Policy* 10(3): 61–73.

Legler, Thomas, Sharon Lean, and Dexter Boniface. 2007. "International and Transnational Dimensions of Democracy in the Americas." In Thomas Legler, Sharon Lean, and Dexter Boniface, eds., *Promoting Democracy in the Americas.* Baltimore, MD: Johns Hopkins University Press.

Legler, Thomas, and Barry Levitt. 2006. *Responding to Democratic Crises in the Americas: A Diagnostic Tool for the Friends of the Democratic Charter.* Prepared for the Friends of the Inter-American Democratic Charter and the Carter Center. Atlanta: Carter Center, July.

Leiken, Robert S. 1994. *A New Moment in the Americas.* New York: Transaction.

Lessard, Geneviève. 2000. "L'OEA dans la dynamique de la ZLÉA-Renforcement ou affaiblissement de l'État de droit?" Centre d'Etudes Internationales et Mondialisation. http://www.er.uqam.ca/nobel/ieim/IMG/html/Lessard.html (accessed March 10, 2005).

Lopez, Ernesto. 2001. "Sobre la indivisibilidad de la seguridad." Presentation at the seminar "Argentina y Brasil frente a las nuevas amenazas," Buenos Aires, March 29. http://www.insumisos.com/Biblioteca/SOBRE%20LA%20INDIVIS IBILIDAD%20DE%20LA%20SEGURIDAD.pdf (accessed March 15, 2006).

Lowenthal, Abraham, F. 1972. *The Dominican Intervention.* Cambridge, MA: Harvard University Press.

Mace, Gordon. 1999. "The Origins, Nature, and Scope of the Hemispheric Project." In Gordon Mace and Louis Bélanger, eds., *The Americas in Transition: The Contours of Regionalism.* Boulder, CO: Lynne Rienner, 19–36.

———. 2004. "Canada and the New North-South Divide in the Americas." *FOCAL Point* 3(2): 1–2.

Mace, Gordon, and Louis Bélanger, eds. 1999. *The Americas in Transition. The Contours of Regionalism.* Boulder: Lynne Rienner.

Mace, Gordon, and Hugo Loiseau. 2002. "Summitry in the Americas and the Institutionalization of Hemispheric Regionalism: A Missing Link?" (unpublished draft).

———. 2005. "Cooperative Hegemony and Summitry in the Americas." *Latin American Politics and Society* 47(4): 107–134.

Mace, Gordon, and Jean-Philippe Thérien. 1996. "Introduction: Foreign Policy and Regionalism in the Americas." In Gordon Mace and Jean-Philippe Thérien, eds., *Foreign Policy and Regionalism in the Americas.* Boulder, CO: Lynne Rienner, 1–9.

Maguire, Robert. 2002. "Haiti's Political Deadlock." *Journal of Haitian Studies* 8(2): 30–42.

March, James G., and Johan P. Olsen. 1989. *Rediscovering Institutions.* New York: Free Press.

Mares, David R. 1996–1997. "Deterrence in the Ecuador-Peru Enduring Rivalry: Designing Around Weakness." *Security Studies* 6: 2.

———. 2001a. *Violent Peace.* New York: Columbia University Press.

———. 2001b. "Boundary Disputes in the Western Hemisphere: Analyzing Their Relationship to Democratic Stability, Economic Integration, and Social Welfare." *Pensamiento Propio* 6: 14.

Margheritis, Ana. 1999. *Ajuste y Reforma en Argentina (1989–1995): La economia politica de las privatizaciones.* Buenos Aires: Nuevohacer Grupo Editor Latinoamericano.

Martinez, Pablo Carlos. 2002. *La reestructuración de las Fuerzas Armadas y el rol del Congreso: La experiencia argentina.* La Paz, Bolivia: EDUBOL for the Center for Hemispheric Defense Studies.

McCall Smith, James. 1998. *Policing International Trade: The Politics of Dispute Settlement Design.* PhD diss., Department of Political Science, Stanford University.

———. 2000. "The Politics of Dispute Settlement Design: Explaining Legalism in Regional Trade Pacts." *International Organization* 54(1): 137–180.

McCallum, John. 1995. "National Borders Matter: Canada-US Regional Trade Patterns." *America Economic Review* 85(3): 615–623.

McCoy, Jennifer. Forthcoming. "Transnational Response to Democratic Crisis in the Americas, 1990–2005." In Thomas Legler, Sharon Lean, and Dexter Boniface, eds., *Promoting Democracy in the Americas.* Baltimore, MD: Johns Hopkins University Press.

Mitchell, Ronald B. 1994. *Intentional Oil Pollution at Sea.* Cambridge, MA: MIT Press.

Moe, Terry M. 1984. "The New Economics of Organization." *American Journal of Political Science* 28: 739–777.

Molineu, Harold. 1994. "The Inter-American System: Searching for a New Framework." *Latin American Research Review* 29(1): 215–226.

Morales, Brian. 2004. "The Viability of the Inter-American Treaty of Reciprocal Assistance in the Post–September 11 Environment as the Foundation for Collective Security in the Americas." US Mission to the OAS. Unpublished manuscript.

Morales, Isidro. 1999. "NAFTA: The Governance of Economic Openness." *Annals of the American Academy of Political and Social Science* 565: 35–65.

Moravcsik, Andrew. 1997. "Taking Preferences Seriously: A Liberal Theory of International Politics." *International Organization* 51(4): 514–553.

———. 2000. "The Origins of Human Rights Regimes: Democratic Delegation in Postwar Europe." *International Organization* 54(2): 217–252.

Moreno Pino, Ismael. 1977. *Origenes y evolucion del sistema interamericano.* Tlatelolco: Secretaría de Relaciones Exteriores.

Muñoz, Heraldo. 1993. "A New OAS for the New Times." In Viron P. Vaky and Heraldo Muñoz, eds., *The Future of the Organization of American States.* New York: Twentieth Century Fund, 67–95.

Murphy, Craig N. 1994. *International Organization and Industrial Change: Global Governance Since 1850.* New York: Oxford University Press.

NAFTA (North American Free Trade Agreement). 1993. Ottawa: Acquisitions and Services Canada.

Nolan, Janne E. 1993. *Global Engagement: Cooperation and Security in the Twenty-First Century.* Washington, DC: Brookings Institution.

Noriega, Roger F., Ambassador. 2003. "The Complex Challenges for the Americas in the Twenty-First Century." Speech to the Graduation Ceremony of the Inter-American Defense College, Washington, DC, June 25. http://www.state.gov/p/wha/rls/rm/21971.htm (accessed July 19, 2005).

North, Douglass. 1990. *Institutions, Institutional Change, and Economic Performance.* Cambridge: Cambridge University Press.

OAS (Organization of American States). 1948. *Charter of the Organization of American States.* Washington, DC: Organization of American States.

———. 1986. *Protocol of Cartagena de Indias.* OEA/Ser.P AG/doc.16 (XIV-E/85) rev. II. February 26.

———. 1991a. *Representative Democracy.* AG/RES. 1080 (XXI-0/91).

———. 1991b. *The Santiago Commitment to Democracy and the Renewal of the Inter-American System.* OAS/Ser.P AG/RES/ (XXI-0/91), June 4.

———. 1991c. "Cooperation for Security in the Hemisphere." AG/RES. 1123 (XXI-0/91).

———. 1992a. *Protocol of Amendments to the Charter of the Organization of American States "Protocol of Washington."* Sixteenth Special Session of the General Assembly of the OAS, 1-E Rev. OAS Official Documents/Sec.A/2/Add 3—Treaty A-56, Amendment to Chapter III of Article IX. December 14.

———. 1992b. *On Cooperation for Security and Development in the Hemisphere—Regional Contributions to Global Security.* AG/RES. 1179 (XXII-0/92). http://www.oas.org/main/main.asp?sLang=E&sLink=documents/eng/documents.asp (accessed March 15, 2006).

———. 1995. "Declaration of Santiago on Confidence and Security Building Measures." OEA/Ser.K/XXIX.2, COSEGRE/doc.18/95 rev. 3 (November 10). http://www.oas.org/csh/english/csbmdeclarsant.asp.

———. 1995–2002. *Annual Reports.* Washington, DC: Organization of American States.

———. 1996. *Declaration of Lima to Prevent, Combat, and Eliminate Terrorism.* April 26.

———. 1997. *Charter of the Organization of American States.* Signed in Bogotá in 1948 and amended by the Protocol of Buenos Aires in 1967, by the Protocol of Cartagena de Indias in 1985, by the Protocol of Washington in 1992, and by the Protocol of Managua in 1993. Washington, DC: General Secretariat of the Organization of American States.

———. 1998a. "Commitment of Mar del Plata." Declaration of the Second Inter-American Specialized Conference on Terrorism (November 23). http://www.oas.org/juridico/english/Docu1.htm.

———. 1998b. *Declaration of San Salvador on Confidence- and Security-Building Measures.* February 25–27. http://www.state.gov/t/ac/csbm/rd/4359.htm (accessed March 15, 2006).

———. 2000a. Electoral Observation Mission (MOE/OEA). *Informe final del jefe de misiòn: Misión de Observación Electoral, elecciones generales de la República del Perú, año 2000,* June 2.

———. 2000b. *Inter-American Strategy for the Promotion of Public Participation in Decision Making for Sustainable Development.* Washington, DC.

———. 2000c. "OAS to Lead High-Level Mission to Peru." Press release of June 15. http://www.oas.org/main/main.asp?sLang=E&sLink=http://www.upd.oas.org (accessed March 11, 2005).

———. 2000d. "Proposals Presented by the OAS Mission in Peru." Press release of June 29, 2000. http://www.oas.org/main/main.asp?sLang=E&sLink=http://www.upd.oas.org (accessed March 11, 2005).

———. 2001a. *The Western Hemisphere as an Antipersonnel-Land-Mine-Free Zone.* AG/RES. 1794 (XXXI-0/01).

———. 2001b. *Inter-American Democratic Charter (2001).* OAS Doc.OEA/Ser.P/ AG/RES.1, XXVLLL-E/01, September 11.

———. 2001c. "Restructuring the Organization of American States to Address the Challenges of the Summit Process on Response to Resolutions AG/RES 1812, 1824, 1936, and 1839." CP/doc.3537/01, December.

———. 2002a. "Executive Order No. 02-3. Subject: Establishment of the Secretariat for the Summit Process." General Secretariat of the OAS, p. 2. http://www.oas.org/legal/english/gensec/EXOR0203.doc (accessed February 16, 2005).

———. 2002b. *Situation in Venezuela.* OEA/Ser.G CP/RES 811 (1315/02). April 13.

———. 2002c. "The Organization of American States: Description." http://www.oas.org/en/pINFO/OAS/oas.htm (accessed June 25, 2002).

———. 2002d. "The Multidimentional Approach to Hemispheric Security ('Declaration of Bridgetown')," AG/DEC XXXII-0/02, Bridgetown, June (accessed March 15, 2006).

———. 2003a. *Declaration on Security in the Americas.* Mexico City, Mexico, October 27–28.

———. 2003b. *Support for the Constitutional Government of the Republic of Bolivia.* CP/RES. 838 (1355/03), February 14.

———. 2003c. *Support for the Constitutional Government of the Republic of Bolivia.* CP/RES. 849 (1384/03), October 15. http://www.oas.org/documents/eng/DeclaracionSecurity_102803.asp (accessed March 15, 2006).

————. 2004a. *Declaration of Nuevo Leon.* Monterrey, Mexico, January 13. http://www.summitamericas.org/SpecialSummit/Declarations/Declaration%20of%20Nuevo%20Leon%20-%20final.pdf (accessed March 15, 2006).

————. 2004b. "Program—Budget of the Organization for 2005." In General Assembly, *Declarations and Resolutions Adopted by the General Assembly at Its Thirty-Fourth Regular Session.*

————. 2004c. *Situation in Haiti.* CP/RES. 862 (1401/04), February 26.

————. 2004d. *Situation in Haiti: Strengthening of Democracy.* AG/RES. 2058 (XXXIV-0/04), June 8.

————. 2004e. "Specific Fund to Support the Participation of Civil Society Organizations in OAS Activities and the Summit of the Americas Process." http://www.civil-society.oas.org/Permanent%20Council/cp_res_864_eng.doc (accessed February 16, 2005).

————. 2005a. *Declaration of Florida: Delivering the Benefits of Democracy.* AG/DEC. 41 (XXXV-0/05). Fort Lauderdale, FL, June 7.

————. 2005b. *Support by the Organization of American States for the Republic of Ecuador.* Permanent Council Resolution 880, April 22.

————. 2005c. *Support to Nicaragua.* AG/DEC. 43 (XXXV-0/05), Fort Lauderdale, FL, June 7.

————. 2005d. "The Role of the Joint Summit Working Group (JSWG)." *Summits of the Americas Informs,* no. 2. Newsletter, Summits of the Americas Secretariat, March.

————. 2006a. "La Junta Interamericana de Defensa como una entidad de la Organización de los Estados Americanos y aprobación de su Estatuto." OEA/Ser.G CP/Res.900(1532/06), March 1. Approved ad referendum.

————. 2006b. "OAS General Assembly Approves Quota Scale and New Budgetary Ceiling." Press release, February 1.

OASGA (Organization of American States, General Assembly). 2005. Minutes of the Thirty-Fifth Regular Session of the General Assembly, Fourth Plenary Session, June 2005. www.oas.org/main/main.asp?sLang=E&sLink=http://www.oas.org/consejo/GENERAL%20ASSEMBLY/default.asp (accessed March 15, 2006).

O'Brien, Robert, Anne Marie Goetz, Jan Aart Scholte, and Marc Williams. 2000. *Contesting Global Governance: Multilateral Economic Institutions and Global Social Movements.* Cambridge, UK: Cambridge University Press.

O'Donnell, Guillermo. 1994. "Delegative Democracy." *Journal of Democracy* 5(1): 55–69. http://www.ispnet.org/documents/cepcidi/estraeng.rtf (accessed March 10, 2005).

Olson, Mancur. 1965. *The Logic of Collective Action: Public Goods and the Theory of Groups.* Cambridge, MA: Harvard University Press.

Oppenheimer, Andrés. 2005. "New OAS Chief's Top Priority: Defending Democracy." *Miami Herald,* May 5.

Osava, Mario. 2005. "The United States Doesn't Understand Latin America." *Inter Press Service,* June 11. http://www.antiwar.com/ips/osava.php?articleid=6290 (accessed via Lexis/Nexis, August 8, 2005).

Ostry, Sylvia. 2005. "The Multilateral Agenda: Moving Trade Negotiations Forward." MCIS Briefing. Toronto: Munk Centre for International Studies, November.

Pagés, Marisol. 2000. "El Area de Libre Comercio de las Américas (ALCA) y la sociedad civil." In Bruno Podestà et al., eds., *Ciudadanía y mundialización: La sociedad civil ante la integración regional.* Madrid: CEFIR, CIDEAL, INVESP, 159–174.

————. 2001. Personal communication with the author.

Pastor, Robert A. 2001. *Toward a North American Community: Lessons from the Old World for the New.* Washington, DC: Institute for International Economics.

Patiño Mayer, Hernan. 1993. "Aportes a un nuevo concepto de seguridad hemisférica—seguridad cooperativa." May. http://www.ser2000.org.ar/articulos-revista-ser/revista-4/mayer4.htm (accessed March 10, 2005).

Pauly, Louis. 2003. " Enforcing the Rules in a Global Economy: The Emergence of Structural Conditionality in the World Bank and the International Monetary Fund." In Albert Berry and Gustavo Indart, eds., *Critical Issues in International Financial Reform.* New Brunswick, NJ: Transaction.

Payne, Mark. 2003. "Civil Society Participation in the Activities of the IDB." Draft paper presented at the conference, "Civil Society and Political Transformations in Latin America." University of California, San Diego, March 24.

Pecly Moreira, Valter, Ambassador. 2002. "National Approaches to Bilateral and Subregional Aspects of Hemispheric Security." Presented by the Permanent Representative of Brazil to the Committee on Hemispheric Security at its meeting of November 5, 2002, OEA/Ser.G CP/CSH/INF.16/02 add. 4, November 14.

Pellicer, Olga. 1998. "La OEA a los 50 años: Hacia su fortalecimiento?" *Revista Mexicana de Politica Exterior* 54: 19–36.

Perina, Rubén M. 2005. "The Role of the Organization of American States." In Morton Halperin and Mirna Galic, eds., *Protecting Democracy: International Responses.* Lanham, MD: Lexington Books, 127–171.

Perry, William J. 1995. *Report on the First Conference of Ministers of Defense of the Americas.* http://www.state.gov/t/ac/csbm/rd/6434.htm (accessed March 15, 2006).

Pevehouse, Jon C. 2002. "Democracy from the Outside-In? International Organizations and Democratization." *International Organization* 56(3): 515–549.

Polanyi, Karl. 1957. *The Great Transformation: The Political and Economic Origins of Our Time.* Boston: Beacon Press.

Pollack, Mark A., and Gregory C. Shaffer. 2001. "Transatlantic Governance in Historical and Theoretical Perspective." In Mark A. Pollack and Gregory C. Shaffer, eds., *Transatlantic Governance in the Global Economy.* Lanham, MD: Rowman and Littlefield.

Pratt, John W., and Richard J. Zeckhauser. 1985. "Principals and Agents: An Overview." In John W. Pratt and Richard J. Zechauser, eds., *Principals and Agents: The Structure of Business.* Boston, MA: Harvard Business School Press, 1–35.

Puryear, Jeffrey, and Benjamin Alvarez. 2000. *Implementing the Education Agreements of the Santiago Summit.* Coral Gables, FL: Dante B. Fascell North-South Center, Leadership Council for Inter-American Summitry, Working Paper Series.

Putnam, Robert D. 1988. "Diplomacy and Domestic Politics: The Logic of Two-Level Games." *International Organization* 42(3): 427–460.

Putnam, Robert D., and Nicholas Bayne. 1984. *Hanging Together: The Seven-Power Summits.* Cambridge, MA: Harvard University Press.

Quebec City. 2001. "Declaration." Third Summit of the Americas. Quebec City, April 20–22.

Rama, Martin. 2003. "Globalization and the Labor Market." *World Bank Research Observer* 18(2): 159–186.

Rasmusen, Eric Bennett. 2001. "Explaining Incomplete Contracts as the Result of Contract-Reading Costs." *Advances in Economic Analysis and Policy* 1(1): 1–37.

Rescia, Victor Rodriguez, and Marc David Seitles. 2000. "The Development of the Inter-American Human Rights System: A Historical and Modern-Day Critique." *New York Law School Journal of Human Rights* 16: 593–634.

Risse, Thomas. 2000. "The Power of Norms Versus the Norms of Power: Transnational Civil Society and Human Rights." In Ann Florini, ed., *The Third Force: The Rise of Transnational Civil Society*. Washington, DC: Carnegie Endowment for International Peace, 177–209.

Robert, Maryse. 2000. *Negotiating NAFTA: Explaining the Outcome in Culture, Textiles, Autos, and Pharmaceuticals*. Toronto: University of Toronto Press.

Rodriguez, Francisco. 2004. "Factor Shares and Resource Booms: Accounting for the Evolution of Venezuelan Inequality." In Giovanni Andrea Cornia, ed., *Inequality, Growth, and Poverty in an Era of Liberalization and Globalization*. Oxford: Oxford University Press.

Rodrik, Dani. 2004. *Rethinking Growth Strategies*. Helsinki: United Nations University, World Institute for Development Economics Research.

Roett, Riordan, and Guadalupe Paz, eds. 2003. *Latin America in a Changing Global Environment*. Boulder: Lynne Rienner.

Rojas Aravena, Francisco. 1994. "Security Regimes in the Western Hemisphere: A View from Latin America." In Lars Schoultz, William C. Smith, and Augusto Varas, eds., *Security, Democracy, and Development in US–Latin American Relations*. Miami: University of Miami Press for the North-South Center, 171–197.

———. 2001. *Diseño y Gestión de la Seguridad Internacional en América Latina*. PhD diss., Utrecht University, Netherlands.

Rose-Ackerman, Susan. 2000. "Is Leaner Government Necessarily Cleaner Government?" In Joseph Tulchin and Ralph Espach, eds., *Combating Corruption in Latin America*. Baltimore, MD: Johns Hopkins University Press.

Rosenau, James N. 1995. "Governance in the Twenty-first Century." In *Global Governance* 1(1): 13–43.

Rosenberg, Robin L. 2000. Interview with the author, December 13.

———. 2001. "The OAS and the Summit of the Americas: Coexistence or Integration of Forces for Multilateralism?" *Latin American Politics and Society* 43(1): 79–101.

Rosenberg, Robin L., and Steve Stein, eds. 1995. "Foreword." In *Advancing the Miami Process: Civil Society and the Summit of the Americas*. Coral Gables, FL: North-South Center Press at the University of Miami, i–viii.

Ruggie, John Gerard. 1998. "What Makes the World Hang Together? Neo-Utilitarianism and the Social Constructivist Challenge." *International Organization* 52(4): 855–885.

Ruiz-Cabañas, Miguel. 2003. Remarks at the National Defense University. Washington, DC, November 21. http://www.resdal.org/ultimos-documentos/art-ruiz-cabanas.html (accessed March 15, 2006).

Salazar-Xirinachs, J. M. 2004. "Proliferation of Sub-Regional Trade Agreements in the Americas: An Assessment of Key Analytical and Policy Issues." In Vinod K. Aggarwal, Ralph Espach, and Joseph Tulchin, eds., *The Strategic Dynamics of Latin American Trade*. Stanford, CA: Stanford University Press, 116–155.

Salazar-Xirinachs, J. M., and Jaime Granados. 2004. "The US–Central America Free Trade Agreement: Opportunities and Challenges." In Jeffrey Schott, ed., *Free Trade Agreements: US Strategies and Priorities*. Washington, DC: Institute for International Economics, 225–275.

Salazar-Xirinachs, J. M., and Maryse Robert, eds. 2001. *Toward Free Trade in the Americas*. Washington, DC: Brookings Institution and General Secretariat of the Organization of American States.

Santa-Cruz, Arturo. 2005. "Monitoring Elections, Redefining Sovereignty: The 2000 Peruvian Electoral Process as an International Event." *Journal of Latin American Studies* 37(4): 739–767.

Scheman, Ronald L. 1987. "Rhetoric and Reality: The Inter-American System's Second Century." *Journal of Interamerican Studies and World Affairs* 29(3): 1–31.

———. 1988. *The Inter-American Dilemma: The Search for Inter-American Cooperation at the Centennial of the Inter-American System.* New York: Praeger.

———. 1994. "Promise and Potential of the OAS." *North-South,* 14–18.

———. 2003. *Greater America.* New York: New York University Press.

Schlesinger, Arthur M., Jr. 1986. *The Cycles of American History.* Boston: Houghton Mifflin.

Schmitter, Philippe C., and Terry Lynn Karl. 1996. "What Democracy Is . . . and Is Not." In Larry Diamond and Marc F. Plattner, eds., *The Global Resurgence of Democracy.* Baltimore, MD: Johns Hopkins University Press, 49–62.

Schott, Jeffrey J. 2001. *Prospects for Free Trade in the Americas.* Washington, DC: Institute for International Economics.

Schoultz, Lars, William C. Smith, and Augusto Varas. 1994. *Security, Democracy, and Development in US–Latin American Relations.* Miami: North-South Center.

Schwanen, Daniel. 2004. *Deeper, Broader: A Roadmap for a Treaty of North America.* Thinking North America, vol. 2, no. 4. Montreal: Institute of Research on Public Policy.

Scott, Robert E. 2003. "A Theory of Self-Enforcing Indefinite Agreements." *Columbia Law Review* 103(7): 1641–1699.

Security and Prosperity Partnership of North America (SPP). 2005. *Report to Leaders.* June 27.

Shaw, Carolyn M. 2004. *Cooperation, Conflict, and Consensus in the Organization of American States.* New York: Palgrave Macmillan.

Shelton, Dinah. 1988. "Improving Humans Rights Protections: Recommendations for Enhancing the Effectiveness of the Inter-Commission and the Inter-American Court of Human Rights." *American University Journal of International Law and Policy* 3: 323–338.

———. 1989–1990. "Private Violence, Public Wrongs, and the Responsibility of States." *Fordham International Law Journal* 13: 1–34.

Shifter, Michael, and Vinay Jawahar. 2006. "The Divided States of the Americas." *Current History* (February): 51–57.

Sikkink, Kathryn. 2005. "Patterns of Dynamic Multilevel Governance and the Insider-Outsider Coalition." In Donnatella de la Porta and Sidney Tarrow, eds., *Transnational Protest and Global Activism.* Lanham, MD: Rowman and Littlefield, 151–174.

Simmons, P. J., and Chantal de Jonge Oudraat, eds. 2001. *Managing Global Issues: Lessons Learned.* Washington, DC: Carnegie Endowment for International Peace.

SIRG (Summit Implementation Review Group). 2004. "Fourth Summit of the Americas, Buenos Aires (2005). Preliminary Document for Discussion." September 16. http://www.summit-americas.org/SIRG/SIRG-MAIN-documents .htm (accessed April 29, 2006).

Slater, Jerome. 1969. "The Decline of the OAS." *International Journal* 24(3): 497–506.

———. 1970. *Intervention and Negotiation: The United States and the Dominican Revolution.* New York: Harper and Row.

Slaughter, Anne-Marie. 2000. "International Law and International Relations." *Recueil des Cours* 285: 12.

―――. 2004. *A New World Order.* Princeton, NJ: Princeton University Press.

Smith, Adam. 1999 [1776]. *The Wealth of Nations.* Mexico City, Mexico: Fondo de Cultura Económica.

Smith, William C., and Roberto Patricio Korzeniewicz. 1997. "Latin America and the Second Great Transformation." In William C. Smith and Roberto Patricio Korzeniewicz, eds., *Politics, Social Change, and Economic Restructuring in Latin America.* Boulder, CO: Lynne Rienner, 1–20.

Stallings, Barbara, and Wilson Peres. 2000. *Growth, Employment, and Equity: The Impact of Economic Reforms in Latin America and the Caribbean.* Washington, DC: UNECLAC and the Brookings Institution.

Stiglitz, Joseph. 2000. *Globalization and Its Discontents.* New York: W. W. Norton.

Stoetzer, Carlos O. 1993. *The Organization of American States.* 2nd ed. New York: Praeger.

Strumpen-Darrie, Christine. 2000. "Rape: A Survey of Current International Jurisprudence." *Human Rights Brief* 7(3).

Summits of the Americas. 1994. *Summit of the Americas Action Plan.* http://www.summit-americas.org/miamiplan.htm. (accessed March 15, 2006).

―――. 2005a. "Creating Jobs to Fight Poverty and Strengthen Democratic Governance." Plan of Action, Mar del Plata, Argentina, November 5. http://www.summit-americas.org/Eng-2004/previous-summits.htm (accessed March 12, 2005).

―――. 2005b. "Creating Jobs to Fight Poverty and Strengthen Democratic Governance." Declaration, Mar del Plata, Argentina, November 5. http://www.summit-americas.org/Eng-2004/previous-summits.htm (accessed March 12, 2005).

Summits of the Americas Information Network. N.d. "Second Summit of the Americas: Building Confidence and Security Among States." http://www.summit-americas.org/Hemispheric%20Security/Confidence&Security.htm (accessed December 20, 2005).

Summits of the Americas Secretariat. 2003a. *Achievements of the Summits of the Americas: Institutional Contributions.* Washington, DC.

―――. 2003b. *Advancing in the Americas: Progress and Challenges.* Washington, DC.

―――. 2003c. *Achievements of the Summits of the Americas: National Accomplishments.* Washington, DC.

Thérien, Jean-Philippe, Michel Fortmann, and Guy Gosselin. 1996. "The Organization of American States: Restructuring Inter-American Multilateralism." *Global Governance* 2(2): 215–240.

Thomas, Christopher R., and Juliana Magloire. 2000. *Regionalism Versus Multilateralism: The Organization of American States in a Changing Global Environment.* Boston: Kluwer Academic Publishers.

Tickner, Arlene B., ed. 2000. *Sistema interamericano y democracia: Antecedentes historicos y tendencias futuros.* Bogotá: Ediciones Uniandes.

Tittemore, Brian D. 2004–2005. "The Mandatory Death Penalty in the Commonwealth Caribbean and the Inter-American Human Rights System: An Evolution in the Development and Implementation of International Human Rights Protections." *William and Mary Bill of Rights Journal* 13: 445–520.

Tobin, James. 1978. "A Proposal for International Monetary Reform." *Eastern Economic Journal* 4: 153–159.

Tokatlián, Juan Gabriel. 2005. "Una cumbre bastante modesta." *La Nación,* November 7.

Tomic, Esteban. 2006. "Address by Ambassador Esteban Tomic, Permanent Representative of Chile and President of the Thirty-Second Special Session of the General Assembly." OEA/SER.P, AG/INF (XXXII-E/06). Washington, DC, March 16.

Treaty of Asunción. 1991. *Treaty Establishing a Common Market Between the Argentine Republic, the Federal Republic of Brazil, the Republic of Paraguay, and the Eastern Republic of Uruguay.* Asunción, March 26.

Tulchin, Joseph, and Ralph Espach, eds. 2000. *Combating Corruption in Latin America.* Baltimore, MD: Johns Hopkins University Press.

———. 2001. *Latin America in the New International System.* Boulder, CO: Lynne Rienner.

Tussie, Diana, and Mercedes Botto, eds. 2003. *Sociedad civil y el proceso de Cumbres de las Américas ¿Nuevos o viejos patrones de participación y cooperación en América Latina?* Buenos Aires: Editorial Tema.

Ubeda de Torres, Amaya. 2003. "Freedom of Expression Under the European Convention on Human Rights: A Comparison with the Inter-American System of Protection of Human Rights." *Human Rights Brief* 10: 6.

UNAM (Universidad Nacional Autónoma de México). 2000. Estudios Básicos de Derechos Humanos, vol. 10, Instituto de Investigaciones Jurídicas de la UNAM. Mexico City. http://www.bibliojuridica.org/libros/libro.htm?l=1844 (accessed March 15, 2005).

UNITAR (United Nations Institute of Training and Research). 1984. "Cooperation in the 1980s: Principles and Prospects," 1–5. New York.

United Nations. 1994a. *An Agenda for Social Change: Human Development Report.* New York: United Nations Development Programme. http://hdr.undp.org/reports/global/1994/en/ (accessed March 10, 2005).

———. 1994b. *Managua Declaration on Democracy and Development.* July. http://daccessdds.un.org/doc/UNDOC/GEN/N94/465/54/IMG/N9446554.pdf?OpenElement (accessed March 10, 2005).

———. 2004. *A More Secure World: Our Shared Responsibility—Report of the Secretary-General's High-Level Panel on Threats, Challenges, and Changes.* New York: United Nations.

———. 2005. *Human Development Report: International Cooperation at a Crossroads.* New York: United Nations.

United Nations Commission on Human Rights. 1999. *Promotion of the Right to Democracy.* Commission on Human Rights Resolution 1999/57. April 27.

United Press International. 2004. "Al-Qaida Recruiting Local U.S. Gang Ties." September 28 (accessed via Lexis/Nexis, August 7, 2005).

US Conference of Catholic Bishops. 2006. Background on Colombia. http://www.usccb.org/sdwp/international/200602colombia.htm (accessed April 14, 2006).

US Department of Defense. 2005. *The National Defense Strategy of the United States of America.* March.

US Department of State. 2001. Central American Security Commission Esquipulas Peace Agreement, August 6–7, 1987, Fact Sheet. Washington, DC: US Department of State, Bureau of Political Military Affairs. http://www.state.gov/t/pm/rls/fs/2001/4265.htm (accessed March 15, 2006).

———. 2005. "U.S. Official Outlines Goals for Fourth Summit of the Americas." http://usinfo.state.gov/wh/Archive/2005/Sep/30-667427.html (accessed April 28, 2006).

US House of Representatives. 1993a. *An Act to Implement the North American Free Trade Agreement.* 103d Congress, 1st Session, House Document 103-159, 1: 3–449.

————. 1993b. *The North American Free Trade Agreement Implementation Act-Statement of Administrative Action.* 103rd Congress, 1st Session, House Document 103-159, 1: 450–680. http://www.oas.org/main/main.asp?sLang=E&sLink=http://www.oas.org/OASpage/eng/latestnews/latestnews.asp (accessed February 16, 2005).

US Trade Representative (USTR). 2005. *CAFTA Policy.* Brief, June.

Vaky, Viron P. 1981. "Hemispheric Relations: 'Everything Is Part of Everything Else.'" *Foreign Affairs* 59(3): 617–647.

————. 1993. "The Organization of American States and Multilateralism in the Americas." In Viron P. Vaky and Heraldo Muñoz, eds., *The Future of the Organization of American States.* New York: Twentieth Century Fund, 1–65.

————. 1997. "The Inter-American Agenda and Multilateral Governance: The Organization of American States." Washington, DC: Inter-American Dialogue.

————, ed. 1983. *Governance in the Western Hemisphere.* New York: Praeger.

Vaky, Viron P., and Heraldo Muñoz, eds. 1993. *The Future of the Organization of American States.* New York: Twentieth Century Fund.

Van Klaveren, Alejandro. 2001. "Political Globalization and Latin America: Toward a New Sovereignty?" In Joseph S. Tulchin and Ralph H. Espach, eds., *Latin America in the New International System.* Boulder, CO: Lynne Rienner, 117–140.

Varas, Augusto, James A. Schear, and Lisa Owens, eds. 1995. *Confidence-Building Measures in Latin America.* Washington, DC: Henry L. Stimson Center Report No. 16.

Villalta Vizcarra, Ana Elizabeth. 2002. "Bilateral and Subregional Aspects of Hemispheric Security: The Framework Treaty." Presentation to the Committee on Hemispheric Security, October 29. www.oas.org/csh/english/documents/cp10431e07.doc (accessed March 15, 2006).

Watson, Alexander F. 1995. "Toward a New Relationship of Western Hemisphere Democracies." *US Department of State Dispatch* 28: 1–5.

Webb-Vidal, Andy. 2005. "Venezuela Plan for Oil Income Will Aid Chávez." *Financial Times,* July 28.

Weingast, Barry R. 2002. "Rational-Choice Institutionalism." In Ira Katznelson and Helen V. Miller, eds., *Political Science: The State of the Discipline.* New York: W. W. Norton and American Political Science Association, 660–692.

Weintraub, Sidney. 1994. *NAFTA: What Comes Next?* Westport: Praeger.

Weintraub, Sidney, Allan M. Rugman, and Gavin Boyd, eds. 2004. *Free Trade in the Americas.* Cheltenham, UK: Edward Elgar.

Wendt, Alexander. 1992. "Anarchy Is What States Make of It." *International Organization* 46(2): 391–425.

————. 2001. "Driving with the Rearview Mirror: On the Rational Science of Institutional Design." *International Organization* 55(4): 1019–1049.

Westley, Glenn D. 2001. "Can Financial Market Policies Reduce Inequality?" Washington, DC: Inter-American Development Bank, Sustainable Development Technical Paper Series.

Whitaker, Arthur P. 1954. *The Western Hemisphere Idea: Its Rise and Decline.* Ithaca, NY: Cornell University Press.

Whitehead, Laurence. 2000. "High-Level Political Corruption in Latin America: A 'Transitional' Phenomenon?" In Joseph Tulchin and Ralph Espach, eds., *Combating Corruption in Latin America.* Baltimore, MD: Johns Hopkins University Press.

Williamson, Oliver E. 1985. *The Economic Institutions of Capitalism.* New York: Free Press.

Wilson, James Q. 2000 [1989]. *Bureaucracy.* New York: Basic Books.

Winters, L. Alan, Neil McCulloch, and Andrew MacKay. 2004. "Trade Liberalization and Poverty: The Evidence So Far." *Journal of Economic Literature* 42: 72–115.

Yarbrough, Beth V., and Robert M. Yarbrough. 1992. *Cooperation and Governance in International Trade: The Strategic Organizational Approach.* Princeton: Princeton University Press.

Zartman, I. William, and Viktor Kremeniuk, eds. 1995. *Cooperative Security: Reducing Third World Wars.* Syracuse, NY: Syracuse University Press.

Zoellick, Robert B. 2001. *Prepared Statement of Robert B. Zoellick, US Trade Representative, Before the Subcommittee on Trade of the Committee on Ways and Means of the US House of Representatives.* Washington, DC, May 8.

———. 2004. *Prepared Statement of Robert B. Zoellick, US Trade Representative, Before the Council of the Americas.* Washington, DC, May 3.

The Contributors

Kenneth W. Abbott is professor of law and Willard H. Pedrick Distinguished Research Scholar in the Sandra Day O'Connor College of Law at Arizona State University, and professor of global studies in the ASU School of Global Studies.

Louis Bélanger is professor of international relations in the Department of Political Science and the Institute of Advanced International Studies at Université Laval. He was public policy scholar at the Woodrow Wilson International Center for Scholars in Washington at the time of writing his contribution to this book.

Albert Berry is professor emeritus of economics at the University of Toronto and research director of the Programme on Latin America and the Caribbean at the Centre for International Studies. He also teaches in the International Development Studies program at the University of Toronto's Scarborough Campus.

Bernard Duhaime is professor of law at the University of Québec in Montreal and director of UQAM's International Clinic for the Defense of Human Rights. Duhaime worked previously as staff attorney at the Inter-American Commission on Human Rights.

Richard E. Feinberg is professor of international political economy at the Graduate School of International Relations and Pacific Studies, University of California, San Diego. He has served in several senior government positions, including with the National Security Council, State Department, and Treasury. He was the first president of the Inter-American Dialogue. Currently he is the book reviewer for the Western Hemisphere section of *Foreign Affairs* magazine.

Paul Haslam is assistant professor of development studies at the University of Ottawa's School of Public and International Affairs.

Margaret Daly Hayes is principal of Evidence Based Research, Inc. From November 1997 to March 2004, she served as founding director of the Center for Hemispheric Defense Studies at the National Defense University. She teaches Latin American security issues at Georgetown University. Hayes has specialized in US–Latin American political economy and security issues throughout her career.

Roberto Patricio Korzeniewicz is associate professor of sociology at the University of Maryland. In 2006, he was a visiting scholar at the Russell Sage Foundation in New York City.

Thomas Legler is a professor in the Departamento de Estudios Internacionales, Universidad Iberoamericana. He is coauthor of *Intervention without Intervening? The OAS Defence and Promotion of Democracy in the Americas.*

Gordon Mace is a professor in the department of political science and at the Institute of Advanced International Studies at Université Laval, Québec. He is also the director of the Inter-American Studies Center and editor of *Etudes internationales.* His research interests include regional studies, inter-American cooperation, and Canadian foreign policy.

David R. Mares is professor of political science and adjunct professor at the Graduate School of International Relations/Pacific Studies at the University of California, San Diego. He was formerly professor at El Colegio de Mexico, Fulbright professor at the University of Chile, and visiting professor at FLACSO Ecuador.

Maryse Robert is acting chief of the Trade Section in the Department of Trade, Tourism, and Competitiveness at the General Secretariat of the Organization of American States. She has authored numerous studies on trade-related issues, particularly investment and services trade.

L. Ronald Scheman is the former US executive director of the Inter-American Development Bank and former director general of the OAS's Inter-American Agency for Cooperation and Development. He is presently senior advisor at Kissinger McLarty Associates in Washington, D.C. He is author of four books on inter-American relations, of which the latest is *Greater America.*

William C. Smith is professor of international studies and political science at the University of Miami. His research focuses on democratic governance and civil society and social movement responses to globalization. He also is the editor of *Latin American Politics and Society.*

Jean-Philippe Thérien is professor in the Department of Political Science at the Université de Montréal and associate scientific director of the Centre d'études et de recherches internationales de l'Université de Montréal (CERIUM). His research interests include inter-American politics, development assistance, and North-South issues.

Index

About the Book

G*overning the Americas* presents the first systematic assessment of the functioning of hemispheric institutions since the introduction of the Summits of the Americas process in 1994.

The authors evaluate the effectiveness of inter-American institutions with regard to core issues of democratic governance, security, trade, and economic development. They consider, as well, the impact of the profusion of multilateral institutions on the coordination and efficiency of hemispheric cooperation. Exploring why some multilateral efforts have worked while others have been more problematic, they also offer a reasoned assessment of the future of inter-American cooperation.

Gordon Mace is professor of political science at Laval University and director of the University's Inter-American Studies Center. He is also director of the journal *Etudes internationales*. Among his publications are *Foreign Policy and Regionalism in the Americas* and *The Americas in Transition: The Contours of Regionalism*. **Jean-Philippe Thérien** is professor of political science and assistant scientific director of CERIUM at the University of Montreal. He is coauthor of *Foreign Policy and Regionalism in the Americas*. **Paul Haslam** is assistant professor of international development at the University of Ottawa.